The Collected Works of
James M. Buchanan

VOLUME 19
*Ideas, Persons, and Events*

*Left to right on the grass: Alberto di Pierro, Roger D. Congleton, Francesco Forte, Yong J. Yoon, Dwight R. Lee, Jennifer Roback Morse, James M. Buchanan; on stairs, back row: Charles Plott, Roger Faith, António Pinto Barbosa, Nicholaus Tideman, Geoffrey Brennan (behind Tideman), Viktor J. Vanberg, Wm. Craig Stubblebine; front row: Gordon Tullock, Robert D. Tollison, Mark Pauly, David Fand, Cotton M. Lindsay. Fairfax, Virginia, April 1994.*

*The Collected Works of*

# James M. Buchanan

VOLUME 19

*Ideas, Persons, and Events*

LIBERTY FUND

*Indianapolis*

This book is published by Liberty Fund, Inc., a foundation
established to encourage study of the ideal of a society of free
and responsible individuals.

𒀀𒈄

The cuneiform inscription that serves as our logo and as the design
motif for our endpapers is the earliest-known written appearance
of the word "freedom" (*amagi*), or "liberty." It is taken from a clay
document written about 2300 B.C. in the Sumerian city-state of Lagash.

Frontispiece photograph by David Scavone

05  04  03  02  01   C   5   4   3   2   1
05  04  03  02  01   P   5   4   3   2   1

*Library of Congress Cataloging-in-Publication Data*
Buchanan, James M.
Ideas, persons, and events / James M. Buchanan.
p.   cm. — (The collected works of James M. Buchanan ; v. 19)
A collection of 34 journal and book articles previously published
1968–1997.
Includes bibliographical references and index.
ISBN 0-86597-249-4 (hc. : alk. paper). — ISBN 0-86597-250-8 (pbk. : alk. paper)
1. Buchanan, James M.   2. Economists—United States.
3. Economists.   4. Social choice.   5. Free enterprise.   I. Title.
II. Series : Buchanan, James M.   Works.   1999 ; v. 19.
HB119.B67A3   2001
330.1—dc21        99-42600

LIBERTY FUND, INC.
8335 Allison Pointe Trail, Suite 300
Indianapolis, IN 46250-1684

# Contents

## 3. Political Economy in the Post-Socialist Century

## 4. Reform without Romance

# Foreword

The personal and the theoretical are often inseparably intertwined in the essays of this volume. For instance, quite a number of the discussions in part 3, "Political Economy in the Post-Socialist Century," even though theoretical along one dimension, are personal along another. Likewise, the autobiographical and biographical essays often address important theoretical questions. As a case in point, consider James Buchanan's account of his relationship to Frank Knight. This account not only sheds some interesting light on the personal element in the development of science, it also offers some new perspectives on the concept of the "relatively absolute absolutes," which has been so central to Buchanan's thinking in general.[1]

Since in this volume's title "ideas" come first, it seems appropriate to dwell somewhat further on the idea of the relatively absolute absolutes. Sometimes, including on occasion in this volume, Buchanan seems to downplay the role of the relatively absolute absolutes to the purely pragmatic principle that the critic of existing norms and institutions would, in general, have good reason to play by the existing rules since ". . . no choices are made *carte blanche*. An institutional structure always exists. . . ." In this institutionalist interpretation, the principle amounts to no more than René Descartes' provisional practical morals as adopted in his *Discourse on the Method*, where he assured the reader that he, while casting doubt on everything in theory, would live up to all the conventional expectations in practice. Yet in other instances, one can sense that Buchanan is willing to go beyond the tradi-

---

1. James M. Buchanan, "Frank H. Knight: 1885–1972," in *Remembering the University of Chicago: Teachers, Scientists, and Scholars,* ed. Edward Shils (Chicago: University of Chicago Press, 1991), 244–52. See also "The Relatively Absolute Absolutes," *Essays on the Political Economy* (Honolulu: University of Hawai'i Press, 1989), 32–46, reprinted in volume 1 of this series, *The Logical Foundations of Constitutional Liberty.*

tional Cartesian maxim. Then the concept of the relatively absolute absolutes expresses a basic principle of practical *reasoning* rather than of practical action. In this much more interesting reading, it expresses the fundamental idea of what may be called "reformist conservatism."[2]

Reformist conservatism must be distinguished from both conservatism and radicalism. As Buchanan himself puts it in the paper "The Epistemological Feasibility of Free Markets," "the conservative's choice may be biased towards that which is; the radical's choice may be biased towards that which is not but might be." The reformist conservative chooses a course between the extremes, and the concept of the relatively absolute absolutes can assist him in finding his way. It makes him aware that at any given time he has to accept certain premises and principles guiding his reason, not only certain rules and institutions guiding his actions. Nevertheless, the principle also tells him that what is accepted at one time is merely relatively absolute and may therefore be changed at another time.[3]

As reformist conservatives, Buchanan and Knight meet not only with Hume the skeptic but also with Hume the reformer, who trusts that rational policy advice can be given even though an absolute, sufficient rational justification of the basic normative and descriptive premises of the reasoning leading to such advice is lacking.[4] The criteria for telling rational from irrational reasons are of necessity those that have, as a matter of fact, evolved. What is plausible or implausible must be determined according to those criteria that we do, in fact, have. Even in our *thinking*, we have to start from where we are. Though we know that our fundamental views may change, we cannot at any time adopt a position outside our frame of reference. Still, that we do not know things absolutely is no good reason either for doing nothing (we do not know that the choice of doing nothing is a sound one) or for assuming that anything is possible and, thus, anything goes. We know that

2. See James M. Buchanan, "The Epistemological Feasibility of Free Markets," in *Post-Socialist Political Economy: Selected Essays* (Cheltenham, U.K.: Edward Elgar, 1997), 153; on this, see René Descartes, *Discourse on the Method*, part 3, in John Cottingham, Robert Stoothoff, and Dugald Murdoch, *The Philosophical Writings of Descartes* (Cambridge: Cambridge University Press, 1984).

3. Buchanan, "The Epistemological Feasibility of Free Markets," 153.

4. For the political views of Hume, see David Hume, *Essays: Moral, Political and Literary* (Indianapolis: Liberty Fund, 1985).

the criteria by which we judge our acts and omissions can conceivably be otherwise, but since they are all that we have at any point, it is certainly not reasonable to accept arguments that are implausible according to the evolved descriptive and normative plausibility criteria.[5] In that sense, the criteria are relatively absolute absolutes.

Buchanan's reformist conservatism is different from a "nonreformist conservative" view. As is obvious from several papers in this and other volumes in the Collected Works, Buchanan distances himself from the view that existing institutions must be rationally accepted simply because they are adaptive in a given institutional environment. A hands-off approach to politics as sometimes suggested by self-declared adherents of Friedrich August Hayek who have been misled by some of the more extreme statements Hayek made later in his life is not acceptable to Buchanan. First of all, as the large-scale experiment of socialism has shown, we can influence our fate by political actions. Second, if we can change our fate for the worse, why should we not be in a position to change it for the better? For Buchanan, that we cannot know for sure whether reforms are for the better is no reason not to evaluate their advantages and disadvantages in comparison with the status quo and according to the plausibility criteria we do have.

Like Hayek, Buchanan diagnoses many failures of our present Western systems. But even though Hayek himself suggested some sweeping reforms, Buchanan tends to think of constitutional reforms of basic political structures in terms of an ongoing contractual process that goes beyond the evolutionist Hayekian vision. Still, Buchanan, though in Hayekian terminology perhaps a "constructivist" of sorts, is certainly not a radical. He accepts the relatively absolute absolutes of time and place and the state of knowledge and ideas. Moreover, he strongly resents imposing his own ideas and visions on society. He insists that his proposals have to be accepted ultimately by their addressees.

So much for a general account of some basic ideas that are operative in the papers reprinted in this nineteenth volume of the Collected Works. More specifically speaking, the volume commences with part 1, "Autobiographical and Personal Reflections," which is followed by "Reflections on Fellow Po-

---

5. This point is argued in the epistemic considerations in David Hume, *Dialogues concerning Natural Religion* (1779; reprint, Indianapolis: Hackett, 1986).

litical Economists." These two sections are closely related to each other. In the first section, we find quite a bit of material about fellow political economists and their views. While in the second section, we find many personal and autobiographical remarks. One should be aware, though, that in "From the Inside Looking Out," Buchanan characterizes the personal as "almost the intellectual opposite of autobiography." In personal reflections, it is not Buchanan per se who forms the focus of attention, but rather the way the world is perceived by Buchanan.[6]

The autobiographical and personal reflections give an account of Buchanan's view of the world and how it has been formed. Because of the strong influence of Frank Knight on Buchanan's thinking, the two pieces on Knight should actually be read in conjunction with the essays in part 1. In fact, most of the reflections on fellow political economists should presumably be read along with the more personal and autobiographical material in the first section.[7]

In somewhat varying degrees, all these essays shed some light on Buchanan's view of the world. In particular, the contrast between Buchanan's own perspective and that of Gordon Tullock as described in the essay "The Qualities of a Natural Economist" is instructive. Buchanan ascribes the qualities of a natural economist to Tullock but does not perceive himself as a "natural economist." Still, Buchanan would certainly insist that he, like Tullock, is an economist. Thus Buchanan must evidently think that one can be an economist without being a natural economist. He agrees that being a natural economist may be fruitful. At the same time, he feels that perceiving all human behavior as the outcome of the narrow motives of *Homo economicus* leads to a distorted view of the world. It is important to look at the world that way, but we have to integrate the *Homo economicus* perspective into a broader vision of the world. At least we must look at the world through both windows—that of the contractarian political economist and

6. James M. Buchanan, "From the Inside Looking Out," in *Eminent Economists: Their Life Philosophies,* ed. Michael Szenberg (Cambridge: Cambridge University Press, 1992), 98–106.

7. Some of the essays in part 4 of volume 1 in the series, *The Logical Foundations of Constitutional Liberty,* and in part 1 of volume 12 in the series, *Economic Inquiry and Its Logic,* contain reflections on fellow political economists as well as extended reflections on economic method.

that of the natural economist. And, as we may add here, if we do it as well as Buchanan and Tullock, respectively, a great book like their famous *The Calculus of Consent* may emerge.[8]

The pieces on Winston Bush and on Jack Wiseman speak for themselves, and so do the personal recollections "I Did Not Call Him 'Fritz.'" However, since the relationship between Buchanan and Hayek is often seen as being characterized by some rivalry, and even tension, it may be helpful if I add a personal remark here. As is mentioned in the piece on Hayek, in 1984 Buchanan and I organized a seminar at the European Forum in Alpbach, Austria, which Hayek attended for some days. One evening Buchanan invited me to dine with him and Hayek. Despite what might be told otherwise about the relationship between the two men, the evening was extremely harmonious. Buchanan developed the conversation with Hayek. He made Hayek recollect and remember in ways that showed Hayek in the most impressive and memorable light to a young academic like myself. Since, particularly in the Hayekian camp, there seems to be a certain tendency to project theoretical rivalry between the two thinkers onto their personal relations, it may be useful to keep such anecdotes in mind when interpreting Buchanan's own piece on Hayek and other accounts of their relationship. As is clearly brought out by his own report on the Ayres-Knight debate, Buchanan regards dissent between political economists, including dissent on fundamental philosophical issues, as healthy and useful for the discipline. And such dissent does not affect his personal relations to others—at least as long as it remains within the limits of the reasonable.[9]

8. James M. Buchanan, "The Qualities of a Natural Economist," in *Democracy and Public Choice: Essays in Honor of Gordon Tullock,* ed. Charles K. Rowley (Oxford: Basil Blackwell, 1987), 9–19; for Buchanan's distinction between *political economy* and *economics,* see volume 17 in the Collected Works, *Moral Science and Moral Order,* and for further comments on that distinction, see also the introduction to that volume; James M. Buchanan and Gordon Tullock, *The Calculus of Consent: Logical Foundations of Constitutional Democracy* (Ann Arbor: University of Michigan Press, 1962), volume 3 in the series.

9. James M. Buchanan, preface to *Essays on Unorthodox Economic Strategies: A Memorial Volume in Honor of Winston C. Bush,* ed. Arthur T. Denzau and Robert J. Mackay (Blacksburg, Va.: Center for Study of Public Choice, 1976), vi; "Jack Wiseman: A Personal Appreciation," *Constitutional Political Economy* 2, no. 1 (1991): 1–6; and "I Did Not Call Him 'Fritz': Personal Recollections of Professor F. A. v. Hayek," *Constitutional Political*

Buchanan's discussion in "Economists and the Gains from Trade" is in one dimension a reflection on William Hutt's contribution to political economy.[10] Along another dimension, this essay really goes to the heart of what, according to Buchanan, economists should do.[11] They should understand how individuals can gain from agreement and trade, or agreement in the widest sense of that term. As far as their normative proposals are concerned, economists should suggest institutional and rule changes that can be brought about in Pareto-superior moves. As far as their explanatory and predictive endeavors are concerned, it is worth noting that Buchanan is quite close to endorsing the unorthodox views of Shackle.[12]

All of this that comes up in one way or other in Buchanan's reflections on fellow political economists does not provoke further comments. One may have some second thoughts, however, about Buchanan's claim that Wicksell is the one most important figure for the development of public choice theory as a whole. Wicksell is certainly the most important figure for the development of what Buchanan nowadays calls "constitutional political economy." But as far as public choice theory as a purely descriptive or positive political theory is concerned, Hobbes may, arguably, be the more important figure. It is not by accident that the qualities of a natural economist are very closely associated with a hard-nosed Hobbesian view, according to which individuals pursue their own ends with their own means and do not feel under any *a priori* obligation to restrain that pursuit to what can be gained from trade and mutual agreement. It should be noted, though, that Wicksell had already discarded the concept of a benevolent despot who supposedly would

---

*Economy* 3 (Spring/Summer 1992): 129–35. "Methods and Morals in Economics: The Ayres-Knight Discussion," in *Science and Ceremony: The Institutional Economics of C. E. Ayres,* ed. William Breit and William Patton Culbertson, Jr. (Austin and London: University of Texas Press, 1976), 163–74.

10. James M. Buchanan, "Economists and the Gains from Trade," *Managerial and Decision Economics,* special issue (Winter 1988): 5–12.

11. This, of course, alludes to the title of a paper reprinted in volume 1 of this series, *The Logical Foundations of Constitutional Liberty,* and to the same title of the volume of collected papers in James M. Buchanan, *What Should Economists Do?* (Indianapolis: Liberty Fund, 1979).

12. James M. Buchanan, "Shackle and a Lecture in Pittsburgh," *Market Process* 7 (Spring 1989): 2–4, and review of *Imagination and the Nature of Choice,* by G. L. S. Shackle (Edinburgh: University of Edinburgh Press, 1979), *Austrian Economics Newsletter.* Also see the papers commenting on subjectivism as reprinted in part 1 of volume 12 in the series, *Economic Inquiry and Its Logic.*

lend the welfare economist his ear. In that sense, Wicksell indeed anticipated the modern public choice perspective.

Buchanan not only contrasts Wicksell's methodology in the *Finanztheoretische Untersuchungen* with a noncontractarian Hobbesian approach, but
also insists that the Wicksellian focus on agreement does not cohere with
the allocationist's paradigm that he ascribes to most modern (welfare)
economists.[13] The allocationist derives what is "right," or "efficient," for the
collectivity as a whole from a point external to the ongoing process of social
interaction. He imagines himself as deciding between alternative uses of
scarce resources in the pursuit of given collective ends. Buchanan's principal
objection to this is not that the underlying means-ends perspective is inadequate in economics in general, but rather that it is inadequate as relating to
society as a whole. There is no efficient allocation of scarce resources to the
pursuit of given collective ends, because there are no ends that a collective
could rationally pursue.[14] As far as individuals do own or control certain resources collectively, interindividual agreement is the only indicator of improvement in the allocation of resources. Independent of interindividual
agreement, criteria for an efficient allocation of resources do not exist. This
criticism is offered by Buchanan in several ways throughout the volumes of
this series, and the reader should be aware of its central place in Buchanan's
thinking in general. But the criticism is of particular importance for
Buchanan's rejection of socialism. Still, it is by no means Buchanan's only
criticism of socialism. The essays in the section "Political Economy in the
Post-Socialist Century" give an account of Buchanan's assessment of why socialism failed and what the implications of this failure for political economy
are.[15] The essays in the final section, "Reform without Romance," take
"Adam Smith as Inspiration" and outline some of the fundamental ideas that

---

13. Knut Wicksell, *Finanztheoretische Untersuchungen: Nebst Darstellung und Kritik des Steuerwesens Schwedens* (1896; reprint, Aalen: Scientia, 1969).

14. On this see, in particular, James M. Buchanan, "Social Choice, Democracy, and Free Markets," *Journal of Political Economy* 62 (April 1954): 114–23, and "Individual Choice in Voting and the Market," *Journal of Political Economy* 62 (August 1954): 334–43, in volume 1 of the series, *Logical Foundations of Constitutional Liberty;* "Rational Choice Models in Social Sciences," in *Explorations into Constitutional Economics,* comp. Robert D. Tollison and Viktor J. Vanberg (College Station: Texas A&M University Press, 1989), 37–50, in volume 17 of the series, *Moral Science and Moral Order.*

15. See also James M. Buchanan, *Socialism Is Dead but Leviathan Lives On,* the John Bonython Lecture, CIS Occasional Paper 30 (Sydney: Centre for Independent Studies,

have been guiding Buchanan throughout his academic career. It seems fitting, too, that Buchanan's related paper, "Politics without Romance: A Sketch of Positive Public Choice Theory and Its Normative Implications," has been reprinted in volume 1 of this series, *The Logical Foundations of Constitutional Liberty,* as the initial paper of the first main section.[16] This, hopefully, indicates that we, at least in a way, came "full circle" with this volume of the Collected Works. But one should be aware that these are *not* the "complete works" of James M. Buchanan. As these lines are written the author is adding to his list of publications with incredible productivity.

Hartmut Kliemt
*University of Duisburg*
1998

---

1990): 1–9, in volume 1 in the series, *The Logical Foundations of Constitutional Liberty;* "Adam Smith as Inspiration," in *The Academic World of James M. Buchanan,* ed. Byeong-Ho Gong (Seoul, Korea: Korea Economic Research Institute, 1996); Korean translation only. Also part 8 of volume 16 in the series, *Choice, Contract, and Constitutions,* contains related material on the reform issue; "Reform without Romance: First Principles in Political Economy," in *Post-Socialist Political Economy: Selected Essays* (Cheltenham, U.K.: Edward Elgar, 1997), 233–39.

16. James M. Buchanan, "Politics without Romance: A Sketch of Positive Public Choice Theory and Its Normative Implications," Inaugural Lecture, Institute for Advanced Studies, Vienna, Austria, *IHS-Journal, Zeitschrift des Instituts für Höhere Studien, Wien* 3 (1979): B1–B11.

# PART ONE

# Autobiographical and Personal Reflections

# Born-Again Economist

I have been tempted to expand my title to "Born-Again Economist, with a Prophet but No God." Both parts of this expanded title are descriptive. I was specifically asked to discuss my evolution as an economist, an assignment that I cannot fulfill. I am not a "natural economist" as some of my colleagues are, and I did not "evolve" into an economist.[1] Instead I sprang full-blown upon intellectual conversion, after I "saw the light." I shall review this experience below, and I shall defend the implied definition and classification of who qualifies as an economist.

The second part of my expanded title is related to the first. It is my own play on the University of Chicago saying of the 1940s that "there is no god, but Frank Knight is his prophet." I was indeed converted by Frank Knight, but he almost single-mindedly conveyed the message that there exists no god whose pronouncements deserve elevation to the sacrosanct, whether god within or without the scientific academy. Everything, everyone, anywhere, anytime—all is open to challenge and criticism. There is a moral obligation to reach one's own conclusions, even if this sometimes means exposing the prophet whom you have elevated to intellectual guruship.

In an earlier autobiographical essay, "Better than Plowing,"[2] I identified two persons who were dominant intellectual influences on my own methodology, selection of subject matter, attitude toward scholarship, positive analysis, and normative position. One of these, Knut Wicksell, influenced me

From *Lives of the Laureates: Ten Nobel Economists,* ed. William Breit and Roger W. Spencer (Cambridge: MIT Press, 1990), 163–80. Reprinted by permission of the publisher.

1. James M. Buchanan, "The Qualities of a Natural Economist," in Charles Rowley, ed., *Democracy and Public Choice* (New York: Blackwell, 1987), 9–19.

2. James M. Buchanan, "Better than Plowing," *Banca Nazionale del Lavoro Quarterly Review* 159 (December 1986): 359–75.

exclusively through his ideas. I used the occasion of my Nobel Prize lecture to trace the relationship between Wicksell's precursory foundations and later developments in the theory of public choice, notably its constitutional economics component with which I have been most closely associated. By comparison and contrast this paper offers me the opportunity, even if indirectly, to explore more fully the influence of the second person identified, Frank H. Knight, an influence that was exerted both through his ideas and through a personal friendship that extended over a full quarter-century.

The paper is organized as follows. In the following section I try as best I can to describe my state of mind, intellectually and emotionally, before I enrolled in the University of Chicago in 1946. Then I offer a retrospective description of my Chicago experience, with an emphasis on my exposure to the teachings of Frank Knight along with a subconscious conversion to a catallactic methodological perspective on the discipline. The next section briefly traces the catallactic roots of my contributions to public choice theory. After that I discuss the remembered events and persons who were important in giving me the self-confidence that was surely necessary for any career success. Frank Knight was important but by no means unique in this evolution (and in this respect the word "evolution" can be properly applied). I then discuss the influence of Knight's principle of the "relatively absolute absolute" upon my own stance, as moral philosopher, as constitutionalist, and as economic analyst. Finally, I defend my use of the title of my earlier autobiographical essay, "Better than Plowing," which has been questioned by colleagues and critics. Here I try to examine the motivations that, consciously or unconsciously, may have driven me throughout the course of a long academic career. Why did I do what I did? It may be helpful to explore, even if briefly, this most subjective of questions.

## Pre-Chicago: Standards without Coherence

From 1940 I called myself an "economist," as my military records will indicate. I did so because after graduating from Middle Tennessee State Teachers College in June 1940, I was awarded a graduate fellowship in economics at the University of Tennessee for the academic year 1940–41, and I earned a master's degree in 1941. By the academic counters, I took courses labeled "economics," and I made good grades. But as I have noted, however, I learned little or no economics in my preferred definition during that Knoxville year. I surveyed the workings and structures of the institutions of Roosevelt's New Deal; I came to understand central banking theory and policy; I learned something about taxation and budgeting processes; I learned a bit of elementary statistics, especially in practice. But neither in these courses nor in my prior undergraduate experience did I have proper exposure to the central principle of market organization. I remained blissfully ignorant of the coordinating properties of a decentralized market process, an ignorance that made me vulnerable to quasi-Marxist arguments and explanations about economic history and economic reality but also guaranteed that my mind was an open slate when I finally gained the exposure in question.

During the Knoxville year I did learn to appreciate the dedication of the research scholar though my association with Charles P. White, whose course in research methods was the intellectual high point. White instilled in me the moral standards of the research process. My experience with him, as both graduate student and research assistant, gave me something that seems so often absent in the training of the economists of the postwar decades, whose technology so often outdistances their norms for behavior.

By subject matter, by terminology, and with a bit of technique I left Knoxville as an "economist," but I lacked the coherence of vision of the economic process that I should now make the sine qua non of anyone who proposes to use this label. I have often wondered whether or not I was relatively alone in my ignorance, or whether something akin to my experience has been shared by others who purport to pass as professional economists without the foggiest notion of what they are about.

## Chicago, 1946

I enrolled in the University of Chicago for the winter quarter, 1946. I had chosen the University of Chicago without much knowledge about its faculty in economics. I was influenced almost exclusively by an undergraduate teacher in political science, C. C. Sims, who had earned a doctorate at Chicago in the late 1930s. Sims impressed on me the intellectual ferment of the university, the importance of ideas, and the genuine life of the mind that was present at the institution. His near-idyllic sketch appealed to me, and I made the plunge into serious study for the first time in my life. In retrospect I could not have made a better selection. Sims was precisely on target in conveying the intellectual excitement of the University of Chicago, an excitement that remains, to this day, unmatched anywhere else in the world.

During the first quarter I took courses with Frank Knight, T. W. Schultz, and Simeon Leland. I was among the very first group of graduate students to return to the academy after discharge from military service during World War II. We swelled the ranks of the graduate classes at Chicago and elsewhere.

Within a few short weeks, perhaps by mid-February 1946, I had undergone a conversion in my understanding of how an economy operates. For the first time I was able to think in terms of the ordering principle of a market economy. The stylized model for the working of the competitive structure gave me the benchmark for constructive criticism of the economy to be observed. For the first time I was indeed an economist.

I attribute this conversion directly to Frank Knight's teachings, which perhaps raises more new questions than it answers. Knight was not a systematic instructor. More important, he remained ambiguous in his own interpretation of what economics is all about. He was never able to shed the allocating-maximizing paradigm, which tends to distract attention from the coordination paradigm that I have long deemed central to the discipline.[3] But Knight's economics was a curious amalgam of these partially conflicting visions. And for me the organizational emphasis was sufficient to relegate the allocative thrust to a place of secondary relevance. In this respect I was fortunate in my ignorance. Had I received "better" pre-Chicago training in economics, as widely interpreted, I would have scarcely been able to elevate the coordination principle to the central place it has occupied in my thinking throughout my research career. Like so many of my peers, aside from the few who were exposed early to Austrian theory, I might have remained basically an allocationist.

There are subtle but important differences between the allocationist-maximization and the catallactic-coordination paradigm in terms of the implications for normative evaluation of institutions. In particular the

---

3. For an extended discussion of Knight's ambiguity in this respect, see my paper "The Economizing Element in Knight's Ethical Critique of Capitalist Order," *Ethics* 98 (October 1987): 61–75.

evaluation of the market order may depend critically on which of these partially conflicting paradigms remains dominant in one's stylized vision. To the allocationist the market is efficient *if it works*. His test of the market becomes the comparison with the abstract ideal defined in his logic. To the catallactist the market coordinates the separate activities of self-seeking persons *without the necessity of detailed political direction*. The test of the market is the comparison with its institutional alternative, politicized decision making.

There is of course no necessary implication of the differing paradigms for identifying the normative stance of practicing economists. Many modern economists remain firm supporters of the market order while at the same time remaining within the maximizing paradigm. I submit here, however, that there are relatively few economists whose vision is dominated by the catallactic perspective on market order who are predominantly critics of such an order. Once the relevant comparison becomes that between the workings of the market, however imperfect this may seem, and the workings of its political alternative, there must indeed be very strong offsetting sources of evaluation present.

The apparent digression of the preceding paragraphs is important for my narrative and for an understanding of how my conversion by Frank Knight influenced my research career after Chicago. Those of us who entered graduate school in the immediate postwar years were all socialists of one sort or another. Some of us were what I have elsewhere called "libertarian socialists," who placed a high residual value on individual liberty but simply did not understand the principle of market coordination. We were always libertarians first, socialists second. And we tended to be grossly naive in our thinking about political alternatives. To us, the idealized attractions of populist democracy seemed preferable to those of the establishment-controlled economy. It was this sort of young socialist in particular who was especially ready for immediate conversion upon exposure to teachings that transmitted the principle of market coordination.[4]

An understanding of this principle enabled us to concentrate our long-

---

4. For a discussion of two kinds of socialism in this setting, see the title essay in my book *Liberty, Market and State: Political Economy in the 1980s* (New York: New York University Press, 1986).

held anti-establishment evaluative norms on politics and governance and open up the prospect that economic interaction, at least in the limit, need not embody the exercise of man's power over man. By our libertarian standards, politics had always been deemed to fail. Now by these same standards markets may, just may, not involve exploitation.

An important element in Knight's economics was his emphasis on the organizational structure of markets, and it was this emphasis that elevated the coordination principle to center stage despite his continued obeisance to economizing-maximizing. Once attention is drawn to a structure, to process, and away from resources, goods, and services, many of the technical trappings of orthodox economic theory fall away. Here Knight's approach became institutional, in the proper meaning of this term.

It is useful at this point to recall that Frank Knight's career shared a temporal dimensionality with the seminal American institutionalists Clarence Ayres, John R. Commons, and Thorstein Veblen. He treated their technical economics with derision, but he shared with them an interest in the structure of social and economic interaction. Knight did not extend his institutional inquiry much beyond the seminal work on human wants that exposed some of the shallow presuppositions of economic orthodoxy. He did not, save in a few passing references, examine the structure of politics, considered the only alternative to markets.

## Public Choice and the Catallactic Paradigm

Public choice is the inclusive term that describes the extension of analysis to the political alternatives to markets. It seems highly unlikely that this extension could have been effectively made by economists who viewed the market merely as an allocative mechanism, quite independent of its political role in reducing the range and scope of politicized activity. I can of course speak here only of my own experience, but it seems doubtful if I could have even recognized the Wicksellian message had not Knight's preparatory teachings of the coordination principle paved the way.

The point may be illustrated by the related, but yet quite distinct, strands of modern inquiry summarized under the two rubrics "social choice" and "public choice." I have elsewhere identified the two central elements in public choice theory as (1) the conceptualization of politics as exchange, and (2) the model of *Homo economicus*.[5] The second of these elements is shared with social choice theory, which seeks to ground social choices on the values of utility-maximizing individuals. Where social choice theory and public choice theory differ—and dramatically—lies in the first element noted. Social choice theory does not conceptualize politics as complex exchange; rather politics is implicitly or explicitly modeled in the age-old conception that there must exist some unique and hence discoverable "best" result. This element in social choice theory, from Arrow on, stems directly from the allocative paradigm in orthodox economics, and the maximization of the social welfare function becomes little more than the extension of the standard efficiency calculus to the aggregative economy.

By contrast, the extension of the catallactic paradigm—the emphasis on the theory of exchange rather than allocation—to politics immediately calls attention to the institutional structure of political decision making. Without Frank Knight as teacher and as role model, would Knut Wicksell's great work have been discovered by the fledgling economist that I was in 1948? I have strong reasons for doubt on this score.

## The Evolution of Confidence

When I reflect on my own experiences over a tolerably long academic career, I come back again and again to identifiable events and persons that built up or bolstered my confidence, that made me, always an outsider, feel potentially competent among my academic peers. The first such event came with the release of academic grade records at the end of my second year at Middle Tennessee State Teachers College in 1938. My name led all the rest. For the first time I realized that despite my rural origins, my day-student status, and my graduation from a tiny struggling high school, I could compete with the town students, the live-in students, and with all those whose earlier education was acknowledged to be superior to mine.

A second such event occurred in January 1942, when I finished a three-

5. James M. Buchanan, "The Public Choice Perspective," *Economia delle scelte pubbliche* 1 (January 1983): 7–15.

month stint as a midshipman and was commissioned an ensign in the United States Naval Reserve. Again, despite my Tennessee heritage and my mediocre academic experience at both Middle Tennessee and the University of Tennessee, I ranked sixth or seventh in a midshipman class of some six hundred college and university graduates from across the land. The Tennessee country boy could indeed hold his own.

After a successful, interesting, exciting, and easy four years on active military duty in the Pacific theater of war, which I spent for the most part on the staff of Admiral Nimitz at Pearl Harbor and at Guam, my confidence was once again put to the test when I entered graduate school at the University of Chicago in January 1946. Here the test was of a totally different dimension. I knew that I could compete successfully in terms of the ordinary criteria—academic grades, degrees, and honors. I do not recall ever entertaining the slightest doubt about my ability to finish doctoral requirements. What I did not know was whether I could go beyond these criteria and enter the narrowed ranks of producing scholars who could generate ideas worthy of the serious attention of their disciplinary peers.

At this point Frank H. Knight again enters my narrative. Had my Chicago exposure been limited to the likes of Jacob Viner and Milton Friedman, both of whom were also my teachers there, I doubt that I should have ever emerged from the familiarly large ranks of Ph.D.'s with no or few publications. Jacob Viner, the classically erudite scholar whose self-appointed task in life seemed to be that of destroying confidence in students, and Milton Friedman, whose dominating intellectual brilliance in argument and analysis relegated the student to the role of fourth-best imitation—these were not the persons who encouraged students to believe that they too might eventually have ideas worthy of merit.

Frank Knight was dramatically different. In the classroom he came across as a man engaged always in a search for ideas. He puzzled over principles, from the commonsensical to the esoteric, and he stood continuously dismayed at the arrogance of those who spouted forth the learned wisdom. Knight gave those of us who bothered to listen the abiding notion that all is up for intellectual grabs, that much of what paraded as truth was highly questionable, and that the hallmark of a scholar was his courage in cutting through the intellectual haze. The willingness to deny all gods, to hold nothing sacrosanct—these were the qualities of mind and character that best describe Frank Knight. And gods, as I use the term here, include the authorities in one's own discipline as well as those who claim domain over other dimensions of truth. Those of us who were so often confused in so many things were bolstered by this Knightian stance before all gods. Only gradually, and much later, did we come to realize that in these qualities it was Frank Knight, not his peers, who attained the rank of genius.

As he was the first to acknowledge, Frank Knight was not a clever or brilliant thinker. He was an inveterate puzzler; but this thought process probed depths that the scholars about him could not realize even to exist. To Knight, things were never so simple as they seemed, and he remained at base tolerant in the extreme because he sensed the elements of truth in all principles.

There were many graduate students, both in my own cohort and before and after my time, who could not take in or relate to the Knightian stance before the gods. To these "outsiders" Knight seemed a bumbling and confused teacher, whose writings mirrored his thought and whose primary attribute appeared to be intellectual incoherence. To a few of us, what seemed confusion to others came across as profundity, actual or potential, and despite the chasm that we acknowledged to exist between his mind and ours, Knight left us with the awful realization that if we did not have the simple courage to work out our own answers, we were vulnerable to victimization by false gods.

My own understanding, appreciation, and admiration for Frank Knight were aided and abetted by the development, early on, of a close personal relationship. Some three or four weeks after enrollment in his course I visited Knight's jumbled office. What was expected to be a five-minute talk stretched over two hours, to be matched several times during my two and a half years at Chicago, and beyond. He took an interest in me because we shared several dimensions of experience. Both of us were country boys, reared in agricultural poverty, well aware of the basic drudgery of rural existence but also appreciative of the independence of a life on the land. Knight left his native Illinois in his teens for rudimentary college instruction in my home state of Tennessee, and he enrolled in graduate studies at the University of Tennessee, where I too had first commenced graduate work. These common threads of experience established for me a relationship that I shared with no other professor. We shared other interests, including an appreciation of the gloomy poetry of Thomas Hardy and the fun of the clever off-color joke.

Of course I was a one-way beneficiary of this relationship. Knight was the advisor who told me not to waste my time taking formal courses in philosophy, who corrected my dissertation grammar in great detail, and who became the role model that has never been replaced or even slightly dislodged over a long academic career. In trying to assess my own development, I find it impossible to imagine what I might have been and become without exposure to Frank Knight.

Let me return to confidence, lest I digress too much. Both T. W. Schultz and Earl J. Hamilton deserve inclusion in this narrative account. Schultz encouraged students by his expressed willingness to locate potential merit in arguments that must have often approached the absurd. I was never a formal student of Earl Hamilton. I did not enroll in his economic history courses at Chicago. Nonetheless during my last year at Chicago, 1948, Hamilton sought me out and took a direct personal interest in my prospects. As with Knight, the sharing of common experience in rural poverty created a personal bond, supplemented in this case by a passion for baseball, reflected by trips to both Cubs and White Sox home games. Hamilton enjoyed giving advice to those he singled out for possible achievement, and with me two separate imperatives stand out in recall: the potential payoff to hard work and the value of mastery of foreign languages.

Perhaps Earl J. Hamilton's most important influence on my career came after 1948, during his tenure as editor of the *Journal of Political Economy*. First of all he forced me to follow up on his recommendation about language skills by sending me French, German, and Italian books for review. Second, he handled my early article submissions with tolerance, understanding, and encouragement rather than with brutal or carping rejections that might have proved fatal to further effort. Hamilton was indeed a tough editor, and every article that I finally published during his tenure was laboriously transformed and dramatically pared down through a process of multiple revisions and resubmissions. Without Hamilton as an editor who cared, my writing style would never have attained the economy it possesses, and my willingness to venture into subject matter beyond the boundaries of the orthodox might have been squelched early. With Earl J. Hamilton as editor, by the mid-1950s I had several solid papers on the record—a number sufficient to enable me to accept the occasional rejection slip with equanimity rather than despair.

I noted earlier how Friedman's analytic brilliance exerted a negating effect on those he instructed. An event occurred early in my post-Chicago years that tended to erase this negative influence by placing Milton Friedman, too, among the ranks of those who take intellectual tumbles. A relatively obscure scholar, Cecil G. Phipps, of the University of Florida, located and exposed a logical error in one of Friedman's papers,[6] an error that Friedman graciously acknowledged.[7] To this day I have never told Milton how this simple event contributed so massively to my self-confidence.

## The Relatively Absolute Absolute

I have already discussed how Frank Knight's willingness to challenge all authority—intellectual, moral, or scientific—indirectly established confidence in those for whom he served as role model. Any account of such an influence would be seriously incomplete, and indeed erroneous, if the philosophical stance suggested is one of relativism-cum-nihilism against the claim of any and all authority. It is at precisely this point that Frank Knight directly taught me the philosophical principle that has served me so well over so many years and in so many applications. This principle is that of the *relatively absolute absolute,* which allows for a philosophical way station between the extremes of absolutism on the one hand and relativism on the other, both of which are to be rejected.

Acceptance of this principle necessarily requires that there exist a continuing tension between the forces that dictate adherence to and acceptance of authority and those very qualities that define freedom of thought and inquiry. Knight's expressed willingness to challenge all authority was embedded within a wisdom that also recognized the relevance of tradition in ideas, manners, and institutions. This wisdom dictates that for most purposes and most of the time prudent behavior consists of acting as if the authority that exists does indeed possess legitimacy. The principle of the relatively absolute absolute requires that we adhere to and accept the standards of established or conventional authority in our ordinary behavior, whether this be per-

6. Cecil G. Phipps, "Friedman's 'Welfare' Effects," *Journal of Political Economy* 60 (August 1952): 332–34.

7. Milton Friedman, "A Reply," *Journal of Political Economy* 60 (August 1952): 334–36.

sonal, scientific, or political, while at the same time and at still another (and "higher") level of consciousness we call all such standards into question, even to the extent of proposing change.

In relation to my own work this principle of the relatively absolute absolute is perhaps best exemplified in the critically important distinction between the postconstitutional and the constitutional levels of political interaction. More generally, the distinction is that between choosing among strategies of play in a game that is defined by a set of rules and choosing among alternative sets of rules. To the chooser of strategies under defined rules, the rules themselves are to be treated as relatively absolute absolutes, as constraints that are a part of the existential reality but at the same time may be subject to evaluation, modification, and change. In this extension and application of the Knightian principle to the political constitution—and particularly by way of analogy with the choices of strategies and rules of ordinary games—I was stimulated and encouraged by my colleague at the University of Virginia, Rutledge Vining, who had also been strongly influenced by the teachings of Frank Knight.

## Why "Better than Plowing"?

As noted, in 1986 I wrote an autobiographical essay called "Better Than Plowing," a title I borrowed directly from Frank Knight, who used it to describe his own attitude toward a career in the academy. To me the title seemed also descriptive, and it does, I think, convey my sense of comparative evaluation between "employment" in the academy and in the economy beyond. This title also suggests, even if somewhat vaguely, the sheer luck of those of us who served in the academy during the years of the baby-boom educational explosion, luck that was translated into rents of magnitudes beyond imaginable dreams.

To my surprise constructive critics have challenged the appropriateness of the "Better than Plowing" title for my more general autobiographical essay. To these critics this title seems too casual, too much a throwaway phrase, too flippant a description of a research career that, objectively and externally considered, seems to have embodied central purpose or intent. This unexpected invitation to write a second autobiographical essay provides me with an opportunity to respond to these critics and at the same time to offer additional insights into my development as an economist.

The many books and papers that I have written and published between 1949 and 1987 make up an objective reality that is "there" for all to read and to interpret as they choose. These words and pages exist in some space analogous to the Popperian third world. There is a surprising coherence in this record that I can recognize as well as or better than any interpretative critical biographer. As Robert Tollison and I have suggested in our analysis of autobiography,[8] the autobiographer possesses a record over and beyond that which is potentially available to any biographer. The person whose acts created the objective record lives with the subjective record itself. And such a person, as autobiographer, would be immoral if he relied on the objective record to impute to his life's work a purpose-oriented coherence that had never emerged into consciousness.

I recognize of course that my own research-publication record may be interpreted as the output of a methodological and normative individualist whose underlying purpose has always been to further philosophical support for individual liberty. In subjective recall, however, this motivational thrust has never informed my conscious work effort. I have throughout my career and with only a few exceptions sought to clarify ambiguities and confusions and clear up neglected pockets of analysis in the received arguments of fellow economists, social scientists, and philosophers. To the extent that conscious motivation has entered these efforts, it has always been the sheer enjoyment of working out ideas, of creating the reality that is reflected finally in the finished manuscript. Proof of my normative disinterest lies in my failure to be interested in what happens once a manuscript is a finished draft—a failure that accounts for my sometimes inattention to choice of publisher, to promotional details, and to the potential for either earnings or influence.

I look on myself as being much closer in spirit to the artist who creates on canvas or stone than to the scientist who discovers only that which he accepts to exist independent of his actions. And I should reject, and categorically, any

8. James M. Buchanan and Robert D. Tollison, "A Theory of Truth in Autobiography," *Kyklos* 39, fasc. 4 (1986): 507–17.

affinity with the preacher who writes or speaks for the express and only purpose of persuading others to accept his prechosen set of values.

In all of this, once again, Frank Knight has served as my role model. His famous criticism of Pigou's road case is exemplary.[9] By introducing property rights, Knight enabled others to see the whole Pigovian analysis in a new light. Something was indeed created in the process. I like to think that perhaps some of my own works on public debt, opportunity cost, earmarked taxes, clubs, ordinary politics, and constitutional rules may have effected comparable shifts in perspective. The fact that these efforts have been commonly characterized by a reductionist thrust embodying an individualist methodology is explained, very simply, by my inability to look at the world through other than an individualist window.

It is as if the artist who has only red paints produces pictures that are only red of hue. Such an artist does not choose to paint red pictures and then, instrumentally, purchase red paints. Instead the artist uses the instruments at hand to do what he can and must do, while enjoying himself immensely in the process. The fact that others are able to secure new insights with the aid of his creations and that this in turn provides the artist with a bit of bread—this gratuitous result enables the artist, too, to entitle his autobiographical essay "Better than Plowing."

Awarded Nobel Prize in 1986. Lecture presented October 28, 1987.

DATE OF BIRTH
October 3, 1919

ACADEMIC DEGREES
B.A. Middle Tennessee State College, 1940
M.S. University of Tennessee, 1941
Ph.D. University of Chicago, 1948

ACADEMIC AFFILIATIONS
Associate Professor, University of Tennessee, 1948–1950

9. Frank H. Knight, "Fallacies in the Interpretation of Social Cost," *Quarterly Journal of Economics* 38 (1924): 582–616. Reprinted in *The Ethics of Competition* (London: Allen and Unwin, 1955), 217–36.

Professor, University of Tennessee, 1950–1951

Professor, Department of Economics, Florida State University, 1954–1956

Professor, James Wilson Department of Economics, University of Virginia, 1956–1962

Paul G. McIntire Professor of Economics, University of Virginia, 1962–1968

Professor of Economics, University of California, Los Angeles, 1968–1969

University Distinguished Professor, Virginia Polytechnic Institute and State University, 1969–1983

Holbert L. Harris University Professor, George Mason University, 1983–present

SELECTED BOOKS

*Fiscal Theory and Political Economy*

*The Calculus of Consent* (with G. Tullock)

*The Limits of Liberty*

*Democracy in Deficit* (with R. Wagner)

*Freedom in Constitutional Contract*

*The Power to Tax* (with G. Brennan)

*The Reason of Rules* (with G. Brennan)

*Liberty, Market and State*

*Economics: Between Predictive Science and Moral Philosophy*

*Explorations into Constitutional Economics*

# From the Inside Looking Out

## Introduction

In the early 1970s, I received a short and strange note from a woman whom I had met at a European conference. In the note she asked me, quite straightforwardly, to outline my philosophy of life in a single paragraph not more than a half-page in length. The challenge was sufficient to make me respond, and my outline summary was expanded into, first, a lecture and, later, a brief chapter in a book.[1] I now interpret that response to be an adequate statement of what I should call my "public philosophy," a statement that requires little or no emendation after a decade's ripening. In this essay I respond differently. Partly in order to differentiate the product and partly to meet what seem the particular desires of the editor of this project, I shall here offer a statement of my "private philosophy" or, rather, a set of statements about separate attributes of my personal stance before my own gods.

I shall limit the autobiographical narrative, because I have traced out portions of my life story in two previous papers.[2] This essay is personal rather than autobiographical. That is to say, I shall describe how I look out at the world beyond, and not attempt to look on myself as an object of narrative

From *Eminent Economists: Their Life Philosophies,* ed. Michael Szenberg (Cambridge: Cambridge University Press, 1992), 98–106. Reprinted by permission of the publisher.

1. See James M. Buchanan, "Criteria for a Free Society: Definition, Diagnosis, and Prescription," in *Freedom in Constitutional Contract* (College Station: Texas A&M University Press, 1977), 287–99.

2. See my "Better than Plowing," *Banco Nazionale del Lavoro Quarterly Review,* 159 (December 1986), 359–75; and my "Born-Again Economist," in W. Breit, ed., *Lives of the Laureates: Ten Nobel Economists* (Cambridge, Mass.: MIT Press, 1990), 163–80.

exposition. There is a sense in which this sort of private or personal statement of a philosophy is almost the intellectual opposite of autobiography.

I hope to treat several distinct features of my window on the world. In the next section, I discuss my approach to scholarship and its responsibility. In the third section I move on to examine the mixture of scientist and artist that I have always felt myself to be. A natural follow-on involves the issues of normative and positive analysis, which I examine in the fourth section. The section following that is more autobiographical and surveys my role as an outsider. Finally, I respond to questions of current motivation as well as more general questions of ultimate purpose.

## Is It My Task to Save the World?

I shall commence this section with a citation from Frank H. Knight:

> It is intellectually impossible to believe that the individual can have any influence to speak of, . . . on the course of history. But it seems to me that to regard this as an ethical difficulty involves a complete misconception of the social-moral problem. . . . I find it impossible to give meaning to an ethical obligation on the part of the individual to improve society.
>
> The disposition of an individual, under liberalism, to take upon himself such a responsibility seems to be an exhibition of intellectual and *moral* conceit . . . ; it is *un*ethical. Ethical-social change must come about through a genuine moral consensus among individuals meeting on a level of genuine equality and mutuality and not with any one in the role of cause and the rest in that of effect, of one the "potter" and the others as "clay." ("Intellectual Confusion on Morals and Economics," *Ethics*)

I have long felt a strong affinity for Knight's position. But I have found it difficult to go beyond affirmation of agreement and to mount a persuasive supportive argument. We face squarely the question: If no individual assumes responsibility for improving society, how can society ever improve, other than through the forces of evolutionary change? I am on record as rejecting acquiescence before the forces of a cultural evolution. I have stated, on numerous occasions, that we have a moral obligation to think that we can constructively design and implement reform in social arrangements.

Any appearance of paradox vanishes if care is taken to read and to understand what Frank Knight says in his statement. He is not advancing a logic of rationally grounded abstention from discussion about changes in the rules of social order. He is defining the limits or constraints under which any individual must place himself as he enters into such discussion. The moral conceit that bothers Knight arises when any individual, or group, presumes to take on the responsibility for others, independent of their expressed agreement in a setting of mutuality and reciprocity. The underlying principle is indeed a simple one: Each person counts equally. And even if this principle counters observed empirical reality in terms of measurable criteria, adherence to the principle must remain relatively absolute, even on an acknowledged "as if" basis.

This principle has been a central element in my own approach to political economy. I have always thought it my task to develop and create ideas and to enter these ideas into the discussion matrix. Once this step is taken, my task is done. I have felt, and feel, no moral obligation to promulgate my own ideas, or those of others. In this, I differ sharply from many of my colleagues in economics. I have never been didactically motivated, despite reasonable success in teaching, especially at the graduate level. For me, utility enhancement stems from working out ideas for myself and with sufficient clarity that enables me to present a coherent and aesthetically satisfying argument. Ultimate publication reconfirms initial judgments in this respect. If my ideas succeed in persuading others to view the social world in a fashion similar to my own, I secure secondary utility gains. But if my ideas fail to persuade, and the implied reforms in social arrangements do not occur, my private utility losses are no greater than those of persons who do not enter the discussion. I do not, in any sense, accept responsibility for the results of the interaction in which I am only one among many participants. I cannot, as Knight suggests, move the world unaided, and it is morally arrogant of me to imagine myself in a position of power sufficient to enable me to act unilaterally.

Respect for the individual, as one among many participants in the social network of interaction, imposes a necessary humility on the social scientist. This humility is a stance that must be deliberately maintained. The natural scientist faces no comparable choice; he works within the constraints imposed by the almost total exogeneity of the subject matter that he explores. The social scientist must acknowledge the endogeneity of the structure of social interaction, at least within broad limits. But the endogeneity applies to the whole community of participants, including the scientist. Imagined, and potentially realizable, structures of social interaction that are alternatives to that which is observed to exist are within the set of those that are made feasible by physical and natural limits, including human nature. The social scientist defaults on his duty if he fails to model structures of interaction "that might be." As the social scientist makes predictions about the working properties of imagined alternative structures, he becomes both internally and externally vulnerable in a manner unknown to the natural scientist. Precisely because the direct linkage between observed reality and theories about that reality is abandoned, the discipline imposed by potential testability (falsifiability) is weakened. The social scientist is internally tempted to bias his argument toward structures that reflect his normative values. And even if he succeeds in thwarting this temptation, his critics will charge that he has not done so.

The fact-value distinction so beloved by second-rate methodologists confuses rather than enlightens. The social scientist who predicts "what might be" is not working within the realm of facts that may be observed in historical reality. The often-observed pitiful efforts to milk empirical data to reinforce hypothetical predictions reflect misunderstanding of the whole enterprise.

## Science or Art?

I have never been attracted to enter the sometimes complex upper reaches of the philosophy of science, and particularly the discussion of "economics as a science." I have not shied away from presenting my own methodological position, which does, indeed, ensure that I remain an outsider in this as in so many other aspects of my endeavors.[3] But discussion among philosophers of science, per se, has always seemed to me to use the natural sciences as a model and to embody a failure to appreciate the distinguishing features of social science, only some of which I noted in the preceding section.

It is precisely because of my conviction that social science is different from

3. See my "Positive Economics, Welfare Economics, and Political Economy," *Journal of Law and Economics,* 2 (October 1959), 124–38; and my "What Should Economists Do?" *Southern Economic Journal,* 30 (January 1964), 213–22.

natural science that I find myself more sympathetic to the interpretist critique than most of my economist peers, save for a few who locate themselves among modern Austrians. Yet while I am more sympathetic to the criticism, I should insist that the social scientist hold fast to the truth-directed morality of his natural science counterpart.

I can perhaps clarify my position by comparing and contrasting the scientist and the artist, with the former described in the role normally assigned to the natural scientist. I return to the exogeneity of the subject matter with which the natural scientist works, the reality that is, independent of his own understanding of its inner workings. The behavior of the scientist is *discovery;* he finds that which exists, and his imaginative talents are deployed in a search process. There is, and should be, no pretense that something new is created.

Consider the artist, however. He is, of course, constrained by the physical limits of his medium, be this paint or stone. But it is totally misleading to model the artist's act as discovery. The artist creates something where there was nothing. Both the act of scientific discovery and the act of artistic creation are intensely private as they are carried out. But the products divide sharply along the public-private dimension, once the acts are done. Scientific discovery is public in the classical sense; once made available to anyone, it can be available to everyone. Artistic creation is available to everyone once it is done; but that which is created may be privately interpreted in many and varied ways.

This comparative sketch should suggest that social science, as an activity, falls somewhere between the two models. Because the social scientist must explore the working properties of imagined alternatives to that which is observed, constrained only by the natural limits of the material with which he works, his activity has elements that are more akin to those that inform the artistic process than the scientific. However, his ultimate motivation matches that of the scientist, not the artist. The social scientist works in the hope that improvement in the processes of social interaction will finally emerge upon agreement both on diagnosis and on effective reform; aesthetic experience plays little role.

My own subdisciplinary prejudices should be evident. Within economics, I look on the efforts of the general equilibrium theorists, even if these efforts are sometimes extended to unnecessarily rarefied abstraction, to be potentially more productive than the works of those empiricists who behave as if the reality of social interaction embodies an exogeneity comparable to that of the physical world.

## Normative and Positive Political Economy

Critics have charged that my work has been driven by an underlying normative purpose, and by inference, if not directly, they have judged me to be mildly subversive. As I noted earlier, anyone who models interaction structures that might be is likely to be accused of biasing analysis toward those alternatives that best meet his personal value standards. Whether or not my efforts have exhibited bias in this sense is for others to determine. I shall acknowledge that I always work within a self-imposed constraint that some may choose to call a normative one. I have no interest in structures of social interaction that are nonindividualist in the potter-clay analogy mentioned in the earlier citation from Frank Knight. That is to say, I do not extend my own analysis to alternatives that embody the *rule* of any person or group of persons over other persons or group of persons. If this places my work in some stigmatized normative category, so be it.

The individualist element in my vision of social reality, actual or potential, has been an important component of my substantive criticism of the work of others in political economy. I have remained unable either to share in the enthusiasm for the social welfare function of formal welfare economics or to participate putatively in proffering advice to a presumed benevolently despotic government. There are at least three distinguishable sources of my criticism of orthodox political economy. First, I have been influenced by Frank Knight and by F. A. Hayek in their insistence that the problem of social order is not scientific in the standard sense. Second, I was greatly influenced by Knut Wicksell's admonition that economists cease acting as if government were a benevolent despot. Third, I rejected, very early in my thinking, the orthodox economist's elevation of allocative efficiency as an independent standard of evaluation.

These three sources seem internally consistent, and properly combined, they have provided me with my own window on the political economy. From this window, I found it relatively easy to mount criticism of much of the conventional wisdom. There seemed to be no shortage of matters to be straightened out, and I have been quite happy to leave to others the classification into normative or positive categories.

Wicksell's was perhaps the most significant influence, but without Knight's teaching and without my conversion to a catallactic perspective, Wicksell's message might not have been so compelling to me. However, once Wicksell's advice is heeded, once we acknowledge that governmental or political decisions are themselves produced by an interaction of persons acting in various roles, the political economist necessarily must extend analysis to the process of interaction and to the relation between process and patterns of results. The theory of public choice, at least my own version of this theory, was an almost natural consequence of my absorption of the Wicksellian message.[4]

Conceptualization of political reality as emergent from the interaction of many persons immediately suggests that patterns of results depend on the rules or institutions within which behavior takes place. Constitutional political economy, in both its normative and positive variants, replaces the political economy of policy at center stage. The shift of focus to rules comes quite naturally to the economist who has been exposed to the approach of modern game theory. But concentration on processes rather than outcomes does not fit well within the orthodoxy of political science, the pre-modern origins of which involve idealizations of parliamentary regimes. Despite our expressed intent to model the logical foundations of constitutional democracy, roughly corresponding to the Madisonian enterprise, Gordon Tullock and I found a very mixed reception to our book, *The Calculus of Consent* (1962).

There seemed to be a surprising reluctance by modern social scientists, economists and political scientists alike, to accept the two-stage decision structure that constitutional understanding requires and that all game theorists necessarily adopt. For over a quarter-century, I have found myself trying to clarify the constitutional perspective on policies, and on the economy as well, with demonstrable but quite limited success.

---

4. The relationship between the precursory ideas of Wicksell and later developments in public choice theory was the subject of my Nobel Prize lecture in December 1986. See "The Constitution of Economic Policy," *American Economic Review,* 77 (June 1987), 243–50.

## An Outsider Comes Inside

Nonetheless, the dialogue has shifted. "Constitutional economics," or "constitutional political economy," has emerged as an entry in *The New Palgrave*. My own emphasis on the importance of the rules of the social-economic-political game was recognized in the Nobel Prize citation in 1986. No longer could I claim status as a genuine outsider whose efforts continue to be largely ignored by my peers in the academy. Within limits, and despite my stance of relative indifference noted earlier, my ideas are beginning to have consequences. I do not yet know how I shall react when and if specific changes in rules are more or less directly traceable to my influence. I do not welcome becoming an "insider" in any sense, and my own efforts over four decades can be understood only in terms of the outsider image of myself that has been an integral part of my personal luggage.

The outsider appellation explains the somewhat singular type of self-confidence that I have always had to a degree and that has been reinforced over four decades. I have been academically successful, far beyond any plausibly predictable range, more or less "in spite of" my limitations rather than "because of" my capacities. I would never have been really surprised had my work failed to prove acceptable for publication, had my published work been neglected far more than it was, had my career advancement been less rapid, had there been no series of alternative opportunities in the competitive academic environment of the United States, had I not been awarded the Nobel Prize in 1986. I have never felt, nor do I feel today, that there is much that is unique or special about what I have done or what I do, write, and say. My surprise, and this surprise has continued to exist for four decades, is not at all that my own work is relatively neglected; my surprise is, instead, that other economists have failed to acknowledge the simple and the obvious, which is all that I have ever claimed my work to be. In a sense I have felt embarrassed at being placed in the role of telling my far more clever peers that the king really has no clothes.

Why was it my task to point out that economists should postulate some model of policies before proffering policy advice? Why, among the many critics of Arrow's important work in the general impossibility theorem, did it fall on me to point out that the satisfaction of his plausible conditions would amount to political tyranny rather than effective democracy? Why was it necessary for me to demonstrate that classical public debt theory was logically valid, in the face of the Keynesian macroaggregation absurdities? Why was it required to show that genuinely sacrificed opportunities must be measured in a utility dimension? These and other "contributions" attributed to me might not have been made had I worked as an "insider" involved in the complexities of analytical discussion along the heated cutting edges of economics. Such an insider might have been unable to take the comprehensive perspective that my outsider position allowed me to assume, almost as a matter of course.

It is in this respect that I do not especially welcome the increasing academic respectability and popularity of my own ideas. As a critic of prevailing orthodoxies, I had no reason to back up and respond to critics of my constructions, which seemed, in any case, to be triturations of the obvious. As my ideas approach mainstream, at least in some aspects, I find myself being challenged to defend foundational normative sources that I had long considered to be widely shared. The fact that my own acknowledged normative starting points do not seem so widely accepted as I should have expected may possibly account for the apparent oversight of propositions that seemed so obvious to me. In other words, my normative mind-set may be more important than I have ever realized.

## Why Not Sit in My Rocking Chair?

I resist, and resist strongly, any and all efforts to pull me toward positions of advising on this or that policy or cause. I sign no petitions, join no political organizations, advise no party, serve no lobbying effort. Yet the public's image of me, and especially as developed through the media after the Nobel Prize in 1986, is that of a right-wing libertarian zealot who is anti-democratic, anti-egalitarian, and anti-scientific. I am, of course, none of these and am, indeed, the opposites. Properly understood, my position is both democratic and egalitarian, and I am as much a scientist as any of my peers in economics. But I am passionately individualistic, and my emphasis on individual liberty does set me apart from many of my academic colleagues whose mind-sets are mildly elitist and, hence, collectivist. And to these colleagues, I can never be forgiven for having contributed to the development of a subdiscipline, public choice, that has exposed the operation of collectivist political institutions to serious scrutiny for the first time in well over a century.

Why do I continue to work? Why do I not retire gracefully to my mountain farm in Virginia, sit in my front-porch rocking chair, bemused at the follies of the world? Since I have acknowledged that I do not presume to move the world unaided, and that I have no urge to do so, what inner forces drive me? My answer, as adumbrated, is simple and straightforward. I work because I enjoy it! I get utility in ideas, in thinking, in organizing my thoughts, in writing these thoughts in coherent argument, in seeing my words in manuscript and in print. In some real sense, I am a writer who enjoys living in his own world, a world that some critics claim to be fictional but that I defend as feasibly attainable territory. I am also a lecturer, perhaps a century out of date, and I get utility from the receptive feedback for an intellectually competent audience. Here again, my ultimate purpose, either in writing or in lecturing, is not so much to convince readers or listeners of the merits of my argument, but to engage them in ongoing discussion.

Above all, perhaps, I am an intellectual reductionist who seeks to cut through the complexities of argument and to understand points in simple terms and homely examples. As noted earlier, much of my work has been in the form of exposé, and hence of a sort that is rarely welcomed by those who are natural obscurantists.

When all is said, I have faced few genuine choices between work and play because there is really no distinction. My work is my play, and I am surely among the fortunate in this as in so many other aspects of a happy and well-ordered life. I have not been plagued by psychological hangovers that make me try to respond to the "whys" of existence or the "whats" beyond. I hope that I seem what I think I am: a constitutional political economist who shares an appreciation for the Judeo-Christian heritage that produced the values of Western culture and institutions of civil order, particularly as represented in the Madisonian vision of what the United States might have been and might still become. Am I grossly naive to think this definition is sufficient unto itself?

# Italian Retrospective

## I. Introduction

The Fulbright year in Italy (September 1955–August 1956) was critically important in influencing the development of my interest in political decision structures and processes and particularly in the participation by individuals in these structures and processes. It is not exaggeration to state that the Italian year allowed me to cross the threshold into what would much later come to be called the research program in "public choice," and, particularly, the more narrowly defined program in "constitutional political economy."

The Italian year was also important in setting off and stimulating my interest in the theory of public debt, which came to be the focus of my efforts immediately on my return to Virginia in 1956. In a more comprehensive, and external, assessment of my work, this public debt effort may be viewed, as it has been by some critics, as a digression from the direct public choice emphasis, as initially suggested in my pre-Italy papers in 1949 and 1954 and carried forward in much of my later work.[1] However, in an internal assessment,

From *Better than Plowing: And Other Personal Essays* (Chicago: University of Chicago Press, 1992), 82–92. Copyright 1992 by The University of Chicago. All rights reserved. Reprinted by permission of the University of Chicago Press, publisher.

The translation of an early version of this chapter was printed under the title "Ricordo di un anno in Italia" as part of the Italian translation of my *Freedom in Constitutional Contract* (College Station: Texas A&M University Press, 1977). *Libertà nel contratto costituzionale,* ed. di Paolo Martelli (Milan: Arnoldo Mondadori Editore, 1990).

1. James M. Buchanan, "The Pure Theory of Public Finance: A Suggested Approach," *Journal of Political Economy,* 57 (December 1949): 496–505. James M. Buchanan, "Social Choice, Democracy, and Free Markets," *Journal of Political Economy,* 62 (April 1954): 114–24. Reprinted in James M. Buchanan, *Fiscal Theory and Political Economy* (Chapel Hill:

the work on public debt falls squarely within the more inclusive research program that describes my career, and particularly with regard to my expressed aim of reducing changes in macroaggregative variables to individually identified utility gains and losses.

I can, indeed, locate precisely the moment when the "theory of public debt burden" became clear to me. This moment occurred near the end of my Italian visit, during a sojourn at the Albergo d'Ingleterra in Rome. Even more precisely, the moment of "enlightenment" came while I was walking down the marbled stairs between floors on the occasion of a mechanical failure of the lift. I treasure the memory of that moment because we rarely are able to locate the emergence of ideas so distinctly. I waxed so enthusiastic over the "discovery" that I commenced writing what later became my book on stationery picked up from the hotel writing room.[2]

## II. Before Italy

I commenced my professional academic career as a straightforward public finance economist, whose concerns were about taxes, budgets, federalism, and fiscal policy. The public finance that I learned included goodly doses of Edgeworth-Pigou normative utilitarianism, of Marshallian incidence theory (of taxes, not of spending), of Keynesian inspired denial of debt burden. In this public finance orthodoxy for the 1940s, government was implicitly postulated to be exogenous to the economy or, when normative discourse commenced, was presumed to take the form of a monolithic and benevolent decision maker. In one of my first papers, I had challenged this presumption; in so doing I had already been stimulated and supported by Wicksell's seminal effort and by an English translation of de Viti de Marco's *First Principles of Public Finance*.[3]

My motivation in seeking a Fulbright research scholarship for study in It-

University of North Carolina Press, 1960), 75–89; and in *Public Finance: Selected Readings,* ed. Helen Cameron and William Henderson (New York: Random House, 1966), 158–75.

2. James M. Buchanan, *Public Principles of Public Debt* (Homewood, Ill.: Irwin, 1958).

3. Knut Wicksell, *Finanztheoretische Untersuchungen* (Jena: Gustav Fischer, 1896); Antonio de Viti de Marco, *First Principles of Public Finance,* trans. E. P. Marget (London: Jonathan Cape, 1936).

aly was a mixture of the scientific and the personal. I did, indeed, want to learn more about what the Italian masters in public finance had written about political decision structures, as these might affect the pattern of results observed. I was curious as to how the Italians had managed to integrate their analyses of taxes and spending, both positive and normative, with the alternative models or theories of collective or political decision making. But I also wanted some exposure to, some involvement in, a European cultural experience. As a Tennessee native whose World War II experience had been exclusively in the Pacific theater and whose graduate training had been in mid-America at Chicago, I sought to "jump over" the cultural atmosphere of the American East, and to acquire, within limits, some sense of the intellectual and cultural sophistication that only Europe seemed to, and did, offer.

Earl J. Hamilton, a professor at Chicago, had encouraged me to seize all opportunities to acquire language skills, and spurred by my initial reactions to de Viti de Marco, I tried to pick up minimal reading competence in Italian. Let me also acknowledge that I estimated my chances for success in the Fulbright competition to be higher in Italy than they might have been for a European year in the United Kingdom.

My application was successful, and from early 1955 I knew that the Italian year was settled. I had minimal personal contacts. Through earlier correspondence, I had exchanged views with Professor Lello Gangemi of Naples, who had encouraged me in my project. My personal assistance in the United States came from a surprising source. I got an unsolicited letter from Professor Oskar Morgenstern of Princeton, whom I had met only once, but who helped me greatly by listing acquaintances of his own whom I might look up when I arrived in Rome. It was Morgenstern who was responsible for my subsequent relationship with both Giannino Parravicini and Sergio Steve.

## III. Culture Shock

My wife and I sailed for Naples on the SS *Independence* in September 1955. At Naples, we—the whole group of American Fulbright recipients, professors, scholars, and students—were bused to Perugia, where we were enrolled for a month at the Universitá per Stranieri, with an intense concentration on learning to speak Italian.

We were lodged with the Giugliarelli family, in the oldest part of Perugia, near the center. The rules required that our hosts speak to us only in Italian. The month was personally rewarding because it helped us to get a sense of Italian family life and a taste for authentic Italian cuisine and to enjoy genuine Italian hospitality. Within a day of arrival we were, almost literally, made a part of the family, taking all our meals in the kitchen that served as the household center. My wife learned to cook Italian while I learned Italian conversational skills from a master instructor, Professor Guarnieri. And Perugia itself offered a fine base for the initial weeks of an extended Italian visit. The Umbrian hill towns—Perugia, Assisi, Gubbio, and others—remain, for me, the best of Italy.

In early October 1955 we were ready for Rome, and I was anxious to commence work on the project that had motivated the visit. Housing was difficult to find, and provisionally we found accommodations as paying guests in the lovely home of Signora Laura Guidi, the widow of a professor of Arabic languages at the University of Rome, and herself a distinguished Roman matron. Her home was ideally located in the Aventino, just across the street from the church of San Sabina, and only a short distance from the famous keyhole of the garden that frames St. Peter's across the Tiber. From my desk in the professor's study, surrounded by many volumes of Arabic grammar, I could look across at St. Peter's and reflect on the grandeur that was Catholic Rome.

## IV. Research Setting

Finding a location where I might conduct my research was even more difficult. I was frustrated early by the limits on days and hours of library opening and on restrictions on the borrowing of books. After some comparisons of the alternatives available, I settled in at the library of the Bank of Italy, on the Via Nazionale. This library had a good collection of books relevant to my inquiry and, importantly, also kept up to date with journal issues in all languages. In addition the research and clerical staffs were cooperative and appreciative of my efforts. In part, my decision to locate at the bank was due to my early contact with Parravicini, who served on the research staff of the bank while, at the same time, holding down the chair of public finance, as professor-in-charge, at the University of Pavia. It was Parravicini who introduced me to the morning ritual of espresso or cappuccino at the nearby bar, always accompanied by good talk on economics.

Officially, I was attached to the University of Rome, but my physical presence there was limited to regular attendance at the seminar organized by Professor Ugo Papi every few weeks, always with presentations by visiting scholars from around the world. These were pleasant and informative occasions, made notably so by the postseminar dinners, always at an excellent restaurant on Piazza Colonna. Professor Papi, even in 1955, was quite a senior figure; I was more impressed by his extensive network of acquaintances among economists worldwide than by his contribution to ongoing discussion. But Papi was, indeed, a fine host figure, and the Italian year would have been less memorable in the absence of those seminars.

In terms of my own research purposes, the most helpful Italian scholar was Professor Sergio Steve, who lived and worked in Rome, and whom I had also contacted early as a result of Morgenstern's indirect introduction. Steve remains closer to being a "pure professor" than any Italian I have ever met, and he proved invaluable in pointing me in productive directions. His wide-ranging scholarship and knowledge of the history of doctrine in "scienza delle finanze" saved me from hours of fruitless search.

While in Rome, I also visited with Professor Cesare Cosciani, whose textbook I had read. He was helpful, but my contact with him was limited to one or two visits.

## V. Procedure and Routine

My research agenda was comprehensive but formless. I carried with me no provisional hypotheses to be tested. I sensed only that the Italian masters in "scienza delle finanze," because of their explicit attention to political decision structures, had worked at a level of analytical sophistication above and beyond that attained by their English-language counterparts. My immediate objective was to *read* the relevant materials, necessarily on a selective basis but broadly enough to give me some grounds for evaluation. My procedure was straightforward. Quite simply, I read and made notes on the treatises, books, monographs, and papers by Ferrara, Mazzola, de Viti de Marco, Pantaleoni, Ricca-Salerno, Puviani, Montemartini, Barone, Einaudi, Fasiani, Fubini, Cosciani, Griziotti, de Maria, Arena—and many others. In this process, at least in its early stages, I had no sense of what the structure of a final evaluation of the whole "tradition" might be, or if indeed a final evaluation would be forthcoming at all.

My routine was one of ordered scholarship, perhaps for the one and only time of my whole career. I arrived early at the library, and I worked a long half-day, almost never returning after the siesta, an institution that I came greatly to respect, then and now. Aside from the cappuccino breaks on those days when Parravicini was in residence (he spent two days per week in Pavia), my personal contacts with fellow economists were minimal. I met the other economists of the bank's research staff, but on little other than a cursory basis. I kept my attention on the books, at least sufficiently to satisfy myself that work was being done.

## VI. When in Rome

I was also *living* in Rome, and enjoying it. Perhaps more than in most cities of the world, there is a categorical distinction there between visiting and living. After two months as paying guests at Signora Guidi's, my wife and I subleased the flat of an economist from FAO (Food and Agriculture Organization) who took an American leave of absence. We moved across the Aventino, to Viale Giotto, only a short distance from Terme di Caracalla, the location of Rome's summer opera.

And we lived as Romans. The hard rolls delivered twice daily to our door spoiled forever our tastes for other breads. My wife made quotidian forays to the local markets, jug in hand, and returned with wines, pastas, fruits, and produce of the campagna. Vini dei Castelli, the wines of the Roman hills, were, for me, introductory to the pleasures of the grape. And the morning snack of the Roman shopper, focaccia or pizza bianca, remains a favorite after decades, so much so that my wife acquires a local reputation for its production wherever we locate for more than a few days.

We wandered about the city; we sampled its wares. We marveled at the delights of the "tavola calda," a glorious Italian precursor of the now ubiquitous fast-food franchise. We located the excellent, the good, the medium, and the bad trattorie; we learned the gustatory rewards of garlic, rosemary, oregano, basil, and so much else that was foreign to the mid-American palate, rewards without which we would now subsist nonexcitingly, if at all.

And, of course, we walked through the monuments of republican, imperial, medieval, and modern Rome, from the forum to the wedding cake. We did not neglect the churches, the museums, the fountains, or the galleries. We fed the communal cats at the Pantheon, those who sought out a bit of winter's sun on raw February days. We were in St. Peter's square on Easter Sunday, when the rain did stop to allow the Pope to appear on the balcony. But we did all this as Romans do, as if we were there rather than merely passing through.

## VII. Beyond the Walls

Aside from Perugia, my academic experience beyond Rome was limited. (Touristic jaunts are quite another matter; both in the initial year, and later, we visited all of Italy's regions and most of its towns and cities.) I traveled to Naples early, and I presented a seminar at the university under Gangemi's sponsorship. My primary recollection is unrelated to the subject matter; it is about Gangemi's flat which was, literally, lined wall-to-wall with original paintings by Italian artists. And my viewing was accompanied by Gangemi's disarming honesty in admitting that his passion for economics had long since been replaced by that for art.

The primary academic extension of the Roman year was Pavia. As noted, Parravicini was professor-in-charge of the relevant courses at the university, and he invited me to come along for a lecture and/or seminar on, I think, two separate occasions during the year. The professorial chair at the University of Pavia had long been held by Professor Benvenuto Griziotti, who had just retired. Griziotti and his wife, herself a distinguished scholar in the history of economic ideas, entertained us graciously in their home. And they also introduced us to Francesco Forte, who remained in Pavia as Griziotti's very last assistant. Forte was assigned the task (perhaps a chore to him as a very busy young scholar) of acting as our tour guide, host, and life arranger during the whole course of a several-day visit to the Po Valley and its environs. We made the circuit, which included two days in Milan.

The Pavia visit is important for me largely in that it marked the start of my relationship with Francesco Forte, whom we came to know much better in later years, both personally and professionally. The young Francesco Forte of 1956 so impressed me that I subsequently invited him as a visitor to my university in Virginia, from which, in turn, there emerged several coauthored papers. For three decades we have counted Francesco and Carmen Forte among a relatively small number of friends for life.

During my initial year in Italy, 1955–56, I did not know Bruno Leoni, who was professor of political science at Pavia at the time. As I noted earlier, I was only beginning to venture beyond the disciplinary boundaries of economics, including public finance, and I had neither the excuse nor the courage to make research thrusts into legal and political philosophy, domains that later came to command much of my attention. Some five years later than my first Italian visit, and after my initial crossing of the disciplinary threshold, so to speak, I read some of Leoni's seminal pieces, and I subsequently invited him for a Virginia visit. This visit was followed up by my own later visits to Pavia, Stresa, and elsewhere under Leoni's auspices. And I maintained a personal and professional association with Leoni until his tragic death.

## VIII. A Meeting with Luigi Einaudi

By late spring 1956, I had begun to block out a draft for a lengthy evaluative essay on the whole Italian tradition in "scienza delle finanze."[4] I had expressed to Giannino Parravicini a desire to meet, if at all possible, the only Italian master in the tradition who remained active. Luigi Einaudi had completed his tenure as president of the republic of Italy, and he had retired from both politics and the academy. But Professor Einaudi he remained to all who knew him, and during one of his periods of residence at his villa outside Rome he invited me to meet him. Parravicini accompanied me, and I recall a pleasant afternoon conversation in a sunlit and surprisingly well-stocked library of current periodicals in all languages and many subjects. Small in stature, but majestic in bearing, Einaudi greeted me with courtesy and respect, despite the awesome gulf between one of the free world's most respected leaders and an unknown, uncultured, and young American aca-

---

4. James M. Buchanan, " 'La Scienza delle finanze': The Italian Tradition in Fiscal Theory," in *Fiscal Theory and Political Economy* (Chapel Hill: University of North Carolina Press, 1960), 24–74.

demic. Most important for me, however, was Einaudi's expressed and sincere interest in my research project. He agreed to read my provisional draft essay and to offer comments and suggestions. As soon as I could do so, I sent off a copy of the draft to him, and he did, as promised, make several constructive suggestions. I was perhaps more proud of my ability to make the footnote acknowledgment for Einaudi's assistance than for any other such attribution in any of my writings.

At several of Papi's seminars, I met Professor Gustavo del Vecchio, who was also of Einaudi's generation, and who was widely respected as one of the most senior economists in Italy. Even though he had not worked directly in public finance theory, del Vecchio knew personally many of those whose works I examined in the essay. He also agreed to read and make comments on my draft, and I was pleased to acknowledge his assistance as well in the same footnote.

## IX. The Italian Legacy

A review of my summary essay, written in 1956 and 1957 and published in 1960, would not convey accurately the impact of the Italian exposure on the direction and development of my own research program over the years subsequent to my visit. As noted, my scientific perspective as of the middle 1950s was that of a public finance economist who was only beginning to recognize the potential explanatory extension made possible by the abandonment of disciplinary constraints. I did not then appreciate that Knut Wicksell and the Italians had left me with an enduring intellectual legacy that insured personal differentiation of "my product" from that of most of my American peers.

This differentiation in perspective, on political economy generally, was in the process of emergence almost from the onset of my research career, as witnessed by the arguments in my 1949 paper and in my 1954 review of Arrow's work.[5] Despite these directional flags, however, my specific work in 1955, just prior to the Italian year, involved a strictly orthodox application of efficiency analysis to current policy, specifically to the financing, production, and pricing of highway or road services. The Italian leave of absence from this project convinced me that the whole argument of the book I had almost finished was

5. Kenneth Arrow, *Social Choice and Individual Values* (New York: Wiley, 1951).

both naïve and misleading, so much so that, upon my return, I gleefully abandoned all efforts toward completion.

Two things had happened during the twelve-month period. I had, while living and working in Rome, completed the final draft of the English translation (from the German original) of Wicksell's seminal essay.[6] (In this effort, I was aided and abetted greatly by Elizabeth Henderson, who lived in Rome only a short distance from my flat.) And, as narrated above, I had also read the Italian masters in "scienza delle finanze," who had emphasized the importance of modeling political decision structures for any exercise in political economy, whether positive or normative.

In retrospect, I do not think that a geographically detached or distanced experience of these two "readings" would have sufficed to push me fully and irrevocably beyond the mindset of the orthodox economists of the day. I was, in this sense, fortunate that these complementary "readings" occurred during residence in Italy. I absorbed what was, for me, an attitude toward "the state" that I could never have quite attained in America (or in Britain). Is it grossly inaccurate to claim that the Italian mind remained almost totally immune from Hegelian mythology, and that "the state" was always viewed through the observed activities of its all-too-human agents? What I might call this Italian perspective on politics, which now seems so natural to me, emerged definitively upon my return to American academia.

This perspective has much in common with eighteenth-century conceptions from which emerged both the ideas of the Scottish Enlightenment and those of the American Founding Fathers. After Italy, I was prepared, intellectually, psychologically, and emotionally, to join in an entrepreneurial venture with my Virginia colleague Warren Nutter, a venture aimed at bringing renewed emphasis to "political economy" in its classical sense. And from these beginnings, the more directed research spin-off into the "economics of politics," initiated jointly with my colleague Gordon Tullock, now seems as but a natural progression.

---

6. Knut Wicksell, "A New Theory of Just Taxation," in *Classics in the Theory of Public Finance,* ed. R. A. Musgrave and A. T. Peacock (London: Macmillan, 1958), 72–118.

# Political Economy: 1957–82

## I. Introduction

I have chosen this chapter's title, "Political Economy: 1957–82," with deliberation. The symmetry of a quarter-century has an appeal all its own, but my choice was also prompted by events at the beginning and the end years of the period selected. It was in 1957 that Warren Nutter and I founded the Thomas Jefferson Center for Studies in Political Economy and Social Philosophy at the University of Virginia. It was in 1982 that I engaged in a modern struggle to sustain an institutional setting for a political economy that Warren Nutter would have endorsed enthusiastically. I want to trace the lineage between these terminus points of my narrative. In so doing, I shall be largely concerned with what members of the academies were and are doing and how they interpret their own social, scientific, and philosophical roles. I do not apologize for this emphasis to those among my readers who are not of the academy. I remain convinced that what goes on in the groves has profound effects on the development and transmission of ideas and, ultimately, on the translation of these ideas into practice.

From *Liberty, Market and State: Political Economy in the 1980s* (Brighton, England: Wheatsheaf Books, 1986), 8–18. Copyright 1986 by James M. Buchanan. First published in Great Britain in 1986 by Wheatsheaf Books Ltd, Brighton, Sussex. Reprinted by permission of Pearson Education Limited.

Material in this chapter was first presented as the G. Warren Nutter Memorial Lecture at American Enterprise Institute, Washington, D.C., 20 April 1983, and was published under the chapter's title by American Enterprise Institute, Washington. © American Enterprise Institute, 1983. I acknowledge permission to reprint relevant portions. I have made some revisions from the initial lecture, both the delivered and the published versions.

## II. Political Economy: 1957

In 1957 the anti-libertarian socialists were in the ascendancy in the academies. I refer to those who were driven by an ideological commitment to the benevolent leadership of the national state on all matters economic. (The French have a more suitably descriptive word, *dirigistes*.) In 1957 the Keynesian "digression," to employ Leland Yeager's apt phraseology, was still accelerating if measured by its acceptance in the universities. Those were the days before the Stalinist terror had fully seeped into modern intellectual consciousness. The debacle of post-war socialist experiments elsewhere had not then been fully recognized. The dirigistes in the academic establishment, those who would have run our lives for us, were in positions of dominance. They controlled major departmental programmes; they made basic decisions on who should be appointed, tenured, and promoted; they approved what was to be published; they controlled the flow of funds from the major foundations, which had by that time floated free of any desires of the initial donors.

When Warren Nutter and I joined the faculty at the University of Virginia in late 1956 and early 1957, we found, I think to our own surprise, an academic setting that was genuinely different, in a commonwealth that had a different history that mattered for its academies. Under the leadership of T. R. Snavely, and bolstered by the imaginative ideas of David McCord Wright and Rutledge Vining, the economics programme at Virginia had already become "different" from its counterparts. The University of Virginia administration was more than passively receptive to our announced intention to make some effort to counter more explicitly the dominating thrust in economics, and in political economy, circa 1957. (Almost surely, any statement of such an intention would have met immediate resistance at most of the leading universities in the United States at that time.) I recall vividly a meeting with William Duren, then Dean of the College of Arts and Sciences, and Colgate Darden, then President of the University. When I somewhat hesitantly put forward the notion that Warren and I had discussed about establishing a political economy center, the simple response was "go ahead." Given this lead, we waxed enthusiastic, and establish such a center we did.

In the initial brochure for the Thomas Jefferson Center for Studies in Political Economy and Social Philosophy that Warren and I jointly prepared, we stated that our purpose was to set up a "community of scholars who wish to preserve a social order based on individual liberty." Little did we reckon on the difficulties that the phrase "individual liberty" would cause us in the intellectual-academic atmosphere of that time. We were told, quite openly, by an officer of a major foundation, that the explicit encouragement of scholars who believed in individual liberty, as implied in the brochure, was "particularly objectionable," and that the Thomas Jefferson Center's stated purpose reflected a clearly defined ideological bias. We were placed under suspicion precisely because we had indicated our intention to study the problems of a free society.

In retrospect I can recognize our naïveté in thinking that rational argument could have been effective in countering the dominant mind-set of the time. But we did make such argument, and I remain pleased with one of my own statements included in a letter to Kermit Gordon, our primary adversary:

> I categorically refuse to acknowledge or to believe that a program such as ours, one that is unique only in its examination of the search of free men for consensus on social issues and which assumes that individuals are free to discuss all issues openly and fully, violates in even the slightest way the Jeffersonian spirit.

But all of this belongs in a much longer story than is appropriate in this chapter.

Let me then shift my level of discourse and try to outline for you what our thinking was in establishing the Thomas Jefferson Center. What differences in programme did we have in mind? How did Warren Nutter and I aim to make the Virginia programme in political economy distinct?

We were concerned, first of all, by what seemed to us to be a developing neglect of the basics of economics. Both Warren Nutter and I were Chicago economists, and Chicago economists of the Frank Knight, Henry Simons, Lloyd Mints, Aaron Director vintage. The basics of economics were those of *price theory,* not formal mathematics, and *price theory applied to real-world issues.* The economic organization, the market process, was the focus of attention, and the working of this organization operating through the pricing structure was the subject matter of the discipline. Political economy was nothing more than this subject matter embedded within the framework of society, described by the "laws and institutions" about which Adam Smith wrote. To us, quite simply, political economy meant nothing more than a return to the stance of the classical political economists. Aside from Chicago, we saw programmes elsewhere in economics neglecting these very foundations of our discipline.

Let me also admit, openly and without apology then or now, that we were motivated by our conviction that if these foundations are neglected, a society in which individuals retain their liberties is not sustainable. We had faith that an *understanding of the price system* offered the best possible avenue for the generation of support for free institutions. We did not feel any need for explicitly ideological polemic. Our faith in *understanding* was intensely personal. Both Warren and I became economists when we were dedicated socialists. We experienced "conversion" as a result of our own enlightenment through an understanding of market process, and we translated our own shared experience into the positions of our peers and students. We were convinced that the apparent persuasiveness of the socialist arguments seemed so only to those who were ignorant in economics. Our ultimate purpose was to enlighten prospective graduate students, to help them reach an understanding comparable to our own, to produce economists who knew what their proper subject matter was all about, economists who might be able, by presenting their own hard-nosed analysis, to then lead generations of others to their own enlightenment. It was as simple as that, even if we could not state our purpose so straightforwardly then as I can do now. And let me also now acknowledge that in the dominant anti-libertarian mind-set of the late 1950s our purpose was indeed *subversive*.

## III. The Charlottesville Decade: 1957–67

By both our own and by external standards, the "Virginia School," over the decade 1957–67, was highly successful. The Thomas Jefferson Center for Studies in Political Economy and Social Philosophy was generously supported by several special, non-mainstream foundations as well as by the university and the commonwealth. The graduate programme was expanded. Leland Yeager, Ronald Coase, Alexandre Kafka, Andrew Whinston, Gordon Tullock, and William Breit were added to the faculty. Visiting scholars, political economists all, and all of worldwide eminence, came to the center for extended half-year visits. These included Frank Knight, F. A. Hayek, Michael Polanyi,

Bertil Ohlin, Bruno Leoni, Terence Hutchison, Maurice Allais, Duncan Black, and O. H. Taylor.

We commenced to attract outstanding graduate students. For a period our graduate students were among the best in the United States. Out of several cohorts, and with my advance apologies to an equally large number whose names could well be added, let me mention only a few by name here: Otto Davis, Charles Goetz, Matt Lindsay, Jim Miller, John Moore, Mark Pauly, Charles Plott, Paul Craig Roberts, Craig Stubblebine, Bob Tollison, Dick Wagner, Tom Willett. These were all products of the "Virginia School of Political Economy." A mere listing of these names is sufficient without elaboration on my part. The Virginia initiative was successful.

During this "Charlottesville decade," which seems so productive when viewed retrospectively, things were, of course, happening in economics and in political economy, both in and out of the academies. As I noted earlier, the socialist ideal, as a motive force for intellectual-moral-emotional energies, was perhaps at its zenith in the 1950s. This force was spent by the middle of the 1960s. The somewhat lagged Keynesian apogee was attained in the very early 1960s, and fine-tuning went the way of all flesh in the latter part of the decade.

The dirigistes of our discipline shifted into neutral or else joined the flower children. The Virginia programme in political economy lost any putative ideological taint it might have had to external observers as its scholars and students produced ideas that came to command respect and attention. There came to be an increasing awareness of the importance of the institutional setting and of institutional constraints for the operation of an economy. Property-rights economics, law and economics, public choice—these three closely related but distinct subdisciplines emerged, each of which is derivative from political economy, broadly defined, and each of which also finds some of its origins in the work of scholars then associated with the Virginia School.

The active and identifiable programme at the University of Virginia was not, however, destined to persevere much beyond the decade. Despite its dramatic success story, the programme was too different from mainstream academic attitudes within the university itself and, notably, from attitudes held by those outside economics. At the very same time that the graduate programme was being so widely praised for its success by those beyond the

Lawn, there were active internal efforts aimed at its destruction. I personally recall that one of my proudest moments was recorded when Jack Gurley, then editor of the *American Economic Review,* sometime around 1963 or 1964, stated in a general meeting of the American Economic Association that Virginia's graduate students were submitting more interesting manuscripts than those of any other institution in the country. Almost simultaneously with this, however, and unknown both to Warren Nutter and to me, the university had, in 1963, organized a secret study of our programme, by a committee explicitly motivated by a desire to offset the "political motivation" of the center, and whose report concluded with a description of the Department of Economics as "rigidly committed to a single point of view" which it labelled as "nineteenth-century ultra-conservatism." All of this was produced with no consultation from the department or the center. The committee went on to recommend, of course, that economists of a "modern outlook" be appointed.

By the mid-1960s, the University of Virginia, which had indeed been so different in the 1950s, had joined the ranks of academic orthodoxy, albeit belatedly and almost out of date. Over a period of some four years, from 1964 through 1968, the university made no effort to hold onto members of the dramatically successful research-educational unit that we had so fortunately managed to organize at Virginia. Through a policy of deliberate neglect and even active encouragement, scholars were allowed to shift to other institutions. By 1968, Coase, Whinston, Tullock, and I had moved to other universities, and in 1969 Warren Nutter became a participating rather than an academic political economist.

At this point my necessarily autobiographical narrative loses direct contact with Warren Nutter. I saw him only rarely after I left Charlottesville in 1968, and after he joined the United States Department of Defense in 1969. I cannot, therefore, bear personal witness to the continuing struggle within the university that was waged by Warren Nutter after his return to academia, a struggle in which Warren was joined by Leland Yeager, William Breit, and others and which continued over the decade of the 1970s. On the few occasions that Warren and I did meet, however, I felt that there had been no change in our long-standing consensus on the purpose and objective of any programme in political economy. There was really no need for us to discuss this commonly held commitment to what we considered to be the moral obligation of those in our discipline. For this reason I feel that it remains appropriate for me to continue my personal approach to developments in political economy after 1968.

## IV. Public Choice—The New Virginia School: 1969–82

As I noted above, "public choice" emerged as an independent, or quasi-independent, subdiscipline within political economy and had its inception at the Thomas Jefferson Center in the early 1960s. What was to become the Public Choice Society was initially organized by Gordon Tullock and me at the Old Ivy Inn in Charlottesville in October 1963. When, six years later, Tullock and I found ourselves relocated in Virginia once again, this time at Virginia Polytechnic Institute, we established the Center for Study of Public Choice.

This new center had a somewhat narrower purpose than the Thomas Jefferson Center. Experience had shown us that an understanding of the market process was a necessary but not a sufficient condition to secure the intellectual-analytical foundations of a free society. This understanding is greatly strengthened in practice by a complementary understanding of the political process. And we found that the study of public choice, which in summary terms is nothing more than the application and extension of economic tools to politics, opened up exciting new vistas for social scientists, some of whom could never have been affected by exposure to old-fashioned, hard-headed price theory alone. Public choice quickly gained prominence in intellectual circles more generally, both in and out of the academies. Our programme in Blacksburg, supported initially by the exciting administrative leadership of T. Marshall Hahn, was a success in a way quite different from the earlier programme in Charlottesville. Graduate students came to Virginia Polytechnic Institute, and many of these now carry forward the public choice perspective in their research and teaching at many institutions. But perhaps the most dramatic impact of the programme was reflected in the internationalization of public choice over the decade of the 1970s. Public choice emerged as the "new political economy" in Europe, Japan, and elsewhere. Blacksburg, Virginia, of all places, became a mecca for economists, political scientists, philosophers, sociologists, and other scholars from all corners of the globe.

As was the case with the Charlottesville center a decade earlier, however, public choice research, like Virginia political economy, its parent, was too unorthodox, too different, indeed too successful, for the orthodoxy, whose members command positions of influence in modern academies. The year 1982 marked a turning point. The Center for Study of Public Choice at Virginia Polytechnic Institute, like the Thomas Jefferson Center before it, was a victim of its own successes. In 1982 a new story commenced. A decision was made to start anew, to shift the center's operations as a unit (faculty, staff, facilities) to George Mason University.

## V. The Orthodoxies of 1982

I repeat my apologies for too many lapses into autobiographical detail that will interest only selected readers. But I have a larger purpose in detailing these experiences. I want to compare and to contrast the challenges that Warren Nutter and I thought we faced in 1957 with those challenges that seem to face anyone who seeks to promote a research-educational programme in political economy in the decade of the 1980s.

Recall that I said earlier that the 1957 mind-set of the academy's members was dirigiste or anti-libertarian socialist. Among economists, market failure was all the rage, and a demonstration that markets could fail by comparison with a totally imaginary idealized construction was widely held to be evidence that political-governmental intervention was justified. The macroeconomic fluctuations in employment, output, and the price level were held to exist only because old-fogey politicians had not yet learned the Keynesian policy lessons. Recall how economists of that time laughed with scorn when President Eisenhower said that public debt imposed burdens on the generation's grandchildren.

It is easy to criticize the attitudes of the economists of the 1950s. But let us also give them credit due. They were wrong on so much; we are allowed to say this in hindsight. But they were interested in ideas, and they thought that ideas mattered. They were not frauds and they were not conscious parasites on the community.

A quarter-century is a long time. But the shift in the mind-set of the econ-omists who dominate the academies seems a whole century away from that of the 1950s. Surely for the better, anti-libertarian socialism has almost dis-appeared. Even under the most inclusive definition that might be possible, the economists of 1982 who could be enrolled under socialist banners would make up a tiny minority of the profession, and they control almost no pro-grammes or funds. The dominant dirigisme of the 1950s has vanished, but it has not been replaced by any comparable offsetting ideological commitment.

Economics, as a discipline, became "scientific" over the quarter-century, but I put the word in inverted commas and I deliberately pronounce it pe-joratively here. As it is practiced in the 1980s, economics is a "science" with-out ultimate purpose or meaning. It has allowed itself to become captive of the technical tools that it employs without keeping track of just what it is that the tools are to be used for. In a very real sense, the economists of the 1980s are illiterate in basic principles of their own discipline, even if in a quite dif-ferent manner from those of the 1950s. Their motivation is not normative; they seem to be ideological eunuchs. Their interest lies in the purely intellec-tual properties of the models with which they work, and they seem to get their kicks from the discovery of proofs of propositions relevant only for their own fantasy lands.

Command of the tools of modern economics is a challenging intellectual achievement, and I do not question for a minute the brilliance of the modern "scientists" who call their discipline by the same name that I call my own. I do deplore the waste that such investment of human capital reflects. The in-tellectual achievement comes at major resource cost, and, as with any such commitment, the opportunity cost is measured in benefits that might be ex-pected from the alternative that is sacrificed. In modern economics, that which is sacrificed is an understanding of the principles of market process and of the relationship of this process to the institutional setting within which persons choose. In other words, learning to master the tools of mod-ern economics, as exemplified in the educational programmes of our major graduate schools today, does not leave time for the achievement of an un-derstanding of political economy in the classical meaning of the term.

Our graduate schools are producing highly trained, highly intelligent technicians who are blissfully ignorant of the whole purpose of their alleged discipline. They feel no moral obligation to convey and to transmit to their students any understanding of the social process through which a society of free persons can be organized without overt conflict while at the same time using resources with tolerable efficiency.

The task faced by those of us who would attempt to restore political economy to its proper place of attention as the central research programme of our discipline is then quite different from that which we faced in the 1950s, and it is in many respects much more difficult. The socialist commitment was dislodged in part by the simple observation of the cumulative historical experience, which finally does affect human consciousness, even of those who are long-immunized within the ivoried towers. The success of some of our earlier efforts in instilling an understanding of the elementary principles of market and political order was made possible only by the sweep of events over the three decades. To say that events overwhelmed the intellectual arguments is not, of course, to deny the relevance of the latter. Public choice theory did offer an intellectually sophisticated government failure analogue to the earlier market failure thrust of welfare economics. But general attitudes about governmental failures were much more directly affected by straightforward observation of those failures in action.

Our job in the 1980s is therefore less one of ideological displacement and more one of methodological revolution in our parent discipline of economics itself. We find ourselves in the bizarre position where those of us who seek to define our central research programme as it was defined for the first century and one-half of our discipline's history are now the methodological revolutionaries.

Our task is made difficult because of the genuine awe that partially trained mathematicians feel for mathematics itself. It is useful to try to understand just why this awe arises and why it tends to create such serious inferiority complexes in those economists who do not fully understand economic process. Why do the acknowledged masters in mathematics itself not feel some comparable awe at the understanding possessed by the genuine political economists? What is the ultimate source of the one-way awe?

I suggest that the asymmetry emerges because of the methodological revolution in economics that did take place, almost unnoticed, in the twentieth century and, notably, since Alfred Marshall wrote his *Principles*. Once the "economic problem" is the research programme of the discipline, and the search is on for maximizing or optimizing solutions within the constraints of specified wants, resources, and technology, we are unwittingly trapped in a *mathematical perspective.* In this perspective, we *must* defer to those among us who have superior command of the tools and techniques that only sophisticated modern mathematics can provide. In this perspective, those among us who cannot "border the Hessians" *are* ignoramuses, and we should be made to feel pedestrian and second rate, left behind by the mainstream scholars of the 1980s.

The basic commitment to the mathematical perspective in economics may be challenged, however, and outside this perspective we need feel no more awe for the mathematicians than we do for the logician, the linguist, or the fiddle player. In comparison with these specialists, we simply acknowledge that we are trained to do, and do, different things. So it should be with the mathematicians. The methodological revolution that is required in political economy must remove the awe by shedding the mathematical perspective; unless this perspective is modified, we shall remain the slaves of the economist-cum-mathematician.

Let me be quite specific at this point, and let me try to illustrate my argument. It is necessary to be clear, especially since many of our colleagues who are outstanding political economists, in the way that I should define the term, remain trapped in the mathematical perspective, even if they remain unconscious of its effect on so many lesser lights. It is their own ability to have become solid political economists while not having been awed by the mathematicians that distinguishes members of this group, but this very ability does tend to blind them to the genuine methodological trap that the mathematical perspective places upon the whole discipline.

I suggest that the mathematical perspective takes hold once we so much as define persons as utility or preference functions and implicitly presume that these functions exist independent of the processes within which persons make actual choices. The utility function apparatus can be properly employed as an *ex post* reconstruction of the choices that may have been made, but it becomes totally misleading to postulate the independent existence of such functions. By postulating such functions independently, and by imposing the resource constraints, it then becomes possible to define, at least conceptually, the "efficient" allocation of resources, quite apart from any voluntary processes of agreement among trading parties. This formalization of the efficiency norm then allows the market to be conceptualized as merely a means, a mechanism, one among others, to be tested or evaluated in terms of its efficacy in attaining desired results in the utilization of resources.

It is indeed hard for almost anyone trained in economics almost anywhere in this part of our century to exorcise the false constructions and presuppositions that characterize the mathematical perspective. It is not easy to give up the notion that there does indeed exist an "efficient" resource allocation, "out there" to be conceptually defined by the economist and against which all institutional arrangements may be tested. Despite the emerging emphasis on process as opposed to end-state philosophizing, economists will only reluctantly give up major instruments of their kit of tools.

## VI. Prospects

In any short-term context, I am not at all optimistic that the required methodological revolution will take place. Academic programmes almost everywhere are controlled by rent-recipients who simply try to ape the mainstream work of their peers in the discipline. These academic bureaucrats will not be easily displaced, and it is only in fortuitous circumstances that favourable academic settings will present themselves to those who would take the foundations of their discipline seriously.

I remain thoroughly convinced, however, in 1984 as in 1957, that those of us who do place a value on the transmission of the intellectual heritage of political economy face a moral imperative. We must exert every effort to ensure the survival of the ideas that were formative in generating what Hayek has properly called "the great society."

Warren Nutter was fond of saying, in the sometimes bleak days of the 1950s and early 1960s, that one of our most important functions was to "save the books." Interpreted in the way that I know Warren meant that statement, our function remains basically unchanged. Classical liberalism—the ideas and the analysis that nurtured these ideals for a society that became a near reality—need not perish from the earth. As the saying on Fred Glahe's Colorado T-shirt goes, "Adam Smith was right—pass it on."

# Virginia Political Economy
## Some Personal Reflections

## I. Introduction

In this chapter I shall discuss what has come to be known as "Virginia Political Economy" from my own personal, and very private, perspective. By "personal" I refer to a subjective vision of persons and events as they affected the academic matters to be discussed. I do not intend to treat details of private lives, either my own or those of others. The chapter is, therefore, autobiographical in an intellectual rather than a behavioral, emotional, or psychological sense.

I have, of course, been pleased by the emergence of the appellation "Virginia" or "Virginian" applied or assigned to the particular research program in political economy with which I have been associated at three separate universities in the commonwealth, and over a period of more than three decades. I have not, and I do not, reject this appellation, and I have never felt embarrassed when my work has been described as its exemplar. I have come increasingly to accept the uniqueness of my perspective on political-economic-legal order. For many years I considered my perspective to be similar if not identical to that which was very widely shared by most if not all persons who emerged from the American culture; I now realize that my estimates of the number of persons who share my perspective were grossly exaggerated.

To the extent that Virginia Political Economy embodies the unfolding and developing articulation of my vision of social interaction, I am alone responsible for both the limits and the credits. In yet another, and quite interesting, sense, I have been placed in the position of being the "front man," the representative embodiment of intersecting strands of ideas that have been created by others with whom I have worked closely. The research program in Virginia Political Economy may be associated with me—properly so—but the program as it developed could never have emerged independent of the efforts and input of G. Warren Nutter, Rutledge Vining, Gordon Tullock, Leland Yeager, Winston Bush, Richard Wagner, Charles Goetz, Geoffrey Brennan, and other colleagues and students over the years. I shall, in this chapter, try to isolate and identify the separate contributions of these charter members, so to speak, of the "Virginia School." Those whose names enter my narrative explicitly may, of course, reject my interpretation both of ideas and of events. And those whose names are not explicitly noted deserve my apologies. I make no effort here to do other than present my considered, but still personal, reflections.

## II. Chicago, Charlottesville, and Thomas Jefferson

Virginia Political Economy was born in the foyer of the Social Sciences Building at the University of Chicago early in 1948. In a casual conversation with a fellow graduate student, Warren Nutter, I discovered that we shared an evaluation and diagnosis of developments in economics, the discipline with which we were about to become associated as licensed practitioners. We sensed that economics had shifted, and was shifting, away from its classical foundations as a component of a comprehensive moral philosophy, and that technique was replacing substance. We concurred in the view that some deliberately organized renewal of the classical emphasis was a project worthy of dreams.

Almost ten years later, in early 1957, Warren Nutter and I found ourselves in a position to actuate the idea we had discussed. We had simultaneously joined the faculty at the University of Virginia in Charlottesville, and we had more or less inherited a leadership role. With enthusiastic support from William Duren, then dean of the faculty, we established the Thomas Jefferson Center for Studies in Political Economy and Social Philosophy. The last three words were necessary to describe our purpose, but these soon proved too cumbersome for practical usage and were dropped.

I shall not, in this chapter, discuss the opposition we encountered; I have touched on this briefly elsewhere.[1] But we were not totally isolated, and we secured solid, and substantial, early support for our projected program. The William Volker Fund deserves special mention. An initial five-year grant enabled us to bring to Charlottesville a sequence of Distinguished Visiting Scholars for periods of a half-year each. We turned immediately to Frank H. Knight and F. A. Hayek and later added Michael Polanyi, Maurice Allais, Bertil Ohlin, Overton H. Taylor, T. W. Hutchison, Duncan Black, and Bruno Leoni. These political economists, defined in the broadest sense, graced the Charlottesville academic scene with formal lecture series as well as informal contacts with students and faculty alike. And, importantly for our purposes, their presence brought external attention to the Virginia program in political economy, attention that was necessary to suggest that the program was, in fact, different from the mainstream.

Let me pause here in my account and discuss briefly the Virginia program in economics that Warren Nutter and I found when we arrived in Charlottesville in 1956 and 1957. David McCord Wright had already departed for Oxford and McGill, but his presence was alive, and our proposal might not have been so well received locally without his preparation of the ground. But Rutledge Vining was very much in residence, before, during, and after the glory days. And Vining's influence on my own ideas in particular deserves consideration in some detail.

Vining had been trained at the University of Chicago, and he, too, had been greatly influenced by Frank Knight. This background made for a shared intellectual heritage that facilitated communication between us. But it was the particular set of Knightian ideas that Vining developed that was to affect me—and to stimulate me, too—to draw heavily on Knightian foundations. Rutledge Vining deserves primary credit for initiating what was to become a centrally important component of Virginia Political Economy, the stress on *rules* as contrasted with the then universal stress on policy alternatives within rules. Vining repeatedly emphasized that relevant political choices are not among separate allocations or distributions, but rather are among alternative

---

1. See James M. Buchanan, Nutter Memorial Lecture entitled "Political Economy: 1957–82," reprinted in James M. Buchanan, *Liberty, Market and State: Political Economy in the 1980s* (Brighton: Wheatsheaf, 1986), 8–18.

sets of rules, arrangements, or constraints, which along with the behavior of utility-maximizing persons generate patterns of outcomes or results that we call allocations or distributions. Vining, of course, went further than this initial statement of methodological principle. He also stressed the difficulty in diagnosing "failure" in economic order until the underlying stochastic patterns might be evaluated. This latter emphasis on the basic need for probability theory in any political economy did not attract my own attention except for peripheral acceptance. But the central emphasis on rules as the appropriate objects for political choice found in me a receptive audience.

I was predisposed to accept Vining's criticism of orthodoxy in this respect because I, too, recalled Knight's discussion of rules and, perhaps more significantly, came armed with Knut Wicksell's very practical admonition that, unless we do pay heed to the rules, to the structure of the incentives faced by political agents, we, as economists, were unlikely to exert any influence at all, even in some potential sense.[2] To my knowledge, Vining, in his own work, did not make the step from the emphasis on rules to the incentive structure of political agents. But his direct influence allowed me to pull out from Wicksell's more applied treatment the two-stage or two-level structure of political decision making that is perhaps the sine qua non of constitutional economics.

My own efforts, before Charlottesville, reflect the combined influences of Knight and Wicksell, as expressed in my criticism of orthodox method in normative public finance, my reaction to critics of Arrow's impossibility theorem, and my emerging discovery that, indeed, economists' understanding of the free society of interaction was divergent from my own. I recall my amazement when I found that no one had bothered to carry out the rather simple comparative exercise involved in relating individual choice in the market to individual choice in politics.

The generalized emphasis of the Charlottesville program in economics should not be neglected. Warren Nutter was a dedicated scholar and an

---

2. I have discussed Wicksell's seminal influence on the development of public choice and, by inference, on Virginia Political Economy in my Nobel lecture. See James M. Buchanan, "The Constitution of Economic Policy," *American Economic Review,* 77 (June 1987): 243–50.

outstanding price theorist. Leland Yeager, who joined us in 1958, was, and is, an outstanding independent scholar, who brooks no nonsense, whether spouted by dominant authority or by anyone else. These colleagues, along with Alexandre Kafka, Ronald Coase, and Andrew Whinston, all of whom joined us later, made for an exciting community of scholarship, one where ideas did matter, and where there was sufficient isolation from mainstream pressure to lend confidence to the unorthodox.

As I noted earlier, Warren Nutter and I were motivated to establish the Thomas Jefferson Center out of our shared conviction that mainstream economics was drifting away from its classical tradition. This conviction had normative foundations and normative implications. Economists seemed to be losing an understanding of the market order, and, particularly, to be losing any appreciation of the market's political function, which is to minimize the need for politicized control over and decisions concerning resource use. The Virginia emphasis was, from the outset, on the limits of political process rather than on any schemes to use politics to correct for market failures.

I cannot, of course, speak for my colleagues, but personally I do not ever recall consciously or unconsciously putting myself in the role of proffering advice to government, the stance that has characterized political economists, then and now, despite Wicksell's early admonition. Government, or politics, was, to me, always something to seek protection from, not something to exploit, either for my own ends or for those that I might define for the public at large.

## III. Gordon Tullock and the Economics of Politics

An element in what was to become the Virginia School was, however, missing in the Knight, Wicksell, Nutter, and Vining influences emergent in my own work in the classically oriented academic atmosphere of Charlottesville in the late 1950s. This element was to be added when Gordon Tullock joined us in 1958, first as a postdoctoral fellow at the Thomas Jefferson Center, and, after a spell at South Carolina, as a faculty colleague. Tullock brought with him his near genius sweep of received knowledge in the sciences and in history, along with a rare ability to make dramatic leaps across intellectual bridges. In all this, however, Tullock acted as what I have called a "natural economist," who reduced any and all human behavior to that of *Homo eco-*

*nomicus,* at least as an initial working hypothesis.[3] This basically hard-nosed vision of the behavior of persons in bureaucratic roles allowed Tullock to "explain" and to "understand" what he had observed in his nine years of experience in the foreign service bureaucracy. And this basic behavioral model gave him an initial handle on analyzing the workings of majoritarian democratic process.

In a real sense Tullock's contribution to Virginia Political Economy was to harden the underlying behavioral model, to make the individualistic approach that I had long stressed more amenable to precise analytical manipulation. The important book in Virginia Political Economy was *The Calculus of Consent,* which Tullock and I actually wrote during the 1959–60 academic year, while I enjoyed the research potential offered by a Ford Faculty Fellowship and while Tullock was laboring in a foreign affairs department at the University of South Carolina.[4] Viewed in retrospect, this book effectively combined the two developing strands of inquiry, the emphasis on the rules within which choices are made, and the economists' model of the behavior of political agents. Furthermore, and importantly, these two strands of inquiry were imbedded in a normative framework that confused and irritated our critics. The book was as much political philosophy as it was either economics or political science, and we did not, then or now, deny or even apologize for its location within the Madisonian vision of the American experience.

In my own personal interpretation these two elements are the necessary components of the public choice research program generally, as I have argued elsewhere. And these two elements uniquely emerged in the Charlottesville setting of the very early 1960s. My own role in this constellation of ideas lay in my entrepreneurial efforts in establishing the institutional structure within which such unorthodox political economy might grow and flourish. (I have already acknowledged Warren Nutter's share in this academic enterprise.) It was in my work that the two strands were integrated. Developed independently and in isolation, neither the Wicksell-Knight-Vining emphasis on rules nor the Tullock emphasis on *Homo economicus* in politics could

---

3. See James M. Buchanan, "The Qualities of a Natural Economist," in *Democracy and Public Choice,* ed. Charles Rowley (Oxford: Basil Blackwell, 1987), 9–19.

4. James M. Buchanan and Gordon Tullock, *The Calculus of Consent: Logical Foundations of Constitutional Democracy* (Ann Arbor: University of Michigan Press, 1962).

have emerged as the far-reaching and influential research program that Virginia Political Economy became after 1962.

## IV. From Political Economy to Public Choice: Positive Economics, Welfare Economics, and Welfare Politics

Lest we forget, it is useful to remind ourselves in the 1990s that the predominant emphasis of the theoretical welfare economics of the 1950s and 1960s was placed on the identification of "market failure," with the accompanying normative argument for politicized correction. In retrospect, it seems naïve in the extreme to advance institutional comparisons between the workings of an observed and an idealized alternative. Despite Wicksell's early criticism, however, economists continued to assume, implicitly, that politics would work ideally in the corrective adjustments to market failures that analysis enabled them to identify.

The lasting contribution of public choice theory has been to correct this obvious imbalance in analysis. Any institutional comparison that is worthy of serious considerations must compare relevant alternatives; if market organization is to be replaced by politicized order, or vice versa, the two institutional structures must be evaluated on the basis of predictions as to how they will actually work. Political failure, as well as market failure, must become central to the comprehensive analysis that precedes normative judgment.

To accomplish this, public choice theory had to be split off or divorced from its parent, political economy. This judgment is made from a quarter-century's retrospective view; it was not at all explicit in our thinking in 1963. My own implicit understanding of the differential impact of the two complementary arguments was surely due to Wicksell's influence, and it should be noted here that this influence was exclusively exerted through my contributions to the research program. Political economy, interpreted as a return to the classical foundations, and always reflected in the work of Warren Nutter, emphasized the positive virtues of the market. As normative argument, this emphasis clearly has its limits. By contrast, public choice, which came to be increasingly identified with my own work and that of Gordon Tullock from the early 1960s, emphasized the failures of politics. This argument offered an appeal to many scholars who could never have been reached by political economy.

The institutional beginnings of this divorce or separation commenced in 1963, when Gordon Tullock and I organized what was to become the Public Choice Society at a small meeting in Charlottesville. For the next four years at Charlottesville, Tullock and I formed a splinter subgroup, one that was not fully appreciated by our peers in the more comprehensive program. But we were very successful externally; the small band of scholars increased rapidly in numbers, and the journal, finally named *Public Choice*, began to attract attention.

During this period, we lived through a different sixties from the chaos that was developing in the other academies. There was a set of successive graduate classes with genuinely outstanding students. And these students were very successful in becoming published economists early, many even while still graduate students. This feat was accomplished, quite simply, because the public choice research program was new and there were many, many applications waiting to be analyzed. We could almost literally say to a student, "Pick any politically organized activity, and proceed to analyze its origins, its support, its operation, with the tools of public choice." Those were, indeed, exciting times.

## V. Blacksburg, Winston Bush, and Hobbesian Anarchy

Had Gordon Tullock and I remained in Charlottesville, public choice would not have been divorced nearly so sharply from political economy as was, in fact, the case. But problems with the university administration insured that the initial research thrust could not survive in Charlottesville. Gordon Tullock shifted to Rice University, and, one year later, I moved on to UCLA. But under the entrepreneurial efforts of Charles Goetz, public choice found a Virginia location of its own at VPI, separated from the Charlottesville context. Gordon Tullock moved to Blacksburg in 1968, and I joined in 1969. The independent public choice program in Blacksburg accentuated the developing differentiation in focus between the Buchanan-Tullock inquiry into political failures and the Nutter-classical-Chicago inquiry into market successes. At Blacksburg, we analyzed political rules, political institutions, and political behavior as affected by these rules and institutions; we did so almost exclusively.

Between Charlottesville and Blacksburg, however, other events in the outside worlds of academia had occurred that were also to have their influence and effects on the way in which the Virginia School developed. The Charlottesville research program, exemplified by *The Calculus of Consent* and by my *Public Finance in Democratic Process,* embodied an underlying positive evaluation of the basic institutions of governance in the United States.[5] Despite the recognition of the necessity of limits, and despite the diagnosis of political failures in many applications, there was an upbeat or optimistic quality to these heady years of public choice. Between Charlottesville and Blacksburg the character of the underlying diagnosis shifted, at least for me, influenced in part by the events that were taking place in our established institutions of social order, including the universities. Anarchy replaced order as the underlying model, as the title of one of my books suggested.[6]

The research problem seemed to be to explain and understand the emergence of order out of anarchy rather than to grasp the meaning of a stable order that already existed. Thomas Hobbes, whose work had seemed only peripherally relevant to me in 1960, moved to center stage as the political philosopher to be pondered. At precisely this point in its history, Virginia Political Economy discovered its brightest short-lived star. Winston Bush was, for two short but exciting years, the catalyst who helped us put it all together. Building on Hobbes as foundation, and using all the tools of modern economic theory, Bush was able to formalize the model of "social interaction" in genuine anarchy. He was the driving force in organizing a series of weekly workshops in which the participants wrote papers on anarchy that Gordon Tullock put together in two small volumes, *Explorations in the Theory of Anarchy* and *Further Explorations.*[7] This research focus inspired both

5. James M. Buchanan, *Public Finance in Democratic Process* (Chapel Hill: University of North Carolina Press, 1966).

6. James M. Buchanan and Nicos Devletoglou, *Academia in Anarchy: An Economic Diagnosis* (New York: Basic Books, 1970).

7. *Explorations in the Theory of Anarchy,* ed. Gordon Tullock (Blacksburg, Va.: Center for Study of Public Choice, 1972). *Further Explorations in the Theory of Anarchy,* ed. Gordon Tullock (Blacksburg, Va.: Center for Study of Public Choice, 1974).

Gordon Tullock and me, independently, to prepare full-length books, Tullock's *The Social Dilemma* and my own work, *The Limits of Liberty*.[8] After Bush's tragic death in 1973, it was difficult to recapture the Blacksburg spirit that had been so alive for the winter in which we studied anarchy.

My book *The Limits of Liberty* was treated by some constructive critics as complementary to works by both John Rawls, whose seminal book *A Theory of Justice* had been published in 1971, and Robert Nozick, whose *Anarchy, State, and Utopia* appeared in 1974.[9] These works marked a rebirth, of sorts, of political philosophy, and one of the continuing strands of my own interests has been in constructing elements of the contractarian position in varying applications and extensions. This interest, joined with the earlier Wicksellian influence, provides the roots of "constitutional economics" or "constitutional political economy," the term coined in the 1980s to differentiate this area of inquiry from the more positivistic and more empirical interest-group theory of politics.

## VI. Constitutional Economics in Application: The Fiscal Constitution

From the early 1970s, public choice, defined comprehensively, came to embody two separate and distinct research programs. The first, constitutional economics, finds its precursors in the work of Wicksell and its modern representatives in those of Vining, Buchanan, Wagner, Brennan, and Vanberg. And, as I have noted, my own emphasis has been almost exclusively limited to this program. The second research program within public choice falls more appropriately under the rubric "the economic theory of politics" and involves the extension of *Homo economicus* to behavior under observed institutional rules. A neglected precursor is Schumpeter, and its modern representatives are Gordon Tullock, who is in a sense the primary influence, along with the Chicago-based interest-group theorists, George Stigler, Sam

8. Gordon Tullock, *The Social Dilemma: The Economics of War and Revolution* (Blacksburg, Va.: Center for Study of Public Choice, 1974). James M. Buchanan, *The Limits of Liberty: Between Anarchy and Leviathan* (Chicago: University of Chicago Press, 1975).

9. John Rawls, *A Theory of Justice* (Cambridge: Harvard University Press, 1971). Robert Nozick, *Anarchy, State, and Utopia* (New York: Basic Books, 1974).

Peltzman, and Gary Becker, and also some Virginia second-generation scholars, notably Robert Tollison and his coworkers.

I shall not, in this chapter, discuss contributions of this second research program to what may be interpreted as the Virginia School of Political Economy. This neglect is not indicative of any relegation of this program to second-rank importance. Especially in the theory of rent seeking, first advanced by Gordon Tullock in the late 1960s, major insights into the workings of politicized arrangements have been secured. My neglect here is motivated exclusively by my own relationship to the other program in constitutional economics. And recall that I promised to present here my private, personal reflections on Virginia Political Economy rather than a comprehensive interpretation or history. This chapter should be taken to be neither of these.

Within constitutional economics itself, two substrands of inquiry can be identified, and my own works since the early 1970s can readily be classified as falling variously within these two separable areas. First, there is the continuing attempt at integration of the analysis into the more general contractarian political philosophy. Second, there is the effort to derive implications of the analysis for issues of practical public policy.

It is perhaps not at all surprising that the public policy applications that have been most thoroughly developed are those in public finance, since this was Wicksell's initial focus, and since I came to all this from training as a public-finance economist. As early as 1954, before both the Virginia initiative and any specific emphasis on what was later to be public choice, I had written and circulated a draft paper in which I argued that the Keynesian theory of economic policy was developed in a political vacuum and that the precepts of this theory were unworkable in democratic settings. For better or worse, I heeded the advice of colleagues who warned me against trying to publish such an argument in the climate of ideas that described the early 1950s; there are costs to being branded a heretic too early in one's career. By the mid-1970s this climate was totally different, and Keynesian dominance had at least been partially punctured. In addition simple observation of the workings of politics suggested that the persistence of deficits had already become a problem that would only get more serious in the 1980s. In Richard Wagner I found a colleague and coauthor who shared my views on the political efficacy of the Keynesian fiscal policy nostrums, and we wrote *Democracy in Deficit,* a book that had less impact than it should have had due to the bad choice of publisher on our part.[10] This book made one central point; politicians enjoy spending and do not enjoy taxing. These natural proclivities must emerge so long as politicians are responsive to constituents. I have often used this example as the simplest possible illustration of public choice logic. The normative implications are clear; ordinary politics contains a procedural flaw that can only be corrected by the imposition of constitutional constraints. The argument of *Democracy in Deficit* became increasingly relevant in the decade after it was published, as the deficits of the 1980s emerged to dwarf those of the 1970s in size. And, in some indirect sense, we can, I think, legitimately suggest that both the Gramm-Rudman-Hollings legislation and the movements toward approval of the constitutional amendment requiring budget balance find their intellectual foundations in the Buchanan-Wagner book.

This book was "closer to" current policy discussion than any other of my works, earlier or later. There were other elements of the fiscal constitution that seemed to warrant examination, but at a somewhat more remote distance and in idealized abstraction from fiscal reality. Behind an appropriately defined veil of ignorance and/or uncertainty, when asked to select among alternative rules to be imposed on governmental fiscal authorities, how much taxing power would be assigned? Again I was fortunate to find a colleague and coauthor who could assist me in working out the answer to this challenging question. Geoffrey Brennan was equipped with the orthodox tools of the trade for a modern public-finance economist, and these tools when mixed with the public choice–constitutional economics emphasis of my own produced two books, *The Power to Tax* and *The Reason of Rules*.[11] Without Brennan's influence I would never have "jumped out" of the central public choice model of politics, even for the purpose of constitutional exercise, and without this intellectual leap *The Power to Tax* would never have emerged. What was required in order to answer the question posed above was a model of how ordinary politics works in the use of the taxing power. Orthodox public

10. James M. Buchanan and Richard Wagner, *Democracy in Deficit: The Political Legacy of Lord Keynes* (New York: Academic Press, 1977).

11. Geoffrey Brennan and James M. Buchanan, *The Power to Tax: Analytical Foundations of a Fiscal Constitution* (Cambridge: Cambridge University Press, 1980). Geoffrey Brennan and James M. Buchanan, *The Reason of Rules: Constitutional Political Economy* (Cambridge: Cambridge University Press, 1985).

choice models could produce a multiplicity of results. We needed something much more amenable to analysis. The revenue-maximizing model of government gave us the "handle" upon which to hang the whole constitutional analysis. We recognized, of course, that the workings of politics in democratic societies are complex. But, if the purpose is one of drawing the constitutional limits on the taxing power, would it not be meaningful to utilize a worst-case scenario and to see model governments, anywhere and everywhere, as revenue-maximizing? That is, given any revenue source, would it not be best to assume maximal exploitation? With this model the book almost wrote itself. There were readily discernible constitutional limits to the taxing power that could be laid down, and the "principles" that emerged from the analysis turned orthodox normative tax theory on its head in many cases.

## VII. Constitutional Economics

The constitutional exercise that was the motivating purpose of *The Power to Tax* was not understood by many of our critics, who took our model of revenue-maximizing government to be descriptive of fiscal reality rather than a worst-case model introduced explicitly for the aim of constitutional design. The second Brennan-Buchanan book, *The Reason of Rules,* is best summarized as a response to these critics. In this book we move beyond the fiscal application and discuss the constitutional approach generally, an approach that has characterized my own work since the initial Wicksellian influence, and particularly since *The Calculus of Consent.*

I have come increasingly to think that the constitutionalist-contractarian methodological framework is, indeed, the central feature of Virginia Political Economy, a framework that, from the start, I have found to be appropriately described locationally in the commonwealth that produced James Madison and the other Virginia Founders. I can, I think, make a plausible case that this framework would be out of place in California, Illinois, or Massachusetts. Despite the opposition that we encountered in Virginia's academies, especially in Charlottesville, I like to think that it was our research program that was, indeed, indigenous and that our antagonists were the aliens.

We owe the precise name "Constitutional Economics" to Richard McKenzie, a former student and colleague, who organized a conference and published a book under this title in the early 1980s. I have often used "contractarian political economy" as an alternative designation. Much of my own work during the decade of the 1980s has been in methodological defense of this approach to issues of social philosophy.

In one sense we may pose the challenge of the 1990s and beyond in terms of the struggle between the practical implications of the two separate strands that I have identified as describing public choice and the Virginia research program in an inclusive way. Positive public choice theory suggests that the rent seekers are indeed to inherit our earth, that our polity is already described by the "churning state" metaphor used by Anthony de Jasay in his book *The State*.[12] Constitutional reform offers the only escape from this gloomy projection. But until and unless the rent-seeking potential embodied in the nonconstrained institutions of governance is fully appreciated, it remains impossible to secure the requisite constitutional attitude or constitutional wisdom that will make reform a realistic alternative.

I have often stated that I feel a moral obligation to hope that such reform can indeed take place. Underneath its abstract analysis, the Virginia research program has always embodied a moral passion that our adversaries have fully appreciated. The program has advanced our scientific understanding of social interaction, but the science has been consistently applied to the normatively chosen question. How can individuals live in social order while preserving their own liberties? Scholars associated with the program have consistently eschewed the question: How can the state exert more effective control over individuals? Those scholars who associate themselves with the interests of "the state" have never found, and will not find, Virginia Political Economy congenial. This differentiation in ultimate normative purpose is a feature of Virginia Political Economy that I value positively and strongly.

In conclusion let me stress again what I stated at the outset. These remarks have contained my private and personal assessment of Virginia Political Economy, of its origins, its history, and its development, along with some reference to people and institutions that describe the research program. Other participants will, of course, write a different story and offer a different assessment.

---

12. Anthony de Jasay, *The State* (Oxford: Basil Blackwell, 1985).

# A Theory of Truth in Autobiography

*James M. Buchanan and Robert D. Tollison*

## I. Introduction

We shall support the proposition that the degree of "truth" reflected in autobiography depends, to some extent, on the factually observable biography of a person, that is, on the historical narrative of a life. We shall go further and argue that in most circumstances the less "attractive" the observable biography, the more "truthful" is the autobiography. This second proposition implies that there is relatively more "gold" for the interpretative biographer in the life of the "attractive" person than in that of the "unattractive" one.

To bring our discussion into both more provocative and more professional focus, our theory suggests that economists who write autobiographies are likely to exhibit more truth in their personal accounts than autobiographical moral philosophers. Our argument requires elements of the spatial theory of public choice, along with an essential presupposition about shared values. The argument does not depend on any presumption of differential personal integrity or honesty as between autobiographers. The basic analysis allows several interesting implications to be suggested.

From *Kyklos* 39, fasc. 4 (1986): 507–17. Copyright 1986 by Blackwell Publishers Ltd. Reprinted by permission of Blackwell Publishers Ltd.

We are grateful to Jan Cohn, Dwight Lee, David Levy, and William Shughart for helpful comments.

The managing editors extend their sincere congratulations to Professor James M. Buchanan, a regular contributor to *Kyklos*, on being awarded the Nobel Prize.

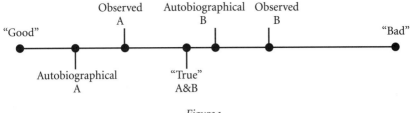

*Figure 1*

## II. Truth or Consequences

We take as stipulated that there exists general agreement, in some broad sense, on the set of personal attributes or qualities that describe a "good" person, and, conversely, a "bad" person. For our purposes, we need not enter into disputes concerning the separate elements in the set of attributes or qualities used for evaluation here, and our model is sufficiently robust to allow for considerable variation in the particular weighting scheme utilized. We require only that persons can be arrayed on a one-dimensional scalar from "good" to "bad." If these inclusive terms are defined by vectors of many elements, internal trade-offs among such elements may allow for an internally consistent agreed-on ranking even with wide differences in particular characteristics. For example, a very compassionate person who has no respect for rules may possibly be ranked alongside a person who lacks compassion but who strictly abides by social norms. Such a scalar is drawn as Figure 1, with a "good" person occupying the position on the extreme left and a "bad" person occupying the extreme right-hand position.[1]

We now proceed to define "a person" in three distinct ways. First, a person is defined by the objective, historical record of his or her life. A person was born at a time and place, to specified parents, was educated at specific institutions, resided at geographically determined locations, entered a profession, established an employment experience, which, possibly, involved speeches, articles, professional papers, books, works of art, photographs, and films that are available for inspection. The biographer who has this rec-

---

1. The correspondence between our left-right and the "good"-"bad" continuum is purely coincidental.

ord available has "something to look at" as he begins his enterprise. This biographer does not commence with a blank canvas upon which he creates a personage. We shall label the person defined by this record as *the observed person.*

The autobiographer must also commence with the record that exists, the historical reality that is "himself"; he cannot escape his history. The recorded actions, deeds, and words are *his.* Attribution has been made. No less than the biographer, the autobiographer cannot start *carte blanche.* For the auto-biographer, however, there is a different, subjectively experienced reality to be described, that which he has lived internally and to which only he com-mands access. By definition, this subjective domain is not recorded in any document.

Why is a person prompted to write an autobiography? We require some presumption about motivation here (beyond the obviously pecuniary). It is, of course, conceptually possible that the autobiographer aims solely and ex-clusively to reconstruct the person he knows himself to be, with no regard to the effects on others. In such instance, however, we would be hard put to come up with a plausible motivation for publication of an autobiography. A private journal would serve the same purpose. If there is any weight given to the larger purpose of describing the person to secure the appreciation of oth-ers, both the writing and the publishing of autobiography become instru-mental to this purpose. Once this motivation is so much as acknowledged, there is a directional bias in the narrative, a bias toward that constructed life that the autobiographer wants others to see as he "really was." The truth of autobiography must, at least in this sense, be defeated by its purpose.[2]

We shall refer to the person whose experiences are recounted in autobi-ography as the *autobiographical person.* Note that this person cannot be to-tally different from the observed person, defined by the objective historical record. A useful metaphor may be one in which the autobiographer is tied to the observed person by an elastic band. The directional bias suggests that the autobiographical person will tend to be located on the "good" side of the

---

2. Under the right circumstances, biography will suffer from the same bias. Thus, "of-ficial" biographies and biographies written with access to living subjects, or with access to personal documents granted by family members of a deceased subject, are suspect on these grounds. One might call such efforts "tutored biographies."

observed person along a uni-dimensional scalar of qualities (or, in Figure 1, to the left).[3]

It has been relatively easy to define both the *observed person* and the *autobiographical person*. It becomes much more difficult to define our third classification, *the true person*. After all, what is the "true" person? We do not propose to enter into murky psychological issues here, and we acknowledge that in a sense there is no uniquely defined "true person" at all. Fortunately, for our purposes, we do not require formal specification that would allow operational definition. We require only some conceptual benchmark that will allow us to develop our central hypothesis. To this end, we can stipulate, without discussion, that the true person is the person that "God" might describe, or that might be ideally reconstructed from the observed person, the autobiographical person, and upon a full recognition of the biases in the latter, as presented.

With the three conceptions of a person, we can outline our model, which is, indeed, exceedingly simple and straightforward. We shall use a two-person comparison. The true persons may be located anywhere along the "good"-"bad" scale of attributes. Although it is not necessary for our conclusions to carry through, we can simplify the analysis initially by postulating that the two persons, A and B, are identical as true persons. That is to say, "God" would locate them at the same place, and, again for simplicity in exposition, assume that this location is midway between the extremes, depicted in Figure 1.

The observed persons differ, however, with A being located to the left of the midpoint, and with B being located to the right, again as depicted in Figure 1. The differences may emerge for any of many reasons. Possibly, A may have been publicly recognized for his philanthropic activity, whereas B's philanthropy was less available for public scrutiny. Both A and B prepare and publish autobiographies. Both will bias their construction in the direction of the set of attributes labelled "good," or leftwards, in Figure 1. Both will tend to stress the positive or favorable elements not available in the observed record; both will tend to downplay or to conceal the negative elements of be-

---

3. For completeness, we should acknowledge the possibility that some autobiographers will deliberately seek to shock others by biasing their narratives toward the "bad." The existence of such eccentrics seems rare enough to permit our basic proposition to hold generally. So, too, for biographies of the "Mommie Dearest" variety.

havior not available in the observed record. It seems reasonable to postulate that the directional bias is roughly equivalent in the two cases, as measured by distance along the attributes scalar.

A glance at the construction in Figure 1 reveals that the autobiographical B, the person who has the least attractive observed record (who is farther right on the scalar), is closer to the "true" B than the autobiographical A is to the "true" A. That is to say, there is more "truth" in B's autobiography than in A's.

We insist that this proposition is not exclusively an artifact generated by the particular structure we have used in the presentation. The results are unaltered if we drop the simplifying assumption that our two reference persons are equal in the "true person" sense. This shift is depicted in Figure 2, which embodies the assumption that A', the "best" person, as observed, is also "best" in the true person sense. As one can see, the same result of autobiographical B' being closer to the true B' person goes through.

We also do not need the simplifying assumption that the length or magnitude of the directional bias in autobiography is identical as between the two persons compared. As both Figure 1 and Figure 2 suggest, our result can hold even if we allow the bias in A's autobiography to be considerably less significant than that in B's autobiography.

Consider the issue in the following way. In Figure 1, autobiographical B would have to leapfrog autobiographical A to destroy our result. In Figure 2, this is not necessarily the case. If autobiographical B' fudges to the left a lot and autobiographical A' fudges a little, our result would not follow. But, in both cases, we can easily argue that the fudge factor is constrained by a recorded reality, and in principle, the degree to which "good" and "bad" types can fudge will be about the same. Someone cannot claim to be 6'4" when he

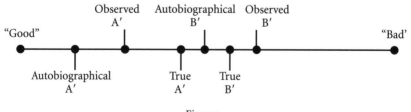

*Figure 2*

is actually 5′4″. In other words, there are constraints generated by readers and acquaintances, who can see through obvious misstatements, on the degree to which any person can fudge his or her autobiography. Constraints are also generated by the entry of potential biographers, who can profit through the correction of autobiographical error. We return to this point below.

Another way to look at the issue is in terms of truth or consequences. Baldly lying about one's self will lead to a general discounting of all elements in one's autobiography. There is an optimal fudge factor, and there is no particular reason to believe that it varies according to our personality types.

As noted earlier, our results depend critically on the presumption that the persons whose autobiographies are being compared share an agreed-on scalar of "goodness" and "badness" in personal characteristics. It is this commonality that creates the uni-directional bias; persons seek to reconstruct images of themselves that exhibit more of the commonly judged "goodness" attributes than mere observation would generate.

Our results also depend on an underlying presupposition about the relative compactness of the distribution of observed persons and true persons along the "good"-"bad" spectrum. If these two distributions are totally unconstrained, almost any result could be generated from our central model of autobiographical bias, and the cases examined above would be isolated examples only. To make our hypothesis generally applicable to a very wide range of comparisons, we need only to presuppose that persons differ less in their "true selves," in the eyes of God as it were, than they differ in their observed behavior. Or, more technically, the presupposition is that the distribution of true persons is more compact than the distribution of observed persons.

This presupposition seems to us to be eminently plausible. The necessary division of labor in a modern economy places persons in widely differing occupational roles. While it may be the case that relatively "bad" persons will be somewhat more attracted to those occupations that require relatively less caring attention to others (Figure 2 illustrates), the fact is that someone must fill the less caring roles if the economy is to function at all satisfactorily. Economists have long hypothesized that, within competing groups, the required equalizing differences in wages imply general preference for those occupational categories that allow persons to "be of service" to others. If the relative compactness of the two distributions should be different from that presupposed here, the equalizing differences would show no necessary relationship to location on the "good"-"bad" scalar.

## III. Economists versus Moral Philosophers

It is time to bring our general analysis back to the provocative and professional application that we alluded to in the introduction. Think of the exercise of comparing the autobiographies of an economist on the one hand and a moral philosopher on the other.

The economist analyzes human behavior in terms of self-interested motivation. His challenge is one of testing the limits of applicability of *Homo economicus*. How much observed behavior can be interpreted as utility maximization in other than an empty sense? How much observed behavior can be explained as attempts on the part of persons to further private economic interest? To what extent does private net wealth assume dominance in human motivation? The economist is required, by the basic tools of his discipline, to concentrate his attention on attributes of human character that are not normally classified as preeminently desirable or "good." As Carlyle is said to have remarked, the economist's inquiry is "pig philosophy." The economist shuns the noble and higher motivations for human action, not because he does not consider these important in some personal sense, but because these motivations are simply excluded from his professional competence.

The moral philosopher, by contrast, spends his professional career discussing, analyzing, criticizing, evaluating the precise motivations that are excluded from the economist's purview. His discourse is concentrated on defining the "good." He seeks normative answers for the questions: What constitutes a "good" person? How "should" a person behave?

The fact that the economist may be classified as a "positive scientist" while the moral philosopher makes no claim to scientific status is irrelevant to our argument here. The positive normative dichotomy in discourse is not the critical difference that attracts our attention. Instead, the relevant distinction for our purposes is that between a concentration of inquiry on the "lower" and on the "higher" motivations of human conduct. The economist is observed to be modelling human beings as if they are self-seekers; the moral philosopher discusses human beings as if they can be saints.

We advance, as an empirically testable hypothesis, that economists are considered to be, relatively, "immoral" or "less good" by their intellectual-academic peers than are the moral philosophers, and that this difference stems from the presumed bias imposed by their disciplinary mindset. If this hypothesis is not refuted, it follows that, *ceteris paribus*, the economist whose life is to be examined would be placed further to the right on a scalar such as those depicted in Figures 1 and 2 than would the moral philosopher. That is to say, the economist, as an *observed person*, would be closer to the "bad" pole than the moral philosopher. If this inference is acknowledged, then the application of the model developed earlier becomes straightforward. The economist who ventures to publish an autobiography is likely to produce a document that contains relatively more truth than the moral philosopher.[4]

Note that this result does not suggest that the autobiographical economist is somehow "more truthful" in some sense of personal integrity or honesty. As in the earlier model, it seems useful here to suggest that the directional bias toward the "good" is identical in the two cases. The relatively greater "truthfulness" in the economist's autobiographical narrative stems exclusively from the differential locations of the two observed persons along the scalar and from the uni-directional bias toward the commonly shared set of attributes that define the "good." A slightly different way of putting this simple point is to say that precisely because the economist, among many of his intellectual-academic peers, is considered as a moral leper, his autobiography must, at least over initial ranges, move toward some more truthful account. The same cannot be said of the moral philosopher who must be, again among many of his intellectual-academic peers, initially accorded quasi-saintly status because of the very questions and issues that he ponders.[5]

---

4. J. S. Mill, *Autobiography* (Boston: Houghton Mifflin, 1969). M. K. Gandhi, *An Autobiography: The Story of My Experiments with Truth* (Boston: Beacon Press, 1966).

5. Adam Smith (the author of *The Wealth of Nations*, not *The Theory of Moral Sentiments*; the economist, not the moral philosopher) did not publish an autobiography, but still provides an example of our argument. According to his biographer, Smith, generally regarded as the father of our discipline, was an incredibly benevolent person in practice. For example, "Carlyle . . . admits him to have been a man of 'unbounded benevolence' " (J. Rae, *Life of Adam Smith* [Fairfield: A. M. Kelley, 1977], 433). Or, upon Smith's death, "the newspapers had an obituary notice of two small paragraphs, and the only facts in his life the writers appear to have been able to find were his early abduction by the gip-

We could, of course, find other applications of our central proposition. The autobiographies of executioners, butchers, policemen, soldiers, prosecutors, criminals, and prostitutes are likely to present more accurate accounts than are the autobiographies of priests, ministers, medical doctors, nurses, actors, politicians, social welfare workers, psychiatrists, and consumer advocates.

## IV. Other Implications and Conclusions

We suggested earlier that one implication of our proposition is that interpretative biography, the effort to use both the observed record and autobiography to describe the true person, is likely to be relatively more productive if the person chosen for scrutiny, as observed, lies toward the "good" end of the scalar. Figure 1 illustrates this point. The fertile ground for the potential interpretative biographer of A lies between the autobiographical A and the true A, which is more extensive than the comparable distance for B. The scandals in the lives of the saints are the interpretative biographers' mother lodes. Comparable scandals in the lives of sinners are direct inferences from the observed record of sin itself. And the "distance" along which search for the anti-scandals of the sinners can profitably be conducted may be short indeed.

Thus, biographers will be relatively more attracted to work on saints than sinners. This might loosely be called a wealth-maximizing strategy for actual and aspiring biographers. They enter the market for biography where the opportunity to correct the record is greatest, all else equal. What can one make of such a result? A non-exhaustive listing of possibilities follows.

1. We have a general explanation for the paucity of biographies of economists relative to, say, saints. Where economists write about themselves, they do not deviate so far from the objective reality of their lives so as to attract much attention or to need much correction. Indeed, economists, relative to other professions, *rarely* write about themselves.

---

sies . . . and the characteristics which the *Advertiser* mentions, that 'in private life Dr. Smith was distinguished for philanthropy, benevolence, humanity, and charity' " (Rae, 436). Dugald Stewart (*Biographical Memoir of Adam Smith* [New York: A. M. Kelley, 1966], especially 77–80) offers a similar portrait of Smith.

2. Our result ought to hold up across the market for biographies. For example, a list of all the new biographies published in a given year should be disproportionately devoted to saints.

3. Dictionaries of national biographies, to the extent that they cover more than basic, existential data about their subjects, should contain more saintly types than economists (again measured relative to the size of profession).

4. The number of times that an individual's autobiography is devalued by an acute biographer ought to be related to his position on the "good"-"bad" scale. Saints will be debunked more often, and more intensely, as measured, for example, by the number of contentious biographies written about them.

5. Biographies of saints ought to be longer, on average, than those of sinners (holding length of life constant).

6. Finally, it seems to us that Stigler is wrong to dismiss the potential usefulness of biographical and autobiographical information. His position is that such data cannot be trusted, which is correct but does not go far enough.[6] Consider the analogy to survey data. Economists often decry the use of survey results; they say, "look at what people do, not at what they say." As our colleague David Levy responds, however, this is only an admission that we do not have an economic theory of what people say, or talk. Talk is relevant, and can be modelled as if it were a economic process. Until we have an economic theory of talk, perhaps it is correct not to look at what people say. But the proposition that talk is irrelevant is *not* correct. The same is true about writing about one's self. We have gone Stigler one better. We offer a theory of the autobiographer and of biographical correction which carries testable implications across professions. We claim that proclamations about self by economists are useful and truthful relative to those by moral philosophers.

6. G. J. Stigler, "The Scientific Uses of Scientific Biography, with Special Reference to J. S. Mill," in *The Economist as Preacher, and Other Essays,* ed. G. J. Stigler (Chicago: University of Chicago Press, 1982), 86–97.

# PART TWO

# Reflections on Fellow Political Economists

# Frank H. Knight

## 1885–1972

For those who swelled the ranks of graduate economics at the University of Chicago immediately after the Second World War, as well as for many who came before us, Frank Knight dominated the intellectual atmosphere. Other professors instructed us, but it was Frank Knight who captured our interest and who seemed, to most of us, to epitomize the spirit of the university. We were stamped with a different logo, one that we display in the small imitative gestures and attitudes that we carry with us, even after almost a half century.

## I

What was there about Frank Knight that made him so different from his peers, at Chicago or anywhere else, and at any time or place? David Hume, whose challenges to established ideas guaranteed his own exclusion from academic employment in eighteenth-century Scotland, was the person whom Frank Knight most closely resembled. The two shared a willingness to question any authority, whether scientific, moral, aesthetic, or institutional. It is perhaps not surprising that Knight proved too persistent a querent for the philosophers at Cornell, who actively orchestrated his initial transfer into economics.

To Frank Knight nothing was sacrosanct, not the dogmas of religion, not the laws and institutions of social order, not the prevailing moral norms,

From *Remembering the University of Chicago: Teachers, Scientists, and Scholars,* ed. Edward Shils (Chicago: The University of Chicago Press, 1991), 244–52. Copyright 1991 by The University of Chicago. All rights reserved. Reprinted by permission of the University of Chicago Press, publisher.

not the accepted interpretations of sacred or profane texts. Anything and everything was a potential subject for critical scrutiny, with an evaluative judgment to be informed by, but ultimately made independent of, external influence. The Knightian stance before gods, men, and history embodies a courage and self-confidence that upsets the self-satisfied propounders of all the little orthodoxies, then and now.

If there are no exemptions from critical inquiry, if there are no absolutes, in science, morals, religion, politics, how, then, does the skeptic keep his bearings? Frank Knight resolved this central question for himself, for me, and for many others by resort to three words. The principle of the "relatively absolute absolutes," which was repeatedly invoked by Knight, can be almost magical in its ability to keep the skeptic from the abyss. This principle stakes out a position between that of epistemological, moral, and cultural relativism at the one extreme and the related absolutisms at the other. To those who raise the relativist accusation, the relatively absolute absolutist can respond: "I acknowledge that there may exist relatively absolute absolutes. By this I mean that there may exist certain precepts, rules, codes, laws, interpretations, explanations, etc., that, for the purposes of getting on with the business of ordinary living, including that of inquiry in the academy, we may want to accept as if they are absolute. But this is emphatically not the same stance as that which exempts some of these ideas from our ultimate critical scrutiny."

Critical intelligence matched by the courage to challenge authority— these are the human faculties that are most desperately needed, and these are the faculties that seem so scarce in the observed discourse that ultimately guides our action. Most of us, most of the time, are fools, in the literal meaning of the term, and the greatest of these are to be found in positions of intellectual and academic leadership. Our aim is to expose error more than to discover and propound new truths, and the precautionary warning must be: Beware of the gospel, no matter when and by whom proclaimed. Frank Knight was a radical critic, who exhibited little respect for the "classical," whether in Greek philosophy or in British political economy. We should, indeed, pay attention to those whose ideas have been influential, but our objective is to learn from their errors, not to celebrate their final achievement of truth.

How did this critical spirit come to be located in time and place?

## II

Frank H. Knight was a product of middle America, of the agricultural economy of Illinois, of the late nineteenth century, of evangelical Christianity. His teenage escape from the large family of McLean County Knights was an extension of "education" in a fledgling "American University" in East Tennessee. By the time this institution failed two years later, Knight had become its star student, an assistant instructor in mathematics, and a part-time administrator. He was then forced to seek employment in the real world for some time before returning to the academy, this time to enroll in a church-related college, Milligan, still located in East Tennessee, where he joined his earlier mentor, Frederick Kershner, who exerted considerable influence on the development of Knight's early ideas. As he had done before, during his years at Milligan (1908–11), Knight assumed several roles—student, teacher, and administrator. His interests covered the whole limited curriculum, but with some emphasis on chemistry and German. Poverty joined proximity to keep him in Appalachia as the academy still beckoned, and he next commenced graduate work at the University of Tennessee, where he worked in German literature. (Precisely thirty-six years later, in 1948, I met an ancient emeritus professor of history while walking on the Knoxville campus. He recalled Frank Knight in these words: "A brilliant young man, but too pessimistic, too much influenced by Schopenhauer.")

After Tennessee, he entered Cornell University as a graduate student to study graduate philosophy, only to be shunted off into economics, where he was more than welcome in a discipline that was just achieving its American independence. Frank Knight once told me, personally, that the only economist from whom he learned much was Allyn Young, with whom he worked at Cornell. Knight's dissertation, which, as revised, became *Risk, Uncertainty and Profit* (1921) is, even now, accorded status as a seminal study.

In one sense, however, this initial work is Knight's only book. The later books, which really indicate his abiding critical interests more adequately by some of their very titles—*The Ethics of Competition and Other Essays* (1935), *The Economic Order and Religion* (1945), *Freedom and Reform* (1947), *Intelligence and Democratic Action* (1960)—are collections of essays or lectures. But the early book, *Risk, Uncertainty and Profit,* established Knight as an economist in the intellectually stimulating times of the 1920s and early 1930s.

There were two early years at Chicago, 1917–19, followed by a stint at the University of Iowa, where he wrote some of his most provocative critical essays. As a final move in a strictly academic career, Frank Knight shifted again to the University of Chicago in 1928. He remained a part of the Chicago academic community until his death in 1972.

## III

There seems relatively little in this biographical account to suggest the origins of the intense critical spirit. To return to my original question: "Why was Knight so different from his peers?" my hypothesis is that he can be explained, phenomenologically, only through recalling his roots in evangelical Christianity. Only through an early experience of having wrestled with God, the source of the ultimate putative authority, and having at least held his own in the encounter, Frank Knight had no difficulty at all in taking on any or all of the lesser gods, as variously represented in the many small dogmas of science, art, politics, and history. His fascination with theological issues throughout his life can, I think, be explained by his implied acknowledgment that God had proved, indeed, to be the most difficult adversary to be faced. If man can use his own critical intelligence in wrestling God to a draw, why should he cower before any other claim to authority?

Why were the representatives of the several monastic orders so attracted to Knight's classroom lectures? Surely they considered attendance a test of faith. If they could return with their faith unshaken after listening to Frank Knight's railleries, they would indeed have measured up.

If I interpret Frank Knight correctly, he was driven by his own intellectual embarrassment at having at one time in his life been ensconced in a faith that no longer seemed remotely plausible. (Professor Donald Dewey, who has worked extensively with the source materials relevant to Knight's early years, and notably his years in church-related schools in Tennessee, differs from my interpretation here. Dewey concludes that Knight was a skeptic from the start.) He was, in any case, sufficiently self-confident to predict that his own lapses were by no means idiosyncratic. He criticized others by way of celebrating his own achievement of intellectual freedom while, at the same time, warning the unwary of the pitfalls of authority. No function of the academy could be more important than the exposure of error, and all who knew Frank Knight recall his frequent reference to Josh Billings' comment to the effect that "it isn't ignorance that does the most damage, but knowin' so derned much that ain't so."

The problems of social order were those that emerge from failures to apply and use our critical intelligence; they are emphatically not amenable to the solutions of science. The continuing task is defined as coming to agreement on the set of rules that constrain our behavior toward one another, and the ethical norm is best described by analogy to sportsmanship in games, playing by the rules, again with the rules in existence accepted as relatively absolute absolutes. Rule-making was to be distinguished from play within the rules. Frank Knight was not a "game theorist," as such, nor was he a "constitutional economist," as these terms apply to research programs too recent for his active participation. But he would surely have applauded both the positive search for solutions to varying game-like interactions and the analysis of alternative sets of rules for social organization.

## IV

Frank Knight was perhaps at the zenith of his influence around the time of the University of Chicago's semicentennial. For a period of a quarter century, his intellectual presence helped to shape the spirit of the quadrangle, and his influence extended, selectively, to the far corners of the academic world. (His works were required reading at the London School of Economics, where he was, I am sure, much better known than at Harvard.) But Knight was very much a man of the academic cloth; he did not succumb to the temptations that destroy the minds of so many of his peers in the social sciences, especially in economics. He remained within the ivory tower; he did not provide consulting services, to private or public agencies.

Aside from his lifelong struggle to keep romantic nonsense from taking precedence over the truth that emerges only from hard thinking, Knight was not a crusader for this or that cause. He resisted taking on the arrogance of academic office that converted "others" into the clay that was to be molded on one's own potter's wheel, even in the realm of discourse. Frank Knight could never have joined those of the self-selected elite who, in idea or practice, seek to plan, steer, or direct the lives of those who are excluded. He was a classical liberal, not because he predicted that only with widespread individual liberty would desired results be generated, but because the liberal order is required to allow individuals, all individuals, to define their own objectives. It is not surprising that Frank Knight opposed Roosevelt's New Deal, Keynesian-inspired macromanagement of the national economy, and any and all proposals for socialist planning.

We should note, however, that these were the prevailing orthodoxies that described the 1930s, 1940s, and 1950s, the three decades that spanned Frank Knight's middle years. During these times his critical focus was necessarily on arguments advanced in defense of politicization, of extension of coercive powers of government. In this context, it is useful to recall that, in the 1920s, Knight aimed some of his most acute critical barbs at those who, blindly, defended market capitalism or free enterprise without recognizing the ethical dimension. Had Frank Knight lived to observe the collapse of socialism, in idea and in reality, his critical fire would surely have been once again redirected, and he would have centered his attacks on those latter-day pundits who would deny the very existence of the moral-ethical elements of market capitalism, elements which, at least in part, made the socialist century possible.

Knight earned his credentials as an economist. His early book clarified the understanding of the competitive model of economic process, including the identification of profit as the distributional return to those who bear uncertainty. He wrote a seminal paper that proved precursory to the much later emergence of the economics of property rights. He also advanced the understanding of the Ricardian model, and he participated in an inconclusive, if heated, controversy with the Austrians over capital theory. But the embroidered nuances on the edges of economic theory were much less challenging to him than the larger issues in moral and social philosophy, upon which the economist could, indeed, say something of relevance. Especially during his Chicago years, Frank Knight's important essays are to be classified, in subject matter, as well outside economics, even of that time. And it was during those years, and especially later, that economics, as a discipline, was to become less rather than more philosophical. As economists came to be captured both by the fascination of mathematical manipulation and by the technology of computational possibilities, they had less time for serious consideration of the issues addressed by Knight, who objected, and strenuously, to the "scientification" of his disciplinary base. Analytical rigor was not to be equated with conversion into symbolic language, and the reality of human interaction was far too complex for much to be learned from the empirical testing of hypotheses analogous to the procedures that describe the activities of the physical scientists.

## V

Unfortunately, the philosophical economics of Frank Knight was not to be kept alive by his rearguard criticisms of the developing orthodoxies. As a result, his penetrating critical essays found increasingly smaller numbers of readers, both at Chicago and elsewhere. Knight's sort of analysis, interesting as it might be, simply did not fit into any research program. It is an intellectual tragedy that modern economists, always busy students, and research scholars know little or nothing of this great man's work.

Although approached always from the perspective of the economist, Knight's subjects were within a broadly defined moral philosophy, and his influence might have been expected to be great among those who professed specialized competence in this ancient inquiry. Again, however, the time was out of joint. Professional philosophy, during Knight's most productive years, was itself passing through its empty phase, only to escape partially in the 1970s, when Rawls and Nozick sparked a rebirth of interest in substantive issues. Frank Knight's essays of the early mid-century would have surely found more receptive readers among the philosophers of today than during the years in which they were published.

I noted earlier that Frank Knight stamped us with a different logo. Let me clarify what I mean here. We accepted Knight as a model of sorts; we sought to be like him in that we sought to achieve a competence to criticize anything and everything, including the ideas of Frank Knight himself. This relationship is totally different from that which describes the student's attitude toward a master, from whom he has learned the gospel and to whom all authority is granted. Discipleship, which describes the student-master relationship, was entirely absent from our linkage to Frank Knight. I could not imagine a Knight student looking for answers to questions by consulting the text as written by Knight, or defending a proposition, in argument, by reference to the word, as spoken by the master. (Indeed, Knight had little or no respect for his own prior statements. He refused to go back and read anything he had previously published, and he commenced each new essay from scratch, as it were. This explains, in part, the appearance of considerable redundancy in the arguments of the separate essays.) The heritage that Frank Knight gave to those of us who would, and could, take it was a critical attitude; it was not a set of propositions, whether these be scientific or ideological.

## VI

I have classified Frank Knight as "Chicago's critical spirit"; I have said little about the man himself. But the qualities that made such a spirit possible also allow some predictions to be made about the person who possessed it. Frank Knight was, at base, a pessimist. He observed the behavior of fools, and he expected relatively little by way of improvement or reform. But he tempered his pessimistic predictions with hope that the application of only a modicum of shared intelligence could put most things right. The apparent emotional tranquillity that could be observed alongside the pessimistic perspective stemmed from the absence of any sense of personal responsibility for the behavior of others than himself. He found no cause for the despair about the course of world events that destroyed the balance of so many of his academic peers. The world was not there waiting to be "saved" by his own efforts, and he would have steadfastly refused to give advice to a reforming despot. Frank Knight was happy in his role; he had found his niche. His self-assigned task was to expose the absurdities of others and nothing more. Would that other academicians could be so humble!

I knew Frank Knight first as a graduate student, but as one a bit more equal than others. An affinity was established based on our shared rural upbringings, along with a Tennessee connection. As a result, I was a one-way beneficiary of many hours of good conversation that ranged from ships and sealing wax through the off-color stories that he enjoyed immensely. He also enjoyed his sherry spiked with peach brandy, and we shared an admiration for the sometimes gloomy poetry of Thomas Hardy. There was always a hint of righteous anger mixed with the bemusement of the cynic in Frank Knight, but there was also an earthiness that removed any sense of social distance. And, yes indeed, Frank Knight did sell off his reprints at varying prices, determined by relative supply and demand. Years later, at the University of Virginia, when I was a host departmental chairman for an extended Knight visiting stint, there was no discernible shift in our relationship. To Frank Knight, there were no members and nonmembers to be treated differently by rank or status.

I shall end this piece with a story that, to me, illustrates Chicago's critical spirit better than almost anything else. "And lo! Ben Adhem's name led all the rest." For most of us who recall this line at all, it would invoke high school memories of some early Victorian poetry. But Frank Knight could not turn off his persistent critical mind, which was always accompanied by a twinkle in his eye and with a bit of the jester about him. So his entry into class one day commenced with the statement: "Abou Ben Adhem, his name led all the rest. Why shouldn't it, it begins with '*a, b*'?"

# Knight, Frank H.

Frank Hyneman Knight was born on a farm in McLean County, Illinois, in 1885. He received a motley education; his higher degrees commenced with a B.A. from Milligan College (Tennessee) in 1911, followed by two degrees (B.A. and M.A.) from the University of Tennessee in 1913, and a Ph.D. from Cornell University in 1916. His major subjects ranged from chemistry, through German literature, to economics and philosophy. At Cornell he studied under Allyn Young, who was perhaps the only man to have exerted an important direct influence on Knight's economic ideas. His academic career included appointments at Cornell, Chicago, and Iowa before he finally returned in 1928 to the University of Chicago. Knight served as president of the American Economic Association in 1950, and in 1957 he was awarded the association's Francis Walker medal.

Knight has always lived primarily in the world of ideas, and he has not compromised his commitment by becoming involved in governmental service or in quasi journalism. He has never been much concerned with defending his own works, once completed, and in these works one senses the struggle of a man who seeks first of all to set his own thinking straight rather than to preach the gospel or to enhance his own professional stature. Frank Knight, the scholar-critic, the self-made intellectual, is a product of the American Midwest, and it is difficult to imagine that he could have emerged from the more sophisticated culture of the eastern seaboard.

## Risk, Uncertainty and Profit

Knight's first major work, *Risk, Uncertainty and Profit* (1921), was written as a doctoral dissertation at Cornell in 1916. It won second prize in the Hart,

From *International Encyclopedia of the Social Sciences,* vol. 17, ed. David L. Sills (New York: Macmillan and Free Press, 1968), 424–28. Reprinted by permission of the publisher.

Schaffner and Marx essay competition in 1917 and after rewriting was published as a book.

The motivation for this work, as with so much of Knight's writing, was the desire for clarification. Ambiguities remained in the formal neoclassical theory of economic organization, notably in relation to the role and meaning of pure profit and its connection with predictive knowledge. Critical of the lack of precision that seemed to be present in the Marshallian treatment, Knight made explicit the distinction between rent, which is a distributive share in the ordinary sense, and profit, which results from imperfect knowledge. In order to do this he was forced to spell out, in considerable detail, the features of a system in which competition is perfect, and his treatment represents, in a sense, the apogee of neoclassical theorizing. He fully recognized and stated quite explicitly that the model of perfect competition is an idealization of reality, not a description.

Lesser theorists who followed Knight overlooked this essential point and erroneously expected real-world institutions to match up descriptively with the idealized model. Their overly simplistic comparisons of theoretical perfection and observed reality have permitted the critics of a competitive economic order to undermine effectively much of its general social support, especially when comparisons failed to consider the flaws of alternative arrangements. Since the rigorous formulation of the idealized competitive model, by Knight and others, did lend itself to this misinterpretation, it is appropriate to ask whether the relevant theory could have been so formulated as to prevent these results. The answer is, of course, that rigorous construction of the model was essential to the development of economic science as it exists.

To construct this model of the perfectly competitive economy, Knight explained profit as the result of uncertainty, which he distinguished sharply from risk. This step involved the differentiation, in degree, between those possible events which can be insured against, to which an objective probability calculus can be applied, and those possible events to which such a calculus cannot be applied. This important distinction between risk and uncertainty found its way quickly into the general structure of theory, and it represents one of Knight's more specific contributions to the standard body of doctrine.

Developments since 1921 in the theory of probability have tended to reduce somewhat the sharpness of the differentiation between risk and uncertainty, at least in any formal sense. The fact remains, nonetheless, that there exist certain uninsurable uncertainties in the institutional environment of modern business operation. Moreover, the distinction retains its formal validity, despite modern notions of probability, when it is recognized that insurance against the possibility of making wrong decisions removes all content from decision itself. To this extent, therefore, genuine Knightian uncertainty must exist in a world where decisions must be made and where decisions may be erroneous. As Knight quite explicitly stated in this early work, where there is no genuine uncertainty, there are no decisions.

## Theory of Economic Organization

Several generations of students at the University of Chicago obtained their "vision" of the whole economic process only after encountering Henry Simons' syllabus (for Economics 201, his course in introductory economic theory) and Frank Knight's monograph *Economic Organization* (1933). The latter was first prepared in the early 1920s at Iowa, and it was later duplicated at Chicago. It was intended solely for student use, and it is in no sense an ordinary textbook, yet it contains the elements of theory that helped to establish for Chicago its eminence in neoclassical economics. There is little in the monograph that is wholly original; its value is in its critical emphasis on key points, its clarification of ambiguous concepts and notions, and, finally, its integrated approach to the economy as a social organization.

In this monograph Knight used his now-familiar double dichotomy of the whole subject field, the sharp distinction between statics and dynamics on the one hand, and between the individual and the social economy on the other. He spelled out in some detail the five functions of an economic system, an approach that has since found its way into many introductory textbooks. He also used the image of the wheel of wealth or income, another standard textbook feature. He emphasized the central position of the economic principle—equalization of returns at the margin. Further, he stated the law of variable proportions, classifying the first, second, and third stages of the production function, and distinguished between the meanings of the law of diminishing returns. Finally, he stressed opportunity cost, a characteristic feature of his economic theory.

Many of the points made in this small monograph had been discussed, earlier and more thoroughly, in *Risk, Uncertainty and Profit* and in journal articles. But for Chicago graduate students, *Economic Organization* was the first encounter with Knight's basic thought. The monograph was not widely circulated beyond Chicago, and Knight's early theoretical contributions became known primarily through his first book and a series of important papers in the 1920s. His influence was notable at the London School of Economics, where, largely at the urging of Lionel Robbins, Knight's work became a necessary part of reading for an economics degree.

## Theory of Capital

In his early theoretical writings Knight accepted without much question the Austrian theory of capital, which utilizes the time period of production as the common denominator for abstract capital. Later he emphatically rejected this theory, and in the 1930s he published a series of important papers designed to show the fallacies inherent in the Austrian view.

Knight held that the Austrian theory is based more or less directly on the classical Ricardian model of an agricultural economy in which capital stock is conceived of as the subsistence for labor over the year until a new crop is harvested. This model of an economy, along with the classical tendency to "explain" all payments as rewards for "pain," produced the notion that the return to capital is a payment for waiting and that capital itself is nothing more than labor embodied in storable product. It is the capital theory that emerges from this model, which attempts to measure the quantity of abstract capital in terms of the time period between input and output, namely roundaboutness in production, that Knight flatly rejected. Capital, he asserted, is not embodied labor; there is no measurable time period of production, and an increase in the quantity of abstract capital need not amount to a lengthening of the production process. While Knight's criticism does not entirely apply to the more sophisticated versions of the Austrian theory, it did much to undermine the more elementary versions of the period-of-production approach.

Knight's own theory of capital is based on a consistent application of the theory of opportunity cost. The rate of return is determined by the real yield on capital investment at the margin, and the economy in equilibrium is adjusted so that the return is equalized in all uses. The long-run demand for investment is extremely elastic at ruling rates of return. There is little need for the tortuous reasoning involved in the Austrian theory, since the rate of return can be explained more straightforwardly.

This theory of capital has been somewhat neglected by other economists. This is largely due to the fact that attention has shifted away from abstract capital theory since the 1930s, so much so that it is now difficult to say just what pure theory of capital the majority of economists do accept. It is to be expected that when the attention of economists does return to this theory, Knight's contribution will be critically re-examined.

## The Methodology of Economics

Knight is the economist as philosopher, not the economist as scientist. Economic theory is for him an idealized construction, a logical system, not an explanatory science. His work represents the search for logical contradictions rather than for conceptually refutable hypotheses, although these two approaches can lead to quite similar results, as evidenced best by Knight's work on realism and its relevance for the theory of demand.

His conception of economic theory as relevant to idealized rather than actual behavior enables Knight to be both an abstract theorist and a severe critic of the "economic" explanation of human behavior. Theory allows prediction to the extent that men do, in fact, act in terms of economic motives and to the extent that they do not make errors. But since, in fact, these motives do not exclusively, or perhaps even primarily, determine behavior, and since there is no way of observing the extent to which they do, theory cannot be operational in the modern methodological sense. Theory can help in the understanding and explanation of behavior, but not in the scientific prediction of behavior.

## Limitations of Economics as a Science

Although he has written several books, Knight is essentially an essayist, and much of his work has taken the form of essays in "criticism of established dogma." It has been suggested that he is the ideal book reviewer, and in a real sense his whole work can be interpreted as a continuing review of the books that are written or read uncritically by so many others. Nowhere is this quality of Knight's work more evident than in *The Ethics of Competition and*

*Other Essays* (1921–1935), a collection of essays (most of which had been previously published) edited by a group of his students.

The pervasive concern here is with the limits that must be placed on the economic way of looking at behavior, on the limitations of economics as a science. Knight's avowed skepticism of any extended application of theory places him alongside the American institutionalists. This question-ridden, almost answerless, set of essays shows that he is that rare theorist who is also an institutionalist, an institutionalist who is not a data collector.

In a classic discussion, he denied the givenness of human wants, emphasizing the continual emergence of wants in creative interplay with the environment. Central to Knight's conception of economic order are the game elements in economic behavior, the deliberate setting of goals designed to make the process of achieving them interesting in itself. This conception, in turn, leads to considerations and more questions regarding the establishment of rules for economic and social behavior, the formation of the social constitution.

## Social Philosophy

Knight's concern with the larger issues of social philosophy is clear in his 1935 essay "Economic Theory and Nationalism" (in 1921–1935). Although written in the mid-1930s, the essay has remained relevant. Basically Knight is a pessimist, and his interpretation of the historical process is a tragic one. Liberalism, as a system of order, failed to realize what it might have become, partly because of its own excesses; socialism emerged as its replacement. While regretting the failure of what might have been, Knight nonetheless conveys perceptively the values inherent in systems alternative to liberalism, and he especially stresses the human desire to be part of a larger organic whole, suggesting the modern necessity of a "social" religion. This essay distills features of national socialism that transcend the disastrous experiments of the 1930s and 1940s, and its predictions continue to be relevant.

Knight's concern with the larger issues of social philosophy is also evident in a second volume of essays, *Freedom and Reform* (1929–1946), which, like its predecessor, was published by students. His shift toward philosophical issues, toward ethics, morals, and values, arises out of his developing conviction that these are the important issues for modern society. The economic problem, as such, is one of Western man's lesser worries; its removal will leave the problem of social order largely unchanged. The difficulties that twentieth-century man confronts are not centrally intellectual; scientific progress offers no panacea.

One of Knight's many crusades has been against the view, which he associates with John Dewey, that science in some instrumental sense can be used to solve social problems in a community of free men. Knight believes that science applied instrumentally implies control, whereas the social problem is one of attaining consensus, of securing mutual agreement. The "social engineer," so prevalent in the background of modern economic models, has no place in Knight's approach to social problems.

Modern man's central problem, according to Knight, is a moral one. Historical liberalism has destroyed conventional religion and has provided no effective substitute for it; as a consequence, men have turned all too quickly to nihilism or to the deification of the state. What men need, therefore, is a common morality founded on truth, honesty, mutual respect, and "good sportsmanship," the ethics that liberalism should have produced but somehow failed to.

It is noteworthy that Knight believes the prospects for a society embodying the liberal ethics improved, if only slightly, in the years after World War II. In his most recent book, *Intelligence and Democratic Action* (1960), he assesses somewhat more optimistically the possibility of a man's applying critical intelligence to his relationships with other men in organized political society. He warns against romanticism in all its varieties, and he calls for an education of the will rather than of the intellect, an education that must, above all, inculcate the critical attitude that is based on a respect for truth. "The distinctive virtue for men in a free society, the essence of the whole liberal view of life, is truth-seeking."

Surveying the history of Western civilization since the Enlightenment, Knight sees no clear indication that man can rise to the challenge presented by the liberation of his own mind. But in his later writings especially, one senses his increased willingness to leave this question open.

Knight's attitude toward organized religion is directly related to his commitment to truth-seeking. As he sees it, the very exercise of critical intelligence requires a willingness to examine all things objectively, to hold nothing sacrosanct. Religion is designed to "fence off" certain areas of inquiry and to ask that the individual accept certain precepts on faith. This represents the antithesis of the critical attitude, which Knight deems so essential. He insists that religious dogma is not different from other dogma and that it should be subject to the same critical scrutiny.

Knight's revulsion from religious dogma resulted from his overexposure in early life to the hell-fire and brimstone of prairie evangelism. His reaction against religious orthodoxy was, perhaps, an essential ingredient in his intellectual development: having rejected it, the less rigid dogma encountered in the world of scholarship became easy prey to the Midwestern skeptic.

## Assessment

In his critical attitude and outlook, in his abhorrence of nonsense even in its most sophisticated forms, Frank Knight has much in common with David Hume, although Hume does not appear to have directly influenced Knight's thought. These two critics share a determination to cut through the metaphysical-linguistic fuzziness that enshrouds the human mind.

Knight is no social reformer in the ordinary sense of this term. He believes that reform, improvement, in social order can come only through man's acquisition of an ability, and a willingness, to use his own mind. Knight's emphasis is always on changing man's way of thinking about social problems rather than on changing social institutions in order to solve problems.

Knight has no "disciples" as such, and those who have been most influenced by his work are as likely to criticize him as others are. This is because as a teacher he has been almost uniquely willing to look for merit in all questions and because he has refused to accept any final answers. His attitude has always been that all principles have their limits, that most of them are both right and wrong, that they hold more or less, and that judgment can never be dispensed with. This is the central point in his 1950 presidential address to the American Economic Association (1951).

Scorning both the relativist and the absolutist, Knight finally insists on the relevance of the "relatively absolute absolutes," a position that makes him refuse to interpret matters in terms of black or white, yet, at the same time, allows him to hold steadfastly that man can, and must, use his own good judgment in making distinctions among the various shades of gray.

WORKS BY KNIGHT

"Interest." In *Encyclopaedia of the Social Sciences,* vol. 8, 131–44. New York: Macmillan, 1932.

"Profit." In *Encyclopaedia of the Social Sciences,* vol. 12, 480–86. New York: Macmillan, 1934.

"The Ideal of Freedom: Conditions for Its Realization." In *The Philosophy of American Democracy,* edited by Charner M. Perry, 87–118. Chicago: University of Chicago Press, 1943.

"The Meaning of Freedom." In *The Philosophy of American Democracy,* edited by Charner M. Perry, 59–86. Chicago: University of Chicago Press, 1943.

*Freedom and Reform: Essays in Economics and Social Philosophy.* New York and London: Harper, 1947.

Knight, Frank H., and Thornton W. Merriam. *The Economic Order and Religion.* London: Routledge, 1948.

*The Economic Organization.* With an article, "Notes on Cost and Utility." New York: Kelley, 1951.

*The Ethics of Competition and Other Essays.* New York: Kelley, 1951.

"The Rôle of Principles in Economics and Politics." *American Economic Review* 41 (1951): 1–29.

*On the History and Method of Economics: Selected Essays.* Chicago: University of Chicago Press, 1956.

*Risk, Uncertainty and Profit.* London School of Economics and Political Science, Series of Reprints of Scarce Tracts in Economic and Political Science, No. 16. New York: Kelley, 1957.

*Intelligence and Democratic Action.* Cambridge, Mass.: Harvard University Press, 1960.

# The Qualities of
# a Natural Economist

## 2.1 Introduction

There are very few natural economists, and most of those who claim professional competence in economics as a discipline are not, themselves, "natural." They tend rather to be reformers, revolutionaries, paternalists, and more frequently of late, mathematicians. Gordon Tullock is an exception to most of his peers in this important respect, and his qualifications as a "natural economist" cut through and thoroughly dominate his own professional training in law. I use the term "natural" here in a manner that is precisely analogous to its usage when applied to baseball players, musicians, and comedians. To designate someone a "natural" is to suggest that he or she has intrinsic talents that emerge independent of professional training, education, and experience. A "natural economist," therefore, is someone who more or less unconsciously thinks like an economist.

But how does an economist think? I leave my designation ambiguous until and unless I answer this preliminary question. An economist, in the sense of the term used here, views human beings as self-interested, utility-maximizing agents, basically independent one from another, and for whom social interchange is initiated and exists simply as a preferred alternative to isolated action. Psychologically, persons remain in a Hobbesian setting, or, as Tullock perceptively suggested in his title for a revealing essay, "The Edge

From *Democracy and Public Choice: Essays in Honor of Gordon Tullock,* ed. Charles Rowley (Oxford: Basil Blackwell, 1987), 9–19. Copyright 1987 by Blackwell Publishers Ltd. Reprinted by permission of Blackwell Publishers Ltd.

of the Jungle," despite the political-legal-institutional trappings of civic order. To the economist who looks at persons in this way, there seems little room for moral or ethical precepts in either positive or normative exercises. Persons are observed to behave in certain patterns, and the economist's task is to offer an explanation-understanding of that behavior in terms of his model of self-interested utility maximization. And, because he considers himself successful in this positive aspect of his science, the economist offers normative guidance grounded on his own self-interest as a participating member of the inclusive political community.[1]

All of us who "do economics" necessarily take on the economist's perspective, as sketched out above, when we engage in analytic enterprise. Those of us who do not qualify as "naturals," however, tend to stop short at the several subjectively determined boundaries of personal behavior. Many of those who call themselves economists are quite willing to incorporate self-interested utility maximization on the part of participants in organized market activity—as consumers, investors, labor-suppliers, owners, entrepreneurs—while at the same time they object, sometimes quite vociferously, to extensions of the *same* motivational-behavioral model to persons as participants in non-market interactions—as politicians, bureaucrats, voters, agents for non-proprietary institutions, criminals, revolutionaries, university administrators, teachers, research scholars, family members, preachers, and judges. It is the "natural economists" such as Gordon Tullock, Gary Becker, and Armen Alchian who have opened up several new areas of interaction to inquiry by extending the economist's standard model. In so doing, they have "dragged" some of us along in the process, despite some initial reluctance on our parts.

My discussion of the qualities of a natural economist will concentrate on Gordon Tullock, and, in part, my discussion must be autobiographical due to my long association with Tullock as a co-author and colleague. Aside from this relationship, however, some treatment of Tullock's influence on my own work can be helpful in developing my central theme. As I noted in the acknowledgment to one of my volumes of collected essays, my debt to Gordon Tullock stems in part from his long-continuing insistence on the economic view of man, which has served to check my own tendencies to wander off

---

1. Gordon Tullock, "The Edge of the Jungle," *Explorations in the Theory of Anarchy,* ed. Gordon Tullock (Blacksburg: Center for Study of Public Choice, 1973).

into ethical and moral discourse. On the other hand, and by contrast, I think that my own continuing reluctance to view man, always and everywhere, as self-seeking, explains my search for ways and means of reconciling self-interest with broader norms for social interaction. Appreciation of the essential tension between these two perspectives provides, I think, some understanding of the success of our major joint effort, *The Calculus of Consent*. Independent of some emphasis on rules, on constitutional structures, straightforward extensions of economic models of behavior to politics might have seemed Schumpeterian, in the sense that they offer no basis for constructive reform. On the other hand, independent of something like Tullock's economic reductionism, my own analyses of politics might have failed to attract the attention of either economists or political scientists. The separate directions of our works after this initial major joint effort illustrates the divergence in our perspectives. My own efforts have been toward the elaboration and development of what we now call "constitutional political economy," the analysis of alternative structures of rules which constrain man's self-seeking. By comparison, Tullock's efforts have involved, for the most part, still further imaginative extensions basically employing the same natural economist perspective on human behavior.[2]

In what follows, I shall discuss several of these extensions briefly to illustrate my main theme. Gordon Tullock's work is, of course, no exception to the general rule that consistency in terms of any classificatory standard is not to be expected. He has, on occasion, applied his imaginative insights to the resolution of analytical problems that cannot readily be brought within the "natural economist" rubric. Such "deviant" contributions will not be surveyed here because, in my judgment, these do represent digressions from Gordon Tullock's more characteristic and consistent path of inquiry.

## 2.2 The Politics of Bureaucracy

When I first met Gordon Tullock in 1957, he had in hand a voluminous manuscript on bureaucracy that he had tried, unsuccessfully, to publish.

---

2. James M. Buchanan, *Freedom in Constitutional Contract* (College Station: Texas A&M University Press, 1977); James M. Buchanan and Gordon Tullock, *The Calculus of Consent* (Ann Arbor: University of Michigan Press, 1962); Joseph Schumpeter, *Capitalism, Socialism and Democracy* (New York: Harper, 1942).

What I took home with me from Philadelphia turned out to be a fascinating analysis of modern governmental bureaucracy that was almost totally buried in an irritating personal narrative account of Tullock's nine-year experience in the foreign service hierarchy. (Then, as now, Tullock's work was marked by his refusal to *write* [everything is dictated] as well as by his apparent inability to separate analytical exposition from personal anecdote.) The substantive contribution in the manuscript was centered on the hypothesis that regardless of role the individual bureaucrat responds to the rewards and punishments that he confronts. This straightforward, and now so simple, hypothesis turned the whole post-Weberian quasi-normative approach to bureaucracy on its head. The bureaucrat becomes an economist actor in his own account, rather than the economic eunuch enshrined in the standard treatment. The economic theory of bureaucracy was born, one that has since been considerably enriched by Downs, Niskanen, Breton and Wintrobe, and others.[3]

Tullock's book *The Politics of Bureaucracy,* the ultimate version of the 1957 manuscript, was published in 1965, after our collaboration on *The Calculus of Consent.* The former was hammered into acceptability to a publisher only after my own heroic scissors-and-paste effort completed during a rain-soaked holiday week in a West Virginia state park—an effort that involved excision of much personal narrative. The rather intensive reading of the initial Tullock manuscript, however, forced me into a much deeper appreciation of the categorical difference between market and political organization—a difference that I tried to elaborate in my own Foreword to the book. This difference, which I discussed in terms of the power relationships among persons, emerges clearly only if one does, indeed, adopt the natural economist's perspective. The implications of the differences between the receipt of opportunity-related wages and situation-related rents for individual well-being and psychological security were clarified. My own tendency is to think in terms of organizational principle, but, even for those for whom political philosophy holds little or no interest, there could be little or no

---

3. Anthony Downs, *Inside Bureaucracy* (Boston: Little, Brown, 1967), William Niskanen, *Bureaucracy and Representative Government* (Chicago: Aldine-Atherton, 1971), and Albert Breton and Ronald Wintrobe, *The Logic of Bureaucratic Conduct* (Cambridge: Cambridge University Press, 1982).

satisfaction in a rent-dependency status. A reading of Tullock on bureaucracy leaves no mystery concerning his own profound disaffection with government as a monopsonist employer.[4]

## 2.3 Voter Abstention and Voter Ignorance

Gordon Tullock, along with Anthony Downs, is credited with having emphasized the basic paradox exhibited in voting behavior in large-number electorates in which majority or plurality rules are utilized to determine the ultimately selected outcome. The paradox emerges directly when the natural economist looks at the behavior of the individual who faces the voting and non-voting options. Attention comes to be placed directly on the privately differentiated costs and benefits anticipated for each of the two alternatives. Because of the extremely low probability that any individual vote will affect the ultimate electoral result, the value differential to the individual between participation and non-participation in the election must be large indeed if rationality considerations are to dictate going to the polls, even if such action involves a minimal cost.[5]

Note that the prediction of rational abstention that emerges from the economist's model of behavior here does not depend on the dominance of individually defined, measurable self-interest, such as net wealth, in the ultimate comparison of the electoral alternatives. A person may well desire that Party A win over Party B for purely ideological rather than identifiable "private" reasons. Nonetheless, unless the differential value weights are very large, rational behavior may still suggest abstention from voting participation. The prediction of rational abstention does require the presumption that when the individual chooses between participation and non-participation in an election he acts in accordance with self-interest, rather than in terms of "duty," "civic responsibility," or similar standards. It is useful to distinguish between the relevance of identifiable self-interest in the individual's ranking of the ultimate electoral alternatives (candidates, issues, or parties) and the rele-

4. Gordon Tullock, *The Politics of Bureaucracy* (Washington, D.C.: Public Affairs Press, 1965).

5. Gordon Tullock, *Towards a Mathematics of Politics* (Ann Arbor: University of Michigan Press, 1967), and Anthony Downs, *An Economic Theory of Democracy* (New York: Harper, 1957).

vance of identifiable self-interest in the ranking of the participation and non-participation options.

The logic of the paradox of voting extends, of course, to the behavior of the individual in determining the level of personal investment in acquiring information about the electoral alternatives. The absence of the direct linkage between the potential act of voting and the final electoral result introduces an element of irresponsibility in the political process that is absent in the comparable market process, where there is one-to-one relationship between individual choice and final result.[6] Even if the individual votes, therefore, he is unlikely to be well informed about the predicted properties of that for which he votes, the pattern of behavior of a candidate, the effects of a particular referendum proposal, or the working out of a party's platform pledges. And note that in this informational element there is no distinction to be made between those persons who do choose to vote and those who do not. Those persons who violate the paradox and go to the polls may behave consistently with the economist's model in remaining uninformed about the voting options. Rational behavior dictates that those who do vote should remain "rationally ignorant."

The basic logic here can be extended further to emphasize the possible dominance of expressive, fashion, or whim motives in the actual behavior within the polling booth. The individual may use voting as means of expressing his whim rather than his genuine ranking over the alternatives because the very institution of the large-number election allows such expression at relatively low cost.[7]

To those who do not accept the economist's model of rational choice, the twin hypotheses of voter abstention and voter ignorance do not warrant serious consideration because they neglect motivational influences that cannot be brought within the rational choice framework. And, empirically, we do observe that many persons vote in large-number settings—an observation which seems to refute the central abstention hypothesis. The basic contribution of Tullock, Downs, and others who have developed the hypothesis

6. See James M. Buchanan, "Individual Choice in Voting and the Market," *Journal of Political Economy* 62 (August 1954): 334–43.

7. See Geoffrey Brennan and James Buchanan, "Voter Choice: Evaluating Political Alternatives," *American Behavioral Scientist* 29 (November-December 1984): 185–201.

lies, however, precisely in the challenge posed to those who would offer alternative explanations. Why do individuals vote? The observed results may well suggest limits to rational choice approaches to behavior, but until and unless the critics of these approaches produce an alternative explanation, we remain with the paradox.

There are important implications here for any normative theory of democracy. If the act of voting must be "irrational" in many settings, and if, in voting, the individual expresses merely an uninformed and whim-driven attitude rather than a genuinely measured preference over the electoral alternatives, how is democratic process to be defined? The natural economist stops at this point and says to all of us "the ball is in your court." It is precisely at this point that the "constitutional economist" draws perhaps most closely on the analysis of the natural economist in his search for institutional changes that may limit the potential for excess in the extension of non-constrained majoritarian politicization.

## 2.4 Revolution, War, and Crime

From the perspective of what I have here called that of the natural economist, perhaps the most difficult, and most questionable, extension of the model is to the behavior of those persons who initiate and participate in revolutionary activity, along with those persons who seem to sacrifice themselves voluntarily in wars. Gordon Tullock has not flinched from such a challenge, however, and has made valiant efforts toward incorporating all such behavior into his inclusive analytical structure (with an apparent delight at the shock effect on his peers).

There is no room for the hero in the Tullock world, and ideology motivates behavior only to some second order of smalls. Yeats description of the worst persons as those "full of passionate intensity" finds no sympathetic reading by Tullock, who tends to shun literary metaphor. The revolutionary leader in the Tullock canon is an entrepreneur, analogous to other entrepreneurs, who recognizes an opportunity for potential personal gain (which may be status- rather than wealth-based), and who sets about to exploit it. Lenin's interest in "saving the world by Communism" was not measurably different from that of anyone else; his interests were his own. The followers of the revolutionary leader, those who actually make the revolution, reach their decisions on the basis of a self-interested utility-maximizing calculus, just as do those who elect to remain non-revolutionaries. The soldier-hero who sacrifices his life for his comrades may, of course, make errors in judgment, but his decision calculus can still be brought within the natural economist's explanatory umbrella.

In my assessment, these are the extensions of the model that are the most vulnerable to criticism, and it is in his willingness to make these extensions that Gordon Tullock has exposed himself to sometime strident attack. By seeming to go too far, these efforts may well have tended to reduce appreciation for Tullock's work in more acceptable applications. (Much the same point might be made with reference to the work of Gary Becker.) In part, the vulnerability here stems from a methodological ambiguity, which was again a tension in *The Calculus of Consent*. Tullock has never clearly distinguished between predictive and explanatory models of behavior. If defined in sufficiently general terms, all human behavior can be "explained" in some utility-maximizing framework, that is, if the arguments in the utility function are left totally unspecified, even as to sign. The utility-maximizing hypothesis becomes tautological, or nearly so, in this setting, although it may remain of some heuristic value in analysis.[8]

On the other hand, if the arguments in the individual's utility functions are defined, along with the assignment of positive and negative signs, operational content beyond formal tests for rationality is put into the model, and refutable implications may be derived. At this level of generality, a significant contribution may be made by looking at non-economic behavior from the economist's perspective, even if it is fully recognized that this perspective is not, in itself, dominant in "explaining" behavior. Even if an individual revolutionary is motivated primarily by ideological conviction rather than measurable net wealth, so long as the latter is positively valued, it follows that changes in the constraint structure can affect behavior in predictable ways. *Some* revolutionaries will respond to increases in rewards for defection or increases in penalties of capture. To the extent that the economist's analytical inquiry concentrates on such exploitable trade-off margins, there is both ex-

---

8. Gordon Tullock, *The Social Dilemma* (Blacksburg: Center for Study of Public Choice, 1974), and "Does Punishment Deter Crime?" *The Public Interest* 36 (Summer 1974): 103–11.

planatory and normative value in having this perspective extended to include overtly non-economic aspects of behavior.

The proponents or advocates of the economist's perspective, including Tullock, have made their efforts more vulnerable to criticism by failing to make clear the operationality of the model, even in such limited motivational settings. Instead, advocates of an "economic" explanation of revolutionary and patriotic behavior tend to go further and to substitute, implicitly if not explicitly, some version of a wealth-maximizing for a utility-maximizing hypothesis. That is to say, and as Tullock has indeed argued, a revolutionary is hypothesized to act so as to increase the expected value of his private net wealth—a much more severely defined objective for choice than the mere signing of net wealth as a positive argument in the revolutionary's utility function. And, perhaps properly, the critics charge that such an extreme economistic model of behavior in such applications becomes caricature.

Extension of the economist's model to criminal behavior is perhaps somewhat less vulnerable to such criticism than the extension of the behavior of revolutionaries. Individuals who commit crimes can be predicted, especially in the more limited usage of the model, to respond to penalties measured in terms of their measured self-interest, for example, longer prison sentences and increased probabilities of capture and conviction. Such changes in the law enforcement structure can safely be predicted to reduce, say, the rate of burglary. This application of the model may be accepted without, at the same time, hypothesizing that individuals become burglars only if their expected "earnings" in this "occupation" equal or exceed those in legal employment (or receipt of welfare benefits). Or, to put the same proposition in the inverse, increases in the rewards to criminal activity can be predicted to lead to increased levels of crime (a simple application of elementary economics), without implying that relative rewards in criminal and legal activities are the primary determinants of the overall level of criminality.

## 2.5 Charity, Cost, and Redistribution

The proclivities of the "natural economist," again exemplified in the work of Gordon Tullock, emerge clearly in analyses of interpersonal transfers of values that remain outside the market exchange nexus. To the extent that one person voluntarily gives a valuable item (money, claims, goods, services) to another, the *Homo economicus* model of behavior seems, on the surface, to be inoperative. The natural economist is prompted to search for ways and means of bringing such behavior within his inclusive explanatory model by looking, for example, at the privately enjoyed benefits stemming from the act of giving *per se,* rather than at the prospects for the existence of genuine altruism beyond minimal limits. He will also tend to look for sources of institutional coercion that penalize the individual who does not voluntarily "join" the charity drive by his firm, community, or church.

It is, however, at the level of collective or governmental, rather than private, transfer that the natural economist's proclivity has led to genuine contributions to our understanding and interpretation of widely observed patterns of behavior. One of Gordon Tullock's most imaginative papers, "The Charity of the Uncharitable," was based on the simple cost-benefit calculus of the person who might vote in support for or opposition to collectively organized transfer programs. The hypothesis is that charitable giving, like all other economic activities, obeys the laws of economics. Individuals are likely to be "charitable" when the costs to them, personally and privately, are non-existent or very low. They become "uncharitable" quickly as these private costs increase. This straightforward cost-benefit calculus on the part of voters, along with the recognition of the publicness of some transfers, and the minimal altruism that persons exhibit, satisfactorily explains those elements of genuine transfers from rich to poor that we observe to take place through our political institutions.[9]

In the modern polity, we observe large government budgets that include ever-increasing shares devoted to transfer payments. Given this budgetary record as fact, there must be some explanation over and beyond that which was noted above. The natural economist is led to explain what we see by hypothesizing that much of the transfer system now in place is not at all motivated by demands for vertical income redistribution, but is driven by the political profit-seeking of competing interest groups. The transfer system inclusively considered is not primarily an altruistically driven welfare system. It is, by contrast, best characterized as a complex structure of inter–interest group pay-

---

9. Gordon Tullock, "The Charity of the Uncharitable," *Western Economic Journal* 9 (December 1971): 379–92.

ments, often with little or no relationship to those ideals for redistribution policy that might be laid out by the philosopher of altruism.

Gordon Tullock, along with Aaron Director and George Stigler, has been a leading figure among those economists who view the transfer structure in this skeptical fashion, a view that is coming to be increasingly accepted by those who do not qualify as natural economists.[10]

## 2.6 Rent-seeking

Many of his peers consider Gordon Tullock's most important single contribution to economics to be the theory of rent-seeking. Tullock's seminal paper was published in 1967, but he did not introduce the now-familiar term which was itself used first by Ann Krueger. Analysis is far from closed in this area of inquiry, but, by 1985, rent-seeking was well on its way toward becoming an integral part of economics.[11]

As with the several other extensions already briefly discussed in this paper, the whole notion of rent-seeking, once introduced, seems to be a self-evident consequence of carrying through the economist's model of rational choice. There is an important difference, however, between this and the other extensions discussed, and one that warrants notice. The applications of the natural economist's model to political, criminal, revolutionary, and charitable behavior are straightforward efforts to widen the explanatory limits of the basic tool kit. The theory of rent-seeking becomes quite different in this respect. Consider Tullock's linking of monopoly, tariffs, and theft in his pioneering paper. The economist's model of behavior had traditionally been applied to the monopolist, and other extensions had already included the behavior of groups seeking tariff protection, and also the behavior of potential and actual thieves. Persons in each of these capacities had previously been analyzed as economic actors. What the theory of rent-seeking does is to ex-

---

10. Gordon Tullock, *The Economics of Income Redistribution* (Boston: Kluwer-Nijhoff, 1983).

11. Gordon Tullock, "The Welfare Economics of Tariffs, Monopoly, and Theft," *Western Economic Journal* 5 (June 1967): 224–32; Ann Krueger, "The Political Economy of the Rent-Seeking Society," *American Economic Review* 64 (June 1974): 291–302.

tend the analysis one stage further back, so to speak, to bring in the behavior of persons before they become successful monopolists, recipients of tariff-cushioned rents, or thieves.

Rent-seeking analysis draws attention to the *process* within which the activity of many persons takes place, a *competitive process,* with a "profit and loss" structure akin to, but quite different from, the market process in its implications for overall efficiency in resource allocation. As I noted in my introductory essay in the volume that collected the seminal works on rent-seeking, rent-seeking behavior is not different in motivation from the ordinary profit-seeking which characterizes the competitive market process.[12] The critical difference lies in the sources of that which motivates the behavior in the two cases. In markets, potential profits emerge from the *increments* to value that are *created* by entrepreneurs who put together new resource combinations, or who meet new demands. In the non-market settings where rent-seeking takes place, there are no increments to value created. Instead, the value that potential rent-seekers attempt to secure is artificially created through interferences with resource adjustment.

## 2.7 Conclusions

I have discussed the qualities of the natural economist, with particular reference to the works of Gordon Tullock, in terms of several extensions of the basic model to unorthodox areas of interaction. My purpose here has not been that of examining any one of these extensions in critical detail, in part because I recognize that other contributors to this volume will take on such assignments. My aim has been the more limited one of utilizing these extensions or applications to indicate, at least indirectly, their potential usefulness to those of us who venture to engage in "political economy" or "constitutional economics," inquiries that focus attention on the evaluation of the working properties of alternative institutional-constitutional structures.

The man that is modelled by the natural economist may fail to attain desired levels of descriptive accuracy in many applications, and especially those

---

12. James M. Buchanan, Robert D. Tollison, and Gordon Tullock, eds., *Toward a Theory of the Rent-Seeking Society* (College Station: Texas A&M University Press, 1980).

interactions that are most removed from the ordinary exchange relationships of the market. However, any evaluation of proposals to change or to reform social institutions that ignores the economic content of human behavior is flawed from its inception. The natural economist provides a necessary input to any such exercise. *Homunculus* (the little man) he may sometimes be, but *Homo economicus* is a part of the reality that is.

# Preface

How can we measure the contribution that Winston C. Bush made to economics, to public choice, to his colleagues, to his university? Those who learned economics by working out the price-theory problems in Henry Simons' Syllabus know the answer. We measure the contribution of any productive unit by taking that unit away and by comparing the result with what has gone before. Those of us at the Center for the Study of Public Choice have lived through this tragic experiment for the year since Winston's death, and each day we observe the differences. His contribution was much greater than any identifiable set of ideas which might find expression and representation in a volume such as this. More than anything else perhaps, Bush had an ability to bring out the best in his colleagues, with "best" defined over more of the elements that enter the utility functions of economists. He was a man with an acute critical awareness who was intensely interested in ideas, both those of his own creation and those of others. But he had no sense of "property," and his willingness to help others with ideas was matched by his willingness to do chore work for his department, to help his friends in farming, and to buy beer for his students. Winston Bush forced an openness, an honesty, a frankness on us all, and the academic temptation to pretense could never have surfaced in his presence.

I can be more specific. Without Winston Bush at least three and possibly four books would not have been written; without him two separate workshops would never have been organized; without Bush at least two young economists would never have stretched their own more traditional econo-

From *Essays on Unorthodox Economic Strategies: A Memorial Volume in Honor of Winston C. Bush,* ed. Arthur T. Denzau and Robert J. Mackay (Blacksburg, Va.: Center for Study of Public Choice, 1976), vi. Reprinted by permission of the publisher.

mist's tools to interesting aspects of public choice theory. All this within three short years.

These are attributes that are easy to enumerate. Others are much more difficult to put in words. In retrospect, Winston offered us "solid ground," a point or place of reference, a haven from the artificialities and superficialities of academia, from the absurdities of the world in which we live and work. A discussion with Winston Bush made me feel much better about modern America, not because he offered hope at all, but because he recognized the alternatives. Winston Bush, along with my own mentor, Frank Knight, knew that life in modern academia is a "lot better than plowing." And in these days of the doomsayers, we need to be reminded of this simple fact.

Winston Bush loved baseball, beer, and country music. And he was not at all ashamed to say so. Matt Lindsay referred to him as a "good ol' Georgia boy." Those who share with me a southern rural heritage will know that these four words suffice.

*Blacksburg, December 1974*

# Jack Wiseman
## A Personal Appreciation

There is so much still to do: may there be enough time. Academics are lucky people. What better life could there be?

—Jack Wiseman, *Cost, Choice and Political Economy*

There was not enough time. Jack Wiseman died on 20 January 1991, less than a month after his seventy-first birthday, and only two months after he returned to Yorkshire from one of his regular visits to the Center for Study of Public Choice, in Fairfax, Virginia. He described this last visit (September–November 1990) as the most stimulating of the five he had made to Fairfax, after earlier visits to both Charlottesville and Blacksburg. He left us full of vigor and determined to get on with the treatise he had already fully organized in his thinking. Cancer was diagnosed immediately on his return home, and in both conversations and correspondence over those last few weeks, Jack stuck fast to the convictions expressed in the last two sentences of the above citation. And, in an electronic message relayed to my colleague, David Levy, just four days before his death, Jack ended with, "Don't be too distressed for me. After all, what has happened is an (unwelcome) vindication of the Wiseman Unknowability Thesis."

The Center for Study of Public Choice has lost an Adjunct Research Associate, and one of its most enthusiastic supporters. *Constitutional Political Econ-*

From *Constitutional Political Economy* 2 (Winter 1991): 1–6. Reprinted by permission of the publisher, Kluwer Academic Publishers.

*omy* has lost a contributing member of its Board of Editors. Professional colleagues and friends on all continents who mourn his death must be counted in the hundreds.

My own is, however, a special deprivation, that I can only partially understand, but which, somehow, I must try to express in this note, the writing of which may, in itself, help me to locate Jack Wiseman in that small (and dwindling) set of persons who have been more than colleagues, more than friends. Jack himself told part of the story in his introductory autobiographical essay in *Cost, Choice and Political Economy* (1989), the closing words of which I used in the preceding epigraph.

I first met Jack in 1960, early during one of my four visits to London and LSE in that turbulent decade. Both of us were, in a sense, outsiders to the Anglo-American academic establishment, Jack with his origins in a Lancashire family of weavers, me as a Tennessee farm boy. And we were both born in 1919, the year that Paul Johnson identifies as the start of *Modern Times*. Both of us had substantial chunks of our lives pulled out of the normal by military services in World War II, Jack's five dull years in the British Army, my own exciting years in the U.S. Navy. And as Jack notes, we soon found that we shared the pleasures of the off-color story, pleasures that so very few of our stodgy academic colleagues can sense at all. Jack took me to the one and only "football" (soccer) game I have ever seen, to Chelsea to see his home team, Burnley, soundly defeated. (Then and now, and despite Jack's talk, I do not understand why this game has so many fans.)

For me, as for others, Jack Wiseman "talked too much," as he acknowledged in his essay, a trait that was attributed to him by his very first teacher. He talked rather than listened, and sometimes with an air of braggadocio that was offputting to some. For me, however, the negatives with Jack were minimal, because I sensed a true kindred spirit, with a shared vision on so much of what seemed to matter to both of us. Jack was not philosophic in his interests, and we rarely reached the lower depths of discourse. But, at base, Jack was a genuine skeptic, a true disciple of David Hume. In this respect, Jack deserves more credit than I do; I had Frank Knight as my professor and role model. None of the LSE grandees could have done so well by Jack.

Someone has remarked that there is only one thing worse than taking life too seriously, and that is not taking it seriously enough. For me at least, Jack

Wiseman struck just the right balance. He did, indeed, enjoy life to its fullest, but always within the constraints of academic conscience.

Jack had sufficient self-confidence to cut through the pretentious arrogance of so much that passes for science and scholarship, and he had no inhibitions about labeling absurdities for what they were. In one sense, however, Jack Wiseman was too unorthodox; he could not, even for pragmatic purpose, work within a paradigm that he despised. We shared a sympathy for Shackle's radical subjectivism, but Jack Wiseman found himself boxed in, like Shackle himself, by the implied nihilism of the extreme subjectivist stance. As a result, he, along with Steve Littlechild, could never finish the textbook-treatise on subjectivist economics that they started.

Jack's best work involved his criticism of the conventional wisdom in particular areas where it was most vulnerable to the subjectivist attack. His paper on marginal cost pricing remains the best that exists, even if few yet understand its message. And thereby hangs a tale.

Jack Wiseman and Michael Farrell had never met each other, and they had engaged in a quite acrimonious controversy in the professional journals over the theory of marginal cost pricing. Michael was a colleague at Cambridge during my year there (1961–62), and he was, like Jack, a personal friend. When "my college," Sidney Sussex, planned its annual feast, I invited Jack up to Cambridge to meet Michael Farrell for sherry in my rooms, followed by the formal feast. With faith in discourse, and knowing both as reasonable men, I was sure that their intellectual differences might be at least partially reconciled. Alas, my efforts were in vain; at the end of the evening the two protagonists were as far apart as when they started; neither could understand what the other was talking about. Mike Farrell was so ensconced in the objectivist mind-set of neoclassical welfare economics that he simply could not make the connection between cost and choice. To Jack Wiseman, by contrast, coming out of the LSE tradition and influenced by Robbins, Hayek, Thirlby and Coase, any conception of cost independent of human choice remained useless at best, and absurd at its worst.

Jack's best pieces are collected in his volume *Cost, Choice and Political Economy,* and the first two words in this title are descriptive of his emphasis. Jack took these words from my own little book, *Cost and Choice,* which directly reflects his influence on my own thinking. Again as Jack notes in his own autobiographical essay, my determination to write *Cost and Choice* emerged in the aftermath of my book on public debt, which to me (and to Jack) seemed so self-evident in its central argument. In my visits to London and in conversations with Jack, I came increasingly to the conviction that economists' elementary confusion about public debt stemmed from confusion about the very meaning of opportunity cost, confusion that could only be clarified by exorcising the objectivist dimension of cost (or debt burden) or, in other words, by relating cost to choice, whether private or public. Jack Wiseman was my personal or conversational entryway into the rich LSE tradition which I later tried to make available to economists more generally in a volume that included Jack's two best papers.[1]

Jack's very first analytical paper, published in 1953, was an intellectually damaging criticism of the claim, then widely accepted among academic economists, that collectivist planning of an economy was possible while maintaining liberal values, provided only that agents for the collectivity should be instructed to follow the rules for efficiency in resource allocation. In the early 1950s, Mises and Hayek were judged by economists generally to have lost the earlier great debate with Lange and his fellow travelers. Mises and Hayek had concentrated on the limits to the availability of knowledge to the central planning agency, by contrast with the knowledge that can be utilized by separate and independent market participants in their localized circumstances. Jack Wiseman's criticism went well beyond that of Mises and Hayek and, for the first time, demonstrated that the problem was not one of dispersed knowledge *that did indeed exist.* The problem was the wholly different one imposed by the necessity that all choices be made in *time* and, hence, under conditions of necessary uncertainty. If the future is unknowable, how can decision-makers, whether they be participants in a market or agents acting for the collectivity, be made accountable? How can any monitor check on the competence and the integrity of the chooser, other than through the observation of results? How, then, can we lay down a rule to be followed, in advance of the conditions to be encountered? Where is the collectivist equivalent of the bankruptcy court?

---

1. J. Wiseman, *Cost, Choice and Political Economy* (London: Edward Elgar, 1989); J. M. Buchanan, *Cost and Choice* (Chicago: Markham Press, 1969; University of Chicago Press, Midway Reprint, 1978); *Public Principles of Public Debt* (Homewood: Irwin, 1958); J. M. Buchanan and G. F. Thirlby, eds., *LSE Essays on Cost* (London: London School of Economics, 1973; New York: New York University Press, 1981).

This early paper contains the basic unknowability thesis to which Jack referred in his very last note to us, and this thesis runs as a central thread throughout all his work. But Jack seemed to draw back from the follow-on implications of this thesis, or rather to put off making the head-on challenge to economic orthodoxy that the thesis suggests. In this sense, his two first LSE papers seem more courageous than his intermediate efforts, and it was only in his Presidential Address to Section F of the British Association in 1981, as well as in later works, that he returned to the fray in full force. And, of course, his unfinished treatise was to be the final part of his career-long challenge.

My own prejudices are already apparent in this narrative. The middle years of Jack Wiseman's career were, by my private standards, less productive than his earlier and later periods. In 1964, he left London and LSE and moved to York, where, along with Alan Peacock, he helped to establish a major research and teaching program in public economics, with a concentration on the applied economics of the modern welfare state, notably the economics of health and social security. By that time, Alan Peacock and Jack Wiseman had attained a measure of academic repute by the reception of their seminal work on the growth of public spending. At York, Jack served as Director of the Institute of Social and Economic Research from its beginning until his partial early retirement in 1982.[2]

The York venture was a roaring success by the ordinary academic standards. The program in public economics soon came to be widely recognized, and York became a locus for visiting scholars and students from many countries. Today it is a common occurrence to run into leading political and academic figures throughout the world who have some connection with York through former visits. And now familiar names such as Alan Hamlin, Charles Rowley and Robert Sugden attribute much of their success to the York years.

But, for me, Jack Wiseman was not using his own comparative advantage well, neither in organizing and supporting the research efforts of others nor in participating directly in research on narrowly applied welfare-state programs, whether project oriented or independently initiated. I have always felt

2. A. T. Peacock and J. Wiseman, *The Growth of Public Expenditure in the United Kingdom* (London: Oxford University Press, 1961).

that there were many other competent professionals who could work on British health services or Canadian fisheries, but only Jack Wiseman could move, full fire, against the basic paradigm that dominated and still dominates our discipline.

Jack Wiseman was early in his recognition and appreciation of the public choice approach to both ordinary politics and constitutional structure. Such appreciation was natural to anyone who commenced analysis of social interaction with an examination of the institutional settings within which persons choose. And Wiseman's emphasis on the necessary uncertainty of choice-in-time allowed him to plug into the public choice relevance of incentive patterns. In discussions about the content of the treatise he had outlined, Jack indicated that the public choice–constitutional framework was to be a central feature of the alternative, and inclusive, "political economy" that he was confident he could finally ascribe.

Early in this note I suggested that in writing it I might be able to locate Jack Wiseman better among those with whom I have felt a sense of shared vision. I now find that my account is much more intellectual and thereby less personal than I might have anticipated, probably to an unbalanced degree. Jack was, for me, always easy to be around, and reciprocal visits between our homes and institutions over three decades were joyous occasions, even if Jack did sometimes overestimate his own talents as a gourmet-gourmand. But perhaps, after all, my kinship with Jack Wiseman was not much related to age, origins or preferences. Perhaps, after all, this kinship was grounded squarely in the only important source, that of ideas about social and economic reality, both actual and potential. I have often remarked to colleagues, both while Jack was in his prime and later, that Jack Wiseman probably came closer than anyone else to an understanding of what my own project was all about. At least that was how it seemed to me. And it is in this sense that Jack's death imposes a loss upon me that is very private, very individualized, and a loss that cannot quite be shared with anyone, even by those of his family and friends who are outside the professional fences that constrain us all.

For Jack Wiseman, there was not time enough. But he was a lucky man, in this as in other elements of his life. Who among us would not want to leave with a treatise left unfinished? We may hope that others will not say that, for us, there was time enough and more.

# I Did Not Call Him "Fritz"
## Personal Recollections of
## Professor F. A. v. Hayek

I did not call him "Fritz." To me he remained always "Professor Hayek," despite his own graciousness in treating me as a peer. I shall not attempt to evaluate Professor Hayek's monumental contribution to our understanding of the events of this turbulent century, to the influence of his ideas on these events themselves or even to the development of economic theory in a strictly scientific sense. My remarks here are limited to a personal account of the man whom I knew over the course of more than four decades.

I first saw Professor Hayek in late 1946, when as a graduate student at the University of Chicago, I attended a seminar that he presented during a visit from the London School of Economics. At the time, I knew Hayek only from the notoriety that had surrounded *The Road to Serfdom* (1944). I do not recall the subject of the seminar itself, but I remember the discussion afterward, in which Hayek surprised some of us by supporting the American loan to Britain, but with the plea that the United States should hold off agreeing to make the loan until reform measures were more or less forced on the Labor government.

My next encounter with Professor Hayek was more extended. For a period of several years during the 1950s, the William Volker Fund financed a series of Volker Fund conferences at academic locations under several local sponsors (Clarence Philbrook at Chapel Hill, Art Kemp at Claremont, Neil McCleod at Appleton, Ben Rogge at Wabash). These conferences were ten-

From *Constitutional Political Economy* 3 (Spring/Summer 1992): 129–35. Reprinted by permission of the publisher, Kluwer Academic Publishers.

day affairs, and each conference normally featured three main lecturers or seminar leaders, each one of whom participated for the whole period of the conference, with responsibility for several lectures. The "students" were a group of some twenty-five young academic economists, who were judged to be potential classical liberals. Hayek, Bertil Ohlin and John Jewkes were the "stars" for a 1955 Volker Fund conference at Wabash College.

Hayek gave a series of several lectures at the conference during which he sketched out most of the ideas that were later to appear in his treatise *The Constitution of Liberty* (1960). He must have already had a quasi-finished draft of this book in hand, since, as I recall, the arguments were well developed. Most of the ideas were, as expected, quite congenial to me, but I recall thinking that Hayek was analytically wrong in his discussion of equal pay for equal work, and that, normatively, I rejected his argument in support of proportional rather than progressive income taxation. On the latter point, the influence of Henry Simons was still too fresh for me to appreciate the political implications of progression, which Hayek may have sensed although they did not appear directly in his discussion. At the time, I was only beginning to escape from the orthodox mindset and to begin to look at politics realistically. In retrospect, what seems most interesting to me about the Wabash lectures is that we judged Professor Hayek as a senior scholar who was presenting to us the well-reasoned product of a life's work. Little did we dream that there were major new and quite different Hayek contributions ahead and that Hayek would develop ideas that he surely did not sense at all at the time.

I was invited to become a member of the Mt. Pelerin Society in 1957, and I vividly recall my first participation in a general meeting, at the Suvretta House in St. Moritz, the most luxurious hotel I had ever seen. I recall the feet cushions in the lobby and the Spanish princess who got so many of us a bit excited by her mere presence. (No connection with the society.) I do not know who nominated me for membership, perhaps it was Frank Knight, but I do know that everyone acknowledged that the society was really Hayek's and that any new member must have been approved by Hayek himself. By 1957, the membership had grown somewhat from its small beginnings a decade earlier, but there was still a club-like aspect to the meeting and with an underlying tension between the central European and American members (the latter mostly with Chicago connections). To those of us who had libertarian-populist blood in our veins, there was too much deference accorded to Hayek, and especially to Ludwig von Mises, who seemed to demand sycophancy.

The tension was kept within bounds, and the Society continued to prosper and expand. Professor Hayek dominated the group, and he was, quite properly, treated with respect that approached awe. But his direct contributions to the discussions were invariably profound as well as relevant, so much so that Hayek seemed to transcend the pedestrian interests of his peers. He was, understandably, human in his judgments, and personal contacts became the basis for some memberships in the Society that were later to be regretted. But when Max Hartwell finally completes his history of the Mt. Pelerin Society, there will be no doubt but that the history will, in large part, be a biography of Hayek's leadership.

Warren Nutter and I joined the University of Virginia faculty in 1956, and, in 1957, we established the Thomas Jefferson Center for Studies in Political Economy and Social Philosophy. Our purpose was to provide a setting for renewed emphasis on and interest in the ideas of classical liberalism and classical political economy. In part, our ultimate success critically depended on an initial grant from the William Volker Fund that allowed us to bring to Charlottesville a series of distinguished political economists, for periods of a half-year each, for special lectures and seminars with graduate students and faculty. And our list was indeed distinguished: Frank Knight, Bertil Ohlin, Bruno Leoni, Michael Polanyi, Terence Hutchison, Maurice Allais, Duncan Black and Overton Taylor. And, of course, F. A. Hayek, who was among the very first scholars that we contacted to arrange for an extended visit.

Professor Hayek came to Charlottesville in January 1961, for a semester-long visit. He had just published *The Constitution of Liberty* (1960), and he expressed an interest in using the Virginia lectures as the format for returning to economic theory and particularly to his early major contribution on the use of knowledge in society, a contribution that was beginning to be widely recognized to be seminal. He announced a series under the overall title "A New Look at Economic Theory," and he presented four lectures: (1) "The Object of Economic Theory," (2) "The Economic Calculus," (3) "Economics and Technology" and (4) "The Communication Function of the Market."

These lectures were failures, at least by Professor Hayek's own standards. Those who listened to them were, of course, rewarded by a careful review of the earlier analysis of knowledge in relation to economic interaction. But Hayek was unable to go beyond that which he had developed two decades before; no new insights emerged as he reviewed the earlier thought processes. His announced ambitions were thwarted. To our great good fortune, frustrated by these efforts to return to economic theory as such, Professor Hayek (increasingly during the 1960s and throughout the remainder of his career) shifted his attention to the philosophical foundations of a liberal order.

For the semester at Virginia, I knew Professor Hayek as a faculty colleague, a scholar who was always interested in ideas. I shall recall only one amusing incident. Hayek came to dinner at our house, and he made the remark that he always judged a scholar by the books on his shelves. He found on my shelves a copy of his book on psychology, *The Sensory Order* (1952), a book that few economists, and apparently few others, possessed. This discovery seemed, from that moment on, to increase my own status in Hayek's subjective ranking of his peers. It was also during this visit that Hayek influenced me in another way that has served me well. He suggested that he simply could not survive, intellectually, without the *Times (London) Literary Supplement (TLS)*. I subscribed immediately and have been an avid reader of *TLS* ever since.

During the 1960s, and after he returned to Germany, then Austria, I saw Professor Hayek only at Mt. Pelerin meetings, although our paths crossed again at UCLA, I think in 1970, when he was a visiting professor in Philosophy. He had, by that time, been working out his ideas on the importance of cultural evolution in the emergence of modern societies, ideas that were to become central to his later work in *Law, Legislation and Liberty* (1973, 1976, 1979).

I remember the 1972 Mt. Pelerin meeting in Montreux, Switzerland, the closest location possible to Mt. Pelerin itself, the site of the initial organizational meeting of the Society, that was large enough to accommodate the now expanded membership. On a pilgrimage to Mt. Pelerin itself, where the small group had assembled in 1947, Hayek addressed the group from the portico of the original hotel on a very hot afternoon. He was enthusiastic as well as nostalgic on the twenty-fifth anniversary, and he more or less forgot the time limits dictated for those of us who stood in the heat of day.

After his award of the Nobel Prize in 1974, Hayek was, of course, in great demand worldwide. The success of Milton Friedman's TV series "Free to

Choose" prompted entrepreneurial effort toward a massively ambitious scheme to put some twenty hours of conversations with Hayek on videotape, to be edited into a six-hour format. A set of conversationalists-interviewers was selected, with each one assigned a two-hour taping on a specific subject matter. My task was to talk to Professor Hayek on political philosophy. In October 1978, we arranged for a studio taping at San Jose, while we were both visiting at the Hoover Institution. The first hour was quite successful, with animated discussion. The second hour was a failure, and, despite my instructions, I was forced to invade any and all subject matter categories. Other conversationalists had some of the same problems, and the grandiose project was never completed. As I recall, an edited two-hour videotape was the final result.

Sometime, late in the 1970s, Hayek had an idea, one that excited his imagination. He wanted to organize a "great debate" between the socialists on the one hand and classical liberals on the other, a debate that was initially projected to have twelve advocates on each side and to be staged over a series of encounters, in Paris, and with worldwide television coverage. I recall that he telephoned me about the scheme, and I promised to write him a letter giving him my reactions to his suggestion. I did respond, and I said that while I would be happy to participate, and while he would have no trouble getting a dozen classical liberals for such a debate, I felt that he would find it difficult to locate twelve socialists who were intellectually respectable adversaries. It is my understanding, although I did not participate and did not attend the meeting, that a group of senior Mt. Pelerin members gave more or less the same advice in Hong Kong when Hayek presented the idea more widely. As a result, Hayek was persuaded to forget about the grand debate and to devote his own time to a major criticism of socialism, the project that did indeed become his last major work, as finally published in *The Fatal Conceit* (1989).

There is more to this story. By the early 1980s, Professor Hayek seemed to be well along with his personal project. Steve Pejovich organized, and Liberty Fund financed, a small conference in Obergurgl, Austria, the site of Hayek's summer retreat for some thirty years, for the express purpose of assisting Hayek in the final stages of preparation of what was then projected to be a three-volume work. There were some fifteen of us assembled in August 1982, a group that included Peter Bauer, Ronald Coase and George Stigler. We were, I must say, not very happy with the draft that we received, and, as critics who, at the same time, maintained the highest respect for Professor Hayek, we felt that we should not recommend publication. The work was eventually published, in one volume, as *The Fatal Conceit,* and we were quite pleased that the book had been markedly improved, due not only to Hayek's diligence in responding to our criticisms, but, probably, also to the help of William Bartley, who took over as editorial assistant in the final stages of preparation.

Aside from the Obergurgl conference, I met Professor Hayek at least four times during the 1980s. During a conference in Freiburg, I sat next to Hayek at a provincial restaurant. He talked at some length to me and others about his early Vienna years, particularly about the Mises seminar, and about the discrimination by the Vienna academic establishment against Mises. A second occasion for a meeting occurred during a visit to George Mason University, where Hayek gave a seminar followed by dinner at my home. The evening was a full one, "gemütlich" in all respects, and Hayek talked more freely about his personal life than I had heard before. For the first and only time, during that evening I did feel close to the man himself, and I may, indeed, have called him "Fritz" when we said goodnight.

The other two occasions for meeting were at the Alpbach European Forum, that loveliest of all quasi-academic settings in Tyrol, Austria. In August 1984, when Hartmut Kliemt and I were joint study group leaders, we actually had Professor Hayek as a "student-participant" for several days running. Hayek had been an off-and-on, more-or-less regular participant in the Alpbach Forum since its inception in the mid-1940s, along with Karl Popper and other notables.

The last time I met Professor Hayek was in August 1988, when Viktor Vanberg, Albert Zlabinger and I drove from Alpbach to Obergurgl one afternoon, especially to talk with Hayek. Already by that time, he tired easily, but, for a full half-hour with us, he was intellectually alert and seemed to enjoy our visit greatly.

Professor Hayek was my senior by two decades. We were separated by a generation. I was not his student in any formal, or even informal, sense. I have never classified myself, and no one else so classified me, as a disciple of Hayek. And, as I have expressed in several published works, I disagree with Hayek on important aspects of his work. Nonetheless, along several dimensions, I feel myself to share in the more inclusive "Hayekian enterprise."

These dimensions extend from the basic understanding of what economics is all about to the concern with the philosophical foundations of a free society. Hayek and his fellow Austrian economists were always cognizant of the subjective bases of economic interaction processes, a position that I came to only after tearing myself away from the still-orthodox mindset. And my conversion to catallaxy, as the proper subject matter of our discipline, came along long after Hayek had laid out the same claim. I have more or less adopted as my own the Hayekian distinction between the moral community and the moral order; my differences with Hayek emerge in my somewhat greater allowance for nonevolutionary construction of the framework for the latter. I have found Hayek's criticism of the purported "scientism" of economics totally congenial. And, finally, and most important, I have tried to share Hayek's interest in understanding how and why the basic organizational and institutional structures of whole societies have changed, may change and may be changed, through time. With Hayek, I consider our role, as economists or other social scientists, to be that of the moral philosopher. Only a handful of my disciplinary peers share this conception.

With Hayek's death in March 1992, coming after the events of 1989 and 1991, we close an era. Socialism is dead, and Hayek's ideas both contributed to its death and helped us to understand why the system was fatally flawed from the outset. But classical liberalism, the other side of the whole Hayekian enterprise, is by no means nearly so resurgent throughout the lands as might have been expected. There has been little or no feedback of the revolutions of 1989 and 1991 on the ordinary politics of Western welfare states. "Socialism in the small" seems alive and well. The task for those of us who follow Hayek remains that of bringing his ideas to bear against the continuing efforts on the part of some persons to control the lives of others.

We have indeed lost a stalwart from the ranks. But the ideas remain alive, whether or not we think of them as lodged forever in Karl Popper's "Third World."

# Methods and Morals in Economics
## The Ayres-Knight Discussion

## Introduction

I base this essay on the 1935 discussion between C. E. Ayres and Frank Knight, the discussion which Ayres entitled "Moral Confusion in Economics" and which Knight characteristically modified to read "Intellectual Confusion on Morals and Economics."[1] An initial reaction is one of vivid contrast between the economist's intellectual world of 1935 and that of the 1970's. Ayres and Knight, leading members of the profession, explicitly concerned themselves with fundamental philosophical issues that emerge naturally from the discipline. By comparison, how many economists in the 1970's debate similar issues or, more critically, so much as recognize that they exist? Surely the basic problems have not been resolved, despite the developments, good and bad, that have resulted from the Robbins, the Robinson-Chamberlin, and the Keynesian "revolutions." These issues have only taken different form, as effected by forty years of additional history.

In this paper, I propose to present the 1935 Ayres-Knight discussion in modern dress, so to speak. I shall argue that developments in economics since 1935 have been such as to bring their positions more closely into

From *Science and Ceremony: The Institutional Economics of C. E. Ayres,* ed. William Breit and William Patton Culbertson, Jr. (Austin and London: University of Texas Press, 1976), 163–74. Reprinted courtesy of the University of Texas Press.
1. C. E. Ayres, "Moral Confusion in Economics," *International Journal of Ethics* 45 (January 1935): 170–99, Frank H. Knight, "Intellectual Confusion on Morals and Economics," *International Journal of Ethics* 45 (January 1935): 200–220, C. E. Ayres, "Confusion Thrice Confounded," *International Journal of Ethics* 45 (April 1935): 356–58.

agreement, although both continue to be sharply divergent from mainstream economic methodology. Both of these scholars should have become increasingly disturbed at the growing mathematization of economic theory, quite independent of the uses to which this might have been put. By "mathematization" here I refer to the conceptualization of economics as a branch of applied mathematics. Both scholars should have been equally, if not more, disturbed by the emergence of the dominating professional emphasis on empirical testing of hypotheses themselves grounded in idealized theoretical constructions, as if the interaction of human beings in society is fully equivalent to the interaction of chemical elements. Ayres might have been at least ambivalent with respect to developments in theoretical welfare economics, properly characterized as "theories of market failure." This might have been matched by Knight's ambivalence toward developments in public choice theory, which could be dubbed "theories of government failure." Both Ayres and Knight would have continued to emphasize the limits to the explanatory potential of purely economic models of man, and both might have maintained their interests in exploring the moral-ethical requirements for social order, requirements that must be met before effective economic interaction begins.

## Theory of Social Order

As we read the 1935 discussion between Clarence Ayres and Frank Knight, their differences emerge; their points of agreement tend to be obscured because these were mutually acknowledged by the participants. This is perhaps most clearly demonstrated by Knight's silence on Ayres's insistence that the function of economics is to offer a theory of social order, of social interaction. "Of course," Knight would have responded here, and students at the University of Chicago, before and after 1935, placed this at the core of Knight's teaching. Modern (post-1935) developments make this elementary methodological principle worthy of reemphasis. By saying that economics offers or should offer a theory of social order, we must, by direct implication, say that economics is not exclusively or even primarily a "theory of choice."[2] Yet the thrust of post-

2. For an elaboration of my own position, see my paper "Is Economics the Science of Choice?" in *Roads to Freedom: Essays in Honour of Friedrich A. von Hayek*, ed. E. Streissler (London: Routledge and Kegan Paul, 1969), 47–64.

1935 development, influenced perhaps too strongly by Robbins's *Nature and Significance of Economic Science,*[3] has surely been toward the latter rather than the former. Once we accept the Robbins formulation of the "economic problem," we are, almost necessarily, forced into a choice-theoretic framework, and the tools of applied mathematics suggest themselves immediately. Economics comes to be conceptualized as a varied set of exercises, all of which involve the maximization of some appropriately selected objective function subject to the appropriately defined constraints, with, of course, the dual minimization problems always offering alternative avenues toward solutions. Formally, the problem faced by the isolated Robinson Crusoe is no different from that facing the political community of persons. Once a utility function is specified and his constraints defined, the economist observer can tell Crusoe just what his "efficient" pattern of behavior must be. Once a "social welfare function" is specified and the constraints are known, the same observer can tell the benevolent despot just how the whole economy must be "efficiently" organized and operated. The role of the economist shifts readily and almost imperceptibly from that of disinterested "engineer" to that of normative counselor, proffering his own judgmental advice as to ends as well as means, if indeed these can ever be separated in fact.

There is a subtle, but vitally important, distinction between this choice-theoretic approach and that which is properly attributable to the theorist of social interaction. In the latter, Robinson Crusoe economics continues to occupy a place, but never to the conceptual or imagined purpose of proffering advice and counsel. We seek to understand Crusoe's isolated behavior as a first and preliminary conceptual stage in understanding the emergent interrelationships among men as they meet in socioeconomic processes. The focus of attention is upon "that which tends to emerge" from the behavioral interaction, and this is not conceptualized as a "solution" to any applied maximization problem faced by some representation or idealization of the whole community of participants. Economists, as specialists, describe characteristics of these results, but it is the structural-procedural aspects that command attention, never the results, as such. To introduce a simple example from the Crusoe-Friday world, the economist is uncon-

3. Lionel Robbins, *The Nature and Significance of Economic Science* (London: Macmillan and Co., 1932).

cerned as to whether the established trading ratio between coconuts and fish settles at 5:1, 1:1, or 1:5. He does not view the exchange process as an "analogue computing device" that makes "choices" for the idealized community. His concern is devoted to the demonstration that in idealized conditions of exchange the trading process insures an equality among the internal trading ratios for all participants.

I am not suggesting here that either Frank Knight or Clarence Ayres fully articulated and consistently held the second position that I have outlined. Through his insistence on the central role of the equimarginal or "economic" principle, even in the multiperson setting, Knight's work is, of course, fully consistent with and can readily be interpreted as falling within the broad choice-theoretic framework. By his query, "Are we going on the rocks?" repeatedly made in his 1935 essay, Ayres implies that he viewed the social economy in a "ship of state" analogue, one which readily translates into "social welfare function" notation. Had he used a slightly different metaphor, he might have asked a more appropriate question for a theorist of social order. Had he said, "Is the island sinking?" he would have implied thereby a potential disintegration or breakdown in the institutional foundations of society within which human interaction takes place and from which outcomes emerge—but outcomes that are not purposefully directed by any single choosing agent. Nonetheless, I should argue that both men equally would view as essentially absurd modern attempts to "compute" equilibrium prices along with both the expressed hopes and fears that advanced computer technology can replace exchange processes or, more generally, can essentially remove human actors from society.

## Homo economicus

Since 1935, technological advances in computers and intellectual advances in mathematical statistics have combined to make the testing of hypotheses in economics less labor intensive and the results more credible. Predictably, economists have responded to this major shift in relative cost-benefit ratios, with the observed modern preoccupation with regression routines. This shift, alone, tends to corroborate Ayres's hypothesis that technology itself independently affects social process. Could the modern emphasis on empirical tests have emerged at all save for computer availability in each research setting?

The larger question, however, concerns the relevance or importance of this development for economics, as a discipline, and the possible distortions in understanding that may have been produced as a result. The opportunity cost of securing proficiency in econometrics is naïveté in basic economic theory itself, naïveté that is manifested in failures to recognize the necessary limits or qualifications with which the elementary propositions of the theory must be hedged. The practical effect is that such limits are ignored, with the result that *Homo economicus* has come to occupy a more central role than it ever assumed in its putative neoclassical heyday. The basic set of hypotheses which are tested in modern regressions is derived directly from the assumption that men behave in terms of narrowly defined and objectively measurable self-interest. There are few, if any, alternative behavioral models behind modern empirical work, although there exist, of course, essentially behavioristic models without any analytical basis. Let us consider an example. Suppose that we organize an experiment by placing coins (nickels or dimes) on a sidewalk in a busy central city, and that we observe passersby with a view toward predicting pickup rates. The experiment is conducted, and, let us suppose, the initial hypothesis of rational economic behavior is falsified. Men do not, as observed, respond to measured self-interest. But these results may also be "explained" by the fact that other motivations, such as time and trouble or "transactions costs," may more than outweigh the measured pecuniary returns. This being the case, however, what will the experimental results have shown? That *Homo economicus* does not exist? That economic theory is tautological?

The elementary fact is, of course, that *Homo economicus* does exist in the human psyche, along with many other men, and that behavior is a product of the continuing internal struggle among these. The task of economic theory is not that of predicting specific patterns of behavior; it is that of providing a structural understanding of the processes within which the divergent behavioral plans of persons are integrated and reconciled. Knowledge of the strength of the definable economic motivation may be important for making comparisons among institutional-organizational alternatives. But economic theory does not relinquish its explanatory role if its central predictive hypotheses fail to be corroborated empirically. *Homo economicus* need not reign supreme over other men, and his failure to do so does not signal his nonexistence. From this there emerges an implicit organizational norm.

When alternatives are possible, social efficiency will be gained by channeling man's self-interest toward mutually compatible goals. This principle, the heart of eighteenth-century wisdom, remains untouched by modern empirical testing, yet the failure of modern economists is measured by their loss of the understanding of this precept.

This does not suggest that economists should desert their econometric playthings and become modern apologists for market capitalism, as Ayres seemed to classify neoclassical economic theorists. Nor does it suggest the more likely opposite, that they become the intellectual vanguard for further socialist experimentation. As Knight often remarked, economists should adopt the morals of the physical scientists even if they should shun the latter's methods. This morality must include a willingness to go beyond the limits of empiricism. In effect, modern economists opt out of their essential moral responsibility by their self-imposed limitation to data-determined inquiries. Ayres's strictures against the neoclassical purists of the 1920's and 1930's should be as nothing when compared with those which might be posed against the sterilities of the econometricians of the 1970's. The hard questions are not readily formulated in terms of testable hypotheses. But this offers no cause for not thinking about such questions, for not discussing them, for not searching for an appreciation and understanding. Empirical science provides solutions to problems posed, solutions which, once obtained, become "truth," to be followed by the invention of new problems and new solutions. "Moral science" (if I may be permitted to use an old-fashioned word in what seems to be its proper meaning) is concerned with age-old "problems," for which "solutions" are, almost by definition, inappropriate. We do not "solve" the "problem" of social order by producing a unique "solution," regardless of the sophistication of empirical techniques. There is no objective "truth" to be established here. The "problem" of social order is faced eternally by persons who realize that they must live together and that to do so they must impose *upon themselves* social rules, social institutions. Economics and economists cannot evade their responsibility in the continuing discourse over such rules and institutions by shifting attention to trivialities. To the extent that they do so, their functional roles can only be filled by the charlatans and the fools, whose presence about us requires no demonstration.

## Market and Governmental Failure

As noted, Ayres viewed the neoclassical economists of his time as imposing a conceptual model upon economic reality that was, first of all, fallacious, and, second, designed and used deliberately to provide an intellectual-moral defense of a particular form of social order, market capitalism or free enterprise. Viewed in modern perspective, Ayres was somewhat out of date, even in 1935, because the central body of neoclassical theory had already been turned on its head by Pigou, whose great influence seems now to be only remotely correlated with his ability. Ayres should have been ambivalent about the post-Pigovian developments in theoretical welfare economics. Insofar as his strictures were laid against the imposition of a behavioral model which he held to be overly restrictive, Ayres could only have been upset by the theories of market failure that emerged from the marginal social product–marginal private product calculus of Pigou because this calculus embodied even more restrictive assumptions about human behavior than those which informed the neoclassical models of competitive order. On the other hand, because this theoretical welfare economics did produce market *failure* results, and as such did much to undermine the neoclassical defense of market organization, Ayres might have independently welcomed such developments. In this aspect of the debate, Knight seems clearly to have been corroborated by intellectual developments within economics itself. In a formal sense, pure economic theory is surely value neutral. The uses to which this theory is put need not be so, and the resort by modern economists to theories of market failure as a means of providing a putative intellectual-moral basis for socialist experimentation is fully comparable to the behavior of the laissez-faire proponents of earlier epochs.

Developments in the 1950's and 1960's have, however, offered something of a Hegelian antithesis. *Homo economicus* was introduced to assist in explaining man's behavior in decision roles outside of and beyond market exchange, including political or public choice decisions. Once this simple step was taken, the theorems of governmental or political failure emerged, at least on all fours with the market-failure theorems of post-Pigovian welfare economics. The synthesis, as and when it emerges, can only be represented in a value-free and strictly pragmatic stance. Economic theory can tell us little or nothing about alternative organizational forms, except on a case-by-case basis. Frank Knight would have welcomed some methodological consensus on this point. We cannot be so sure about Clarence Ayres, although some of his students have indeed expressed approval of the "modern institutionalism" that is descriptive of the work of an increasing number of scholars.

## The Limits of Self-Interest

Markets fail; governments fail. Demonstration of these propositions is straightforward once *Homo economicus* is plugged into the model of interaction. Even in those aspects of economic intercourse that involve no externalities or spillover effects in the Pigovian sense, some limits must be imposed on the working of pure self-interest. Individuals must abide by behavioral standards which dictate adherence to law, respect for property and personal rights, and fulfillment of contractual agreements—standards which may not, in specific instances, be consistent with objectively measurable economic self-interest. Absent such standards as these, markets will fail even when there are no imperfections of the sort that have attracted the attention of the welfare theorists. And, of course, even when such standards prevail, markets fail once any of these more familiar imperfections are introduced, failure here being measured against the conceptual ideal. But political attempts at correcting market breakdown also founder on the rocks of measurable economic self-interest of the participants. No person is motivated to undertake the costs of organization that may be required to generate the "public good" that corrective reform represents. Elected and appointed politicians and bureaucrats are not different from other men. They are motivated at least in part by their own interest, not by some higher version of the "social good."

"Social order" requires general acceptance of a minimal set of moral standards. Well-defined laws of property and freedom of market exchange minimize the necessary scope and extension of such standards, but they by no means eliminate them. As individual property rights become confused, and as markets are replaced by or subverted with governmental interventions, the dependence of order on some extended range of moral responsibility increases. (So long as the individual confronts market *alternatives*, his dependence on the behavioral pattern of any single person or administrative unit is correspondingly reduced. If he confronts a single governmental or political alternative, his well-being is of necessity put at the mercy of the behavior of a single person or decision unit. In the limit, his dependence is complete.)

Markets do not, however, carry moral weight comparable with their organizational alternatives. Then and now, critics become disturbed at the inequalities that result even from the idealized workings of market processes. These objections, made by Clarence Ayres and other critics, do not really concern the division of the gains-from-trade generated by exchange, the realizable surplus that only markets make possible. At base, the objections are to the basic assignment of property rights among persons and families, the allocation of potential "tradeables" among persons *before* they enter market activity. But, somewhat surprisingly, market institutions themselves are held responsible for their failure to redress these initial imbalances among unequals. Markets are condemned for their failure to produce distributive justice, even if the injustice observed arises in premarket distribution rather than in any sharing of the gains. Comparable failure of the political apparatus to accomplish similar objectives does not seem to mitigate the continuing force of this morally based criticism of market orders.

Maintenance of a viable social order characterized by substantial individual liberty depends critically on the widespread acceptance of a common set of moral precepts. Such acceptance is by no means assured in our world of the 1970's. These precepts include respect for individual rights, once these are defined in law and/or customary standards of behavior, along with the recognition that the historically determined assignment or allocation of rights among persons may embody significant departures from assignments or allocations that might plausibly emerge from a "renegotiated social contract."[4] This recognition, in turn, should suggest that adjustments may be needed in the structure of rights, as such, rather than interferences in the social process through which assigned rights and titles are exchanged among persons. Moral energies should be diverted away from criticisms of markets, as such, and distributionally motivated, politically implemented attempts at redress of premarket injustices should be shunned. Distributional

---

4. For a further discussion of this point, see my paper "Before Public Choice," in *Explorations in the Theory of Anarchy,* ed. Gordon Tullock (Blacksburg: Center for Study of Public Choice, 1973); also, my book *The Limits of Liberty: Between Anarchy and Leviathan* (Chicago: University of Chicago Press, 1975).

objectives should be furthered through instruments that operate directly on the underlying extramarket assignment of individuals' rights.

Historical evidence offers little grounds for optimism that the moral energies will be channeled as suggested. Market organization, which minimizes the dependence of man on the morality of his fellows, may continue to be subverted in the mistaken hope that inequalities can be erased. In the attempt, the realizable surplus made available to society only through the working of markets may be dissipated, and the grosser because less tractable inequalities of political power increased.

## Institutions, Technology, and Moral Values

Clarence Ayres might not have accepted these conclusions, but the insistence of Ayres and his institutionalist compatriots on the independent importance of institutions and of technology becomes germane to any current examination of the moral requirements for social order. Institutions and technology affect the behavior of men, including their acceptance of ethical-moral precepts. Major changes have occurred in the forty years since Ayres and Knight addressed these issues. The institutions of order—the family, the church, and the state—have undergone dramatic change, and the directions of effect on individual adherence to traditional moral standards seem clear.

The family's role in transmitting moral values, including a sense of respect and honor for the institution itself, has been undermined by the shift from the extended unit to the nuclear cell. Ayres might have intervened at this point to add, appropriately, that this changing role for the family is itself traceable to the dramatic changes in technology which moved us off the farms and into the great conurbations. Can urbanized man be expected to live by the moral precepts ideally characteristic of the sturdy yeoman farmer?

The decline of the church as an institution of order, and of orthodox religion as a shaper of the attitudes of men and women, has perhaps a more tenuous relationship with technology. But this decline is fact, and one that must be reckoned with in any attempt to assess moral requirements. "God Will Take Care of You"—this hymnal statement was meaningful to many more persons in 1935 than it is in the 1970's. Orthodox religion has, by now, almost abandoned its role in softening man's urge to moral wrath against the social structure in which he finds himself. If anything, the modern church has become itself subversive of existing and traditional moral standards, changing its color from an institution of order to one promotive of disorder and instability.

There has been an accompanying change in man's vision of "the state," the governmental-political process. In 1935, man did not know about the Stalinist purges; Hitler was only partway toward his final solution; the post-war failures in socialist democracies were in the future; the debacles of Great Society programs, the weirdness of the Warren Court and of Watergate were more distant still. Despite the Great Depression, individuals in 1935 honored politics and politicians, and patriotism remained extant as a major motive force. There was widespread respect for "law," as such, and rare indeed were those who felt themselves morally capable of choosing individually determined norms of obedience.

Alongside this partial disintegration of those institutions which tended to establish and to maintain order and stability in society, with the predictable effects of such disintegration on individual adherence to traditional moral norms, the parallel role of the school must also be examined. Within the context of strong and stable institutions of family, church, and state, the school can appropriately combine a rational transmission of moral values with a critical and searching reexamination of these values. As the offsets are weakened, however, and as the internal mix, within the school, changes toward criticism and away from value transmittal, this institution becomes one of disorder and instability in modern society.

The institutional developments alone, independent of technology, would have placed increasing pressure on the sometimes fragile stability of social order. This pressure has been enhanced by technological change, which has exerted independent influence. The genuine revolution that has occurred in transportation and communication has helped in creating a highly mobile society, with the result that "locational loyalty," as a force making for moral value stability, has largely disappeared. Perhaps even more important, what has been, and what will be, the impact of television on individual attitudes and behavior in all sorts of social interaction, in the marketplace, in the voting booth, in the day-to-day adherence to ordinary standards of conduct, in manners? Will mass television so modify behavior patterns as to make adjustments in the institutional constraints, in legal order, necessary, or, if not necessary, desired? Can the basic norms of a free society be extended to cover this medium? Is "freedom of the press" automatically extendable here, or do we require a new definition?

## Conclusion

These are not "economic" questions, as such, and few modern economists bother to ask them, much less attempt to provide answers, to their shame; for it is precisely these issues and these questions that would have occupied the minds of both Clarence Ayres and Frank Knight in the 1970's. These two would have, no doubt, continued to disagree sharply on both diagnosis and prescription, but, at the same time, both would have treated the piddling trivialities that occupy modern economists with the contempt that they deserve.

Retrospectively, we might say that both Ayres and Knight should have been admonished in 1935 by the Adam Smith statement: "There's a deal of ruin in a nation." Forty years later we live in a more affluent but still tolerably free society that has not suffered moral collapse. The optimistic critic would be tempted to apply much the same admonition to my own assessment. Despite the institutional and technological changes that have occurred, there may be major elements of stability in our society that I have tended to overlook in my discussion. Perhaps the excesses of the 1960's were aberrations from the more orderly development of a social order embodying affluence, justice, and freedom. Perhaps. But hoping will not make things so, and those of us who do sense the vulnerability of social order to what seem to us to be gradual but unmistakable changes in the moral bases of this order would be derelict in our own duty if we did not raise warning flags.

# Economists and
# the Gains-from-Trade

*Abstract:* This paper examines William H. Hutt's work in terms of
two early books, *Economists and the Public* (1936) and *A Plan for
Reconstruction* (1944). Hutt is presented as a consistent reductionist, who concentrated attention on the elementary principle of
mutuality of gains-from-trade. This concentrated attention led
him to reject any and all observed restrictions on voluntary exchange as inefficient and, hence, damaging to welfare.

The consumer is sovereign when, in his role of citizen, he has not
delegated to political institutions for authoritarian use the power
which he can exercise socially through his power to demand (or
to refrain from demanding).

—William H. Hutt, *Economists and the Public* (1936), 257.

## Introduction

In a recent paper I contrasted two starting points for the inquiry of economists: (1) the two-person, two-good exchange model which immediately
calls attention to the mutuality of gains-from-trade, and (2) the one-person,
or Crusoe model, which immediately draws attention to the allocation of
scarce resources among alternatives aimed at maximizing utility.[1] These

From *Managerial and Decision Economics,* special issue (Winter 1988): 5–12. Copyright
1988 by John Wiley & Sons, Ltd. Reproduced by permission.
1. J. M. Buchanan, "Better than Plowing," *Banca Nazionale del Lavoro Quarterly Review* 159 (December 1986): 359–75.

two initiating methodological thrusts can, of course, be integrated, and the work of almost any economist incorporates elements of both. It is nonetheless helpful to classify economists in terms of these two starting points. Such a classification can offer a basis for evaluation that enables us to identify and appreciate the internal consistency of apparently disparate contributions.

For somewhat different, although related, reasons, I should place Knut Wicksell, Ronald H. Coase and William H. Hutt squarely in the first, or gains-from-trade, category, the category that I apply self-consciously to my own efforts. As I have argued at some length in another paper, I should locate my own professor, Frank H. Knight, in both categories simultaneously, a characterization that explains a source of ambiguity in his work.[2] The overwhelming majority of modern economists fall clearly into the second category; identification by name is unnecessary.

My volunteered assignment for this special issue of *Managerial and Decision Economics* was the preparation of a paper on two early books by William H. Hutt, *Economists and the Public* and *A Plan for Reconstruction*. These books can be best appreciated if the gains-from-trade emphasis is stressed as the characteristic feature. In these books, as in all of his works, Hutt is an articulate reductionist. He demonstrated early in his career an ability to cut through mazes of analytical complexity and to isolate and to identify the elementary principles relevant to the issues discussed.[3]

In the next section I shall show how reductionist use of the gains-from-trade model allows Hutt to mount effective criticism of observed economic policy and to suggest directions for institutional reform. In the third section I relate Hutt's proposals to those advanced by Knut Wicksell four decades previously. In particular, I identify what seem to me to be differences in epistemological presuppositions for normative analysis. In the fourth section I compare Hutt's analysis with that associated with Ronald H. Coase, and in the fifth section I describe Hutt as an authentic classical liberal, distinguish this position from those who do not quite qualify and, finally, point out

---

2. J. M. Buchanan, "The Economizing Element in Knight's Ethical Critique of Capitalist Order," *Ethics* 98 (October 1987): 61–75.

3. W. H. Hutt, *Economists and the Public* (London: Jonathan Cape, 1936), and *A Plan for Reconstruction* (London: Kegan Paul, 1943).

some of the problems that the classical liberal faces in public persuasion. The final section offers summary conclusions.

## Gains-from-Trade

Let me first follow up the distinction between a gains-from-trade or exchange perspective and an allocational or maximizing perspective by comparing and contrasting both the diagnostic and the reformist proclivities that emerge more or less naturally from each. The economist whose foundational base is catallaxy tends to locate breakdown or failure of an observed or imagined economic process in restrictions on or prohibitions of the freedom of individuals to enter into mutually beneficial exchanges. Market failure, by definition, means that there exist unexploited gains-from-trade, and the economist diagnoses such failure by identifying the barriers that prevent the potential gains from being exploited by the persons whose interests would be served by their removal. By comparison, the economist whose foundational logic lies in a maximizing calculus tends to define breakdown or failure as a shortfall in aggregate value below that which might maximally be achievable. More familiarly, his emphasis is put on the inefficiency reflected in the misallocation of resources that he observes. Market failure, as defined, implies inefficiency in resource usage, and the economist performs his diagnostic task when he identifies departures from those conditions that must be satisfied to insure optimality. The observed relationships between and among prices and costs, as these seem to be faced by market participants, offer the basis for evaluation.

The two approaches to diagnoses of market failure yield differing normative implications concerning potential correction. The gains-from-trade economist, having diagnosed failure through identification of a restriction on the liberty of participants, calls, quite simply, for a removal of the barrier, independent of explicit reference to the subsequent predicted shift in allocational results. By contrast, the allocational economist, having identified failure by specific distortions in resource use, calls explicitly for a shift in allocation, independent of direct reference to the institutional setting.

The seemingly straightforward comparison of the two positions taken by economists, as sketched out above, masks a difference in the definition of the individual economic actor implicit in each position. The gains-from-trade economist defines an individual, as potential trader, by both preferences *and* endowments. Further, the distribution of resource endowments among individuals is presumed settled and legally protected. The allocational economist defines an individual strictly in terms of a preference or utility function without necessary reference to resource endowments. In this analytical construction, efficiency or optimality in resource use is defined in terms of individual values, but these values are "disembodied" in the sense that they are not directly tied to endowments. For this reason, the allocationist, as such, may have difficulty even in identifying restrictions on economic liberties to exchange, and especially in distinguishing such restrictions from those involved in establishing the pre-trade distribution among individuals.

Nowhere is the gains-from-trade source of Hutt's inquiry more clearly evident than in the early chapters of *A Plan for Reconstruction*. Here the institutional setting under examination was the economy-polity of Great Britain upon entry into World War II. This political economy was characterized by many and varying restrictions on the economic liberties of individuals, restrictions that were defended in each and every case by the arguments of presumably sophisticated economists as well as by those persons and groups who held putative claims to the capital values embodied in the existence and continuation of the restrictions. The potential gains in capital values that would have been produced by a removal of the restrictions existed only as an imagined opportunity foregone, and this was sensed only by the economist who thoroughly understood the principles upon which the market order functions. In the earlier book, *Economists and the Public,* Hutt had laid out these principles, and he had also traced out the subversion of these principles in the work of economists, commencing with the ambiguities that emerged in the influential work of John Stuart Mill and carried forward in the work of W. S. Jevons and many others.

I suggested earlier that Hutt was a reductionist in his application and usage of the gains-from-trade criterion to condemn restrictions on economic liberties whenever and wherever these were observed to be present. Hutt made no attempt to classify restrictive practices, whether publicly or privately organized, into two sets, those that were to be condemned and those that were, somehow, to be condoned. Hutt was among a very small band of social scientists who exhibited elementary consistency in the normative stance accorded to economic value. If persons are restricted in their liberties to engage in voluntary exchange, value is, by definition, less than it could be in the absence of such restriction. What criteria may be introduced to distinguish those exchanges that exclusively or primarily increase value to the exchanging parties from those in which the values to these parties are achieved at the expense of parties external to agreement?

In *Economists and the Public* Hutt introduced the now-familiar notion of "consumers' sovereignty," which provided the criterion he needed here. (Hutt's introduction of consumers' sovereignty in and of itself should warrant him a significant place in the history of economic terms in this century.) Value to consumers of final products and services—this becomes the test that may be used to make the distinction between voluntary agreements that pass the ultimate value test and those that do not. Any restriction or barrier to freely negotiated economic exchanges of the ordinary sort must harm consumers. Similarly, and conversely, any implementation of an agreement through which agreeing parties gain at the expense of third parties may also generate net harms. John Stuart Mill, along with many others, did not understand this critically important difference. Their whole normative edifice crumbled because of the failure to condemn voluntary contracts (or public surrogates) that reduced value to ultimate consumers.

From the mid nineteenth century, normative discourse, with accompanying developments in economic policy, was drained of the clarity that had been present in the works of the earlier classical writers, notably Adam Smith. Further, the increasing politicization of the economy weakened the carryover force of the common law, which had embodied, in rough terms, the appropriate distinction between value-enhancing trades and restrictive agreements. The gains that parties sought to secure, through either public or private agency, from agreements on sharing or dividing markets, on fixing prices or wages, on joint negotiations—these are not properly enforceable as gains-from-trade. These are, instead, gains from restrictions on trade, and as such, they are subject to normative condemnation on the principle of consumers' sovereignty. The state's enforcement and protection of individuals' liberties of contract cannot be extended to contracts made in restraint of trade.

As noted, there was no distinction made in Hutt's analysis between privately and publicly organized restrictions on trade. There was no argument for direct government restrictions on exchanges based on some putative "general interest" until and unless such restriction could be demonstrated to be beneficial to consumers. State intervention in markets to protect or to enhance value positions attained or potentially attainable for or by producer interests, including particularly the interests of the owners of factor inputs, stands condemned on the principle of consumers' sovereignty.

## Restrictions and Reform

The normative implications that follow from an identification of restrictions on value-enhancing exchanges seem straightforward. If the objective for policy reform is the maximization of utility for individuals, as consumers, subject to the preferences of others, along with a distribution of endowments, then such reform consists in the elimination of the identified restrictions. Indeed, such has been the convention of reformist advice proffered to governments and to political leaders by economists generally, who have normally assumed, even if implicitly, that governments would act benevolently upon and therefore follow the advice so offered.

As early as 1896 Knut Wicksell warned against such a presumption by economists, and he called for a totally different approach to normative political economy. He was concerned directly with the structure of taxing-spending decisions, and his criticism was specifically aimed at the rather empty pronouncements of the public-finance economists on principles of taxation, which they advanced independent of any consideration of the spending side of the fiscal account and also independent of any consideration of the institutional structure within which fiscal choices are made. Wicksell suggested that if improvements in fiscal outcomes are desired the advising economist should concentrate attention on the structure of the political decision process, on the incentives that were faced by legislators who were ultimately responsible, electorally, to their constituencies. The interests of constituents, in turn, must reflect both tax costs and spending benefits.[4]

As I have argued at length, and variously, Knut Wicksell deserves recognition as the most important precursor of the whole research program in public choice, or at least those aspects of the program with which I have been

---

4. K. Wicksell, *Finanztheoretische Untersuchungen* (Jena: Fischer, 1896).

personally identified.[5] Wicksell's objective was to construct a criterion for efficiency in fiscal decisions, by which he meant the satisfaction of the demands of individuals, as consumers of collectively financed goods and services, analogous to the satisfaction of consumer demands in the competitive market for private goods and services. In Hutt's later terminology, Wicksell was seeking to establish institutional requirements that would insure that the principle of consumers' sovereignty is met through governmental provision of goods and services, alongside the operation of the market or private sector. By the very nature of the problem that he confronted, Wicksell was forced to adopt what I have called a gains-from-trade perspective. He could not call on the formal properties of decentralized competitive equilibrium to assist in any diagnosis of failure or success or to provide criteria for satisfaction of the welfare norm. By necessity, Wicksell was compelled to adopt the criterion of *agreement*, interpreted as that which emerges as the end state of any voluntary exchange process. As this criterion was extended to the fiscal choice process, the "voluntary exchange theory" of normative public finance was born.

I had discovered Wicksell's major contribution in 1948 (by accident), and my translation of the central part of this contribution was published in 1958. Somewhat later, in 1959, I used the basic Wicksellian construction to lay out what I considered to be an internally consistent methodological position.[6] Sometime after publication of my methodological paper, probably in 1961, Professor F. A. Hayek called my attention to William H. Hutt's book, *A Plan for Reconstruction*, a book that was unknown to me. Hayek recognized the parallel between the Wicksell-Buchanan analytical structure for normative economics and that which he recalled in Hutt's book. Hayek's suggestion made me search out and read Hutt's 1943 book. (I was already familiar with *Economists and the Public.*)

5. My Nobel Prize Lecture in 1986 was devoted to a detailed elaboration of the Wicksellian foundations for normative economic policy. See J. M. Buchanan, "The Constitution of Economic Policy," *American Economic Review 77* (June 1987): 243–50.

6. The translated part of Wicksell's book appeared as "A New Principle of Just Taxation," in *Classics in the Theory of Public Finance*, ed. R. A. Musgrave and A. T. Peacock (London: Macmillan, 1958), 72–118. The methodological essay was J. M. Buchanan, "Positive Economics, Welfare Economics, and Political Economy," *Journal of Law and Economics* 2 (October 1959): 124–38.

There were parallels in the two analyses, but I discovered that there were also major differences between the Wicksellian and the Huttian normative perspectives. These differences seem reinforced by my recent review of these two contributions, a review made in the course of preparing this paper. The epistemological presuppositions of the two constructions are quite different, along with several points of relevant emphasis. We can perhaps better understand Hutt's book by juxtaposing his whole enterprise with that of Wicksell.

As I have noted above, Wicksell was required by the nature of the problem he faced, and as he conceived it, to utilize *agreement* as the ultimate test for the mutuality of gains from the complex exchange that any taxing-spending choice represents. He was led, therefore, to introduce the rule of unanimity as the benchmark institution for fiscal decisions. Only if some tax-sharing scheme should at the same time be agreed to unanimously and provide sufficient revenues to cover outlays could a spending project be guaranteed to be value-enhancing or efficient. Although he presented the whole construction under the rubric of "justice," Wicksell's emphasis, as I interpret it, was on the epistemological properties of agreement. That is, it is only upon the observed agreement of all parties that the observing economist could adjudge a project to be value-enhancing in net. Absent such agreement, as revealed, there was no means through which the values placed on the project by benefiting parties might be ascertained. The rule of unanimity was required, ideally, in order to establish the existence of consensus, without which a project proposal could not be evaluated.[7]

A second feature of the Wicksellian construction deserves notice as we compare it with Hutt's reconstruction exercise. Wicksell was aiming to establish rules for making fiscal choices in a legislative assembly that would remain in being for a sequence of budgetary periods, during which many ordinary taxing and spending projects would be presented for acceptance or rejection. None of the projects described institutions that were already in existence and which carried with them valued claims held under putative ownership of separately identified persons and groups.

---

7. The Wicksellian construction was shifted to the constitutional level of choices among rules in J. M. Buchanan and G. Tullock, *The Calculus of Consent* (Ann Arbor: University of Michigan Press, 1962).

With this summary statement of Wicksell's construction, we may proceed to examine Hutt's plan for postwar reconstruction. The first difference refers to the institutional setting, tied to the Wicksell objective discussed immediately above. By contrast with Wicksell's, Hutt's target was the whole structure of restrictions that was embodied in the more or less permanent institutions of the British economy, as it had existed prewar. These restrictive institutions had established for identified persons and groups specific claims that were highly valued, and which rational persons would seek to protect. Hutt considered the wartime emergency disruption as a once-and-for-all opportunity to put matters right, to eliminate long-established practices, through one fell swoop of reform and reconstruction. Hutt's enterprise was genuinely "constitutional" in the sense of structural change rather than a Wicksell-like change in political rules for making decisions. Once the restrictions were swept away, the only requirement was that heed be paid to the normative advice of classical liberal political economists. Hutt did not sense the possible policy consequences of majoritarian rules in legislative bodies. In this respect, his enterprise was less sophisticated than that of Wicksell.

The central parallel between Wicksell and Hutt lies in their common recognition that effective normative economics required something more than railing against either arbitrary tax schemes or observed restrictive practices on some absurd presumption that a benevolent government would, willy-nilly, act directly on the advice so offered. However, there were subtle differences in the epistemological grounds for such commonly shared departures from the orthodox stance of political economists. As noted earlier, Wicksell recognized that governments are driven by the interests of constituents, and that *consensus* is required in order to get political change. Hence, reform proposals must embody a set of changes that will secure consensus which will, in its turn, serve to ratify, on normative grounds, the changes themselves.

Hutt was substantially more self-confident, and confident in the ability of the observing economist, to locate market failures through the identification of restrictions on economic liberties, a confidence that stemmed, perhaps justifiably, from the type of exercise involved. Hutt did not seek *consensus* for its own sake, either as the unique means of determining whether or not an observed practice was value-reducing or value-enhancing. Nor did he refer explicitly to consensus or consensus-building in terms of the politics of reconstruction, although this may well have been an underlying element in the discussion that seemed too obvious to discuss. Explicitly, Hutt seemed to ground his plan, which did embody buy-out and compensation schemes on a large scale, on the injustices and inequities that might accompany any major institutional change. The following statement indicates the thrust of Hutt's argument:

> . . . the vested interests may be, and on grounds of social justice, indeed, *must* be "bought out," "compensated." And we shall suggest . . . firstly, that this be done in such a way that the distributive injustices of restrictive privileges will dissolve in posterity; and, secondly, that the burden on the productive system may be immediately dissolved and so incidentally furnish the funds requisite for compensation.[8]

Note that this statement appears in Hutt's 1936 book, which suggests that *A Plan for Reconstruction* can be interpreted as little other than a detailed working out of the general position outlined seven years before. The argument seems to be that individuals and groups, perhaps through no fault of their own, found themselves locked into positions of being beneficiaries of various restrictive practices. They held claims under the existing scheme with some legitimacy, and the wholesale confiscation entailed in any noncompensated reconstruction would violate all precepts for justice.

Examined from our vantage point in 1987, *A Plan for Reconstruction* seems naive and unsophisticated in its implicit presumptions about the political efficacy of bureaucratic administration. In keeping with the intellectual fashion of the 1930s and 1940s, Hutt's overall plan involved the operation of a complex set of commissions and boards, peopled by lawyers, civil servants and economists who would genuinely serve the "public interest." Hutt acknowledged that in proposing the plan he was engaged in an act of social engineering, put forward in the institutional chaos and disruption of war as a means of "seizing the day" before the structure should be allowed to rigidify into its established prewar patterns of restrictiveness. In this particular respect, Hutt's vision matched that of Mancur Olson, some forty years in advance.[9] Hutt clearly saw that a relapse into restrictionism would insure unnecessary harm and suffering.

---

8. Hutt, *Economists and the Public,* 65; italics in original.

9. In his book (M. Olson, *The Rise and Decline of Nations* [New Haven: Yale University Press, 1982]), Olson argues that the relatively rapid growth rates of Japan and Germany

We should not, as we celebrate Hutt's ninetieth birthday, be too critical of him for his failure to anticipate contributions made by public choice economists decades after these books were written. Almost necessarily, Hutt wrote these books burdened with a part of the economists' mind-set of the times. What is important is that *A Plan for Reconstruction* is driven throughout by Hutt's reductionist emphasis on the simple equation between the existence of restrictive practices on the one hand and unexploited gains-from-trade on the other. The set of direct and indirect compensations, the income guarantees, the devices for bureaucratic administration and adjudication—these aspects of the book tend to be rejected out of hand by modern classical liberals. However, the Hutt of the 1940s considered these to be small costs to pay for the improvement promised, and costs that could readily be paid from the value surplus that full exploitation of the potential gains would make possible.

(As a digression, we may ask a question about the general intellectual mind-sets of the decades of the 1890s and the 1940s. Did Wicksell's much more skeptical attitude toward political decision makers reflect a characteristic of his times, a characteristic that changed markedly over the forty years that separate these two economists?)

## "Reform" without Restriction

William H. Hutt and Ronald H. Coase are a half-generation apart in age, Hutt being the senior of the two. Both economists were educated at the London School of Economics, and both have explicitly acknowledged the direct and indirect influence of the same two scholars, Edwin Cannan and Arnold Plant. We should, therefore, expect to find parallel strands in their analyses and attitudes, despite the genuine originality that makes each of these economists a man unto himself.

Parallels there are, parallels that we may readily identify if we return to my initial classification of both as gains-from-trade economists. I have suggested that the main theme of Hutt's efforts may be described as: "If restrictions on

---

during early postwar years, as compared with the growth rate for Great Britain, were due, at least in part, to the destruction of institutional rigidities consequent on military defeat, a destruction not matched in the economic structure of the victors.

economic liberties exist, there exist unexploited, and hence potentially exploit-able, gains-from-trade." This theme leads Hutt to look persistently for restric-tions, whether privately or publicly organized, and to advance normative schemes for removal of such practices whenever and wherever they occur.

This theme has its obverse: "If there are no restrictions on economic lib-erties to exchange, there exist no nonexploited gains-from-trade." This ob-verse rendering of the theme can be readily associated with the contribution of Ronald H. Coase,[10] in a sense more specifically than any association of the first version with Hutt. If ownership rights are well defined and legally pro-tected, and if no restrictions exist, individuals will act so as to exploit all of the opportunities from exchanges among rights independent of the pattern of ownership. This now-famous Coase theorem has been central to the de-velopment of the whole "law and economics" research program since the early 1960s. We can predict, retrospectively, that Hutt, who was always en-gaged in the development and applications of the positive variant of the theme here, would have found the Coase theorem to be an almost self-evident proposition.[11] The shock waves that the theorem sent through the ranks of professional economists, even among those who were normatively sympathetic to the positions taken by Coase (or by Hutt), provides clear, if indirect, proof that the allocationalist mentality dominated the discipline in 1960, as indeed it does in 1987. Only by some institutionally blind and epistemologically arrogant concentration on the conditions required for optimal or efficient resource allocation (the equalities between marginal private and marginal social costs, à la Pigou) could the self-evident char-acter of the Coasian proposition be called into question.

The normative implication of the Coase theme is, expectedly, also the ob-verse of that associated with Hutt's obverse. For the latter, if restrictions exist, let us remove them in order that gains-from-trade may be exploited. For the

10. R. H. Coase, "The Problem of Social Cost," *Journal of Law and Economics* 3 (Oc-tober 1960): 1–44.

11. I can justify my classification of Wicksell, Hutt and Coase in the same gains-from-trade category by recalling, autobiographically, my own initial reactions to the Coasian proposition, when first presented among faculty colleagues at the University of Virginia in the late 1950s. Coming at the Coase theorem from a Wicksellian perspective, I found the theorem almost self-evident, and I specifically recall the surprise felt when Coase re-ported back to us about the controversial reaction to his presentation of the theorem at the University of Chicago.

former, for the Coasian theme, if no restrictions are observed present, *laissez-faire*. The appearances of inefficiency, based on observations of apparent market failures, are just that, mere appearances, and presumably reflect some failure of observers to reckon on the accompanying existence of transactions costs that must be present in any exchange, which can occur only with an institutional setting. There is no inconsistency between the sometimes zealous reformist thrust that identifies restrictive practices in order to seek to eliminate them and the apparent quiescence in the face of apparent allocational failures in the absence of observed restrictions. Both attitudes are cut from the same cloth; both are characteristic of the gains-from-trade economist.

## The Limits of Classical Liberalism

William H. Hutt is an authentic classical liberal, and this characterization is nowhere better exhibited than in the book *Economists and the Public,* which remains, in several respects, his best work. As I have noted above, Hutt does not commit the libertarian blunder of extending his defense of the liberties of individuals to enter into ordinary voluntary exchanges to a defense of the liberties of individuals to enter into voluntary agreements in restraint of trade. His measuring rod is always ultimate value to consumers, the role that is universally shared among all individuals in the economy-polity. The norm of consumers' sovereignty carries through in all of Hutt's discourse.

There are very few authentic classical liberals, and especially if we require internal consistency between their positive analysis and its normative implications. For the economist whose methodological starting point is allocational, such consistency is likely to be difficult if not impossible to maintain, since there is no central emphasis on process as opposed to results. The dominance of the allocational thrust in modern normative economics, along with the inconsistencies that this fosters, has been partially responsible for the failure of classical liberalism to be more effective as a coherent social philosophy. I suggest, however, that there are also more fundamental limits to the persuasiveness of classical liberalism, limits that may be identified even in the works of authentic representatives, such as William H. Hutt.

I should commence, however, with a more targeted criticism leveled against those economists who share a broadly classical liberal persuasion but who, nonetheless, fall strictly within the allocational camp. Their normative emphasis is, as suggested, on efficiency in resource usage. Also, as has often been noted, arguments promoting abstract efficiency as a social objective gain few adherents. Hence, these arguments carry relatively little by way of potential for garnering votes in any electoral process. Efficiency, as a norm for policy, carries little or no emotive thrust, and economists should never have been surprised that their unqualified advocacy of efficiency-enhancing changes in structure falls on deaf ears.

The authentic classical liberal who adheres to the basic gains-from-trade perspective on his discipline of economics represents an advance on his counterpart who comes from the allocational camp. The gains-from-trade economist, if he remains consistent, does not place arguments from efficiency, as such, in the front rank of his rhetorical presentation. His reform emphasis is directed toward the removal of restrictions, with the enhanced value in exchange relegated to a position of necessary consequence. This, roughly stated, is the stance that describes Hutt's economics.

A further step could readily be taken by the gains-from-trade economist that is more difficult for the allocationalist, but it is a step that Hutt does not himself explicitly take. All emphasis on gains in exchange value could be dropped, and an argument against restrictions on liberties to exchange could be mounted on grounds of simple justice. Adam Smith's "justice of natural liberty" could be moved to center stage. It has always seemed to me that this offers a more persuasive base for generating public and political support for the freedom of exchange than any argument from utility, value or efficiency. On the other hand, the argument from justice may lapse more readily into a generalized defense of the liberty of voluntary contract, with no readily available means of making the distinction between contracts, exchanges or agreements that concentrate benefits on the trading parties and those in which the benefits are secured from the imposition of spillover harms on others. Some criterion analogous to Hutt's consumers' sovereignty must enter the evaluative exercise at some point.

The modern public choice economist, who may also seek to further the normative principles of classical liberalism, may succeed where his colleagues fail, at least with some of the unpersuaded. Rather than stressing either the superior allocative efficiency of the market process or the potential for exploiting unenjoyed gains-from-trade through the removal of restrictions on economic liberties, the public choice economist calls direct attention to the predicted and the observed failures or breakdowns in the institutional alternatives to market interactions. Markets fail, especially when evaluated against idealized efficiency norms. Institutional correctives to market failures also fail, even if these are cleverly designed by authentic classical liberals like Hutt. *A Plan for Reconstruction,* in particular, conveys the notion that if only the institutional structure could be redesigned by economists who are guided by the precepts of classical liberalism, all just might be well. In that small book, Hutt, along with his economist peers of all ideological persuasions, remained an institutional-political idealist of sorts, while he, again with his peers, looked quite critically at the economic process.

There remains, however, a more fundamental weakness in the position of the classical liberal, again as exemplified in the early works of W. H. Hutt, a weakness or deficiency that very substantially reduces the normative impact of the total argument. I refer to the absence of an ultimate ethical criterion against which reform measures are to be tested. Hutt himself recognizes the problem here, in his defense of his norm of consumers' sovereignty. Consider the following statement:

> It will now be suggested that values under natural scarcity in response to consumers' sovereignty are the only ones that can be taken as providing the ideal control of society's activities. The basis of our contention is as follows: Rejecting all systems of absolute ethics and aesthetics, judgment as to the goodness or badness of the result of any valuation process can only be personal; so that we have no more satisfactory criteria of the goodness of society's preferences in the objective expression than we have of the goodness of individual taste. But under our assumption of the absence of absolute standards, it seems that there is only one *conceivable* criterion of the desirability of values for which we can expect general acceptance, namely, that the forces determining them have been social, not private. It is for this simple reason that *liberty* (which we regard as practically synonymous with *tolerance*) must be regarded as a higher over-ruling principle.[12]

The appeal here to consumers' sovereignty (carefully qualified and interpreted) is perhaps persuasive to economists, but there is no easy response to someone who asks: Why consumers? A response that calls upon a value-

---

12. Hutt, *Economists and the Public,* 282; italics in original.

maximization criterion is likely to be misunderstood, and vague references to utility maximization will quickly run foul of distributional objections. The alternative that appeals directly to the rights of persons to engage in exchange freely, which is the base of any argument from justice, may seem to rest on arbitrary assertion.

What is the most satisfactory underlying political philosophy for classical liberalism? If we reject both the utilitarian and the natural rights positions, what are we left with? The answer here has always seemed obvious. *Contractarianism* is the one generalized philosophical position consistent with the classical liberal defense of freedom of exchange. Indeed, contractarianism can be interpreted as little more than an extension of the paradigm of free exchange to the broader setting. Also, importantly, the extension adds ethical content that seems absent in the truncated stance that describes Hutt's efforts.

Is a specific collective action justified, or can a justificatory argument in its support be made? Is a specific rule or institution justified, or can a justificatory argument be mounted in its defense? Hutt would apply his consumers' sovereignty test. Does the action or the rule operate so as to benefit individuals acting independently as ultimate consumers? However, why single out this role of individuals to the exclusion of all others?

The contractarian can offer a way out of the dilemma that may seem to be left dangling in the Hutt enterprise. The contractarian shifts the question to the following: Could the proposed action or the observed rule possibly secure unanimous consent (in the limit) of all participants affected if the direct effects, positive and/or negative, cannot be imputed to identified parties? Alternatively, in terms that have been made familiar since the seminal work of John Rawls, could the proposal or the rule have been agreed on by all persons behind a sufficiently thick veil of ignorance and/or uncertainty such that no identification of prospective gainers and losers is possible?[13] This elementary contractarian test does lend operational support, at least conceptually, to Hutt's norm of consumers' sovereignty, properly interpreted, but it does also possess a more appealing ethical base because it applies to individuals in *all* roles. Further, the contractarian test becomes conceptually more precise in its ability to make the required distinction between acceptable and unac-

13. J. Rawls, *A Theory of Justice* (Cambridge, Mass.: Harvard University Press, 1971).

ceptable voluntary agreements. By shifting "voluntary exchange" upward to the constitutional level of choices among rules, the consensual or general agreement test may be applied.

I do not suggest here that the contractarian logic can be used to generate ethical support for the whole comprehensive program of classical liberalism, as this program is normally understood and presented. The contractarian test cannot rule out the possible influence of what Sen has called "meddlesome preferences,"[14] even if identification of the holders of such preferences is removed from the exercise. There are "gray" areas of potential institutional change and policy action over which the contractarian test remains silent, whereas the consumers' sovereignty test may seem definitive.[15] I should argue, nonetheless, that the contractarian foundations do lend support to the classical liberal principles for social order over most of the domain that interest such authentic representatives of the tradition as W. H. Hutt, and that this ethical support may more than offset the apparent losses in definitiveness on the in-between or "gray" areas of normative political economy.

## Conclusion

I have not reviewed in detail the two books discussed in this paper. I have, instead, used some of the arguments in these two samples of Hutt's work as bases for developing and elaborating my characterization of the gains-from-trade economist, in both his positive and his normative roles. *Economists and the Public* stands as one of Hutt's best contributions, and it deserves much more attention than it received when it appeared and subsequently. It warrants reading by modern social scientists. (I have long urged that this book be reprinted.)

*A Plan for Reconstruction* is a dated effort that reflects, in part, the engineering urges of the economists of its time. Further, it includes rather tedious discussion of institutional proposals that retain little modern relevance. This book does not warrant careful reading in 1987. On the other hand,

---

14. A. K. Sen, "The Impossibility of a Paretian Liberal," *Journal of Political Economy* 78 (1970).

15. See J. Gray, "Contractarian Method, Private Property, and the Market Economy" (Jesus College, Oxford, 1986, mimeographed).

credit must be given to Hutt for his recognition that fundamental institutional reform requires that attention be paid to the interests of those persons and groups that have legitimately valued expectations embodied in any *status quo.* Such recognition alone places William H. Hutt among the select few political economists and classical liberals who are, at base, realist rather than romantic reformers.

ACKNOWLEDGEMENTS

I am indebted to my colleagues Roger Congleton, Jennifer Roback and Viktor Vanberg for helpful comments.

# Shackle and a Lecture in Pittsburgh

It is both intellectually and emotionally stimulating to be drawn back to the radical subjectivism of G. L. S. Shackle, who has consistently exhibited the courage to state the implications of his perspective for the whole realm of scientific inquiry in economics. Along with many others among my disciplinary peers, I have found it too easy to slip into orthodox methodology when its applicability beckons, thereby implicitly expressing a lack of concern with the apparent logical incoherence that describes my work upon any inclusive evaluation. The invitation to write this short review article provides me with an opportunity to reevaluate my own position specifically as it relates to that taken by Shackle, which is restated severally in this volume.

*Business, Time, and Thought* collects twenty papers, most of them short, almost all of which have been quite recently written and published, well beyond the productive years of most economists. But, as we have long been aware, George Shackle is no ordinary economist, and his ability to present even familiar ideas in a prose that sparkles with enthusiasm remains characteristic of this new volume.

I can commence my reevaluation by a direct citation:

> The elemental thing we study is *choice*. If choice means anything, it means *origination*. The making of history (on however small a scale) is the making possible one path of affairs rather than another. By origination, I would say (and here take a decisive step outside all orthodoxy, even the

Essay Review of *Business, Time, and Thought,* by G. L. S. Shackle, edited by Stephen F. Frowen (New York: New York University Press, 1988). From *Market Process* 7 (Spring 1989): 2–4. Reprinted by permission of the Mercatus Center at George Mason University, Arlington, Va., formerly the Center for Market Processes.

Austrian) we ought to mean an act of thought that is a *first cause,* so that choice in its essential nature is unpredictable in its effects, its sequel. Many "choices" are of course mere response or obedience to habit or simple reckoning. By choice we ought to mean a *momentous* act of thought. If such an act is truly originative, it cannot be foreknown in character or timing, and thus we are essentially denied the power to specify the sequel of any present choice as a singular path. . . . (p. 206)

I want to suggest that Shackle's definition of choice, expressed here and elsewhere, tends to conflate two distinguishable mental events, both of which can, with qualifications, be brought within his definition but which remain categorically different in their implications for both economic theory and the whole scientific enterprise of economists.

I propose to introduce a personal, autobiographical example to develop the distinction between the two quite separate conceptions of choice, and I hope, in so doing, to construct a bridge of sorts between the implied scientific nihilism in Shackle's position and the positivism that describes orthodox neoclassical economics.

In late 1987, an officer-agent for the National Association of Business Economists invited me to deliver the annual Adam Smith Lecture at the association's scheduled meeting in Pittsburgh in September 1988. This lecture, as delivered by me, involved two quite distinct choices that illustrate the category differences I want to emphasize. There was, first of all, a decision, a choice, made by some officer, officers, or committee on behalf of the association. This choice was expressed by the sending of the initial invitation to me. This choice was *creative* in that a sequence of events was made possible, a sequence that did not exist prior to choice and that was brought into being, literally, by the choice itself. This creative choice seems to be the sort that occupies Shackle's attention almost exclusively, and, by inference, his treatment relegates all other "choices" to the status of behavioral responses.

I suggest, however, that the lecture, as delivered, involved a second genuine choice, this time a choice on my part concerning acceptance or rejection of the invitation. In one basic sense, my choice in this instance was not creative; it was, instead, *reactive.* I found myself confronted with a modified set of environmental alternatives, but I had done nothing directly or indirectly to create the change in conditions that had brought the new opportunity into realization. Clearly, however, I did face a genuine choice that fits within the inclusive Shackle definition. I was not merely responding to a stimulus in my act of acceptance.

There is a categorical difference between *creative* and *reactive* choice when we come to the realm of predictability, the domain of scientific inquiry. My reactive choice could have been, probabilistically, predicted by those who advanced the association's invitation. By contrast, there was no way that I could have, even probabilistically, predicted that such an invitation would have been forthcoming. The matching of the name "Buchanan" with the "1988 Adam Smith Lecture" was creative in a Kirznerian entrepreneurial sense.

I need not push the personal illustration too far. But it does allow me to clarify my own position, as expressed variously, which may have seemed to embody inconsistency by my acceptance of much of the Shackle critique while continuing to use the neoclassical framework of analysis. Neoclassical analysis is, and must be, restricted entirely to the domain of *reactive* choice, which is always predictable, at least within probabilistic limits. A genuine science of reactive choice is possible, and patterns of order can be predicted to emerge, even if each choosing participant retains the fullest Shacklian freedom to originate his own sequence of future events. The domain of reactive choice extends over a wide spectrum of possible choice settings. At the one extreme, the individual actor is genetically programmed to respond uniquely and predictably to the alternatives that are confronted; in this limit, "choice" in any meaningful sense disappears. As we move beyond this limit, *individual choice* becomes possible, and indeterminacy replaces determinacy in any attempt to predict individual behavior. Such indeterminacy need not, however, extend to *patterns* of behavior that describe the choices made by many persons, comparably situated in at least some respects, or, alternatively, the choices made by a single person over a whole series of comparably defined circumstances.

I should stress that the *reactive* choice of an individual may meet the Shacklian criterion for *originative* choice, when examined in perspective of the individual who chooses. Such a person does, indeed, originate the particular sequence of events that can come into existence, *for him,* only after genuine choice is exercised. In my acceptance of the invitation to deliver the

Adam Smith Lecture in Pittsburgh, I originated a sequence of events, for myself and others, that would not have been within the possible had my choice been rejection. I suggest, however, that my choice in this instance was not itself *creative* because it was at least probabilistically predictable, as indeed all reactive choices must be. The *pattern* of response might have been such as to allow for my private choice to have been either one of the alternatives that I faced, while retaining some appropriate appellation of stochastic determinacy. And, of course, as we move back along the spectrum of reactive choice toward generalization over persons and over time sequences, the determinacy of reactive choice patterns increases and with this comes enhanced productivity of scientific inquiry.

All such reactive choices are, however, categorically distinct from genuinely creative choice, which does indeed bring into being a sequence of events that remains indeterminate, not only at the level of individual action but also at the level of any conceivable pattern of behavior generalized over many persons and many periods. In creative choice, the behavior of the individual is not probabilistically predictable because such choice, in itself, *creates* alternatives from which the other individuals choose. The creative chooser does not select from among competing "forks in the road" that remain "out there," thrown up to him either by natural circumstance or by the action of others, privately or collectively. The reactive choice I faced in accepting or rejecting the invitation to deliver the Adam Smith Lecture came into being by the creative decision of the agents who acted on behalf of the association. This choice was dimensionally different from that which I faced in reacting to the modified opportunity that I found.

The essential contribution of G. L. S. Shackle, who is surely one of the most neglected economists of this century, lies in his emphasis and insistence on the indeterminacy of choice. And the related emphasis of modern Austrian economists, notably that of Israel Kirzner, on the necessary role of entrepreneurial choice in the dynamic operation of any economy, deserves our praise. Understanding how the economic order works requires that we give due attention to both dimensions for choice, and neoclassical orthodoxy has surely neglected creative choice as the necessary complement to the reactive choice that must be its central focus. But all "choice" that deserves to be so labelled is originative, while not all "choice" is creative (entrepreneurial).

In this short essay, stimulated again by reading Shackle, I have shifted my

own position toward a more catholic and less critical attitude on the orthodoxy of neoclassical economics than that expressed in separate essays published in celebratory volumes in honor of Hayek and Mises.[1] I remain a
Shacklian, but I now recognize, more than before, the essential distinction
between individual and pattern indeterminacy.

I apologize to those readers who might have expected me to offer a more
comprehensive review of the particular contents of this new Shackle book.
In terms of the central subject matter discussed, at least two earlier books
by Shackle are more focused,[2] because the essays reprinted here are necessarily the sometimes unrelated reflections of a senior scholar. But it is difficult for me, here as before, to read anything by Shackle without being
stimulated to reflect on issues that are, indeed, central to our whole enterprise as economists.

1. See my "Is Economics the Science of Choice?" in *Roads to Freedom: Essays in Honor
of F. A. Hayek,* ed. Erich Streissler (London: Routledge and Kegan Paul, 1969), reprinted
in my *What Should Economists Do?* (Indianapolis: Liberty Fund, 1979), 39–63; and my
"The Domain of Subjective Economics: Between Predictive Science and Moral Philosophy," in *Method, Process, and Austrian Economics: Essays in Honor of Ludwig von Mises,* ed.
Israel Kirzner (Lexington, Mass.: Lexington Books, 1982), reprinted in my *Economics: Between Predictive Science and Moral Philosophy* (College Station: Texas A&M University
Press, 1987), 67–82.

2. G. L. S. Shackle, *Epistemics and Economics* (Cambridge: Cambridge University
Press, 1972), and *Imagination and the Nature of Choice* (Edinburgh: Edinburgh University
Press, 1979).

# Review of *Imagination and the Nature of Choice*

This small book is distilled vintage Shackle. I choose this metaphor carefully, for what we have here is best described as the core of Shackle's ideas on choice, variously presented in other books, distilled into their essential elements. The casual, even if peripherally interested, reader should be forewarned. A cursory reading, a dipping into the discourse here and there, may suggest redundancy and repetition, both with other works and within the book itself. But cursory reading cannot suffice. The argument in this book is tightly packed. It is an integrated and carefully constructed whole designed to present Shackle's genuinely revolutionary ideas on choice, cognition, uncertainty, creativity, and, indeed, on the human condition. The argument rewards close attention.

I shall be honest here and state that I am not sure that I fully understand what Shackle is discussing. And, as Austrian and quasi-Austrian economists know, I come to Shackle from a sympathetic and congenial subjectivist perspective. There are at least three possible reasons why I may be confused in my interpretation. First, I may simply be incapable of comprehending elements of Shackle's argument, which is highly complex even if not technical in the terminological sense. Secondly, Shackle himself may be confused, or at least ambiguous, in the development of certain implications of his argu-

"Review of *Imagination and the Nature of Choice,* by G. L. S. Shackle" (Edinburgh University Press, 1979), 159 pages. From *Austrian Economics Newsletter* 3 (Summer 1980): 2–3. Reprinted by permission of the Ludwig von Mises Institute.

ment. Finally, the implications of the argument may offer up many more basic issues than even Shackle himself realizes. I suspect that my own difficulties are some combination of these three reasons.

Let me first try to sketch out briefly the essentials of the argument as a means of offering a basis for some of my concerns and questions.

"Decision," taken literally, is a cut in time. "Choice" is among alternative "choosables," which are imagined possibles in time-to-come. The results of choice cannot be knowable. Choice itself creates time-to-come; the chooser creates that which he chooses by the act of choice itself. He makes his own history. Psychologically, choice is commitment that antedates the action that is required to carry out that commitment. The action consequent on choice is a beginning, an uncaused cause. It is totally inappropriate to apply a probabilistic calculus to choice.

Choice is commitment to one of a skein of rival choosables. This commitment is internal to the mind of the chooser, and hence, unknowable to others outside this mind. And choice initiates action, which brings into being the single one of the rival choosables selected. But the consequences of choice, the results in time-to-come, of the selection of a single rival choosable may themselves be more or less predictable. It seems to me that Shackle fails to clarify his analysis in this respect. He seems to suggest that the consequences of choice must also be unknowable to the chooser in some sense analogous to the unknowability of choice itself to an external observer. But two types of "unknowledge" (Shackle's term) require distinction. There is unknowledge about choice itself, which limits the predictions of any observer external to the chooser. But internal to the potential chooser himself, the consequences of specific choices (commitments) may be predictable, at least within limits.

Let me clarify my point with an example. Robert Frost's traveler confronts two paths in the wood. His choice is between the two. Clearly, there is no "choice" involved in his predictions as to the physical terrain along each path. Given uncertainty about the latter, the traveler may possibly resort to a subjective probabilistic calculus in an attempt to clarify his predictions. Other persons, if they apply the same subjective probabilities, might make the same predictions about the physical attributes of the two paths in the wood. But all such predictions are prior to choice itself, and they do not determine choice. The traveler commits himself to one path or the other, given his set of predictions. In the action consequent on choice, the traveler himself determines the events in time-to-come. He creates history, and this history must remain unknowable to any external observer. If genuine choice could be predicted in advance, even probabilistically, it will not be choice.

If the chooser, as well as others, knows in advance the weights to be assigned to the whole set of elements that might be valued (positively or negatively) in "choice," then we might seem able to model such "choice" in the orthodox manner of modern economic theory. But, as Shackle stresses, this procedure is absurd, since, if I know everything in advance, I do not choose in any meaningful sense. I am not initiating action from commitment; I am not generating an uncaused cause; I am not involved in a beginning. The attempt to bypass genuine choice by postulating specific utility functions of persons is essentially fraudulent. It removes genuine choice to some prior level which remains undiscussed.

If choice is to be taken to create one of the elements of the environment that may be observed in time-to-come, it cannot itself be thought of as part of a deterministic experiment. The chooser is not modelled by analogy to the ball in the urn; his choice behavior is unique.

Shackle would, I think, suggest that the word "choice" is wrongly used if a well-defined maximand is assigned to some putative chooser in advance and if each element that may inform "choice" could be predicted under some pattern of stochastic uncertainty. Nothing is created in such a setting, and it seems that Shackle has the better of the argument when he implies that choice simply does not exist in such situations. The individual becomes an automaton who is programmed, even if the results are only stochastically determined. It is this removal of the individualization of choice that lies at the heart of Shackle's objection to orthodox analysis. To bring choice within some inclusive probabilistic calculus, even in the most tolerant subjectivist sense, is to deny that persons determine their own destinies.

Shackle's perspective on choice is likely to be highly congenial to Austrian economists, and especially to those who follow Kirzner in his emphasis on the role of the entrepreneur in dynamic competition. Shackle deserves a more comprehensive place in modern economic theory. Despite his many books, he has remained only a peripheral influence on the received wisdom in the theory of choice under uncertainty, with relatively few of his works being referenced even by the increasingly rare number of young scholars who bother to read anything beyond the works of their own professors and colleagues. Shackle's ideas on choice can represent a standing challenge to those young Austrian economists who tire of standard methodological disquisition and want to sink their intellectual teeth into tougher stuff. Even if, in some final assessment, the criticism is negative rather than positive, the result would be wider dissemination of Shackle's perspective, a dissemination that will surely not emerge from analyses by non-Austrian scholars. Make no mistake, Shackle's ideas are "radically subversive" of orthodoxy, as Professor Stephen Littlechild has noted.

Despite its rigor which places high demands on thought processes, Shackle's prose is a pleasure to read. At one point it seems to me to be almost poetic, and warrants extended citation as the endpiece to this review:

> Formal treatment, the diamond facets of logical rigour, are intellectually beautiful, they cut the hardest materials. Beauty is a proof-devisers' ultimate clinching satisfaction, the classic intellectual glory. But it is the desire for a perfect formalism which, it seems to me, has impelled theorists to mistake the nature of unknowledge. It goes against the grain of western man's whole history and ambition to recognize an ultimate stop to his progress towards "control" of his affairs. The inspired creative power, the *original* Promethean gift, original in its continuous power of perhaps *ex nihilo* contribution to history, which drives the human affair along, is incompatible with foreknowledge. The gift of choice (if choice means anything worthwhile) denies us the gift of knowledge of time-to-come. For how should there be knowledge, in every present moment, of what men are about to *originate* in the extreme sense, to draw from the void?

# Review of *Politics and Markets: The World's Political Economic Systems*

I am sorry that I was persuaded by Warren Samuels to undertake this critique. It is sometimes stimulating to review bad books by scholars or pseudoscholars whom one does not know and/or does not respect. Such, alas, is not the case here. I know and respect C. E. Lindblom as a dedicated scholar who has made significant contributions in both economics and political science. It is painful for me to condemn this book as bad, but to do less would be intellectually dishonest.

One of my primary impressions is that Lindblom comes off as a "bifurcated Rip Van Winkle." I should briefly explain both parts of this characterization. By the judgment of his peers in both disciplines, Lindblom qualifies as an economist and as a political scientist. But this is not a book by an economist who extends his analysis to politics and political institutions, nor is it a work by a political scientist who analyzes markets. It is, almost literally, as if Lindblom discusses markets as an economist and then dons another hat to discuss politics. There seems to be little or no carry-over of his quite sophisticated and critical understanding of the market process into his analysis of politics, which becomes more or less standardized modern political science.

Why the Rip Van Winkle label? There is nothing in the book to indicate that Lindblom has been awake to changes in either the scholarly or the real world for the past decade. The book smacks of the early 1960s, and it reads as if it was largely written before the counterculture, before the failures of the

From "Three Reviews of Charles E. Lindblom—*Politics and Markets: The World's Political Economic Systems*," *Journal of Economic Issues* 13 (March 1979): 215–17. Reprinted by special permission of the copyright holder, the Association for Evolutionary Economics.

Great Society, before Vietnam, before Alexander Solzhenitsyn, before Watergate, before the post-1965 transfer revolution, before Ralph Nader, before Leviathan, before the inflation of the 1970s, before public choice, before the economic theory of regulation, before the demonstrated failures of Keynesian policy precepts. Even many of the statistical tables contain data no more current than the mid-1960s.

These flaws, although important ones, might have been excused by the pressures of modern academic life on a scholar who has served his country internationally and his university administratively. But two additional major flaws in the book cannot go unchallenged. The first, which Lindblom makes into a central theme, is the argument that the interests of business necessarily take on predominant importance in democracy. This argument is based on the notion that business interests must supercede those of all other groups because only "business" is in a position to do what government wants. Only "business" can produce, employ, innovate, distribute, invest, create capital, and ensure economic growth. Hence, so the argument goes, "business" can, by threatening to withhold the carrying out of these universally necessary functions satisfactorily, secure its own private demands from those who allegedly control the society's destinies through the offices of governance. But who or what is "business"? The lie can be given to the argument quite easily by making the simple assumption that no "business" exists at all. Suppose, strictly for purposes of discussion here, that each and every industry were organized on ideally competitive principles, with literally thousands of small producers, employers, and investors in each product and service line. Precisely the *same* economic functions would need to be performed, and in order to ensure that these functions are performed with tolerable efficiency, precisely the *same* governmental policy set would be dictated. Where does this leave the claim that "business" interests dominate, as if there is some grand and quasi-mysterious two-party game between government and the business monolith? I am not, in posing the counterfactual example, denying the existence of a "business" interest in perhaps several organized variants. I am suggesting that public or governmental policy dictated by elementary efficiency considerations cannot, and should not, be attributed to the power of "business interests." Personally, I find it difficult to understand how anyone, viewing the political-economic setting of 1978, could argue that "business interest" dominates much of anything.

This bizarre theme is matched by one that deserves more discussion than is possible in this review. While acknowledging the excesses in institutional reality, Lindblom argues that communism offers a *Weltanschauung* in which intelligence is respected, relative to classical liberalism, which depends on invisible-hand processes of mutual coordination and adjustment to organize major areas of human interaction. What can he mean here? Somehow, Lindblom seems under the delusion that the idealized notion of a single mind (of an individual or a ruling elite), coordinating everything in society, elevates and honors the intellect of man more than the notion of mutual and spontaneous adjustment among men, each one of whom utilizes the information available to him. But where does he leave those whose actions are to be coordinated by the imaginary mastermind? What implicit respect is given to the intelligence of those who are to be the putty to the master's modeling? Where is there room for individual preference? He gives no answer to these questions and apparently does not even consider them.

Readers who come to this book with sufficiently critical attitudes will find useful positive analyses of comparative institutional structures. I have not discussed the positive features because my primary concern is with the reactions of other potential readers who will find vulgar prejudices reinforced by arguments that simply will not stand up to critical examination.

# Liberty, Market and State[1]

I recall hearing "my professor" Frank Knight say on numerous occasions that he could never tell whether those who opposed the market did so because they thought the market worked well or because they thought it failed. Like so many other statements made by Frank Knight, this one is worth a bit of pondering. I want to suggest here that opponents of the market or market order fall into two quite distinct groups along the lines Knight indicated, and, further, that the two groups are quite different in terms of the potential receptiveness to the ideas of economic theory on the one hand and to public choice theory on the other.

The theme for these remarks emerged from my resolution of a puzzle that I had thought about for more than three decades. I was invited to deliver the G. Warren Nutter Memorial Lecture in April 1983. In that lecture, I referred to the experience that Warren Nutter and I shared at the University of Chicago in the late 1940s. I noted that both of us had initially come into economics as dedicated socialists, an experience shared by so many members of our age cohort. But I also noted that both Warren Nutter and I had been converted into strong advocacy of the market organization of the economy, in my own case through a mere six-week exposure to Frank Knight. My puzzle was why the other dedicated socialists in our group, who shared precisely the same academic experience, including the exposure to Frank Knight, did not undergo comparable conversion. Why did they remain as firmly dedicated

From *Liberty, Market and State: Political Economy in the 1980s* (Brighton, England: Wheatsheaf Books, 1986), 3–7. Copyright 1986 by James M. Buchanan. First published in Great Britain in 1986 by Wheatsheaf Books Ltd, Brighton, Sussex. Reprinted by permission of Pearson Education Limited.

1. The material in this chapter was first written for presentation as an occasional lecture at a Liberty Fund conference, Fairfax, Virginia, in July 1983.

to the socialist alternative after they "learned economics" as they did before. And they obviously did "learn economics," since there was no distinction in levels of observed academic achievement.

Only after I had written the draft for the Nutter lecture, and as I was going over the draft for presentation, did I come on my answer to the puzzle. I had always assumed implicitly that most of those persons whose attitudes might best be described as "socialist," broadly defined, were in most essential respects similar to me before I was converted, before I became a born-again free-market advocate. I now realized that this essential similarity applies only to a subset, only to members of one of the groups who oppose market organization, and that the distinction has important consequences. Members of one of these groups, those who may be described as having basically my own preconversion mentality, are vulnerable to the analytical arguments of economic theory. Members of the other group, by contrast, remain almost totally immune to such arguments. By comparison, the analytical arguments of public choice theory may be considered unnecessary, irrelevant, redundant or worse (after conversion) by members of the first group, but for members of the second group the public choice arguments may possibly engender a paradigm shift, even if not accompanied by a conversion to any positive alternative.

I want to discuss these two quite distinct anti-market mentalities in some detail. It is useful, even if sometimes misleading, to assign labels. I shall refer to a member of the first group as a *libertarian socialist*, and to a member of the second group as an *anti-libertarian socialist*.

Objection may be raised to the juxtaposition of the two words "libertarian" and "socialist"; my joining them may seem internally contradictory. Nonetheless, I think that the term "libertarian socialist" does best describe the position I held before I "saw the light." (There did exist a Libertarian Socialist party in Weimar Germany.) The person who shares this perspective places a primary value on *liberty*, as such. He personally disputes, rejects, resents, opposes attempts by others to exercise control or power over his own choice behaviour. He does not like harness. There is an exhilaration in simply being free.

Consider, now, the thought processes of such a person who does not really have the foggiest notion of the way the market works. He remains blissfully ignorant of economic theory and, notably, of its central principle of spontaneous coordination, and he is not blessed with any intuitive sense of the interaction process. At the same time, however, the person observes what goes on about him. He lives in and participates in an economy. He works for his wages; he pays money for his consumables. Economic decisions are made by someone, somewhere.

How can such a person fail to view the economy as a system through which some persons control and exploit others? The direction and control of the economic process seems totally arbitrary, and a single participant seems to be at the mercy of those who manipulate the lives and fortunes of others to further their own private greed, to promote their own whims and fancies. If such ideas did not emerge more or less naturally, they would be encountered almost universally in the popular media and in the academic-intellectual establishment. And these ideas would find alleged intellectual legitimacy in the many variants of the Marxian dialectic, the "science of historical development." The abiding genius of Karl Marx lies precisely here, in his acute understanding of the possible reaction of the ignorant intellectual to the workings of the capitalist or market order.

In the attitude of the person whose mentality I am trying to describe here, there is little or no positive value placed on collective action, as such. There need be no sense of community, no thought about the organic unity of the social group, the state or any such things. The person that I am describing here is socialist only because he is strongly anti-capitalist. In a very real sense, his socialism stems from his very libertarianism. Rejecting the control over his own destiny by the whims of the arbitrary "money managers," "robber barons," "Wall Street tycoons," "gnomes of Zurich" and "members of the Eastern establishment," what is left as the organizational alternative? "Throw the rascals out," but who is to replace the rascals? The libertarian socialist falls back, almost desperately, on some form of populist democracy. At the least, he reckons, come the revolution, he will exercise potentially equal powers in shaping his own fate, powers equal to those exercised by others. The person I am trying to describe here probably never goes much beyond his negativism. He really does not think much about the pragmatic problems of organizing a genuinely democratic socialism. (Again, witness the genius of Marx in remaining silent on the postrevolution organizational problems.)

Consider now how such a person will respond when he encounters the solid arguments of economic theory. Think about his reaction when he finally comes to understand the principle of spontaneous order of the market economy. Consider how his whole vision of the world might be affected by exposure to someone like Frank Knight, whose intellectual honesty and integrity were beyond question. Such a person now *understands* that the choices in the market are not arbitrary, that there are narrow limits on the potential for exploitation of man by man, that markets tend to maximize freedom of persons from political control, that liberty, which has always been his basic value, is best preserved in a regime that allows markets a major role. Such a person is both morally consistent and intellectually honest when he undergoes the apparent conversion into market advocacy. He has, quite literally, seen the light.

Let me now try to contrast the position of the libertarian socialist, just discussed, with that of the anti-libertarian socialist. Description of the mentality of a member of the latter group is much more difficult for me since, after all, in describing the first position I am describing my own former self. But let me try to get into other persons' minds. The anti-libertarian socialist is not an individualist, and he does not place primary value on individual liberty. He could never have written, or sympathized with, the slogan of the American revolutionaries, "don't tread on me." His initial anti-market or anti-capitalist mentality stems not from any anger, rage or loathing at the arbitrary powers that others seem to exercise over him, and not from any apparent limits placed on his own liberty by others. Instead, this person opposes the market order for a much more basic reason. He does not think that individuals *should* choose their own destinies. He objects to the market just as much if he knows how it works as he does if he remains ignorant. And he objects just as much to a market that works well as to a market that fails. The level of economic understanding and sophistication possessed by the anti-libertarian has little or no influence on his ideological stance in opposition to market order.

The socialism of the anti-libertarian is essentially positive rather than negative. He actively supports collective control over the lives and liberties of men because he does not consider that persons should be allowed to control their own lives, that they should retain their liberties. There is a "better" way. The community, the society, the organic unity of the group, the state—these entities command his loyalties. The anti-libertarian may be, but need not be, paternalist. He may, but need not, think that his own values should be imposed on others. The central element in this position is the rejection of the notion that individuals should be allowed to determine their own values, independent of the collective, which is presumably guided in its search for "truth" and "goodness."

Consider how such a person might react to the teachings of the economic theorist. He may take these teachings as the duck takes water off its back. He may fully understand the logical structure of the market, while at the same time he remains an ardent advocate of socialist or collective initiatives. Such a person is basically immune to economic argument. The dispersion and limitation of power that the market insures is precisely the reason for his opposition to this organizational form, rather than the converse. The anti-libertarian remains anti-libertarian.

Interestingly enough, however, it is precisely this sort of person who may, if he remains intellectually honest, be reached by the teachings of public choice theory. If such a person comes to recognize that the idealized collectivity does not, and indeed cannot, exist, that persons in politics are like persons elsewhere, including the market, that they remain pursuers of their own private and individualized interests, despicable as these might be, he may waiver considerably in support for collectivistic schemes. How much waivering will take place is unclear, however, since such a person cannot really be expected to become a market zealot. There is no way that the true anti-individualist can be brought to a position of advocacy for the market order, regardless of some removal of romance from his image of the state. The socialist god may die for the anti-libertarian, but no other god appears. The temptation toward drift into nihilism is strong, and this stance does seem to me to be descriptive of many jack-socialists in our world of the 1980s.

In this preliminary chapter I have done nothing more than to share with you how I resolved the puzzle I mentioned. I have found the excursion useful in clarifying my own confusions about the anti-market mentalities. I do not want to argue that my two ideal types are located in their pure forms anywhere, in any person, past or present, living or dead. We are all mixtures of many persons, so that those who oppose the market order may well reflect some blending of the two abstract positions I have tried to outline here, as well as others that may be constructed. Further, even among those of us who remain basically proponents of market order, there remain remnants of the two mentalities I have sketched. For myself, I can empathize much more closely with those who advance the pseudo-Marxist criticisms of monopoly capitalism than I can with those who advance the arguments about the potential benevolence of the state.

My ultimate justification for these remarks is the hope that understanding the mind-set of those who differ with us is a first step toward commencing dialogue and discussion at the most fundamental level of political philosophy.

# PART THREE

# Political Economy in the Post-Socialist Century

# America's Third Century
## in Perspective

In 1976, the United States will enter its Third Century of nationhood. This offers an appropriate theme for my lecture. I want to look critically and carefully at American society as it prepares to enter this Third Century. By profession, I am an economist; by interest, I am a social philosopher. I want to look at modern America in sociophilosophical terms, and to try to identify elements of change that often escape attention as we carry on in our separate petty existences. Adam Smith, a philosopher who was also our patron saint in economics, once remarked that the task of the philosopher was to do nothing, but to observe everything. I want to play this philosopher role here.

There is always a strong temptation to view society in terms of romance, not reality. For traditional liberals, society is compared against an unreal and romantic age of what it might become if only its destiny should be shaped on all-knowing, benevolent wisdom. Hence, the liberal's emphasis on social reform, his frustrations at the *status quo*, his willingness to experiment with the unknown. Against this, there is the equally romantic image of the golden age, the benchmark used by the traditional conservative when he evaluates the *status quo*, which frustrates him as it does the liberal. Hence, the conservative's emphasis on stability, on the glories of the past, his negative attitude toward change.

From *Atlantic Economic Journal* 1 (November 1973): 3–12. Reprinted by permission of the publisher.

This paper was presented as the banquet address at the first conference of the Atlantic Economic Society held in Richmond, Virginia, on 28–29 September 1973. I am indebted to my colleague Gordon Tullock for helpful comments on an earlier draft.

Let me try to be a realist here, rather than slip into romanticism in either of these two familiar guises. Society cannot be transformed into utopia, and there was no golden age. We live in a social order that can surely be improved, but, because we are individuals, the idealized liberal society can scarcely be approached. On the other hand, there were elements of our historical experience that we have destroyed to our peril, and which may never be restored. One of these was the widespread faith in the American dream itself. Label this as myth if you will, but its loss has wrought havoc in our social fabric.

Let me start at some beginning. In an elementary idealized sense, anarchy would clearly be the most desirable of all social arrangements. I have often called myself a philosophical anarchist. By this I mean that if all persons could be depended upon to adhere voluntarily to rules for mutual tolerance, mutual respect, there would then be little argument or basis for anything like government or law, empowered to coerce individuals against their wills. It seems to me that anyone who values individual freedom, instrumentally for his own sake, or ideologically, as a social objective, must accept this philosophical anarchism as a base for evaluating social institutions. Even here, however, there is a basic conceptual issue. Suppose that all persons agreed to respect the rights of others, agreed to observe rules of voluntary behavior, and that the same rules should be agreed to by all in the community. What would define a person? How would rights, property rights (by which I mean simply the rights to do things), be distributed among persons? Anarchy, as an organizing principle for social order, begins to break down, even in a world of nice people, once conflict emerges.[1]

Constructively, therefore, I am a constitutionalist, by which I mean that I acknowledge a basic legal structure, a constitution, must be established. This constitution must specify just what the rights of individuals and groups are, who may do what with what and who may do what to whom, including the rights, and the limits, of the government to take action. In other words, law is an essential feature of ongoing society. Viable society becomes possible

---

1. For a positive analysis of the workings of an anarchist in society, see Gordon Tullock, ed., *Explorations in the Theory of Anarchy* (Blacksburg, Va.: Center for Study of Public Choice, 1972).

only when it is given a legal or constitutional structure that details procedures for avoiding and for resolving interpersonal conflicts. If all persons could be depended on to abide by the law, once laid down, there would, even here, be no need for government, as such, although there would be a minimal role for jurists.

As we move closer toward reality, however, it is necessary to realize that all persons cannot be relied on to abide by the constitution, by the law. All cannot be expected or predicted to obey the law as defined (any law), to respect the property rights of fellow citizens. When we come to this elementary recognition, we make a major but necessary step away from any idealized social order. If men will not voluntarily respect rules or standards of behavior *vis-à-vis* other men, they must somehow be ruled. This requires the establishment of a ruler, a sovereign, as Thomas Hobbes so perceptively noted three centuries ago. The basis for government, as an independently coercive power, is provided, that of enforcing the law. This is full of consequences. It would be desirable, perhaps, if a robot enforcer could be invented, one that would strictly limit its own activities to the enforcement of existing law. But in the real world who is to impose limits on the enforcer? How is Leviathan to be chained?

This has now become the critical question of our time. This is the issue that the Third Century faces. Unless it meets this challenge, the United States of America will join the other nations in history that have slipped from regimes in which men remain tolerably free into regimes that subject large numbers of men to the arbitrary whims of a few.

This problem is not uniquely modern in either reality or conception. It has existed in all ages, in all lands, and on it political philosophers have written learned treatises in all languages, dead and living. The solutions that have been proposed and tried have taken two distinct forms. First, there have been various institutional devices designed to restrict government interferences with the lives of ordinary citizens. The Roman Republic attempted to share executive power among two or more officials, appointed simultaneously to the same office. Medieval Europe opposed a centralized church against the power of feudal lords. Montesquieu urged the separation and division of political power within a single polity, largely along procedural lines. The federalist idea, which has been successfully used by Switzerland for so long, embodies a division of sovereignty between an inclusive central government and quasi-autonomous regional units. The philosophers of the 18th century discovered market organization of the economy as a means of keeping powers of the state limited.

Secondly, there has been the explicit promulgation of the mystique of some "higher law," one that guides the actions of sovereigns as well as of ordinary men. The tablets of Moses and the Book of Mormon offer us ancient and modern examples of "law" externally derived from "God." The natural-law philosophers of the late Middle Ages hoped that rulers would be held in check by belief in the higher laws of nature, whether or not these be God-given. Scholars of the 18th-Century Enlightenment evoked the "social contract" to explain the origins as well as the limits on the state. The written constitution, carrying a specified historical date, presumably had as a primary objective the guarantee of some predictability about the limits on governmental powers.

The Founding Fathers faced this issue squarely as they confronted our First Century. In conceiving their grand design for the nation that was to be America, they incorporated a mix among several of the devices that I have mentioned. By necessity as well as by design, they tried to construct a genuine federal system, one in which the powers of the central government were limited by definition, with residual powers held by quasi-autonomous state governments. Equally, if not more, important was their resolve to keep government, at any and all levels, out of the nation's ordinary business.

Influenced by the discovery of the 18th-century philosophers that the economy, if allowed to function without overt governmental direction, would generate tolerably efficient results, they assigned a noninterfering role to government. (It is, of course, no accident that 1776 was also the date of publication for Adam Smith's great book, *The Wealth of Nations*. The Third Century of this book's history appropriately coincides with that of this nation.) "That government is best which governs least" was Thomas Jefferson's succinct expression of this fundamental notion.

The Founders recognized and understood a principle of elementary economics that is understood by few men today, not even by many of those who profess to call themselves "economists." This principle is that one of the major advantages of a market or free enterprise economic system is its implied limits on the powers of the government. To the extent that markets work, there is no need for government decision or direction. It is as simple as that.

Within the structure of government itself, the Founding Fathers accepted the teaching of Montesquieu. They deliberately introduced a separation of powers, among the executive, legislative, and judicial branches, hoping that each would serve as a check on the potentially expansive urges of the others. All of these devices were embodied in a written constitution, which was initially amended to include a Bill of Rights, which suggested the strength of natural-law philosophy. The American government, almost uniquely, was derived from the conception of the people as the ultimate constituent power, from which a legal order in the form of a constitution emerges, but a constitution which, once chosen and written down, was acknowledged to define the set of rules under which the nation was to operate.[2] This was, indeed, a grand, in fact a glorious, design. And it was one that excited the world.

Fortuitous circumstances held back the actual growth of central government power until well into the Second Century. Before the end of the First Century, however, elements of the design had been effectively destroyed. Viable federalism, as a means of checking the expansion in power of the central government, has scarcely existed since the horrible civil war of the 1860's. With the Great Depression of the 1930's, the second major pillar of the American structural design collapsed. Governmental noninterference in economic life was replaced by that of governmental interference in details. The doctrine of intervention was accepted much earlier. Since the Great Depression, we have witnessed a continuing and accelerating growth in the American Leviathan.

Descriptively, we now live in what might best be called "constitutional anarchy," where the range and the extent of federal government dominance over all our lives, over all of our private behavior, is largely dependent on the accidental preferences of politicians in judicial, legislative, and executive positions of power. Increasingly, men feel themselves at the mercy of a faceless bureaucracy, itself irresponsible and subject to unpredictable twists and turns that destroy and distort personal and private expectations. Furthermore, men have little or no opportunity for redress or retribution. George Wallace's reference to the "brief-case carrying bureaucrats" strikes

2. This unique element in the American historical experience is emphasized by R. R. Palmer, *The Age of Democratic Revolution*, vol. 1 (Princeton: Princeton University Press, 1959).

home to many because of the demonstrable absurdities promulgated every-where in the name of liberal progress.

Far more serious than the bureaucratic invasion of our private world, however, is the judicial usurpation of power that proceeds apace, and which shows no sign of stopping. Judges have long since forgotten that their role is one of umpire, one of enforcing the rules of the game that are pre-established and quasi-permanent. Judges, and the law schools that train them, now con-ceive their own role to be that of making new rules as we go along, that of rewriting constitutional documents piece-meal to fit the whims of their own passing fancies.

This picture is perhaps even more frightening if we look, not at the spe-cific and illustrative instances of government interferences with our lives, but at the sheer quantitative impact of government, and, most notably, at its rate of growth in this century. In 1902, total government spending was but $1.7 billion. In 1970, it was $333 billion, and, of course, it is higher now. This means that total government spending has increased more than 200 times over during the seven decades.

A large share of this increase is obviously due to general inflation. But when we deflate these figures to constant dollar terms, to real terms, we still find that spending has increased 40 times over. As a share of GNP, govern-ment spending has moved from an eighth to a third. Government has come to dominate a larger and larger share of the economy, and, furthermore, the central government has been growing more rapidly than state and local gov-ernments.

If we project current trends forward, it is relatively easy to see that by the middle of the Third Century the whole of GNP would be required to support the public sector. But, of course, long before this point might be reached, the economic base for public sector growth would dry up; there would be no private economy left from which to collect revenues to finance the growing governmental sector.

It should be clear to everyone that our own particular Leviathan is on the loose; indeed it is on a rampage. It is high time that this monster in our midst be recognized for what it is. The government now exists and operates quite independent of the desires of citizens. It has a structure, and a will, of its own, and those of us who once might have hoped that the demands of the people could be translated easily into the actions of government must be grossly disappointed.

Let me be more specific. We can explain some of this massive growth of government by our own demands for more public goods and services. We have called on the government to do more for us, and we have all wallowed in the myth that there are governmental cures for all of our social ailments. If this were all there is to it, we might, in fact, hope to turn things around once we recognize the myth for what it is, once we give a new set of directions to our elected politicians.

Something of this sort may be happening, but I use the word "may" reservedly and with great caution. There are indeed signs and signals that suggest reaction against governmental dominance, against the expanding governmental influence over your lives and mine. This is, to me, one redeeming feature of the counterculture movement of the 1960's. Amidst much of the sound and fury, amidst the romantic sloganeering, amidst the violence and quasi-violence, amidst the hypocritically uncritical concern for social ills, there is a consistent rejection of bureaucratic-governmental solutions, or at least there was a rhetoric of rejection. There are paradoxes here, to which I shall return, but at the level of rhetoric, the whole movement is anticollectivist, antisocialist. It is, at base, anarchistic, and this, in itself, offers grounds for hope.

Quite apart from and far more significant than the emergence of the quasi-anarchistic counterculture are elements of a populist revolt, a revolt against the oppression of taxes imposed by governments at all levels, taxes that are increasingly seen to support unproductive and essentially parasitic members of society. George Wallace exploited this attitude successfully and expressed it in his slogan, "send them a message." It was in recognition of the strength of this attitude that Richard Nixon patterned his major electoral victory, and it was this that offered the origin for his second-term theme of budgetary restriction.

Before the Watergate disclosures, the "battle of the budget" dominated the 1973 policy discussion. What was this all about? President Nixon had, apparently, decided that continued explosive expansion in federal spending was neither popular with the citizenry nor desirable in itself. He had chosen this battleground deliberately; control over this aspect of our Leviathan had apparently become a major second-term objective. In this, the President appealed to all of us in our common role as taxpayers, but he also opposed many of us in our separate roles as beneficiaries of the federal gravy train, roles that are quite effectively represented by members of the Congress. Even before Watergate intruded, the outcome of this struggle was not at all clear, but should we not have found in the struggle itself some cause for optimism? Should we not have rejoiced that the issues were at least joined for the first time in this century?

There was indeed cause for optimism, and I personally applauded the President's efforts, whether these were based on personal conviction or political expediency or some combination of both. If, as the aging Walter Lippmann suggested in an interview,[3] Nixon's role was that of carrying forward and putting into action a general shift in the popular will, a generalized loss of faith in the ability of government to accomplish all good things, my own private concerns about our Third Century might not have materialized. But I was never so sanguine.

As my comments have suggested, President Nixon had the weight of logic and of history on his side in this struggle, and I also think that his position was, at base, much more closely attuned to what I have called mainstream American values than is that of his opposition. His electoral victory supports this presumption. Despite this correspondence with mainstream values, however, even before the Watergate disclosures, I predicted that the President's cause was a losing one, that his efforts to place checkreins on the growth of the federal establishment would fail.

If my supposition holds, if the President's efforts were both right and representative of mainstream values, then should he not have won the struggle with Congress, with those who represent special interests? Unfortunately, few who have looked carefully at the workings of American democracy would dare predict that the general interest can prevail over divergent special interests. Precisely because they do have special interests, offering them measurable and directly identifiable gains, individuals and groups are willing to invest both time and financial resources in influencing political outcomes.

Take an example, the university professor, like me, who secures occasional research support from the National Science Foundation. I am, personally, af-

3. Walter Lippmann, *Washington Post*, March 25, 1973.

fected much more directly by a cut in the budgetary allocation to NSF than I am by the minimal tax reduction that this cut would facilitate. Hence, I should, normally, be much more likely to write my congressman urging him to support appropriations to NSF than I am to write him urging him to keep my taxes down. Multiply this by several millions, and you may begin to get some idea as to why the workings of Congress are biased against overall, general programs designed to limit budgetary growth and to keep taxes down, and biased in favor of continued expansion in spending programs and increases in tax rates.

This is a flaw in our basic constitutional structure, a flaw that is now coming to be recognized by many, including political leaders in the Congress itself. But it is not a flaw that is going to be eliminated readily, especially since the pattern of continuous expansion in programs has been so long established.

If we expect individual members of Congress to shift their fiscal attitudes, to take a more comprehensive and long-run view of the whole taxing and spending process, their constituents must first modify their own behavior. Members of Congress represent constituencies; changes in the expressed attitudes of potential voters must precede changes in congressional views.

The larger question becomes: Can the American public adopt the more comprehensive view? Can the man-on-the-street, the middle American, the member of the silent majority, change his behavior *vis-à-vis* politics and politicians? Can he succeed in making articulate his intuitive sense that the time has come to do something about Leviathan? Is he willing to forego the immediate and apparent gratification that he seems to secure from government handouts in exchange for the additional freedom that he might gain in the Third Century?

As I have noted, I think that the potential for some reversal of priorities does exist, but I am not so certain as Walter Lippmann that this potential will be, or can be, made reality. Individual citizens, nonpoliticians, spend most of their time going about their ordinary affairs. They devote relatively little time and effort in acquiring information about social policy alternatives, about political programs. Aside from those specifics of policy that bear directly on their own interests, they economize. They rely on summary information offered by commercial media outlets, TV network news and commentary, newspaper reporting and editorializing. They accept what they are told, or they analyze the facts informed by their own educational training and experience.

Practical observation forces us to recognize that the inchoate, intuitive worries and concerns of the average citizen about the high level of taxes and government spending, about governmental interferences with his life, will not emerge as effective political programs until and unless these are formulated, expressed, and presented by the appropriate outlets in the intelligentsia, including the media.

There would be no cause for alarm here if the intelligentsia and the media were genuinely "representative" of constituency attitudes. But I fully share the increasing concern about the bias of the academic and intellectual establishment, about the increasing "distance" between the attitudes reflected in our schools, colleges, on our TV screens, and the attitudes that are genuinely expressive of the thinking of the ordinary man. I must be careful here. I am not saying that the role of the intellectual leader, including the journalist, is to mirror the prejudices of those he serves. Quite the opposite. I am recognizing that the academy and the intelligentsia can shape personal attitudes, can influence individual behavior, within certain wide limits. What concerns me is that the intellectual establishment, considered in the large, is now dominated by a point of view, a bias, if you will, which will simply not allow for a full articulation of the policy alternatives.

Any political leader or party that proposes to haul down the flag of federal government internal imperialism faces frustration at almost every turn. He finds himself advancing proposals that seem derived from "gut" reactions, and without the academic, intellectual respectability that is considered proper for serious media discourse. This is not because such proposals are inherently less amenable to such treatment. They can, in fact, be derived from arguments that are equal to if not more sophisticated than those which often accompany proposals advanced in opposition. Such arguments are absent because of the dominance in the media and in academia of a near-monolithic point of view on social issues, a point of view that is, at base, dirigiste or collectivist.

The conventional wisdom of the intelligentsia embodies a passionate defense of the collectivizing *status quo,* based on a naive and romanticized faith in the ability of the petty intellectuals to plan utopia for us all. In this respect, the establishment intellectuals, those who now hold positions of influence in the academy and in the media, are out of date, both when compared with their sometimes vocal student adversaries and with their less vocal or silent adversaries among the public at large.

The alienation of the intellectuals, the widening of the differences in attitude between the academicians-journalists and the general public, is now acknowledged to be increasing. This alienation provides the basis, in part, for my own predictions about America's start into its Third Century.

Two broad-based coalitions are forming, and there are signs of permanence in each. We can sense the emergence of a "new majority," geographically concentrated in the South, Middle and Far West, and functionally including the ethnic blue collar workers in the Northeast. Against this coalition there is arrayed the upper Eastern Establishment, the media and the intellectuals everywhere, and more importantly, the vast and expanding federal, state, and local bureaucracies whose direct interest lies in continued exploitation of the taxpayer.

Notably, these bureaucracies include the educational industry almost in total. This second coalition will include most of those who are the direct beneficiaries of federal spending programs, the special interest lobbies, and Congress will probably continue to be responsive largely to these groups. In addition, the damage done by Watergate to Nixon's attempts to weld permanence into the "new majority" may be mortal, in which case the governmental share in the economy will continue to grow almost without opposition, and more seriously, the government's interferences in all aspects of our lives will proceed apace.

The nation's Third Century promises, therefore, to commence in paradox. There is widespread disillusionment with bureaucracy, with taxes, with arbitrary judicial fiat. The productivity growth of the governmental sector is acknowledged to be zero if not negative. We have come to predict that most government programs will be failures. Yet we acquiesce as more and more programs are added while few, if any, wholly disappear.

Taxes that are introduced as temporary soon become permanent fixtures of the fiscal landscape. Clamors for tax reductions somehow get translated into proposals for tax reform, which, once again transformed, become proposals for soaking the rich as a means of securing more revenues for the government.

Something is amiss. How can we reduce the government's dominance over our lives when we do not know that other histories are possible? How can we have faith in an unknown even when we have lost most of our faith in the known? Collectively, we are as Hamlet. All of us have been born to the socialist gospels; we have lost the faith, but nothing has emerged to capture our imaginations as its replacement. If government cannot cure ailments, where are we to turn? This is the dilemma of our Third Century.

For us, in the 1970's, it is difficult to say, "let us dispense with governmental programs for this and that." It is as difficult for us as it was for Adam Smith to say almost the same thing in the 1770's. What was Adam Smith's central message, and what does it tell us now? It was simple yet profound. If government will get out of the act, if government will cease and desist, if government will leave things alone, many problems will solve themselves.

Note this message carefully, Adam Smith did not propose alternative solutions to particular social problems, which might have merely called forth a different set of plans and planners. Adam Smith said something far more shocking and much more profound. He said, "throw the rascals out, and don't let any other rascals in." "Quit trying too hard, and you will be surprised at the results." This simple truth is more basic than those applications that describe the economic theory of markets.

Put yet another way, Smith told his colleagues to "take a leap toward anarchy and away from Leviathan, if you do, the results will be better than you expect. Throw away your crutches, which are filled with lead, and you will find that you can walk."

Does this really tell us anything today, in 1973, almost at the start of the nation's Third Century? It is hard to think that it does; but does not this admission, in itself, suggest that we are all trapped in a collectivist ideology? Above all else, let us be honest with ourselves. We do not have the faith required to leap toward *anarchy*, despite our heightening disgust with Leviathan. And this includes those of us who come closest to philosophers who observe everything. We do not have a modern Adam Smith who can offer an intellectually satisfying description of a nongovernmental alternative. Until and unless we do have, our Third Century will be one of frustration, confusion, and paradox.

But this is not a counsel of despair. Within the limits of our talents, we can do much. Those of us in academia who do not blindly accept the prevailing fashions in social ideas can begin to construct effective counterarguments. We can, as some of us have been doing, analyze the failures of governments. We can begin to compute and measure the costs of collectivist follies.

These are steps that can be taken. These are things that may be done. Large things start with small beginnings, and there is nothing inevitable about failure. Carefully and constructively, a counterintelligentsia can be mobilized. It must be small at first, and its ideas must be developed so as to command respect even by those who are our ideological enemies. This task is not nearly so difficult as it might have been a decade past, during the obscenities of Camelot.

There are many intellectually honest men, and even those who cling to the socialist dreams are beginning to find gaping holes in the conventional arguments.[4] Many of these men, who combine intellectual honesty with a love of individual freedom, will join us in attempts to forestall the despot which lingers even more closely as governmental power expands. Out of this counterintelligentsia may come our Third Century Adam Smith, who will supplement our largely negativistic arguments with positive descriptions of some modern quasi-anarchistic alternatives.

These remarks summarize my hopes for the Third Century. Note that these hopes, even if realized, do not embody my own working plans for the Good Society. If I were God, I do not know what form of social order I should lay down for Third Century men. My hopes are grounded in humility and in faith. Humility in admission that no matter who does the planning, no man or group can plan the lives of other men effectively. Faith in the common sense of the common man, and faith that the processes of human interaction among free men will produce results grander than any man can foresee.

---

4. The shift in intellectuals' attitudes may be more significant than I have indicated here. This seems to be the opinion of Daniel P. Moynihan, as evidenced by the following statement: ". . . in the course of the 1960's the left adopted wholesale the arguments of the right. . . . By the end of the 1960's, an advanced student at an elite Eastern college could be depended upon to avow . . . that the growth of Federal power was the greatest threat to democracy. . . . The 1950's and 1960's was a period when conservative thinking had neither social nor intellectual status. A fairly traditional liberalism . . . was dominant in the national media and the academy . . ." (Daniel P. Moynihan, *The Politics of a Guaranteed Income,* New York: Random House, 1973).

My predictions and my hopes must be kept distinct. Even partial realization of my hopes will falsify my predictions. Given my choices, I much prefer to be a bad scientist living in the exciting Third Century of my hopes than to be a good scientist existing in the frustrating Third Century of my predictions.

# Analysis, Ideology and
# the Events of 1989

## I. Introduction

We have all been challenged to think about the consequences of the momentous events of 1989. My initial comment here is by way of confession; I continue to feel a sense of inadequacy in confrontation of the current history that we have observed. I find it difficult to think clearly, to organize analysis, to model reality so that it makes sense, even in an abstracted structure that only those of us who deal mainly in ideas would find helpfully explanatory. It is no excuse to suggest that our mind-set is appropriate only for relatively stable nonrevolutionary circumstances, and that the revolutionary events of 1989 must, necessarily, remain outside the limits of current interpretation. For me, reliance on such an excuse would undermine the legitimacy of the whole academic-intellectual enterprise. If those of us who earn our keep by thinking are confused by the onrush of events, how can we expect others, who work while we philosophize, to accord us the respect that we sometimes claim?

An American political scientist, Fukuyama, provoked a spirited discussion in 1989 and 1990 with an article entitled "The End of History."[1] For the most part, Fukuyama's critics failed to acknowledge the central challenge that was contained in his article. We may, of course, suggest that "history" was the wrong term to deploy, but we may restate the challenge in a set of questions: What was it that ended in 1989 and the years immediately preceding? Can we

(Zürich: Bank Hofmann AG, 1991), 7–23. Reprinted by permission of the publisher.

1. Francis Fukuyama, "The End of History," *National Interest*, no. 16 (Summer 1989): 3–18.

deny that something has, indeed, ended? Can we think about the world in the same way that we did before 1989? Are we not required to look, not merely through a different window, but at a different world?

That which has ended is a vision of socio-economic-political reality, a vision that was itself an integral part of the world, if for no other reason than the fact that individuals made choices on the basis of that vision. The set of ideas from which that vision was constructed, which we may label "collectivist-socialist," which derived initial inspiration from Hegel and which was converted into revolutionary reality by Marx, no longer exists as a meaningful intellectual-emotional foundation for social organization, either as an idealized alternative to that which is observed or as an idealized description of any system of socio-political order in existence. That is to say, we must now look at the complexities of social interaction among persons and associations of persons without resort to the collectivist-socialist utopia or dystopia as a helpmate in our analysis, interpretation and evaluation.

If we accept the proposition that "ideas have consequences," then we must predict that the unanticipated disappearance of the collectivist-socialist vision of socio-political order will ultimately generate profound changes in the course of history. But what form will these changes take? Will some new dialectic emerge, and, if so, what conflicts in principle will describe it?

It is here that I feel most embarrassed intellectually. I think, along with Keynes, that ideas do exert influences on events. But I find it difficult to "get handles" on an analysis of possible futures in the post-socialist epoch. Are we poised on the verge of some as yet undiscovered and unexploited motivating idea that will excite individuals sufficiently to generate political action?

In what follows, I want to advance some "speculations on a theme," which should be taken as little more than that. They surely do not deserve to be called predictions; possibly they might qualify as conjectures.

## II. Politics in the Large and in the Small

For another lecture I have used the title "Socialism Is Dead but Leviathan Lives On."[2] The collectivist-socialist vision that has lost all of its appeal is that

---

2. James M. Buchanan, "Socialism Is Dead but Leviathan Lives On," the John Bonython Lecture, CIS Occasional Paper 30 (Sydney: Centre for Independent Studies, 1990).

of the centrally planned and controlled economy, with individuals finding their own realization as integral components in socialist community. It is now universally acknowledged that this sort of economy does not work; it does not produce goods. And, further, the experience of the century indicates that individuals do not shed their individuality in artificially collectivized communities. Politicization in the large has, in this sense, been almost totally discredited.

That which has not been discredited by the demise of socialism is politics in the small, by which I mean piece-by-piece interference with market processes. The economies of the nations that have not been subjected to centralized planning and control are described by literally hundreds of politically imposed controls, regulations and restrictions, in the form of quotas, tariffs, price, wage and rent floors or ceilings, prohibitions on investment, on entry, exit, occupational mobility, etc. The list could be extended. There has been no crossing of the bridge between the rejection of socialism, that is, politicization in the large, and politicization in the small. Individuals, as members of the body politic, or their intellectual and/or political leaders-agents, have not, generally, come to any acceptance of the notion that if politicization does not work when applied over all markets it will not work when applied for particular markets, taken one at a time.

The crossing of this particular intellectual-evaluative bridge will be difficult for reasons that are well known to those who have followed developments in modern public choice theory. Economists, since Adam Smith, have been almost unanimous in their scientific judgment that politicized interference with single markets, one at a time, destroys potential economic value.

Throughout the two centuries of its existence as a body of scientific discourse, political economy has provided the positive basis for the normative condemnation of piecemeal intervention with the workings of markets.

There have been precious few economists who have claimed that price controls, tariffs, entry barriers, etc., increase economic value. By contrast with the fundamental intellectual oversight that characterized economists' attitudes toward socialist organization (the oversight that Hayek has aptly called the fatal conceit), there has been no epistemological failure represented by a misunderstanding of the effects of politicized piecemeal controls over markets.[3]

---

3. F. A. Hayek, *The Fatal Conceit* (Chicago: University of Chicago Press, 1989).

Over many decades, economists have experienced frustration as they observed politicians and political forces continue to impose and to implement restrictions, controls and regulations, market by market, in the apparent total disregard for the acknowledged effect of destroying potential economic value. Why have, and why do, politicians, and especially those directly responsive to electoral constituencies, seem so uninterested in the generation of value? Why does economic efficiency carry so little political weight?

Public choice theory supplies a relatively easy answer to these questions. Politicians are indeed responsive to the evaluations of those constituents whom they represent. But a characteristic feature of any single market intervention, taken in isolation, lies in the concentration of benefits and the dispersal of costs. The costs of the market restriction, taken overall and measured inclusively, may exceed the benefits, and, by the theorems of economics, will normally do so, but so long as there is a disparity in the distribution, as between the two sides of the account, political response is likely to be favorable to the more concentrated set of persons affected, the beneficiaries. The relative concentration of benefits prompts investment in information about the consequences of political action, and this is matched by investment in efforts to influence political agents. At the same time, and in parallel with this, the larger number of potential losers, each of whom is affected slightly, remain rationally ignorant and invest neither in information nor in political influence.

This elementary "logic of collective action," to use Mancur Olson's terminology here, applies, however, only if the destruction of potential value can be organized and implemented on a piecemeal basis, that is, by interfering with one market at a time.[4] If politicized interventions are extended, simultaneously, over many markets, the shortfall in value will become evident for all to see, both constituents and leaders. In this case, we should predict some rough equivalent, politically, to the reaction against centralized planning and socialist organization that we now observe.

4. Mancur Olson, *The Logic of Collective Action* (Cambridge: Harvard University Press, 1965).

## III. The Future for Laissez-Faire

We should not, of course, expect to observe any simultaneous extension of politicized control to all or even to many markets in an economy. The politics of constituency response will proceed in steps, as political entrepreneurs build up interest group support, not necessarily one group at a time, but in minimal coalitions as required by logrolling within the allowable decision rules. And even if the effects, overall, may be the destruction of a major share of the value potential of an economy, any simultaneous dismantling of the politicized control network, as extended over many markets, will prove exceedingly difficult to organize.

But let us return to the possible relationship between ideas and events. The 18th century was marked by the genuine discovery that depoliticized and decentralized markets allowed to operate within a framework of law produce more wealth than the mercantilist organizational alternative. This discovery, by Adam Smith and his peers, excited the minds of those who came to the new understanding, and classical political economy provided the intellectual-analytical basis for major political reforms that embodied the dismantling of much of the mercantilist apparatus.

The situation in the 1990s is, in some respects, comparable to that of the late 18th and early 19th centuries. We have discovered (rediscovered) that socialism as an economy-organizing principle does not work, that efforts at politicized displacement of a market economy must fail to produce the goods and services that citizens desire. And we share in a broad understanding of this observed failure. Major reforms have taken, and are taking, place that involve the privatization-marketization of previously socialized economies.

As I have noted, however, piece-by-piece politicization of those national economies that were never explicitly socialist in either a structural or an ideological sense has proceeded apace. And there has been little or no idea-generated feedback that motivates political reform here, because the controls in these economies were put in place in the face of a ruling scientific consensus to the effect that potential value was thereby being destroyed. Hence, there is no discovery or rediscovery waiting to be made, no newfound understanding of the simple principle that free markets do, indeed, produce more highly valued bundles of goods and services.

Nonetheless, the standard arguments for the extension of politicized control over particular markets may prove less persuasive in the post-socialist epoch. The claim that "politics works better" as applied to a single market or group of markets may seem more questionable with the widening recognition that "politics works worse," in the large, as applied over all markets. But it would be naive to expect something akin to public renewal, of the general principle of laissez-faire, except possibly in those economies that were formerly under socialist organization. In western welfare states, there will be no recapture of the imagination that could be even remotely comparable to the understanding and enlightenment that followed on the teachings of the classical economists. The intellectual leaders have understood how markets work; and they have rejected markets, almost universally, in favor of the socialist alternative, on the false notion that socialism "works better." Now that they must, however reluctantly, acknowledge socialism's failure, in both a relative and an absolute sense, where will they turn?

## IV. Legitimacy and Liberty

My speculation (and I insist that it is no more than this) leaves the intellectuals in the western welfare states out of account, more or less as the Marxists were allowed to lapse into irrelevancy during the last decades of socialism's effective life. I am able to think about a post-socialist future in which significant political change emerges from a shift in the attitudes of ordinary citizens, from, as it were, a genuine revolution in "public philosophy," and one that the intellectuals can only follow, and very reluctantly at that.

Return to the events of the 1980s. By 1989, there came to be a near universal acknowledgement that socialist organization of an economy fails to produce goods and services, as desired by citizens. In short, socialism has been proven to be grossly inefficient in producing value. A second, and equally important, feature of socialist organization was also widely acknowledged, and particularly by those who were direct participants. The socialist economy maximizes the control of the bureaucracy over the lives of ordinary citizens, while most persons share in the normative precept that dictates minimization. The excessive bureaucratization of life under socialism was as significant in causing the system's collapse as the deficiency in generating valued output.

The public reaction against bureaucratization had been working its way throughout the structure of social interaction long before any formalized reform in the socialist structure took place. Persons in socialist regimes learned to seek out and to find ways and means to subvert the ubiquitous bureaucratic restrictions. "Free markets" emerged, even if these were variously described as "shadow," "black" and "underground" and, in all cases, remained formally illegal. As socialism came to be formally supplanted, nominally on grounds of efficiency, there was a carryover of attitudes to the effect that the bureaucratic intrusions characteristic of socialism were "illegitimate" as well as inefficient. Politicization of economic life in the large was universally seen to fail, on efficiency grounds, but politicization, as bureaucratization, was also seen to be illegitimate, on fundamental moral principle. Persons claimed the rights to trade when, as, if and with whom they choose. "Free to choose" assumed moral force.

This reference to the shift in attitudes in formerly socialist economies may exert important spillover effects on attitudes in western welfare states. I have already suggested earlier that the arguments from efficiency alone will offer relatively little assistance in the depoliticization of particularized restrictions on the separate workings of markets. There are gainers as well as losers from each such restriction, and the concentrated gains are more likely to stimulate political response than the dispersed losses, despite the preponderance of losses over gains, in the aggregate. But the argument from legitimacy cannot be countered so easily. To the extent that citizens claim that they possess moral rights to participate in voluntary market exchanges, free of politicized interferences, those who would deny such claims are forced into a defense of political-bureaucratic coercion, with the failed socialist experiments of the century standing omnipresent in the background.

Might we not expect that attitudes toward the politically orchestrated coercion of the western welfare states will undergo major shifts as the philosophical grounding of collectivism is discredited? Why should the politicians and bureaucrats who act for the welfare states be accorded a degree of public respect and honor that is so totally at variance with the status of their counterparts in the now-despised institutional residues of socialism? (There may, of course, be some difference in public attitudes when democratic procedures themselves lend legitimacy to the actions of bureaucratic agents.)

I suggest that the argument from liberty, the argument that advances the claim of the individual to freedom from state coercion in voluntary economic transactions, may provide the emotional-evaluative source for the breakdown and erosion of the "legitimacy" of western regulatory politics. And it is important to recognize that legitimacy matters. The bureaucratized regulatory intrusions in the market economy in western welfare states require widespread voluntary acquiescence. A simple shift in perception, in attitudes, followed by action, on the part of a relatively small number of market participants would, very quickly, lead to an erosion of the effectiveness of the political control apparatus. How long could a price ceiling imposed on the sale of a standard commodity remain effective in a setting where persons almost universally deny the legitimacy of majoritarian politics to interfere in market pricing?

I am not, of course, imagining a scenario that is nonexistent, even in the best-ordered western societies. Secondary and nominally illegal markets are present wherever and whenever political control establishes artificial scarcities. Illegal drugs are produced, supplied, demanded and consumed; prostitution persists; "key" prices supplement controlled rents; persons are employed at subminimal wages; street vendors peddle contraband goods; currency transactions replace traceable funded exchanges. And, as attempts at politicized regulation of markets extends further, the share in total economic value originated in and processed through the "underground" sector increases, as witness experience in Latin America and, for Europe, in Italy.

This discernible erosion of the control apparatus in the welfare state may, prior to the late 1980s, be attributable largely to those in the citizenry who have little or no respect for law generally. What I am suggesting here is that these persons will be joined in increasing numbers by others who gradually come to the realization that political restrictions on their voluntary choices, imposed for the explicit benefit of specialized interests, no longer command legitimacy. Once the bloom is off the romance that was collectivism, a romance that captured public imagination in all parts of the world for more than a century, politicized restrictions on individual liberties must meet a much more severe standard in order to be accepted.

## V. The Politics, Law and Economics of Disorder

The socio-political-economic setting that may emerge, in both western and eastern countries, is perhaps equidistant from George Orwell's totalitarian dystopia and the ideally ordered utopia of the classical liberal followers of Adam Smith. Centralized collectivist controls over the economic interactions of citizens may be less extensive than might have been predicted in 1980. And, even where such controls nominally exist, they may be treated with more disdain and contempt, even to the extent that fully effective enforcement becomes impossible. This side of the equation in the post-socialist epoch may seem, taken alone, to gladden the heart of the classical liberal, whose idealized polity is described by a state that is constrained constitutionally while remaining powerful within its authorized limits. But the predicted loosening-removal of collectivist controls, and public attitudes toward politics generally, may also extend to those institutions of political order that the classical liberal judges to be minimally necessary for viable social interaction.

Having rejoiced in the destruction of the collectivist myth that the "state knows best," the classical liberal may also observe a weakening and erosion of the "civic religion" that embodies general agreement that "on some matters, the state, as reflecting a set of shared values, indeed, does know best." It seems at least within the possible that the collectivist-socialist mystique that has provided one source legitimacy to politics generally will, like a ball of yarn, unravel so rapidly that fully legitimate, and indeed necessary, political processes will be undermined, in which case libertarian anarchy may offer perhaps a useful descriptive analytical model for the post-socialist epoch.

In this sense, disorder rather than order might be characteristic of the societies in the next decades. The university campuses of the 1960s may prove to be the demonstration models for the inclusive communities of the upcoming century. Agitators in the streets, subject to crowd psychology and highly vulnerable to demagogic persuasion, may become even more commonplace than today. Governments, manned by responsive political agents, will be unable to act because there will be no moral force behind a will to govern. Citizens may increasingly refuse to pay taxes, both in their private capacities as evaders and avoiders and in their public choice capacities as potential voting supporters of tax proposing parties and politicians. Governments may come to rely, increasingly, on the residually remaining power to levy taxation through inflation. Public goods, even within the narrowly defined limits of conservative argument, may not be provided, or, if financed at all, may be minimally extended, accompanying services badly performed and facilities poorly maintained.

Crime, against both persons and property, may continue to increase as the legitimacy of basic enforcement is reduced as a necessary complement to the erosion of the legitimacy of politics. The public image of the policeman as the agent of the state, the potential enforcer of law that may itself not be legitimate, may further encourage citizenry collusion with criminals. And those who are themselves policemen may come to fear the prospects for citizens' reaction against possible overzealous enforcement more than they value the law that they exist to enforce.

The individual may find himself or herself relatively free from bureaucratic restriction imposed through political agency, but an alternative source of inefficiency may be present in the form of vulnerability to opportunistic behavior on the part of other persons with whom mutually advantageous economic interchange might seem possible. Contracts for delivery of services may be difficult to enforce, and agreed-on terms of exchange may lose meaning in the absence of well-defined legal rules. Economic transactions may, necessarily, come to be based more on personal relationships of trust, surely a retrogressive step in the historical evolution of markets in western countries.

The courts of law in western countries will, themselves, have aided and abetted in the emergence of the disorder that I have sketched briefly here. Lawyers, and judges, were, like their peers in other leadership roles, caught up in the romantic vision of politics that described the socialist epoch. They justified, and formally legitimized, discretionary bureaucratic restrictions on the economic liberties of persons, regardless of the consistency of such restrictions either with the letter or the spirit of the historical constitutional structures.

In contradistinction with the politically subservient courts in socialist regimes, courts in western democracies, and particularly in the United States, attempted to erect and to maintain wholly arbitrary and artificial differences between the economic and the noneconomic liberties of persons in terms of protection from political intrusion. The noneconomic liberties, such as those of speech, press, assembly, religion and franchise were zealously protected, while the economic liberties of trade, location, entry, exit, occupation, etc., were held to be subject to the dictates of majoritarian politics and its accompanying bureaucracy. The situation in the United States has reached absurd limits; in 1990, it is unconstitutional for the government to restrict an individual's liberty to burn the flag of the country, but fully constitutional for the government, central or local, to restrict an individual's liberty to make a mutually advantageous and voluntary exchange with another person, on terms of their own choosing. Such absurdities in the law cannot, of course, find any justification in ideas, and, ultimately, individuals must be allowed the simple economic liberties.

Again, if treated in isolation, this possible spillover from the demise of the socialist vision must be applauded. But if economic liberties are defined to include exchanges in rental housing, what is to prevent them being defined to include exchanges in addictive drugs, body parts and babies? The answer must, of course, lie in a generalized public understanding of the differences between those politically imposed constraints that are "constitutionally legitimate" and those that are not.

## VI. Order within Constitutional Limits

I have labelled my remarks as speculative rather than predictive (and a respected critic has suggested that the preceding section is wholly out of place). I should stress that the symptoms of disorder described above need not emerge in the decades ahead when the citizenry must, in some fashion, learn to live with post-socialist reality. Hayek has stated that he wrote his great polemical essay, *The Road to Serfdom,* not so much as prediction but as warning. He sought to tell his temporal peers that unless counterposing ideas were promulgated and actions taken, the serfdom that was socialism was indeed the likely future.[5] For western countries his warning may, in small measure, have prevented the future that he feared. My speculations here should be taken in the same spirit. The constitutional-legal-political-economic anarchy that I have sketchily outlined to be within the possible need not occur, in eastern or western societies, if the central ideas of classical liberalism can be rediscovered and understood, and if the political choices made by individual citizens come to reflect these ideas.

As I indicated by the subtitle of one of my own books, the society within which we can live in peace, prosperity and liberty lies "between anarchy and Leviathan."[6] For well over a century, social scientists and social philosophers

5. F. A. Hayek, *The Road to Serfdom* (Chicago: University of Chicago Press, 1944).
6. James M. Buchanan, *The Limits of Liberty: Between Anarchy and Leviathan* (Chicago: University of Chicago Press, 1975).

have failed in their task of providing the public with a general understanding of the ordering principles of viable social order. We now have the totally unanticipated opportunity to move into the intellectual vacuum that the demise of socialism has created. There will be no rebirth of socialism as an intellectually respectable ideology; of that we can be certain. But some modern variant of the Hobbesian warre of "each against all," defined over groups, may find its own persuasive ideological advocates, with the result that we may, once again, find ourselves in a disordered "solution" that insures minimal rather than maximal benefits to all.

Citizens, either in single polities or as combined, have a common purpose in organizing politics to allow persons to get on with their lives, while at the same time living with some assurance that politics will not get beyond its duly constituted limits. The voluntary interactions among persons in sets of interlinked markets generates social order, even if the results, as such, are not within the grand design of any person, party or state. But the social order of the market can degenerate into the disorder of anarchy unless market relationships are embedded within a constitutional-legal framework where individual rights of person and property are well defined, mutually respected and enforced. This constitutional framework that is necessary for the functioning order of the market must also contain well-defined and enforceable limits on the range and scope for political action. The legitimacy of politics must track the constitutional limits.

# Politicized Economies in Limbo
## America, Europe and the World, 1994

---

Nineteen ninety-four is a useful year for taking stock. We are five years on from the revolutions of 1989; we are a full decade past the celebration of George Orwell's exemplary year, 1984. Now, we knew long before 1984 that George Orwell's precautionary predictions were going to be falsified. And we should have known well before 1989 that the communist socialized regimes in Central and Eastern Europe and the Soviet Union—regimes that reigned at centralized command and control—were not sustainable over a long term. But we paid little or no attention to what the extensively politicized economies of the West or the East would look like in the era following the Cold War, when Germany was reunified and when there was no longer the hovering threat of superpower nuclear conflict.

If only Francis Fukuyama's grand predictions could have become reality, or more soberly, if only we could in mid-1994 discern some signs that the world would be moving in the directions Fukuyama dreamed about.

Let me digress for a minute and tell those of you who are not familiar with him, who Francis Fukuyama is and what his dreams are about. Francis Fukuyama is a young American political philosopher; being a Hegelian he was very strongly influenced by the work of a French Hegelian who wrote in the 1930s. He developed this view that we really were at the end of history in terms of Hegelian dialectic. The dialectic between individualism on the one hand and collectivism on the other had now been played out with the revo-

From *Nobelpreisträger James M. Buchanan in Jena, München und Bayreuth, 7–15 Juni 1994* (Munich: Herbert Quandt Stiftung, 1994), 18–23. Reprinted by permission of the publisher.

lutions of 1989, so therefore we had come to the end of history. He wrote a book published in 1992 called *The End of History and the Last Man*. In the book he argues not only that we have come to the end of history in this Hegelian dialectical sense, but also that henceforward all economies would be organized on market principles: the great scientific truths of classical economics would be accepted as scientific truth, so all societies would organize their economies in terms of markets, and at the same time they would organize their politics as liberal democracies because this was the only type of system that would generate mutual respect for all citizens. Well, so much for Fukuyama's grand dreams. I'll come back to that in a minute. That was his book, and it stirred up a lot of excitement and a lot of criticism, as you can imagine.

Yes, indeed, there is a science of economics. Economists find their *raison d'être* in laying out for the public and politicians alike the conditions that must be met if economies are to grow and prosper. We know what those conditions are, but there is a considerable difference between the applicability of economic scientific teachings and those of the natural sciences. I am going to discuss that in some detail in a minute. After that I will shift perspective a bit and offer some suggestions about the failures of economic science. Why have these findings of economic science not found emplacement in democratic reality? After that I will look a little bit at what we call the equilibrium of interest in the politicized economies of modern democracies. How much total value that might be produced will we sacrifice to what has been appropriately called the "black hole of distributional politics"? I think the metaphor there is very useful. Is there some natural limit to how much value we are potentially going to destroy by distributional politics? After that I am going to introduce the necessary competitiveness among nations as the phenomenon of modern history that may check the implosion of value that majoritarian democracy now seems to promise us. In that discussion I shall examine the role of a European confederation and the workings of competitive federalism more generally; both for Europe and beyond. Finally, at the end, I will return to more familiar territory and discuss the constitutional interest that may well reflect the teachings of economic science. After all, we have to recognize that constitutional revolutions do occur, and the interdependence of the global economy can serve political as well as economic purpose.

Now let me go to that comparison I suggested between the sciences of nature and the sciences of man. Recall what I said about Fukuyama's prediction: His prediction was to the effect that with this century's dramatic falsification of the socialist hypothesis that command and control of economic activity can generate value at levels comparable to those generated under market institutions. That hypothesis has been totally falsified. On the basis of that falsification Fukuyama argued that nations everywhere would reorganize their economies, so as to reflect a final—maybe begrudging—acceptance of the truth of classical political economy. So then markets would become the standard or normal form through which persons and groups would be allowed to carry on their ordinary economic activities. Governments would than presumably back off, pull back from an activist interference stance, the dirigiste mindset would disappear and governments would limit themselves to the establishment, maintenance and enforcement of supportive constitutional legal frameworks.

But of course, as we know, Fukuyama's grand prediction shows no sign of becoming reality. There is no indication that economic science, in the broad sense that's relevant here, carries any more respect and authority in this post-revolutionary moment of 1994 than it did in 1984 or even earlier. Observed political and policy discourse, whether this be in America or in Europe, proceeds as if the revolutions of 1989 simply didn't occur. The rhetoric of the Clinton Administration in the United States today marks a return to that of the 1960s, to an era when policy activism was in flower, when the fatal conceit that was descriptive of political and public attitudes was present and well before the incentives that were allegedly rediscovered in the '70s and the '80s.

The question is why? Why economic science is so different from its natural science counterpart. Technological advances that are based on developments and experiments in the natural sciences continue to generate changes that allow us to get more valued outputs from the inputs that we have available. There are, of course, distributional losses imposed on persons who may have invested human or nonhuman capital in technologies that are displaced, but, at worst, those persons can delay changes through political action. Because, however, it always remains in the interest of some persons to introduce the technological advances that are resultant from scientific progress, the ultimate direction of change is guaranteed.

But matters are quite different with reference to changes in economic structure that may promise increases in the overall generation of value. Potential gainers from the teachings of economic science are likely to be spread among the whole population and to be very large in numbers. There is unlikely to be very high differential profit to anyone in particular upon the introduction of economic reform that simply opens up markets. Efficiency-increasing structural changes may be introduced only through concerted political action. And organized private support for such change may be very difficult to organize, despite the promised increase in total value. Even when reforms are proposed, organized groups may use the same avenues of political action deliberately to reduce or to destroy value potential.

Each person's direct economic interest is in the size of total value under his or her control or command or that of his or her group. But this objective may be gained by getting a larger share in an aggregate that remains unchanged or even falls, and by holding the same or even a smaller share in a larger aggregate. Consider a person who thinks of the prospects of getting, through politically organized action, an increase in income from two to three deutschmarks, even with the full knowledge that the aggregate value in the whole economy is going to fall by two deutschmarks in the process. The person gains a deutschmark; others in the economy lose two. The game is negative sum, as we say. In the distributional politics of modern majoritarian democracies there is little scope for the application of straightforward economic science.

But who has any direct action interest in the aggregate wealth of a nation? And who should have such an interest?

Now, here is the normative contradiction that does confront anyone who takes a classical liberal position. Margaret Thatcher, as you recall, was roundly chastized for her statement that there is no society as such. Her intent in that statement was to suggest that only individuals offer the loci of value and evaluation. But taken literally, there could then exist no national interest, no national purpose, no national vision—whether for Germany, the United States or any other nation-state or group thereof. Yet almost all commentators—academicians and media alike—proceed as if such an aggregate of interest exists, and regardless of their own position on some ideological spectrum. It's almost as if we are forced willy-nilly to adopt an organicist conception of society, while simultaneously mouthing individualist norms in our philosophies.

There is indeed a problem, and this problem finds acute historical placement in this post-revolutionary moment of the middle 1990s. During the long Cold War the normative claims of individualism could be shunted aside, and adherence to the rhetoric of national goals could go unchallenged and unchallengeable. Germany, the United States, the West generally; these entities took on moral significance, and the wealth of nations, defined as the aggregate value of production along with the rate of growth in this value, became a criterion of comparative measurement. To survive in the international conflict with communism, the West required a productive economy. There was a truly common interest in the economic prosperity and growth over and beyond that reflected in privately separable shares of value. Purely distributional objectives with the consequent domestic conflict over these objectives could, at least to an extent, sublimate it to furtherance of this more comprehensive purpose. That is to say the Cold War held the welfare transfer state somewhat in check.

But the Cold War is over, and the West won. But what does this portend for private interest in the wealth of nations? Why should the citizen be concerned with other than his own private separate share in economic prosperity, except for probabilistic calculations? Can we not predict a veritable explosion in the basic distributional politics of democracy once the partially relevant encompassing interest dictated by the Cold War disappears totally from public and political consciousness?

Now, we seem to observe what this model predicts. In the United States in 1993, we witnessed a return to class warfare rhetoric that we had not heard for half a century. In 1994, we are now witnessing a massive effort to transform a major sector of our economy that is motivated primarily by distributional objectives. These 1993 and 1994 initiatives will almost surely reduce, and perhaps substantially reduce, the potential wealth of the nation as conveniently measured. But to what matter? There is simply no calculus of interest that can stand as a board against the political entrepreneurs who always seek to exploit opportunities for differential distributional games. The only criterion for acceptability becomes political success. The winning coalition of interest legitimizes itself as it succeeds independent of any effect on aggregate value.

The politicized economies of Western countries then are in deficit, to return a bit to the more general title. They are in deficit along many dimensions. This includes, of course, the obvious fiscal transfer of value from future taxpayers to current beneficiaries, as represented in the actual deficit financing of governments. Claimant client groups—whether organized geo-graphically, as is the case in Germany, or by age, as in the United States and elsewhere, and by other shared features—are sufficiently strong to prevent any political curbs on rates of growth and entitlement subsidies. On the other hand, productive income-earners surely will resist further tax increases that promise no return in measurable private benefits.

Anthony de Jasay wrote a book in 1985 which he called *The State,* and he talked about different stages. One stage he talks about is the "churning state," where these different groups are transferring money back and forth through the state. Well, his "churning state" is with us, but the transfers are not limited to those who are current givers or current takers. Massive deficit financing burdens future taxpayers who aren't with us. Thereby they guarantee that the conflict between welfare state dependence and productive income-earners is going to get more serious in future years. Someone surely must pay for the spending that now goes through the public budgets, all the spending. Are the income-earners of the next century likely to quietly accept their personal obligations to pay off the accumulated debts that we are incurring in the 1990s? Why should they do so? I think the whole question of the obligation of future generations to meet the debts that we are accumulating is a subject that economists and ethicists ought to study a good deal more thoroughly.

Now let me move on and talk a little bit about the possibility of there emerging some equilibrium interest. Almost all observers agree that the politicized sectors of Western democracies are too large. They are too large in the sense that more economic value could surely be produced from the available resources that we have if we could reduce the size of the public sector, however you want to measure it. Surely a national economy does not produce its highest value when more than one-half of the gross domestic product is in public outlay, at one level of government or another. And in Germany, as you know, that share is now fifty-five percent. If socialism in the large fails so dramatically that we could all observe it, how can socialism in the not so small be expected to work?

The question of most relevance here does not really concern the absolute size of the public sector so much as the perspective change in this size. So long as the politicized sector could stay relatively stable in share of total product, the overall economy might work tolerably well, despite the obvious opportunity cost that would continue to be in lost value potential.

But what are the prospects for either more or less politicization in Western democracies over the remaining years of this century and the early years of the next? In other words, have we already in 1994 got to an equilibrium of sorts? Have all of the groups who might successfully get their profits through political action, even at the expense of overall economic productivity, exhausted their potential opportunities? Will they then acquiesce in their current measured claims on others? Will the German public sector stabilize its current fifty-five percent of gross domestic product? Will the United States shift its priorities from defense to transfer spending while maintaining its relatively low public-sector share? Or will the increase in transfer spending level off? Or will, which I would predict and I fear, political interest succeed in moving America toward European levels?

I have studied these questions, and I don't find a simple analytical logic that allows me to identify what we could call an equilibrium level for the size of the politicized sector, even in the stylized sense that economists might like to use. We could work with tax reaction functions, and we could work with Laffer-curve-type speculations that work with public choice models. All of these might yield us some interesting results, but relatively little that is generally definitive could be produced from these models. As I noted earlier, when the Cold War was on, in the Cold War game between East and West, there were both economic and military targets, and there was a trade-off that was recognized. There was a trade-off point beyond which distributional interest might have been held in check. But without such a trade-off, where is the ceiling? As I say, I haven't been able to work out a logic of an equilibrium.

Now let me shift to a little bit more hopeful note and talk about competitiveness among nations. Limits on the destruction of potential economic value owing to the distributional politics of majoritarian democracy may be indirectly imposed by the necessary competitiveness among separate political units—that is, among the nation-states—in an increasingly interdependent worldwide economic nexus. In a very real sense, the emerging international competitiveness has replaced, and will continue to replace, the economic elements of the Cold War, even if the results are generated very differently in the two cases. A single nation-state that is totally isolated from the world economic nexus might well allow its internal distributional politics to destroy a very large share of the potential economic value that its resource base would make possible.

But to the extent that the economy of any nation-state is integrated with those of other political units, efforts to extend fiscal transfers as well as regulatory intrusions into its economy may well be thwarted. A single country cannot readily impose, for example, rates of tax on its resources or goods that are much above those levels in other countries with whom trade takes place without setting off undesirable shifts in the terms of trade or outward resource flows. That is to say, the basic discipline of the market is to place severe limits on the nonproductive enterprise of political rent-seeking.

Technological developments, especially those stemming from the information communications revolution, may guarantee increase in economic interdependence among separate nations. When you can transfer funds around the world at the speed of light, maybe the technology itself may have an economic effect of significant importance. A former student of mine and a former colleague—Richard McKenzie and Dwight Lee—have written a book which they called *Quicksilver Capital*, in which they argue to the effect that the technology of the information communications revolution itself is going to guarantee that the size of politicization in economies is going to be more limited in the future. To the extent that this historical trend does take place, the value-destroying activities of rent-seeking coalitions are going to be internally inhibited. The overextended welfare state may find its days numbered in that case, unless coalitions among separate states can effectively curtail the welfare sectors of several states, thereby preventing the pressures of international competitiveness. Of course, this is precisely what Brussels is trying to do to Europe.

It is useful at this point to discuss briefly the prospect for the countries of Western Europe in the movement toward European confederation. As I have stated in other connections, my current assessment is that Europe has already missed out on a once-in-history opportunity to achieve economic greatness through integration into a genuinely competitive federalism, in which the advantages of a larger market might well have been secured, while at the same time the forces of interstate competition could have been relied on to forestall undue internal politicization. But prospects in Europe do not seem so bright in 1994 as they were in 1990. Largely because of the offsetting forces of Brussels' bureaucratization and nationalistic intransigency, the urge toward regularization and harmonization of the several economies as dictated by and from Brussels and as reflected in the Maastricht Treaty runs counter to any unleashing of the potential efficiency-enhancing forces of interstate competitiveness.

In 1990, I gave a lecture in Paris in which I was strongly urging Europe's chance to take this once-in-history opportunity and move into a genuine competitive federalism. I was very surprised about the reaction to that talk, because I assumed that the forces of Brussels' socialism would have been changed by the events of 1989, and I was surprised how strongly Delors' position was still maintained. Furthermore, I was very surprised by the intransigency of, particularly, the British view of a refusal to give up any national sovereignty. So, I found myself right down the middle with attacks from both the right and the left, which made me think I must have been saying something right.

A strong but severely limited central authority for Europe is needed, an authority that can effectively enforce the free flow of resources and goods across national frontiers. But this authority should not extend to include the imposition of regularization requirements on the separate political units. Nor should a single currency and a single central bank be a part of the whole competitive federalism scheme. Europe has over the last few years—it seems to me—faced an almost ideal time for the introduction of something like Hayek's proposal for competitive monies. Each nation's central bank should be allowed to issue its own currency, as it does now, but each and every citizen of Europe should be constitutionally protected in the liberty to make contracts in any currency, including the payment of taxes. Just think what discipline that would impose on the central banks. I realize, of course, that the Europe of 1994 seems a long way from attaining this ideal of a competitive federalism that did seem possible, to me, in 1990. But let's recall that there are forces of history at work, and the failure of the dirigiste to secure docile acceptance of Maastricht does offer some lingering hope to all those who are true federalists.

Let me now talk, and talk more generally, about constitutional interest, economic science and international interdependence. My aim in this lecture has been to offer you a brief but broad and inclusive summary assessment of the politicized economies of the world, and particularly those of America and Western Europe in 1994. I have deliberately added the words "in limbo" to my title in order to suggest that so much remains in transition from where we were, pre-1989, to somewhere else. A post–Cold War equilibrium has not been attained.

I have organized these remarks around the themes stimulated by Fukuyama's optimistic and provocative prediction that economic science will emerge triumphant and that polities everywhere will reorganize their economies along market principles. But why have we not witnessed more support for markets and marketization and privatization in the highly politicized economies of Western Europe and America? Why has the public sector continued to grow as a share of gross domestic product?

There is no respected challenge afoot to the basic principles of economic science. We know that markets which allow for free entry and exit and allow for prices to be set by supply and demand unrestricted by political intrusion generate more economic value as measured by standards that emerge in the market process itself—value that is defined by the evaluations of those who participate. We know those structures produce more value than any other organizational structure. Economic value is valued by everybody in a certain sense. Each of us prefers to live in a community, or a region, or a nation, or a world that is prosperous and provides abundance, goods and services along with increasing abundance over time. Each of us, no matter who we are or where we are, has an abiding constitutional interest in economic prosperity.

But we have none or little of what I would call a direct action motivating interest. Instead we have non-general, non-constitutional interests, as these are measured in gains for our own small, less than totally inclusive communities, whether these be defined geographically, occupationally, industrially, professionally or otherwise—interests that come into conflict with the general or constitutional interest. It is these particular interests, as they come to be exploited in the politics of majoritarian democracy, that prevent the implacement of the basic teachings of economic science into observed institutional reality.

There always remains, of course, some residual ignorance of basic economics. I have just read a recent book by Nils Karlson, a Swedish economist, which he calls *The State of State,* and in it he talks about the logic of conceit where people really do think they can manipulate the economy so as to increase value; fundamental ignorance of economics still remains present, even among sophisticated political leaders, even in 1994. But I should empha-size that the primary force that prevents the dominance of the constitutional interest or the general interest is the presence of particularized distributional interests rather than economic ignorance. An American economist, Mancur Olson, has written a book which he calls *The Rise and Decline of Nations,* published about a decade ago, in which he elaborates this point in great de-tail—that it is the absence of an all-encompassing interest in our politics, in the politics responsive to particularized separate interests that generates the problem.

How can the constitutional interest of all the members of a polity be ad-vanced? How can persons be persuaded to act politically in pursuit of their generalized interest, even if in opposition to their particular distributional interest? Well, I spent a good part of a lengthy academic career trying to ad-dress that sort of question. And I'll tell you here and now, I am no closer to an answer in 1994 than I was in 1954, which was about the time I commenced to be concerned with such issues. I am often asked to classify myself as to whether I am a pessimist or an optimist. My response is that looking pro-spectively, looking forward, it's all too easy to be pessimistic, as indeed my remarks in this lecture may suggest to you. But if we turn around and look retrospectively, look at what has happened, there are reasons for optimism. Who could have predicted two decades ago the momentous events of the 1980s and early 1990s? Hence, I don't despair, because I do sense the possi-bility in the offing that somewhere, sometime there's going to emerge a set of political entrepreneurs in some country that will put in place their own institutional variant of what are the basic principles of classical liberalism. That is to say, one country's leaders may act to further their citizens' consti-tutional interest, and the internal politics may be such as to leave time for that experiment to work. In this way there may arise one or more exemplars for other leaders to emulate. Italy, of course, offers a current possibility. The countries on the Asian rim come to mind here, along with those of Latin America. The United States and the overly politicized countries of Western Europe may possibly be goaded out of their political arteriosclerosis of the extended welfare transfer state by the observed growth of smaller nations.

# The Epistemological Feasibility
# of Free Markets[1]

One of F. A. Hayek's most important achievements is his contribution to an understanding of how markets utilize knowledge. However, Hayek himself did not specifically examine the epistemological underpinnings of market institutions or rules that must, themselves, emerge from some process of "choice." Presumably, he did not make such an extension of inquiry because of his concentration on the evolutionary origins of institutions, with the consequent implication that no choice, as such, need inform the historical record.

It is first necessary to clear up a possible ambiguity that may arise from a failure to distinguish between the claim for evaluative or normative superiority of evolutionary *laissez-faire* and the much more sweeping claim that the course of evolutionary development cannot be modified by human action. In his persuasive criticism of what he called "rational constructivism" (or "constructive rationalism"), Hayek can be interpreted as making the first of these two claims. Although he may not himself have been clear here, Hayek should not be interpreted as making the second claim that efforts at institutional reconstruction, no matter how bungled and misguided, and no matter how inefficacious in results, do not, and cannot, exert effects at all. After all, "socialism happened," a fact of history that Hayek surely did not choose to ignore.

From *Post-Socialist Political Economy: Selected Essays* (Cheltenham, U.K.: Edward Elgar, 1997), 151–59. Reprinted by permission of the publisher.

1. Material in this chapter was presented at a Hayek Conference, Bleibach, Germany, in June 1993.

Over the course of two centuries, efforts have been made to reconstruct the order of societies, and institutional structures have been changed because of these efforts. Hayek is convincing when he suggests that the development of these societies would have been "better," by several agreed-upon standards, had the efforts at reconstruction not been made at all. But, to my knowledge, Hayek did not directly recognize that once any effort at social reconstruction was made and was observed to have effects explicit "social choice" became a necessary element in the human condition.

We start from the social order that exists and as shaped in part by past efforts at reconstruction. The institutions of order have been chosen in some process, and this fact of choice is understood to have occurred. Any direction for change, for future development, is also recognized as something to be chosen, quite independent of the causal nexus between choice and consequences. Even to allow the process of cultural evolution to work, to leave institutional change alone, requires choice. "To leave alone" is, itself, a choice alternative.

Once this elementary point is recognized, it becomes appropriate to examine the epistemological environment within which choice takes place. If to leave alone is one choice alternative among many, what sort of generalized public understanding is required for this alternative to emerge? The classical liberal, in the role of social engineer, may, of course, recommend institutional *laissez-faire* as a preferred policy stance. But why, and under what conditions, should members of the citizenry, or of some ultimate political decision authority, accept this advice more readily than that proffered by any other social engineer?

## Preliminary Stipulations

For purposes of clarifying the discussion here, let me stipulate that if there should be adequate understanding of the working properties of market institutions, then these institutions would be chosen as the basic framework within which persons carry out their economic activities. My concern in this stipulation is to set aside all argument about the efficiency-enhancing attributes of markets. I simply postulate that market organization does, indeed, generate a higher-valued bundle of goods and services than alternative forms of organization, with evaluations based on the preferences of those persons who are participants. In this stipulation that the market organization of the economy produces more value than alternative institutional arrangements, I am quite deliberately bypassing the whole set of issues concerning the scientific content of "economics" as a discipline. The stipulation implies that the required understanding of the working properties of markets is achieved through scientific inquiry, in all respects analogous to other fields of knowledge. The initial stipulation also implies that efficiency in the standard sense is the agreed-on objective for economic organization. Neither distributional considerations nor extramarket environmental concerns are relevant for the choice calculus of the political decision maker.

I want also to emphasize that my subject of inquiry is *epistemological* rather than *political* feasibility. There may exist many types of constitutional-political decision structures that fail to generate organizational choices for the polity that correspond to results that would emerge from considerations of the generalized interest of participants. Decision structures may be such that special or differential interests may dominate any selection of alternatives that would further the general or all-encompassing interest. I can circumvent this difficulty either by postulating that the constitutional rules are so stylized as to prevent any subversion of the general interest or by assuming that political choosers are classical utilitarians.

Given such preliminaries, the problem to be addressed can be simply stated: do persons, as political choosers in their roles as participants in political processes, possess the capacities to make informed selections among the relevant organizational alternatives, which, in this case, would be the selection of the market? And, if they do not possess such capacities, can they be expected to defer to the experts, in this case, the economists, who are presumably competent to make accurate institutional comparisons?

We must, of course, recognize that only on a few occasions in history are persons faced with choices among inclusive and comprehensive institutional-constitutional alternatives. The effective choices are rarely in such stark form as that between "socialism" and "the market," even in those societies that have gone through genuine revolutionary upheavals. The choices actually faced by participants in the politically organized communities are likely to be incremental or piecemeal, with particular reference to identified subsectors of the economy. The choices are likely to take such forms as: should the existing politicized and bureaucratized production and/or distribution of, say, bread be abandoned, wholly or partially? Or, vice versa, should the existing decentralized and nonpoliticized market for bread, both in its production and distribution, be replaced by a collectivized alternative, again in whole or in part? Or, even less comprehensively, should the market price for bread be collectively controlled, either directly or indirectly through taxes or subsidies?

Consider, then, the position of the potential political chooser, whether citizen, elected politician, party leader or bureaucrat, who is confronted with such institutional choice. (Recall that I have explicitly ruled out motivations based on narrowly identified interests; the chooser is presumed to act on estimates of the general interest.) Clearly, some understanding of how the institutional alternatives work must inform the choice calculus. It is this understanding and its relationship to the market in particular that I want to examine in some detail.[2]

Before proceeding, however, institutional history must be acknowledged to be relevant for any such choice. As noted earlier, no choices are made *carte blanche*. An institutional structure always exists, and this structure has worked, after some fashion, whether efficaciously or not, and persons have observed its working properties. Effectively, institutional choice is always between some institutional-organizational *status quo* and some proposed alternatives, the working properties of which cannot be observed directly, except possibly in foreign settings. Institutional choice is not analogous to the choice among items in a Greek restaurant kitchen, each one of which is observed to be available. Institutional choice is between that which is and that which might be but is not. This fact alone suggests that the temperament of the chooser may become relevant. The conservative's choice may be biased towards that which is; the radical's choice may be biased towards that which is not but might be.

Again, however, the presence or absence of such a temperamental bias or its direction is not my primary concern in this chapter. My concern is exclusively with the understanding or knowledge of the institutional alternatives that is present in the mind of the potential chooser, whichever alternative may describe the *status quo*.

---

2. In an earlier paper, Viktor Vanberg and I made a distinction between "interests" and "theories" in constitutional choice ("Interests and Theories in Constitutional Choice," *Journal of Theoretical Politics* 1 [1989]: 49–62). In this terminology, my concern in this paper is exclusively with "theories."

## Minimal Economic Understanding

I suggest that there is a minimal level or degree of elementary economic understanding required in order that the potential chooser be led to select the market alternative, under the conditions stipulated, through the process of an internal rational calculus, whether the dimension for choice involves small or incremental adjustment towards or away from an operative market system or comprehensive change in overall economic organization. Absent such minimal understanding, the collectivized alternative tends to be chosen over the market because it tends to be more in accord with the "natural" mind-set of the person who remains nonsophisticated in economics.

This vulgar mind-set has been reinforced rather than offset by the allocation-maximization paradigm of the economic theory of this century— the paradigm that provided the central logic upon which the idealized models of collectivization were constructed. To the extent that the market is conceptualized as a "device" or a "mechanism," or even is discussed in terms of its "functions," it is necessarily seen to be more complex in its operation than the more directly focused, and centralized, control process of the collectivized alternative. Adequately, even if minimally, understood, the market is not to be conceived as analogous to a mechanism, but, instead, as a process within which separate persons interact in furtherance of their own purposes and, in so doing, generate an order. This order of the market may, of course, be described in terms of its results by a vector of valued inputs and outputs, but this vector itself emerges from the process and does not, and cannot, exist independent of the process through which it is generated.[3]

It is an elementary or minimal understanding of this *order* of the market that must inform the choices that are to be made among institutional alternatives, in the small or in the large. Absent this, the collectivization alternative will tend to trump the market in the chooser's rational, even if ignorant, calculus. The collectivist alternative is clearly sensed to have an order, no matter how badly it may be predicted to work, and it stands opposed to what must seem to be a chaotic pattern of results with no internal logic. Order takes precedence over disorder. Quite literally, the market is, indeed, "out of

---

3. See James M. Buchanan, "Order Defined in the Process of Its Emergence," *Literature of Liberty* 5 (1982): 5, for an elaboration of this point.

control" by any person or any authority, and this absence of control is taken to imply the absence of any order in the pattern of results. "The blind forces of the market"—this derogation reflects the unknowledge of those market critics who mouth it.

It is as if those who do not possess the minimal understanding here think of demand and supply relationships in total independence of any incentive response behaviour on the part of persons who participate in economic activities. It is as if both input and output prices (terms of trade) are arbitrarily settled through some complex bargaining among groups that possess varying degrees of effective economic power, with all participants in the economy being recipients of pure rents (producers and consumers). And, of course, in such a setting, resource allocation among end-uses is also quite arbitrary, within broad limits. In such an imagined model of economic reality, the results would, indeed, be chaotic, with no discernible order, and no predictability, either to an observer or to an internal participant.

As this somewhat forced and artificial image might suggest, however, the understanding required to make more informed choice may be quite minimal. As between the market and the collectivist institutional alternatives, under the conditions stipulated, the person who chooses need only know that demand for any good or service is inversely related to price and that, conversely, the supply of any good or service is directly related to price, that markets clear and that resources move to the most valued uses. (That is to say, demand curves slope downward, supply curves slope upward, prices are set at the intersections, resource returns are equalized among uses.)

## Economic Learning and Feedbacks from Reality

The minimal understanding of economic *science* sketched out here is not a part of our intuitive perception of social reality. Such an understanding must be learned, either through some intellectual exposure to the elementary principles of economics or some directly sensed feedback from personal experience. And it is in this latter feature that economic science differs dramatically from natural science. If I choose to deny the existence of gravity and jump off a building, the harsh realities of physics catch up very quickly to bring me into recognition and acceptance, if, indeed, I survive at all. If, however, I should, analogously, deny the existence of the laws of demand and supply and proceed to join with others politically in efforts to impose some preferred allocative and distributive result, the feedback from reality is likely to be much more complex and to require a longer time for general recognition. This century witnessed the grandest social science experiment in all of history. The whole socialist scheme was based on a denial of the elementary laws of economics. And, as we know, seven decades were necessary before the efforts at centralized collective control failed sufficiently to force acceptance of basic institutional-organizational change.

At a less comprehensive level of institutional choice, the feedbacks from reality are likely to prove even less effective in modifying the natural mindset of the economically nonsophisticated. Throughout history, political communities, with the acquiescence of citizens, have destroyed potential economic value by the deliberate restriction and control of markets, based in part on a simple failure to understand the most elementary principles of economic science. It is important in this context to recognize that piecemeal politicization of markets destroys value that *might have been* generated but that was never brought into existence. That is to say, the choice-influenced opportunity costs of market restriction are never observed directly by those who bear them.[4] There is nothing here that is akin to the hard surface of the ground for forcing immediate recognition of error as in the gravity analogue.

The low-skilled person who might have been employed in the absence of the politically imposed minimum wage restriction will never, personally, experience the loss of value from that which exists. And the utilitarian participant in the collective-political choice that considers imposing the minimum wage restriction will not experience the feedback relationship from reality that might substitute for an absence of elementary economic understanding. Modern empirical economists might raise objection at this point and suggest that persons who do not really understand the principles can be convinced as to the truths of basic propositions by confrontation with empirical evidence. But the relationship between empirical evidence and the structure of belief remains mysterious, and in economics particularly the difficulties and lags in experimentation make it unlikely that the marshalling of evidence will genuinely convince those who remain ignorant of the causal sources in behaviour.

4. James M. Buchanan, *Cost and Choice* (Chicago: Markham, 1969; Midway Reprint, University of Chicago Press, 1974).

The institutional-organizational failure of "socialism in the large" seems to have done nothing towards generating an understanding of the elementary logic of markets. The grand experiment served to refute the hypothesis that centralized control of a national economy can produce goods and services of value comparable to those produced through the workings of a market order, along with the complementary hypothesis that the rate of growth in value under collectivized control is comparable. But the linkage between the observed failure of socialism in the large and the value-reducing effects of piecemeal efforts towards "socialism in the small" can be appreciated only by those who do possess the required minimal knowledge of economic science. Until and unless it is recognized that the failures of the grand experiments were rooted in the denial of the behavioural laws that elementary economics teaches, there can be no carryover from the evidence of the failure of these experiments to the assessment of the potential success or failure of piecemeal market intervention which is informed by similar denials of the basic economic regularities.

## A 1993 Example

In his press conference on 23 March 1993, President Clinton made the following statement:

> I was astonished that the Bush administration overruled its own customs office and gave a $300 million-a-year freebie to the Japanese for no reason (referring to estimates of minivan tariffs) and we got nothing, and I emphasize nothing, in return. (*Wall Street Journal*, 24 March 1993)

This statement can be interpreted, I submit, only on the supposition that Clinton does not understand elementary economics. The statement makes sense only on some presumption that the supply of Japanese minivans exported to the United States is totally invariant with the net return to supplying firms, in which case the exclusive beneficiary is the US Treasury, while the Japanese firms bear the full cost. (The supply curve of Japanese minivans is vertical.)

The Clinton statement is particularly disturbing since it was made by someone who is clearly in a position of decision-making authority and also by someone who has demonstrated a high level of general intelligence. As we shift attention to the degree of possible economic sophistication attained by the citizenry, generally, those to whom ordinary politicians seek to respond, the prospects become discouraging indeed. How can free markets survive at all in the face of generalized economic ignorance?

## Deference to Experts

One way out of the morass created by widespread economic unknowledge might seem to be that offered by some enhancement of the authority of the experts, in this case, the professional economists, to whom citizens and politicians might defer in some acknowledgement of their own scientific limitations. Professionals in this discipline, however, have never come close to commanding such intellectual authority, and economics has been plagued from its disciplinary establishment by the proclivity of everyone to act as his or her own economist. This phenomenon is due in part, but only in part, to the ambiguity in feedback between error and reality noted earlier. It is also due in part to the failure of economists themselves to stick to their knitting, to keep attention focused on the elementary verities.[5] Further, the public's disrespect for economists as intellectual gurus stems from the economists' own misunderstanding of what the basic principles of their science tell them. Economists, too, were victims of the "fatal conceit" that allowed socialism to happen.

Above all these, however, there remains still another important reason why the scientists and the science of economics fail to command the intellectual respect that seems to describe public and political attitudes towards natural scientists and science—a reason that was noted by Thomas Hobbes more than three centuries ago. The laws of natural science, of physics and chemistry, do not seem to bear directly on the interests of persons and groups, because these laws are not considered to be amenable to human choices, whether private or public. The laws of natural science are, indeed, "natural."[6]

By contrast, the laws of economics seem to be artificial because both the

5. William H. Hutt, *Economists and the Public: A Study of Competition and Opinion* (London: Jonathan Cape, 1936).
6. Some qualification should be introduced here with reference to modern developments in science that do suggest prospects of interfering with "laws of nature." But note also that precisely as these potential interferences have seemed to become possible, controversy has emerged on the scientific level that did not describe behaviour in earlier periods.

objects of inquiry, the choices of animate human beings and the outcome of such choices, describe a social reality that is, itself, clearly not invariant. There is a general failure to make the distinction between choices made within the institutional parameters that contain incentives for personal behaviour—choices that can be scientifically analysed and tested—and choices of the parameters themselves—choices that cannot, at least not directly, be scientifically predictable. Because institutional structures are themselves subject to choice, and can be modified deliberately, it becomes relatively easy for misunderstanding to arise concerning the ultimate malleability of economic actors. From such a misunderstanding the idea emerges that there are no laws of economics comparable to those of the hard or natural sciences, and that the so-called "science" is without content, leaving institutions vulnerable to shaping by the pressures of particular interests, with little or no feedback from reality.[7] These considerations are independently important and warrant extended treatment. However, they are not my central concern here. I have stipulated that there is, indeed, scientific content in economics. The discussion here is intended only to suggest that dispute over this scientific content, if present, makes it more difficult for the professional scientists to command respect.

## Are Free Markets Epistemologically Feasible?

Public choice economists perhaps have rushed too hurriedly towards the discovery of interest-based explanations for collectivized restrictions on market activity, although the major contribution of public choice in dispelling the romantic myth of the benevolent state should be acknowledged. But, relatively, there has been a neglect of explanations for market restrictions based on economic ignorance and/or illiteracy. Political choosers, whether these be voters, elected politicians, bureaucrats or judges, may lack an understanding of even the most elementary principles of economic science, in which case

---

7. In his provocative book *The End of History and the Last Man* (New York: Free Press, 1992), Francis Fukuyama suggests that after the great revolutions of 1989–91 political communities everywhere will organize economic activities through markets. He argues that this result represents an acceptance of the central hypotheses of economic science. From my perspective, Fukuyama ignores the required linkage between the public-political understanding of these hypotheses and the constitutional choice for market institutions.

the choices made among institutional alternatives may reflect honest error rather than any direct promotion of narrowly defined and special interest.

The capacity to understand elementary economics may be less general among even the most informed elements of the citizenry than we may have implicitly assumed. Free markets may be vulnerable to politicization that is motivated neither by differential interest nor by some rejection of the efficiency norm but, instead, by simple misunderstanding of how markets work. Frank Knight once remarked that he could not distinguish between those critics of the market who based their criticism on the market's failure to work as it was supposed to work and those critics who based their criticism on the results that emerge because the market worked as economists described. My thesis is that there is an important third source of criticism; persons seek to subvert the market order because they do not understand how it does work.

The implication for pedagogy is clear. Economists have failed to promulgate the elementary principles of their science so as to secure the generalized understanding for informed political-constitutional choice. Think of the enormous value of the marginal product of some economist who might have taught President Clinton the elementary principles that would have caused him to think differently about Japanese minivans.

Somewhat more specifically to the point of this chapter, the implication is that we should pay more attention to the human capacity to understand social processes as a basis for making informed choices among institutional-organizational alternatives. Such choices will be made, willy-nilly, and the limits of understanding may be a more serious impediment to the exploitation of maximal value potential than any limits imposed by physically measured resources. The capacity to understand, to know, is also a valuable resource, and this capacity must surely extend to economic interaction. Economists, back to our blackboards!

# Consumption without Production
## The Impossible Idyll of Socialism[1]

## I. Introduction

Social scientists, historians, and philosophers will devote years of research effort in attempts to explain why socialism failed so dramatically in the last decades of this century. Perhaps more productively, they will seek to explain and to understand why social scientists, and especially economists, did not predict such failure. Professor F. A. Hayek is one of the acknowledged few who both warned fellow scientists of socialism's fatal flaws and predicted the ultimate breakdown. It is appropriate, therefore, that in this 1992 Hayek lecture, I relate my argument to socialism's failure.

At the outset, I should acknowledge my own prior failure to examine more critically the basic structure of socialism. It is only in my search for understanding of the observed organizational failure that I have come to the realization that elementary relationships, perhaps too obvious to attract earlier attention, more or less insured the results we see. In this respect, I suggest that even those few critics, such as Hayek and Mises, who did sense socialism's eminent demise, tended to concentrate on features of structure that are unnecessarily complex, while overlooking the more basic flaw. Stress was placed on the potential for the exploitation of knowledge, which is, admittedly, an important source of difficulty, but which is, I suggest, not the most critical element in the socialist construction.

This element is the rupture of the nexus between production and con-

(Freiburg, Germany: Haufe, 1993), 49–75. Reprinted by permission of the publisher and the Walter Euken Institut.

1. I am indebted to my colleague Viktor Vanberg for helpful comments.

sumption, a rupture that would have guaranteed socialism's failure, even in some imaginary world where knowledge might have been perfect. The incentive to produce value is missing in the idealized socialist construction, and thereby poverty is insured.

In one sense, the argument of this lecture is embarrassingly simple, so much so that I apologize in advance for the apparent insult to the intelligence of my audience. But, in some defense here, let me suggest that often the elementary verities are indeed overlooked precisely because they are so self-evident. And recall the fable where only the small boy really did see that the king had no clothes.

I shall proceed as follows: In Section II, I shall offer a summary sketch of the whole argument of the lecture. I then follow this summary with the presentation in Section III of an economic parable that is an alternative to that which informs the analysis of modern economists. The simplified and abstracted model of "an economy" requires no allocation, as such, and there is no evaluation, by anyone, as among separate goods and services in the ordinary sense. The model is designed, in part, to eliminate the market's role or function both in setting a value scale and in allocating resources. In Section IV the model is modified to allow for the introduction, first, of collectivism, second, of authoritarian control, and, third and finally, of rent extraction by those who control. Only in Sections V and VI do I shift discussion and analysis to more "realistic" models of economic interaction, in which evaluative, allocational, organizational, and distributional functions of regimes, whether market or hierarchy, must be compared and contrasted. In Section VII I discuss briefly some of the possible reasons why economists have neglected the elementary principle emphasized in the lecture. Finally, in Section VIII I examine some of the implications of the analysis for an understanding of both the "post-socialist" and the "nonsocialist" regimes emergent in the 1990s.

## II. Consumption and Production

In Munich's Alte Pinakothek, there is a Breughel painting ("Schlaraffenland") that depicts the eternal idyll of men who can think of worlds other than their own. Fat peasants lounge about and find their open mouths filled immediately with morsels of the finest foods. Consumption by everyone without production by anyone—this state of existence describes that which can be imagined but never realized. The myth of the fall jolts the dreamer into sobering reality; in order for anyone to consume, someone must produce. Only by the sweat of some brow does the food for Breughel's peasants come into being. The myth of Eden before the apple was eaten—the myth of nature's abundance—must be entirely exorcised from scientific thought if we are to understand man's many failures, as well as his successes, in attempts to better his own condition.

The source of socialism's failure is located precisely in the scientific error that allowed a divorce between production and consumption, a scientific error that is ultimately derivative from the flawed analytical parables of both classical and neoclassical economics. Both parables embody the presupposed reality of scarcity, of land in the strict classical setting, of resources more generally defined in the more sophisticated neoclassical alternative. And, as all economists are wont to remind us, scarcity makes choice necessary. Hence, some allocation of that which is scarce must be chosen, by someone, somehow, or by some process. And, as David Hume suggested, scarcity also opens up avenues for considerations of justice.

I submit that these familiar parables of scarcity have prompted scientific error because they allow analysts to forget the necessary linkage between production and consumption, a linkage that a more appropriate parable might have placed in full light. In some ultimate sense, we live in a world that is accurately described by neither "abundance" nor "scarcity." These two imagined states do not exhaust potential reality. We need go no further than biblical mythology. Abundance in the garden is not simply replaced by scarcity beyond the boundaries. Post-Eden man must produce that which he desires to consume, even to survive at all. A "choice" to produce is a "choice" to consume; and production does involve the allocation of "something" to "something" rather than to "something else." But the ordinary calculus of allocative choice that is familiar from the economists' models does not capture the elemental behavioral enterprise at all, and, indeed, distracts attention from common sense understanding. Ab initio, there is no glob of value to be allocated, no manna from heaven, nature, or anywhere else. Value must first be produced in order to exist, and the production of value of one sort does not imply the sacrifice of produced value of yet another sort, at least not in the standard meaning of these terms. As Jeremy Bentham implied, the calculus is one of pain *and* pleasure, and the pleasure of anticipated consumption is achieved only by the incurrence of pain. That which is avoided by not producing is the pain or disutility of effort rather than the sacrifice of some produced alternative that might have been consumed. Opportunity cost must be related to choice, and the cost of the choice to incur pain to produce value is measured by the pain itself, by the disutility of effort. This cost is captured only in some reckoning of the pleasure of pain avoidance.

Production takes place in real time, of course, and time itself does seem to have an objective limit. But time, as such, need not be the operative constraint on productive activity. Production of that which has value requires adjustment among many margins simultaneously, only one of which involves the time dimension that is objectively measurable. Physical exertion, time rates of action, carefulness in observation, alertness to environmental change, applied cause-effect reasoning, behavioral attitudes toward risk, personally expressed rates of discount—these seem to be only a few of the many possible attributes that enter into productive effort that cannot be reduced to the unidimensional measure of real time. Shifts along any of these, and other, behavioral margins will affect the measured value that emerges from productive effort.

As a producer-consumer, the individual may be modelled as maximizing utility by adjusting along the several margins, but such an exercise is little more than a forced translation into economists' jargon. It may be nonetheless helpful to think of the individual as consumer motivating the individual as producer and to define a personalized equilibrium, of sorts, where the promised utility of that which is produced to be consumed matches the promised disutility or pain of the production effort required to produce it, always at the appropriate margins.

This simple exercise in personal economics may be contrasted with a model in which the linkage between production and consumption does not exist. Consider a setting in which persons are expected to produce without consuming that which they produce, currently or in future time periods, either directly or indirectly. In the total absence of such linkage, why should any person produce value at all?

This sketch is perhaps sufficient to indicate the thrust of my simplistic argument in this lecture. But I shall try to make the structure of analysis more interesting to skeptics by outlining some details of an alternative parable to either the classical or neoclassical economic world as modelled.

## III. The Parable of the Buffalo

In early America, the Plains Indians produced and consumed a single good: buffalo, which met all of their basic needs—food, clothing, shelter. (Reminder: This is a parable, not a history.) Neither buffalo nor land was scarce. But the buffalo did not convert themselves into directly consumable articles of food, clothing, and housing. These articles came into being only through a process of production that required effort embodying time, imagination, dexterity, strength, speed, and many other attributes. The final products, meat, hides, and fur, were "scarce" in the sense that no one attained satiety. Any person would have preferred more product, provided that he or she was not required to produce it.

The family was the economic unit in this society, and we assume that the advantages of specialization were internal to the family producing-consuming unit. We assume, further, that each family, along with all of its members, respected the "rights" of other families to the product values, in varying form, that had been produced but not yet consumed.

In this imagined economy, each family would extend its productive effort, as described in the several dimensions of adjustment noted above, to the point at which the expected positive value in consumption equals the expected negative value involved in further production. In the language of economists, we can say that each family attained a position that could be classified to be "efficient." But note that there is no meaning of the term "efficiency" as applied to any unit larger than the single family. There is no interdependence; each family produces that which it consumes. And there is no aggregative or overall "resource" capacity that is "allocated." Similarly, there is no interfamily set of "prices," even shadow prices, that may be compared, one with another.

In this imagined world, families would, of course, be predicted to differ both in their relative preferences for produced goods and effort avoidance and in their relative capacities to convert effort into produced goods. The "society" including many families would not be characterized by equality either in observed outlay of effort (including time) or in production-consumption of buffalo in its finally used form.

## IV. Collective Production, Communal Consumption, and Authoritarian Allocation

Remain within the basic parable of the buffalo and suppose that members of the inclusive buffalo producing-consuming society observe the inequalities among the constituent families. Suppose, further, that all of the many families agree to collectivize production by placing all that is produced in a single common depot, from which each family is to get back an equal share (per person). Each family is now expected to exert effort to produce buffalo, as before, but that which is produced is now for common rather than own consumption. Production and consumption are now separate rather than simultaneous choices.

The predicted results are familiar. A family will attain personal equilibrium in its productive activity when the disutility associated with extended effort matches the value that it places on its proportionate share in the consumption of that which is produced plus whatever value might be placed on the consumption of others in the inclusive society. If there are $N$ families in the society, the producing family's own share in that which it produces is only $1/N$. Unless the family values the consumption of others equally with its own, it will attain production equilibrium at some lesser input of effort along all of the dimensions of input adjustment. Each family will produce a lower value of product than it produced in the autarkic setting before the production and consumption decisions were divorced.

In its consumption choices, each family will move quickly to the limit allowed by the equal-sharing rule, and, at this level of consumption, each family will seek, if at all possible, to extend its own consumption, at the expense of other families if possible. A lower value of product will be produced and consumed in the inclusive society, and the product that is produced will be of a quality that is inferior to that previously generated. Further, each family will find itself dissatisfied with its share of that which is produced.

Note that this result will tend to emerge even in the setting where all families, initially, might have agreed on the collectivization of production and the equal sharing of that which is produced. The basic organizational change will have succeeded in its presumed objective of equalizing consumption of produced goods as among the separate families in the society. But the overall quantity and quality of production and consumption will be lower, perhaps substantially lower, than in the private property regime. Productive effort will not, however, be equalized after the regime change examined here, and the disparities in effort as among the separate families may be increased rather than decreased by the collectivization of production. Those families that are more productive in converting effort into output and those that suffer less disutility from any outlay of effort will find that they place higher values of product into the common depot than they are allowed to take out. And those families that are less productive and those that are less willing to endure the disutility of effort will find that they take out more than they contribute to the common pool. The first group, which we may call the *net producers*, will consider themselves to be exploited by the second group, which we can call the *net consumers*. And the sense of unfairness generated among members of the first group will tend to alter the equilibrium adjustment toward lowered rates of production and lowered quality standards.

The failures of "pure" socialism, in the form described, will seem evident to everyone, and the next stage of "reform" must involve the assignment of authority to some agent who will be empowered to set production quotas and to modify consumption shares. In some idealized omniscience, the agent might assign to each family in its capacity as a producing unit a quota that is the same as that which might have been observed under the autarkic equilibrium adjustment. In this idealized setting, full equalization in consumption might be achieved without sacrifice of production; the producing units would be coerced into supplying effort over and beyond that which they would voluntarily choose to supply.

In practice, however, there is no way that even the most benevolent agent might find out just what the personalized equilibria of producing units might have been under the earlier regime. At best, productive effort can be monitored only along the objectively measurable dimensions of adjustment. As noted, hours or days spent in supplying work seem to be objective units, but these involve only one of the many dimensions of productive effort. The agent can assign working times to persons and families, but there seems to be no way that adjustments along the other dimensions can be brought under the agent's control. Forced out of the preferred level of effort, the producer surely will pay less attention to quality. At best, the authority who is empowered to assign production quotas can increase output in the society somewhat above that level attained under "pure" socialism. But total product will remain well below that observed in the autarkic private property model, and the quality of produced goods will be inferior.

The next stage in "reform" will involve some relaxation of the equal-sharing rule for consumption. Even the most benevolent agent will recognize that total production in the society can be increased if the net producers are given shares in consumption in some positive relationship to shares in production. Such reform may take shape by allowing all producing units to retain, for their own usage, some specified share of the value that is produced. Each producing unit may, for illustration, be allowed to retain one-half of the value its effort generates, with only the remaining one-half allocated to the common depot for subsequent sharing along all units in the society.

Such a modification in the incentive structure will restore, to the extent measured by the relevant share, the nexus between production and consumption, and the change can be predicted to increase, and perhaps dramatically, the size of the total value of product along with the quality of output. Such a partial restoration of the nexus cannot, however, be predicted to return production to that level that would have been attained under autarkic production-consumption in this parable. The partial socialization of the economic process will have directionally predictable results. And, of course, the effects on total product value will be directly related to the size of the socialization-privatization ratio. A society that socializes one-half of its value produced will produce less than a society that socializes one-fourth.[2]

The collectivization-socialization process, whether this be total or partial, requires the establishment and continuing operation of an authority that is empowered to act to set production targets and/or quotas, if desired, and to police whatever consumption-sharing arrangements are chosen. Only in the setting where production and consumption are strictly tied together, the autarkic model of this parable, is the authority strictly limited to a protective role. To this point, I have assumed that the allocative-distributive authority is be-

2. Some economists may suggest that a larger product may be forthcoming when producers are allowed to retain less than the total value produced because of the possible presence of a strong income effect that may offset a substitution effect. This logic is, however, inapplicable here because, for the society as a whole, the income effects are canceling. The return of the socialized share of value, in any sharing arrangement, insures that in net only a substitution effect remains.

nevolent in the sense that it acts exclusively as an agent for the members of the society and behaves in such fashion as to exhibit no interests of its own. Even in this limit, of course, persons who act in such positions must themselves receive consumption shares, thereby inserting a bureaucratic wedge, of sorts, between total value generated and value returned to ordinary persons in the society.

The assumption of benevolence on the part of those in positions of authority cannot be sustained. These persons will have their own economic interests, and their positions will be such as to allow these interests to be furthered without directly related checks. It becomes relatively easy for persons charged with allocative and distributive authority, even in the confines of the simple buffalo parable here, to exact rents from the economy, rents over and beyond those consumption shares that would measure their alternative contributions to production. The bureaucratic rents will insure that the rupture between production and consumption is larger than that indicated directly by the share in product devoted to communal purposes. As a partial offset to this effect, the control authority will have an all-encompassing interest in promoting the highest possible production, because such authority becomes a residual claimant of sorts.[3]

I have gone to some length to show why and how socialism, whether total or partial, would fail in the overly simplified economy modelled in the parable of the buffalo. I have extended the discussion for the purpose of suggesting that even in the absence of allocative and evaluation problems of the standard sort any attempted separation of the production and consumption choices creates value shortfalls by comparison with the setting in which these choices merge into one.

## V. From the Simple to the Complex Economy: Production and Consumption in Market Exchange

It is a relatively straightforward procedure to shift from the simple parable of the one-good buffalo economy under autarkic organization toward a complex exchange economy characterized by input specialization, many fi-

---

3. On this point, see Mancur Olson, "Autocracy, Democracy, and Prosperity," in *Strategy and Choice,* ed. Richard Zeckhauser (Cambridge: MIT Press, 1990), 131–57.

nal goods, and an operative market structure in which exchanges are facilitated by a set of prices defined in terms of a numeraire. For my purpose, the important point of note is that this conjectural shift from a simple to a complex economy may be effected without any rupture in the production-consumption nexus. The individual production of one good followed by exchange for a numeraire good that is, in turn, exchanged for units of some finally desired good becomes a process through which the individual indirectly produces the final items of consumption. Nor is the nexus broken when a person or family sells its productive input services for money wages which are utilized, in turn, to purchase final end items in other markets. Despite the apparent circuitousness of the process, participating individuals fully understand that, in making choices to offer inputs to the market, they are indirectly producing the consumption services that they desire. Adam Smith's butcher produces the meat that we desire out of his own interest, as an ultimate consumer of other goods.

The science of economics, commencing with Adam Smith, is that body of analysis that provides the understanding of how the complex network of market interdependence operates so as to maintain the production-consumption linkage while at the same time achieving the coordination among the separated individual choices that is required to generate the maximum value of total product, as determined by the preferences of those who participate in the process.

How does "the market," which necessarily places separate producing-consuming units in positions of mutual dependence, achieve a result that is analogous to that achieved only in fully autarkic independence in the simple buffalo economy sketched out in Sections III and IV? As economists (and perhaps only economists) know, these results emerge without the operation of any consciously registered allocative or evaluative choices on the part of anyone. "The market," as an organizational structure, exploits the separated, and independent, choices made by individuals and groups, in many input and output exchange processes, in such a way that an allocation of productive effort among many possible uses is made, and that a value scale, represented by a set of input and output prices, is established, a scale that, in turn, allows disparate bundles of goods to be compared, one with another.

As in the one-good economy, individuals attain their own equilibria when the disutility of production effort at the margin matches the promised utility of that which such effort produces, and these equilibria can be labeled to be "efficient" in some meaningful sense. Because of the interdependence of separate individuals through the network of markets here, however, the term "efficiency" can also be applied to the whole structure of results, provided care is taken to avoid the confusion generated by some presupposition that there exists some "scarce" resource to be allocated independent of individuals' actions in production. To the extent that there may exist gains from further exchanges, some persons have not attained their own personalized equilibria, and, as a consequence, the overall results may properly be labeled to be "inefficient."

In the idealized workings of the complex exchange economy, with many goods produced by highly specialized inputs, individuals and families would be predicted to differ both as to preferences between productive effort and value produced and as to rates at which valued output can be generated from productive inputs. The interdependent market economy will be characterized by observed inequalities both in effort supplied and in rates of consumption of final goods.

## VI. Collective Production, Communal Consumption, and Authoritarian Allocation in a Complex Economy

Let us now suppose that the observed inequalities prompt a revolution in the economic regime and that the complex market economy is replaced by a full-fledged socialist order. (The presence or absence of a consensus in support of such a revolutionary change is not relevant to the analysis here.) Production is collectivized in the sense that all of the value generated is collected into a common depot from which equal-consumption shares are assigned to all participants in the society. As was the case in the one-good economy examined earlier, individuals (families) as producers will no longer have an incentive to supply effort, whereas individuals as consumers will seek to increase their aliquot share beyond the limits assigned. An authority empowered to assign production quotas and to enforce consumption-share limits will be necessary. But whereas the task of such an authority may have seemed large even in the simple one-good setting, here the task is enormously increased by comparison. Producing units must not only be assigned rates of input supply, they must also be assigned to this or that productive process or "industry." Persons must be directed to work in the brewery, on the wheat farm, or in the steel factory. And the making of any such assignment among the many possible uses of productive effort, even as monitored, requires the presence of some value scale that will allow trade-offs to be made as among the different end items. Is the additional wheat that might be produced by a shift of inputs from steel production "worth" the loss of steel production involved in the shift?

The early critics of socialist central planning, and notably Mises and Hayek, were clearly on target in their emphasis on the magnitude of the task that any putative planning authority must face in any economy that involves many goods. And the stress on the informational-knowledge requirements necessary to accomplish any results, even to a tolerable degree of "efficiency," was well placed. Further, the dramatic contrast drawn between the market's unique ability to exploit information through the voluntary choices of individuals in an interlinked network of exchanges and any bureaucratic authority's effort to achieve comparable results should have been (but was not) convincing to everyone. In the absence of a value scale emergent from the choices of individuals as producers-consumers in a market order, the allocative choices made by any authority must be, to some degree, arbitrary. As a result, the bundle of goods finally produced fails to correspond with that bundle that persons might have preferred. That value which is produced in such an economy and becomes finally available for consumption is not directly related to that which might have been desired by those who actually do the producing, under the coercion of the authority. The allocative "distortion" acts to drive a further wedge between production and consumption, over and beyond that which is represented by the mere separation of production and consumption choices, along with the extraction of bureaucratic rents.

The task that faces the authoritarian agent in a complex economy is incomparably more difficult than that which might be faced in a simple economy, and, indeed, so difficult that it may be considered to be impossible. For this very reason, however, once the socialist order is politically emplaced, the potential for the extraction of bureaucratic rents is enhanced. Because it is called upon to do so much more, the bureaucracy must be larger, and must claim a larger share of rent, even if it remains totally benevolent. And the enormous expansion in the dimensions of allocative control create like expansion in the opportunities for rent extraction by those agents who use office to further their own economic interests. In sum, we can say that the distributive, allocative, and bureaucratic sources of the separation between production and consumption become increasingly constraining as the economy grows more complex.

## VII. Sources of Scientific Distraction

My purpose in Section V, above, was not to show how a complex economy functions under a set of market arrangements, and my purpose in Section VI was not to show why any attempted socialist organization of such an economy must fail. My purpose was, instead, to suggest that concentration both on the positive analysis of the workings of a complex market economy, with normative overtones, and on the potential disastrous consequences of any attempted collectivization of such economies may have acted to distract attention from the most basic element in the whole socialist experiment, the attempt to divorce the production from the consumption of economic value. The ultimate sources of this relative oversight may be located in the parables of resource scarcity that are foundational in both classical and neoclassical economic theory.

My point here can be demonstrated by accepting, for purposes of argument, and working within one simplified version of the scarcity parable. Suppose that there does, indeed, exist a scarce resource, in the usual sense, a glob of potential "capacity," from which may be generated a whole set of desired end items of consumption goods and services, but a set that is not sufficient to satiate persons in the relevant group. This resource exists, as potential capacity; it does not require production. The "function" of the economic process or economic order is to allocate this scarce resource among alternative end uses. We are squarely inside the classic Robbins' definition of what "the economic problem" is.[4]

Relevant and useful economic analysis can be brought to bear which will suggest that the assignment of separate ownership shares in the scarce resource to many persons, along with the liberty to organize processes that convert the resource into end items of consumption, and the liberty of en-

---

4. See Lionel Robbins, *The Nature and Significance of Economic Science* (London: Macmillan, 1932).

tering into voluntary exchanges will generate allocative results that maximize the value of the scarce resource in terms of the preferences of the economy's participants. This sentence summarizes the neoclassical paradigm, which I presume is cleansed of all its peripherally discovered "failures," which are, in any case, unrelated to my discussion.

Assume now that a socialist transformation is implemented. The scarce resource is placed under collective ownership and control, and a planning authority is assigned the task of allocating the resource among uses and of organizing the conversion processes. I submit here that it was within this paradigm that Mises and Hayek mounted their criticism of socialism, a criticism that did, indeed, demonstrate the infeasibility of the socialist effort, and which based such a demonstration on the relative superiority of market arrangements in utilizing information available to individuals throughout the economy. That is to say, Mises and Hayek argued that even if no production of the source of economic value is required socialism fails as an allocative mechanism relative to the market, provided only that the ultimate objective is the satisfaction of the preferences of members of the economy.[5]

Within its limits, this argument is now acknowledged to have been successful, despite its failure to gain early acceptance. What was overlooked, however, was the central socialist element, the separation of the production of value from its consumption. We must ask, and try to answer, the question: Why did economists fail to understand that value must first be produced before it can be allocated?

I suggest that one answer may be identified in economists' failure fully to escape from the classical notion that value is embodied in objectively observable "things," and conceptually separate from the evaluation process that takes place within the consciousness of persons. In other words, the dimensionality of economic value is considered to be objective rather than subjective. Persons exchange "commodities for commodities," as embodiments of objectified value, rather than anticipated utilities. In part, economists' reluc-

5. Ludwig von Mises, *Socialism* (Indianapolis: Liberty Fund, 1981); Friedrich A. von Hayek, ed., *Collectivist Economic Planning: Critical Studies on the Possibilities of Socialism* (London: George Routledge & Sons, 1935); Fredrich A. von Hayek, *Individualism and Economic Order* (Chicago: University of Chicago Press, 1973).

tance to incorporate the utility dimension fully in their formal structure of analysis stems from their desire to apply the readily available mathematical logic of the calculus. A scarce resource, objectively measured, can be "allocated," and the simple principle of maximization can be used readily. But do we not also observe this principle being extended to utility, with much of formal theory couched in terms of utility maximization? As economists all recognize, however, utility as employed in such exercises has no independent objectifiable existence; it is merely a term meaning "that which is maximized," and with no operational content. The "utility" of theory comes into being with choices among alternatives; it does not exist as a potential value subject to allocation, as such. A shift from the basic scarcity parable, in which objectively measurable resources are available to be allocated, to a parable in which utility gains emerge only when, as, and if some evaluation process prompts productive effort, the disutility of which is overmatched by the utility value of that which such effort brings forth, would require a reformulation of the foundations of economic theory. The idealized market order would maximize value, as determined by the preferences of participants and as constrained by the capacities of participants to produce values, but, even conceptually, there could be no "calculus of maximization" independent of the voluntary choices made by participants themselves. The intellectual exercise that socialism embodies could never have been undertaken.

In the introduction to this lecture, I apologized for the elementary nature of the whole argument. Hence, I should not be interpreted at this point to suggest that the basic flaw in the socialist experiment, the attempted divorce of production from consumption, has been totally neglected. The thrust of the argument is as old as Aristotle's defense of private property, and incentive compatibility is an important research program in modern economics. I do suggest, however, that those who have made early contributions to analysis here have not directly extended the argument's logic to the socialist enterprise. The incompatibility of the incentive structure was not a central feature of the socialist calculation debates of the 1930s.

Incentive structure entered modern economics by way of the theories of property rights, bureaucracy, and entrepreneurship. In each case, however, the analysis was largely, if not wholly, limited to institutional comparison within the partially politicized Western-style economies. Armen Alchian's early work on the economics of property rights[6] led him to advance predictions about observable differences between proprietary and nonproprietary institutions, but he did not, to my knowledge, extend discussion to socialist economies, as inclusive organizational structures. Gordon Tullock's pioneering effort to use incentive structures to analyze modern bureaucracies was limited in application to Western countries.[7] Israel Kirzner's emphasis on the entrepreneurial component in all economic behavior can be interpreted to embody a recognition of the necessary production-consumption nexus. However, Kirzner directed his criticism at the economists who sought to understand market structures.[8] My own early work was motivated by a concern to clarify the notion of opportunity cost, and although I did include a section on socialist choice that may now be interpreted as precursory to my argument in this lecture, I did not sense extended relevance and applicability of my own analysis.[9] To my knowledge, only in a short recently published paper by di Pierro[10] has the argument been applied directly to the collapse of socialism.[11]

## VIII. Implications and Prospects

In my interpretation the presumed motive force for socialist transformation is distributional. Production is separated from consumption in order to achieve distributional objectives. By contrast, in an idealized market structure, persons, if they so choose, may consume that share in economic value that they produce. Any increase in a consumption share beyond that which is produced must, *pari passu*, imply that someone else in the economy produces more value than he or she retains for consumption.

6. Armen A. Alchian, *Economic Forces at Work* (Indianapolis: Liberty Fund, 1977).

7. Gordon Tullock, *The Politics of Bureaucracy* (Washington, D.C.: Public Affairs Press, 1965).

8. Israel M. Kirzner, *Competition and Entrepreneurship* (Chicago: University of Chicago Press, 1973).

9. James M. Buchanan, *Cost and Choice* (Chicago: Markham, 1969; Midway Reprint, University of Chicago Press, 1974).

10. Alberto di Pierro, "Istituzioni e modelli produttivi," *Politeia* 6, no. 18 (1990): 4–6.

11. The inverse form of the argument was presented by Joseph H. Carens, *Equality, Moral Incentives and the Market* (Chicago: University of Chicago Press, 1981). That is, the critical importance of moral incentives for the efficacy of socialist organization was recognized, but still within the context of potential, even if idealized realization.

This interpretation suggests that there is a spectrum along which the socialization of an economy may be conceptually measured. At the one extreme, there is the pure market economy, with no separation between production and potential consumption. At the opposing limit, there is pure or total socialization, where all value that is produced is placed in a pool for common sharing among all persons in the collectivity. Real-world economies are located variously along this spectrum. The modern welfare states, which coercively transfer large shares of produced value to persons who produce little or nothing, are not different, in kind, from socialist states that offer enhanced consumption shares as incentives to producers. In both cases, a wedge is driven between production and consumption, with predictable shortfalls in value generation.

In the highly simplified buffalo economy described above, the welfare-transfer state and the socialist state are essentially similar in all respects, since all that matters for productive incentives are the shares of value that producers are allowed to retain. In a complex economy with many end uses of value, there may be major differences between the operation of the welfare-transfer state and the socialist state. These differences stem, of course, from the fact that in a complex economy there does exist an allocation problem that is not present in the simple one-good model. The welfare-transfer state may be organized so as to allow market organization to direct production without political or bureaucratic intervention in the process. By contrast, the socialist state may be characterized by bureaucratic barriers to market forces. As a consequence, in any comparative evaluation, the welfare-transfer state can be predicted to secure a somewhat higher value of economic product, for any given size wedge between production and consumption, than can the state that retains the apparatus of socialist organization. But the basic feature that separates production from consumption remains common to the two organizational structures.

The political economies of Western countries have been transformed gradually over the course of this century toward the socialist pole. The share of total value taken in taxation, largely if not wholly for distributional purpose, has increased dramatically. The separation between production and potential consumption has been less than total, but, nonetheless, has been extended beyond any limits of earlier predictions. For the most part and with some exceptions, these political economies have retained market structures for the organization of production; collectivist-socialist organization, as such, has been avoided in most settings, and even where experiments in nationalization have been carried out there has been a movement toward denationalization (privatization) in the most recent decade. For these Western economies, there seems little prospect for movement toward socialist organization, but, at the same time, there seems almost no prospect for any dramatic reduction in the size of the transfer sector.

Political and economic revolution has occurred in those countries that carried out the grand socialist experiments early in the century. This revolution was sparked in large part by the demonstrable failure of socialist organization to produce economic value, a failure that seems attributable, first, to the effort to separate production from consumption, and, second, to the infeasibility of authoritarian allocation. These countries are now in periods of transition, with unpredictable prospects. For some of these economies, however, there surely exists the unparalleled opportunity to locate closer to the pole of market organization than those positions that describe Western welfare states. The "baggage" of the welfare state, reflected through the complex interplay of client and bureaucratic pressure groups on the political process, need not emerge to prominence immediately in the post-socialist settings. If, and to the extent that, post-socialist countries can "seize the day," we can predict that their prospects for development are relatively unlimited.

In conclusion, I return to the central, and very elementary, point of the lecture. If individuals are allowed the liberty to produce value in the expectation that they are, themselves, to be allowed to consume that which they produce, they can surely be predicted to produce a higher value of whatever it is that they may want than in any other setting.

My whole discussion has been restricted to the simple economics of the matter. I have deliberately left aside any treatment of ethical considerations. What ethical claims do those who produce no value have on those who do produce such value? The economics seems clear enough; the ethics remain, for me, shrouded in mist.

# Economics in
# the Post-Socialist Century

My title specifically suggests that the focus of scientific inquiry in our discipline is not independent of history. Nor are the events of history independent of developments in economics. In our roles both as citizens (public choosers) and as economic analysts, we have learned from this century's experiments in politicised direction of economic activity, and this learning must, itself, affect both socio-political processes and the shape of further scientific inquiry. In both of these symbiotically related capacities, we simultaneously learn from and make our history.

The verb "make" deserves emphasis, because it points to the basic difference between the subject matter of the social and the natural sciences. There is no set of relationships among persons that we can label to be "natural" in the definitional sense of independence from human agency. The political economy is *artifactual;* it has been constructed by human choices, whether or not these have been purposeful in any structural sense. And the political economy that exists is acknowledged to be subject to "unnatural" change. As the great experiments of this century demonstrate, attempts can be made to *reform* social structures, in the proper meaning of the term. By comparison and by contrast, it would be misleading to use the word "reform" with reference to the natural world even with the dramatic advances in our scientific understandings. From the artifactual quality of that which is the subject of

From *Economic Journal* 101 (January 1991): 15–21. Reprinted by permission of the copyright holder, the Royal Economic Society.

I am indebted to Geoffrey Brennan, Hartmut Kliemt, Robert Tollison, Viktor Vanberg and Karen Vaughn for helpful suggestions.

inquiry in economics, we infer, firstly, the necessary interdependence between science and history and, secondly, the relatively more direct linkage between science and purposive design.

In Section I, I shall argue that the post-socialist century will be marked by a convergence of scientific understanding among those who profess to be economists. This convergence will contrast starkly with the sometime acrimonious controversy that described discourse in the century past. This relatively clear difference in the economics of the two centuries will, itself, prompt inquiry into the sources of the earlier conflict. Section II previews the possible re-evaluative enterprise that may take place in ensuing decades and introduces the suggestion that in such an enterprise, profound methodological transformation may be accomplished. The convergence of understanding will also modify the relevance of the positive-normative distinction that became familiar only in this century. Section III elaborates the argument, and here I suggest that the political economy of the next century will indeed become more normative in the now conventional meaning of this term. But the normative focus will necessarily be quite different from that which seemed appropriate in the setting where all economies, to greater or lesser degrees, were subjected to politicised direction and control. The revised normative focus will be on the constraints within which economic actors, individually or corporately, make choices among alternatives. And the accompanying, and indeed prior, positive analysis will involve comparisons among alternative sets of constraints, or rules. As Section V suggests, "constitutional economics" will command increasing scientific attention in the upcoming century, whether or not the relevant research programmes are explicitly classified under this particular rubric. Section VI adds a postscript.

## I. Toward a Scientific Consensus

Consider the following statement by a widely respected observer:

> They (the diverse parties in Eastern Europe in 1990) are also saying—and for the left this is perhaps the most important statement—there is no "socialist economics," there is only economics. And economics means not a socialist market economy, but a social market economy.[1]

1. Timothy Garton Ash, "Eastern Europe: The Year of Truth," *New York Review of Books*, vol. 37, no. 2 (15 February 1990), 21.

In 1990 few who profess to call themselves economists in East or West will challenge the elementary proposition to the effect that economies that are described by individual (private) ownership of the means of production work better than economies where individual ownership is absent. And there exists widespread agreement on what is meant by the descriptive predicate "work better." More goods and services are produced, with "more" being measured in terms of the values placed on such goods and services by individual participants. This convergence of scientific judgment within economics has already been evident for three decades. Since the 1960s, there have been relatively few claims advanced by economists concerning the superiority of centrally planned economies. And, indeed, few modern economists are either old enough or honest enough to recall the frequency of such claims during the middle decades of the century. This still-emerging consensus on the relative efficiency of market and socialist systems of economic order will characterise the first several decades of this journal's second century.

Since the emergence of economics as an independent discipline, there has been near-unanimity in analysis of the effects of particularised constraints on voluntary exchange. The destruction of potential value generated by tariffs, price floors or ceilings, or prohibitions on entry and exit—the demonstration of this result has remained a central emphasis over two centuries and can be predicted to remain in place over a third. But scientific advances have been made in understanding why collectivities impose such value-reducing constraints, and, in addition, economists can now measure the opportunity losses more accurately. Differences will continue as analysis comes to be applied and especially if policy alternatives are presented in piecemeal fashion. But emerging scientific consensus will be indicated by the crossing of the intellectual-analytical bridge between the acknowledged failure of socialist organisation in the large and the inefficacy of politicisation in the small (market by market).

Predictions of convergence seem more dicey when attention shifts to macroeconomics, the domain of inquiry opened by the Keynesian revolution. Market organisation works, but within what set of parameters? And how detailed need political direction be in determining the values of the relevant parameters here? Controversy rather than consensus describes the state of play in the early 1990s. What might be projected for the 2000s?

Convergence here will occur in what might seem a reverse order. Economists will attain broad consensus on choices among policy options *before* observed agreement on underlying analytical models of macroeconomic interaction. The lasting Keynesian contribution will be the emphasis on the dominance of man's "animal spirits" in the subjectively derived definitions of the expectational environment within which entrepreneurs, in particular, make future-oriented choices. The attempted extension of rational choice models to intertemporal and interdependent choices within an equilibrating adjustment framework will, ultimately, be deemed a failure. Both strands of inquiry here will converge early in application to policy. Those economists who stress expectational instability will move toward recognition that only structural reform can serve the implied macroeconomic purpose. And those who extended rationality precepts have already restricted reform efficacy to structural parameters.

Ultimately, this convergence on policy norms will be matched by broader consensus in the underlying analytical exercise. And here the Keynesian heritage will win the day even if, in yet another sense, the implied results may seem non-Keynesian. The limits on man's capacity to choose rationally in any operationally meaningful way must, finally, be reckoned with and the scope for subjectively determined choice behaviour acknowledged. At the same time, however, those and additional limits on the choice behaviour of political agents, and the interaction of these agents within the institutions of politics, will be incorporated into the whole macroanalysis.

## II. Re-evaluation of the Economics of the Socialist Century

If my central prediction proves accurate, economists must, increasingly, begin to raise—and try to answer—the following set of questions: Why did economists share in the "fatal conceit" that socialism represented?[2] How were economists who claimed scientific competence in analysis of human choice behaviour and the interdependent interactions of choices within institutional structures duped or lulled into the neglect of elementary principles? Why did economists who model man as *Homo economicus* in analysing markets fail to recognise that incentives remain relevant in all choice settings? Why did economists forget so completely the simple Aristotelian de-

2. F. A. Hayek, *The Fatal Conceit* (Chicago: University of Chicago Press, 1989).

fence of private property? Why did so many economists overlook the psychology of value, which locates evaluation in persons, not in goods? Why did so many professionals in choice analysis fail to recognise the informational requirements of a centrally controlled economy in both the logical and empirical dimensions? Why was there the near total failure to incorporate the creative potential of human choice in models of economic interaction?

These and similar questions will occupy many man-years of effort in the century ahead. In the examination of the flaws in economics over the socialist century, the perspective of the discipline itself will be challenged and perhaps changed in dramatic fashion. Economists may come to recognise, finally, that the dominance of the implicitly collectivist allocationist paradigm, elaborated in a setting characterised by developing mathematical sophistication, lies at the root of much of the intellectual confusion. The alternative perspective that conceives of the economy as an *order* of social interaction should gradually gain adherents.[3] The accompanying mathematical representations will shift, and game theory's search for solutions to complex interactions under complex sets of rules will surely replace extensions of general equilibrium analysis at the frontiers of formalism.

The shift toward emergent order as a central perspective will be paralleled by a corollary, even if not necessary, reduction of emphasis on equilibrium models. The properties of systems in dynamic disequilibrium will come to centre stage, and especially as economics incorporates influences of the post-Prigogine developments in the theory of self-organising systems of spontaneous order, developments that can be integrated much more readily into the catallactic than into the maximising perspective.

## III. A Recovery in Normative Relevance

A predictable by-product of the ideologically driven controversy that characterised the socialist century was concerted effort to separate positive from normative elements of the economists' enterprise. Methodologists variously reiterated the is-ought and fact-value distinctions. With controversy receding, we can predict some increase in reasoned discourse in defence of nor-

---

3. James M. Buchanan, in *The State of Economic Science: Views of Six Nobel Laureates*, ed. Werner Sichel (Kalamazoo: Upjohn Institute, 1989).

mative standards. Such a return to respectability of normative argument applying economic analysis can serve to re-invigorate the discipline for aspiring young scholars who have been turned away by the antiseptic aridity of a science without heat. A bit of the excitement that described the zeniths of both classical political economy and early Keynesian macroeconomics seems well within the possible.

No direct challenge to the logic of the naturalistic fallacy need be invoked in the recognition that the very definition of the "is," which itself depends critically on the perspective adopted in looking at the subject matter, will influence the shape of the "ought," which emerges when a value ordering is applied to the analysis of the "is." The possible "deconversion" of economists away from the allocationist-maximisation-equilibrium paradigm and toward some vision of the economic process in subjectivist-catallactic-disequilibrium terms must, in itself, have implications for the sort of institutional change that *any* ultimate value stance might suggest as appropriate. The complementary shift in the perspective on politics and political process, a shift that has already occurred, will force normative evaluation to incorporate comparisons among institutional alternatives that remain within the possible. From this evaluation there must emerge, even at the level of practical proposals for reform, a much wider range of agreement among economists than that which described the past century.

## IV. Toward a Revised Normative Focus on Institutional Constraints: The Emergence of "Constitutional Political Economy"

The predicted convergence of attitudes among economists at the level of normative evaluation will take place only within, and in part because of, a dramatically revised focus of the whole of the enterprise. A century ago, Knut Wicksell warned his fellow economists against the proffering of normative policy advice to government implicitly modelled as a benevolent despot.[4] He suggested that improvements in policy results could emerge only from changes in the structure of political decision making. The normative attention of the economists must be shifted from choices among alternative

---

4. Knut Wicksell, *Finanztheoretische Untersuchungen* (Jena: Gustav Fischer, 1896).

policy options within given sets of rules to choices among alternative sets of rules.

As we know, Wicksell's advice was totally ignored during the first two-thirds of this journal's first century. Only since the middle of this century have economists increasingly come to appreciate the force of Wicksell's message. In several research programmes, economists have commenced to turn some of their attention to *choices among constraints* and away from the exclusive focus on the familiar *choices within constraints*. At the level of individual behaviour, the economics of self-control has emerged as a viable research programme on its own. And at the much more important level of collective action, constitutional economics or political economy has come to command increasing scientific interest, especially in the 1970s and 1980s. These research programmes, along with the closely related programmes in the "new institutional economics," broadly defined, seem almost certain to become more dominant in the next century.

The extension in the range of possible agreement on the ranking of alternatives, whether treated at the level of the analysts' normative discourse or at the level of direct choices by participating and affected persons, is a logical consequence of the shift of focus away from in-period, or within-rules, choices to choices among constraints or sets of rules. The necessary increase in uncertainty over the predicted sequences of outcomes generated by the workings of differing rules will force any rational chooser to adopt more generalisable criteria for choices among rules than for choices among outcomes. Any attenuation of identifiable interest produces this convergence effect; the conceptual model need not extend to the limits of the familiar Rawlsian veil of ignorance.

Wicksell was the most important precursor of the public choice "revolution" in the analysis of politics and political process. His call for attention to structure, to constitutional rules, reflected an early recognition of interest-motivated choice behaviour in politics that might be incompatible with ideally preferred results. By contrast, the normative economics of both the classical and the ordinal utilitarians incorporated comparisons between imperfect markets and idealised politics. Almost in tandem with the development of public choice, which in its positive analysis simply extends the behavioural models of economics to persons in varying roles as public choosers, the events of history during the last decades of the century have offered observers demonstrable evidence of the failure of politicised direction of economic activity.

As this journal enters its second century, economists in their normative capacities must, by necessity, compare institutional alternatives on a pragmatic basis, as informed by an understanding of organisational principles in the large. They will be unable to rely on the crutch of an idealised political order which seemed to make the task of their predecessors, the theoretical welfare economists, so easy and, in consequence, made their arguments so damaging to the standards of discourse. As they enter the second century of publication of this journal, the economists will find, because of the emerging consensus in both positive and normative elements of their task and in both micro and macro applications, a greater role to play in political dialogue.

Economists, almost alone, understand the notion of choice itself, and the simple intrusion of opportunity cost logic into continuing debates provides, on its own, sufficient *raison d'être* for the profession's existence. And, having got their intellectual house in order after the internal confusion that described almost the whole of the first century, with a renewed inner-disciplinary confidence economists can expose the arguments of the intellectuals who discuss policy alternative as if there are no limits on the possible.

## V. Postscript

I acknowledge that my predictions are tinged with hope. I sense some moral obligation to believe that preferred developments remain within the set of possibles. Little would be gained by speculation about worse-case scenarios, especially when I do not consider myself to be issuing precautionary warnings.

One caveat: I have limited discussion to possible developments that retain at least some relevance to economic reality. I have not speculated about the intellectualised irrelevancies that will continue to command some "economists'" attention so long as the discipline's ultimate *raison d'être* fails to exert positive feedbacks on the structure of inquiry.

A more significant qualification to projections here, and to those advanced by my peers, stems from the necessary limits imposed by temporal constraints. We can, perhaps, speculate meaningfully about developments in research programmes that have emerged or are emerging, and we may offer up descriptive narratives that extend over three or possibly four decades. But even to imagine developments over a full century must reckon on the emergence of research programmes that remain now within the unthinkable.

An instructive exercise is one in which we imagine ourselves to be time-transported to 1890, and to suppose that we were then asked to speculate about developments in economics over the century 1890–1990. The record would tend to confirm the hypothesis set out earlier; the subject matter of our discipline was, indeed, influenced strongly by the events of history, and, to some much lesser extent, these events were themselves influenced by the scientific inquiry of economists. But history, inclusively considered, also embodies technological change. And who could question the critical importance of the information processing revolution in shaping the very questions that economists ask and attempt to answer? The veritable rage for empirical falsifiability of the ordinary sort may be near to running its course. But the still-developing technological frontier has enhanced economists' ability to simulate interactive behavioural results in complex institutional arrangements. Experimental economics, and especially as applied to imaginative game-like settings, seems to be a research programme in its ascendancy.

As an endnote, let me suggest that prediction, in any strict sense, is impossible. Rational expectations models have re-emphasised the point that all information we can have about the future is contained in the data that we now observe. Any prediction will, therefore, be nothing more than an articulation of that which already exists. But, if "the future," as embodied in such predictions, exists "now," we are frozen in the time-space of the present. If we accept real time, we must acknowledge that the real future remains unknowable for the simple reason that it does not yet exist.[5]

5. G. L. S. Shackle, *Epistemics and Economics* (Cambridge: Cambridge University Press, 1972).

# Post-Socialist Political Economy[1]

In this chapter, I shall speculate about prospective developments in "political economy," by which I shall mean the generalized application of the lessons from economic science, as well as those to be drawn from the historical experiences of this century, to the understanding of and the possible reform in the institutions of human interaction.

I want to discuss the demise of socialism *as an idea,* as opposed to the demise of socialism as historical fact. In the 1990s, we are in a period where intellectual discourse is best described by the presence of a generalized acknowledgement that socialism in its historical meaning is dead, but also by a generalized unwillingness (on the part of many participants in the discourse) to allow the spirit to depart in peace. We seem to be caught up in a setting closely analogous to that which describes any religion that incorporates the immortality of the human soul, where death of the body does not imply death of the spirit. We can say, with considerable accuracy, that socialism is dead in body but not (for many) in spirit or soul; and my central theme in this chapter is that the political economy of the next decades, in both West and East, will be described by the struggle of socialism's spirit, or idea, to find embodiment in varying institutional forms, against the continuing forces of Western liberalism (individualism) as an idea, within the developing scientific consensus that defines the feasible opportunity set of social-economic-political arrangements. The outcome of this struggle is not predictable, at least not in any of its institutionalized particulars. Individual independence,

From *Post-Socialist Political Economy: Selected Essays* (Cheltenham, U.K.: Edward Elgar, 1997), 36–47. Reprinted by permission of the publisher.

1. A version of this chapter was presented at the Jerusalem Center for Public Affairs, Jerusalem, Israel, in June 1991.

or *liberty*, will always be valued, both directly and instrumentally, but individuals will also seek to exercise collective control over some of the resources at their disposal. It is much easier to imagine institutional utopias that will simultaneously satisfy these conflicting values than it is to suggest practicable means to get there from here. But more serious research, examination and discussion of federal, confederal and other relationships that combine autonomy with interdependence are more or less dictated by the urgency of events.

## Socialism, the Economy and the Nation-State

In its classically received definition, *socialism*, as an organizational system, is described by *collective*, as opposed to *private*, ownership of the means of production, by which reference is to the ownership of capital in all of its productive forms, including land and natural resources.[2] More generally, we may define socialism to be characterized by *collective* control over the allocation of productive resources and the distribution of the final product. Note that in this second definition collective control is not contrasted with private or individual control over resource allocation and product distribution. The proper contrast here is that between collective control and the absence of control. In the nonsocialist or market economy no one controls either the allocation of resources or the distribution of product. Allocations and distributions emerge from the workings of the economy in which many persons and groups make interdependent but separated choices, not as among final allocations or distributions, but as among the alternatives that they separately confront. The ideological urge toward socialism, or collectivism generally, has stemmed, and does stem, in part from a failure to understand and to appreciate that in the absence of collective control it is not necessary that someone—some person or group—must, indeed, control allocation and distribution. Such understanding of spontaneous order will surely not emerge full-blown from the generalized observation that in practice socialism failed to work as it was supposed to work by the romanticized models of its early proponents.

But let me return to the relationship between socialism and collective

2. Alec Nove, "Socialism," in *The New Palgrave: A Dictionary of Economics*, vol. 4, ed. John Eatwell, Murray Milgate and Peter Newman (London: Macmillan, 1987), 398.

control. If allocation and distribution are to be collectively controlled, the collective entity or unit must be specified, in terms of membership, territorial boundaries, extent of authority and other relevant characteristics. If "the economy" is to be collectivized, what does "the economy" mean? This question, and similar ones, cannot be answered independent of historical experience, which yields an empirical record that describes the development of culture, technology, economic institutions and political structure. And, although the linkages must be recognized, the emergence of socialism as an organizational ideal coincided with the apogee of the nation-state as the dominating political unit in a culture of nationalism. Despite the internationalist rhetoric of early Marxism, socialism (defined as "collective control") would have carried significantly differing implications for any attempts at application either globally or locally. In historical fact, the nation-state defined the unit for the collectivization of national economies that took place under socialist ideological impetus. It is important to emphasize that the failures of socialism commonly discussed after the events of 1989, especially those of the USSR and the countries of Eastern Europe, are, strictly defined, failures of the collectivization of the economies of nation-states.

## Failures of Socialism Identified

There are, generally, four bases for failure of collective controls over economic interaction, whether these controls be attempted at the national, the international or the local community level. There is, first, the information or *knowledge* gap between any controller, or control group, and that level of information that might be available to the many participants in the economic nexus, each of whom necessarily confronts knowledge that is localized to his own situation. This argument was the basis upon which Mises and Hayek projected their early diagnoses of socialism's collapse.[3] There is, second, the *incentive* incompatibility as between the objectives sought by the controllers, whatever these might be, and those sought by individuals who participate variously in the economy. This argument is, in one sense, as ancient as

3. Ludwig von Mises, *Socialism* (1932; Indianapolis: Liberty Fund, 1981), and F. A. Hayek, ed., *Collectivist Economic Planning: Critical Studies on the Possibilities of Socialism* (London: George Routledge and Sons, 1935).

Aristotle's defence of private property, but it has been introduced into modern discourse primarily by the property rights and public choice strands of political economy. Third, and an argument that is an amalgam of sorts between the first and the second arguments, there is the stifling of the *creative* potential for individual entrepreneurship under collective control. Finally, and an argument that is not often explicitly listed as a basis for socialism's failure, there is the impossibility of taking advantage of *scale* in a collectivized economy, which must, in order to carry out its central objective, be closed to extensions of the economic nexus.

The failures of the attempts at collectivized control over the economies of the large nation-states in this century, and notably in the Soviet Union, are attributed to the first three of the bases noted above. Large national economies, for the most part, are presumed to be sufficiently large to internalize many of the scale advantages. As the size of the collectivized economy diminishes, however, scale elements may emerge to become important. (In 1989, Albania still made its own tractors.) It is also important to note that the scale factor exerts its influence in a direction that is opposed to the first three factors. As the size of the collective units falls, scale does become increasingly significant, but both the knowledge and the incentive problems become less important. A small socialist community, existing in isolation from economic interaction with others, may effectively exploit most information and may not face enormous incentive difficulties, but it must, by its smallness, remain grossly inefficient due to its failure to capture scale advantages.

## Socialism in Market Economies

I think that it is appropriate to label the epoch that we are now entering as "post-socialist," because, for the reasons noted, socialism, as a general organizing principle, is acknowledged to have failed demonstrably. In all countries that previously identified their economies to be socialist, there exist reform efforts aimed at introducing markets and market institutions. As noted earlier, however, these efforts are often accompanied by redefinitions of "socialism" so as to eliminate reference to centralized collective control institutions and to substitute reference to collective objectives independent of organizational forms.

It is important to recognize that nowhere, either in those countries previously calling themselves socialist or in those that carry the label "mixed" or even "capitalist," is there strong public or political support for elimination of socialist sectors, that is, for a pure market economy. We are not, surely, entering what we might call the "capitalist market epoch." There has been little or no spillover from the observed failures of socialism, in the large, to the possible failures of socialist organization, in the small, as applied to sectors of those national economies that remain organized broadly on market or capitalist principles. This absence of transference in ideas deserves examination. How is it possible to acknowledge the failure of socialism as a principle for the organization of the total economy and, at the same time, continue to lend ideological as well as practicable support for collective control over relatively large shares of production and distribution in an economy—control which, in many countries, extends to include more than one-half valued product as measured?

The categories of production and distribution that are socialized in economies that are often classified to be nonsocialist are familiar: national defence, police, education, health, transport, communication, radio and television, housing, external trade, insurance, energy. Some or all of the broad industry groupings listed are socialized in all countries. And we can use the term "socialism" in its classical sense here—the means of production are collectively owned and managed. For example, educational services are provided through collectively organized, collectively operated and collectively financed schools, the physical facilities of which are owned collectively. The investment in providing educational services is determined collectively, and the distribution of these services among potential demanders-users is settled through collectivized-bureaucratic channels. The same, or closely similar, institutionalized description could be applied to the other socialized categories. Significant variations could, of course, be observed in the usage of direct pricing both as a means of rationing the distribution and of financing total outlay.

My concern here is neither with such variations in the use of direct pricing of collectively produced services nor with the precise boundaries between the socialist and market sectors of mixed economies. My concern is with the possible spillovers, in assessment and in practice, between the acknowledged failures of socialism, as an inclusive or quasi-inclusive system of organization, and the viability of socialist sectors that may exist alongside private or market sectors of modern mixed economies. The first point to be made is one of classification and distinction. The appropriate distinction is not that between "collective," in some generic sense, and "private" ownership and control, but rather it is that between patterns of ownership and control that allow competitive discipline to exercise an influence and those that do not. And here reference to the relationship between socialism and the nation-state, as previously discussed, is again necessary. To the extent that productive sectors are collectivized by communities that compete, one with another, within the larger economy defined by the boundaries of the nation-state, it is inappropriate to classify these sectors to be "socialist" for the purpose at hand.

As an example, we may return to education. If the provision of educational services is organized and financed by local units, by localized collectives, that exist alongside each other in a more extensive national economy, the educational services industry is surely closer, descriptively, to the market pole than to that of centralized, monolithic socialism. In a real sense, the separate local units simply replace individuals (families) or firms as units in the working of market organization. And the total investment in, and final distribution of, educational services in the national economy is *not* collectively determined at all; these are, instead, emergent outcomes of the many locally collectivized but decentralized choices that are made separately and independent of each other. The competition with other units must, of course, severely constrain the operation of the activity or enterprise that is locally collectivized, even to the extent of eliminating the semblance of collective control, as such. There may be, however, institutional arrangements that will, simultaneously, allow for some exploitation of competitive forces and some satisfaction of collectivist urges.

The failures of centralized socialism should carry a message for reformers who would shift toward more centralized organization and control of locally collectivized or socialized productive sectors. In the United States, we should beware of efforts to nationalize the educational industry, along with other parts of the public sector that remain largely, if not totally, under localized collective control. Standardization will almost surely reduce, if not eliminate, the competition among localized collectives, thereby exacerbating the informational and incentive problems, with little or no gain in scale economies.

I propose, now, to concentrate attention on those sectors that are centrally socialized, by which I mean that the collective unit is coincident in authority with the broadly inclusive national economy or economic nexus. What lessons can be drawn from the failures of socialism, as a general principle of organization, for these centrally socialized industries, and what reforms might we expect to see proposed and possibly implemented?

The response to this question depends on the extent to which the demise of socialism, as fact, carries with it the demise of socialism, as an idea—the distinction mentioned earlier. If the failures of socialism, in practice, have served to undermine the intellectual-ideological bases that have served to legitimize the institutions of socialist organization, we might, indeed, predict such carryover. Those socialized sectors of mixed economies will, in this case, be subjected to increasing critical scrutiny in the decades ahead, and reforms that are summarized under the "privatization" rubric will become even more frequently observed to become potentially effective. If, however, the intellectual-ideological foundations for socialist order are able substantially to withstand the events of 1989, we may predict minimal carryover impact on the operation and support of socialist sectors of Western economies. Is socialism now rejected as an ideal or does its failure refer only to attempted practical implementation of an ideal that remains?

What is the socialist ideal? And to what is it counterposed in ideological argument? As noted earlier, the central normative thesis is that the allocation of resources and the distribution of product should be controlled collectively—that allocation and distribution should not be left to emerge from the coordination processes of the market in which individuals, separately, make choices without consideration of economy-wide allocative or distributive consequences. In this definition of the central normative thrust of socialism, so-called "market socialism" appears to be an aberration. An organization of the economy that would serve to satisfy the separate demands of individuals, as expressed in some artificially constructed institutional analogues to markets, would totally fail to advance the socialist ideal, which is precisely that of replacing the spontaneity of decentralized individual choice with explicit collective control.

My own assessment is that despite the events of 1989 there has been little flagging in intellectual support for socialism as an ideal. The demonstrable failures have produced a begrudging recognition that informational, incentive and entrepreneurial difficulties encountered in efforts collectively to control whole economies are overwhelming, and that decollectivization is dictated in many sectors. But the necessary trade-off is seen to be that between the sacrifice of collective control—a sacrifice that is intrinsically undesirable—and the promised gains in productivity, an objective that is valued. The liberal position that rejects the desirability of collective control, quite apart from its efficacy, has not informed the thinking of more than a very small number of the participants in the post-1989 discourse.

If my interpretation is correct here, we should not expect dramatic shifts in the organization of currently socialized sectors of those countries whose economies have not been described to be within the explicitly socialist group. Reform movements that include privatization have been and will be observed, but these movements will be motivated primarily by pragmatic objectives of internal efficiency rather than by a reversal of the underlying socialist ideal. There will, of course, be a greater awareness of the efficiency-damaging features of collectivized control, wherever exercised. But there will also be increasing recognition that the presence of a substantially large market sector, alongside the socialist one, must, in itself, place limits on the inefficiency of collectivist organization.

So long as resources, and especially labour, are allowed to move between the market and socialist sectors, while, at the same time, persons are allowed to enter into private production of close substitutes for goods and services that are produced collectively, there are "inefficiency boundaries" that socialized or nationalized industries cannot go beyond. If collectivized industries are open to market competition, both in input and output markets, both domestic and foreign, there could be little or no basis for depoliticization *per se*. The critical element is, of course, that collectivization, as it operates, tends to carry with it monopolistic restriction that allows for the exploitation of resource suppliers and product demanders. (An example is the US Postal Service which could scarcely be viable except for its legally protected monopoly position.) As noted earlier, it is the absence of competition that is crucial here, and it is competition, as the embodiment of the spontaneous forces of the market, that the socialist ideology categorically rejects.

## Welfare Transfers in Market Economies

I have defined socialism, generally, as collective control of the allocation of resources among separate uses and the distribution of products among persons in the political community. This definition has the advantage of facilitating a categorical distinction between socialism, so defined, and the welfare or transfer state. By the latter, as a generalized organizational structure, I refer to an economy-polity in which individuals are allowed to determine the allocation of resources through decentralized markets, both for inputs and for outputs. Consumers are the ultimate sovereigns, as in the idealized market economy of the classical liberals. In its idealization the welfare state embodies no collective control over allocation, but it does claim collective authority and control over the *distribution* of economic value among persons of the community.

The distinction between socialism and the welfare state, as idealized forms of organization, may be illustrated by reference to Bentham's famous utilitarian comparison between pushpin and poetry. The socialist position requires a collective evaluation as between these two uses of scarce resources, presumably with a bias toward elevating poetry to priority status. The position of the welfarist would not, ideally, allow for a judgment as between such uses of resources; rather, the position would imply that if the distribution of economic value is arranged to meet collectively determined norms any allocation as between pushpin and poetry might be indirectly legitimized. Again by comparison, and in its idealized form, the classical liberal position would legitimize any allocation and any distribution that emerges from the free play of market forces.

Of course, we should rarely expect to find personal representatives for either of these ideal-type positions. Many of those who are classified as classical liberals, myself included, may assign normative legitimacy to limited collective redistribution and may also recognize that collective allocation is necessary in technologically defined public goods interactions. Similarly, many supporters of modern welfare transfers, although they place their primary normative emphasis on distribution, may extend collective norms to the allocation of basic goods such as education and medical care. Some mixture of ideal types may be anticipated, but the distinction made here between socialism and welfare statism is important because, post-1989, many of those who espoused socialism have made efforts to shift the meaning of this term so as to make it apply primarily to the welfare state idealization of collectivized distribution. In the face of this apparently determined effort to capture terminological ground, the categorical distinction between socialist allocation and welfarist distribution deserves emphasis.

What elements in socialism's failure extend, at least in principle, to the organization and operation of the redistributionist welfare or transfer state? Listed above as sources for socialism's failure were knowledge, incentives, entrepreneurship and scale. Because allocation is not explicitly collectivized in the welfare state, problems of knowledge, incentive incompatibility and entrepreneurship are substantially attenuated by comparison with the socialist order, despite the collectivization of distribution. Individuals in their capacities as producers, organizers of firms, entrepreneurs and input suppliers are at liberty to respond to the demands of individuals as demanders of outputs. They can take advantage of localized information, and they face incentives that are ultimately consistent with the demands of consumers. Indirectly, the distortions induced by the tax-transfer mechanism must, of course, reduce efficiency in some ways comparable to full-scale collectivization. But there remains a difference in kind as between socialism and the transfer state.

The welfare-transfer state encounters its own difficulties, however, in the form of *motivational,* as opposed to *directional,* incentives. The worker-investor-producer-entrepreneur in the redistributionist state may face proper directional signals, but these signals are weak by comparison with those present in the liberal order. For example, an investment or profit opportunity may promise a differential return of $100 over alternative prospects, pre-tax and pre-transfer. But, with a relatively large transfer sector, this differential may be reduced to, say, $40, post-tax and post-transfer. Clearly, the effect is to make the response more sluggish and to make the aggregate economy less flexible in adjusting to changes in technology as well as to other exogenous shifts in the environment.

Closely related to, but different from, the generalized motivational problem, the welfare-oriented collectivity also finds it impossible to levy charges and pass out transfers in a nondiscriminatory manner. Some producers of economic value will be taxed heavily, some lightly and some not at all. Some claimants for transfers will secure large stipends, some small stipends and some no stipends at all. And the existence, and the persistence, of such differentials in treatment will, in turn, offer incentives for persons, as producers and as claimants, to shift from disfavoured to favoured positions. The result is allocational distortion by comparison with the efficiency norms of the ideally neutral structure. These "excess burden" costs may become large in the large welfare state, and they are over and beyond those identified to emerge under the generalized motivational rubric above. I shall discuss still a further incentive related basis for partial failure of the welfare state in the section following.

The welfare-transfer state, like the socialist state, can only with difficulty remain open to the necessary competitiveness of international markets. The incentive difficulties noted above ensure that the country that attempts relatively more comprehensive redistribution than its trading counterparts must suffer the consequences in its rate of economic growth. Recognition of this elementary fact exerts dual pressures: toward limits on the size of the transfer sector internally and toward national autonomy. If the second of these influences predominates in policy direction, there must be losses from the failure to exploit the scale advantages that are captured only in the international trading nexus.

## Political Economy and Democratic Governance

This book, as well as this chapter, is entitled "Post-Socialist Political Economy," which suggests that the political and economic elements of social organization cannot be readily disentangled. The demise of socialism involves both the acknowledged economic failures of collective control of resource allocation and product distribution and the accompanying failures of governance processes to secure individual rights and liberties. Socialism, as a totalitarian political regime, has been rejected by the regime's members, almost independent of its economic record. Unfortunately, it is also the case that many persons remain under the delusion that the introduction of democratic governance will, as if by some magic, ensure the satisfactory resolution of all problems of economic organization. This view imputes the failures in historical experience to those of politics rather than economics, and the romanticized contradiction of "democratic socialism" is still encountered in quasi-serious argument. In terms of current ideological impetus, the thrust toward democratization of the politics of the socialist bloc countries seems more powerful than that toward decollectivization of the economies. And the painful transition of these countries toward some post-socialist political economy will surely be marked by some shattering of the roseate dreams of democratic deliverance.

The post-socialist political economies of Western countries will be democratic, in both form and substance. The demise of communism as the socialist embodiment has substantially eliminated any threat of totalitarianism. But democratic governance creates its own problems, and especially democratic governance that operates without satisfactory constitutional constraints. These problems ensure that those sectors that are socialist in organizational form are not operated at levels of efficiency that would be attainable, even given the standard incentive and knowledge constraints. Over and beyond these familiar efficiency-reducing elements inherent in socialist organization as such, there are particular constraints that emerge in democratic settings. Employees in socialized industries make up a natural interest group that is able to bring pressure on democratically elected legislators. The socialist equivalent to bankruptcy in the market does not exist. Producing interests, whether in socialized or market sectors, will always seek differential protection. But a major transactions cost barrier is supervened by the monopolistic structure of socialized industries. A private industry must first bear the costs of internal cartelization before seeking legislative protection. A socialized industry is effectively cartelized from the moment of its establishment.

The interactions between the institutions of democratic governance and the welfare-transfer sector of modern states accentuate one efficiency-reducing feature of any collective intrusion into market order. If a substantial share of the total economic value produced in an economy is coercively transferred from those who initially receive payments as pre-tax distributive shares to those who qualify as claimants or recipients, there arise incentives, not only to avoid assigned tax liabilities and to qualify for claims, but, in addition, to change the structure of the tax-transfer system through the political process. Investment in rent seeking seems to offer profit opportunities. Individuals and groups will seek not only to capture the rents that any existing tax-transfer system makes possible, but also to modify directly the structure of the system itself. This sort of rent seeking activity is "socially wasteful" in a way that differs from the more familiar excess-burden destruction of potential economic value. The interest group that secures favourable tax or transfer treatment for its members may find its investment profitable, but other competing groups incur losses. And the total investment may far exceed the politically created gains that seem to be promised.[4]

---

4. The rent seeking research programme dates from the seminal paper by Gordon Tullock, "The Welfare Costs of Tariffs, Monopolies, and Theft," *Western Economic Journal*

Overt exploitation of democratic politics as a means to further differential advantages by particular groups in the economy will increase as the ideological "temperature" falls from that level that described the long socialist epoch. To the extent that individuals considered themselves to be members of an inclusive, economy-wide collectivity, as opposed to identification with separated interest groups, there was less motivation to seek gains at the expense of others within the larger nexus. If, and to the extent that, this collective mind-set becomes weaker, separate groups will try to use institutions of democratic politics along with those of markets to secure differential advantages. The "end of ideology," whether total or partial, is not without major costs. This effect is perhaps especially important in those countries that previously organized their economies on socialist principles, but the spillovers will also apply to any countries that contain large socialist and/or transfer sectors.

## Utopian Speculations

To this point, I have confined discussion largely to positive analysis of the political economy of the post-socialist epoch that we are now entering. In sum, I have suggested that this period will be described as one in which the socialist-collectivist mind-set will not have disappeared, although it must exert a significantly reduced influence on events. There will be general, although begrudging, acknowledgement that market organization is superior in the generation of economic value. But this attitude will have minor spillover effects on the socialized or transfer sectors of nonsocialist economies. A genuinely revolutionary establishment of the ideal structure of political economy as envisaged by the classical liberals will not take place. Individuals remain unwilling to jettison romanticized notions of collective control over economic processes. Economic understanding, in itself, does not produce ideological conversion to *laissez-faire.*

Effective reform must incorporate both the advances in economic understanding, based on the experiences of history and on progress in analysis,

---

(now *Economic Inquiry*) 5 (1967): 224–32. Most of the early contributions are contained in James M. Buchanan, Robert D. Tollison and Gordon Tullock, eds., *Toward a Theory of the Rent-Seeking Society* (College Station: Texas A&M University Press, 1980).

and the inner collectivist-communitarian urges that motivate the behaviour of many individuals. These two elements carry implications that are directly contradictory only in those institutional settings that are described by a precise correspondence or mapping between the political and the economic nexus—a correspondence that was rarely questioned in the epoch of the political nation-state and the attempted socialist organization of national economies. Reform that is aimed toward some breaking of this correspondence offers the genuine opportunity of the coming decades.

Markets succeed in producing higher-valued bundles of goods and services because they exploit the forces of *competition*; socialism fails because these forces are not allowed to operate. The emphasis here is on the presence or absence of competition rather than upon the presence or absence of collective organization, as such. The implication is that if the collective unit that might be organized to meet the collectivist urges can be placed in competitive settings the limits to inefficient operation are built into the system. To the extent that the economy of a nation-state can be opened up to the competitive forces of international markets, the potential failures of internalized collective controls, even if attempted, are severe. Further, if a devolution of activities to locally organized collective units can generate competitive forces within the nation-state as among these units, that will ensure at least tolerable efficiency in operation. Federal, confederal and consociational structures, both within existing nation-states and between and among such nation-states, surely become the subject matter of research programmes of increasing importance. The European community of nations offers perhaps the critical testing ground here. Will the historical nation-states of Western Europe move toward a common market economy that will exploit the forces of competition among the separate national units, or will these nation-states try to implement Europe-wide collective control over the whole economy? In the first case, Europe will, indeed, become the dominant economy of the next few decades. In the second case, Europe will stagnate.

Technology may be important in shaping the events of history. The information-communication revolution has served to bring all parts of the world closer one to another. In an optimistic projection, this technology might guarantee that the economies of the world will become more open, and that the increased competitiveness, on many levels, will act to constrain severely the efficiency-reducing effects of attempted collective controls.[5] The utopian realist, by comparison, will not rely on technology to produce deliverance, but will, instead, advance and support constitutional-institutional change in both the internal political structures of nation-states and the external relationships among these units. Three decades ago, Michael Polanyi, the distinguished chemist turned philosopher–political economist, gave a series of lectures at the University of Virginia under the title "History and Hope."[6] Let me end by using this combination of words to suggest that the history of this century does offer hope for the post-socialist century that will follow. But hope alone is not enough; hard-headed recognition of both the potential and the limits of man's ability to control his destiny is required. And such recognition must replace the romance, or in Hayek's terms, we must shed the "fatal conceit" that described the socialist century.[7]

5. For a presentation of this optimistic projection, see Richard McKenzie and Dwight Lee, *Quicksilver Capital: How the Rapid Movement of Wealth Has Changed the World* (New York: Free Press, 1991).

6. Michael Polanyi, *History and Hope* (London: Routledge, 1962).

7. F. A. Hayek, *The Fatal Conceit: The Errors of Socialism* (Chicago: University of Chicago Press, 1989).

# The Triumph of Economic Science
## Is Fukuyama Wrong and, If So, Why?

## I. Introduction

Francis Fukuyama's book *The End of History and the Last Man* has stimulated too much criticism of its details and too little discussion of its nobler themes. Fukuyama's Hegelian theses involve two components. Liberal democracy and the market economy describe the social order that the dialectic of history has finally produced. But the two components of this order find their separate legitimizations. Liberal democracy offers the only politics that can, even proximately, deliver to persons a felt sense of individual dignity, worth, and respect on terms of equality, even as roughly defined. On the other hand, the market economy represents the institutional embodiment of the long delayed but not universalized acceptance of the scientific truth of classical political economy. "Economic science," defined in its most inclusive sense, has finally carried the day. The social science equivalents of the flat earthers have been put to flight.[1]

In this short paper, I want to concentrate attention on the Fukuyama thesis concerning this ultimate triumph of economic science. I shall discuss the companion thesis dealing with liberal democracy only as it relates to the organization of the economy.

To what extent have the revolutionary events of 1989–91 finally falsified

From *Government Auditing Review* 3, no. 7 (1993): 5–14. Reprinted by permission of the publisher.

1. Francis Fukuyama, *The End of History and the Last Man* (New York: Basic Books, 1991).

the scientific hypothesis that a collectively controlled and managed economy can produce and distribute economic value in any measure remotely comparable to the results emergent in a market economy? To what extent has the empirical evidence been effective in causing skeptics to acknowledge the central truth of economic science? Does the falsification of the collectivization hypothesis carry with it the understanding and acceptance of the alternative hypothesis that embodies the predicted working properties of market organization? In the absence of the underlying ideology of "scientific socialism" working its way through history, can pragmatic collectivist arguments successfully counter those advanced from within the corpus of economic science, as such?

These are questions worth discussing, and, perhaps not surprising to those who may know my own works, I find myself somewhat more sympathetic to Fukuyama's thesis than many of his critics. I hold no naive trust in the persuasive powers of scientific truth, and especially as applied to deliberative institutional change, an attitude that Fukuyama on some reading might be interpreted to express. In the social sciences in particular, there are forces that make for scientific inefficacy, forces that have, until quite recently, been almost wholly absent from the natural or hard sciences. On the other hand, and by contrast, I cannot think that we have yet observed the effects of the removal of the ideological crutch that the socialist ideal offered to all collectivizing efforts, even for those that seemed to be most blatantly motivated by factional interests.

## II. Natural Liberty and the Wealth of Nations

A summary overview of classical political economy may be useful. The great scientific discovery of the eighteenth century was that of the spontaneous co-ordination properties of the market economy. If persons are left to act in their own interests, whatever these may be, within a legal framework of private property and contract (see Part III below), the wealth of a nation will be maximally enhanced, if this wealth is defined in terms of the evaluations that individuals, themselves, place on goods and services. The market economy is, in this sense, "efficient," but more importantly, because the market, in its totally decentralized fashion, carries out the allocative-distributive function, any need for collectivized or politicized management of the economy is obviated. The "natural" proclivity of the scientifically uninformed is to think that in the absence of management chaos must result. The task of economic science, or more appropriately, of political economy, became, and remains after more than two centuries, one of conveying the general understanding of the coordinating properties of markets in increasingly complex institutional reality.

This central idea of "order without design," or consequences that are not within the intent or choices of any person or group, was indeed a discovery of momentous proportion, and, in retrospect, we should be able to appreciate the genuine excitement that was shared by the classical political economists. But, as with many new ideas, the first stages of discovery involve vague and intuitive understandings that emerge well in advance of formal proofs, whether logical or empirical. Classical political economy was, and remained, immature and incomplete in its particulars, and was, in part for this reason, highly vulnerable to critics, and perhaps especially due to the excessive enthusiasm of its own adherents. The bridges between the validity of the central idea and its application to institutional reality were not well or carefully constructed, and the disparities between the idea and reality were seized upon, to great effect, by those who were able to work within the science itself to derive apparent implications that seemed to undermine such validity. I refer, of course, to the genius of Karl Marx, who was masterful in his juxtaposition of the apparently observable flaws in the workings of the imperfect institutional reality of early industrial capitalism with the logical implications of those elements of the classical model that were precisely most in need of correction and revision.

The triumph of classical political economy, if indeed triumph could be claimed at all, was both short-lived and geographically confined. The "discovery of the market," as an institutional-organizational alternative to collectivized management of economic interaction, was embodied in the British politics of the nineteenth century, illustrated in the repeal of the Corn Laws and the opening of markets across national boundaries. The classical understanding also informed the thinking of the American Founders, and United States constitutional history over a century and a half did operate to constrain the politicization of the economy. To a lesser extent, liberal forces, in continental Europe and elsewhere, motivated by the classical idea, emerged in continuing opposition to the developing socialist ideal. But, despite the empirically observed successes, as evidenced in British growth in the nineteenth, and American emergence in the twentieth, century, the idea of the market considered as a scientific proposition did not succeed in getting established firmly for the two centuries following its discovery.

## III. The Legal Order for Laissez Faire

The classical political economists failed to develop their central idea with sufficient rigor and precision to insure against its vulnerability to arguments in support of ideas that were directly in opposition. In some part, this failure involved an insufficient understanding of, and attention to, the critical dependence of an effective market order upon the existence of an underlying legal-institutional structure or framework, which must, in some basic sense, be political in nature and origin. In a crude and naive interpretation, some of the classical advocates of laissez faire, including some modern counterparts, seem to argue that markets emerge and work well quite independent of the characteristics of the legal order.

Adam Smith did not make this mistake. He referred to the "laws and institutions," the existence of which is a necessary condition for market efficacy. Without well-enforced and widely dispersed holdings of private property along with enforcement of binding contracts, a production-exchange nexus cannot function. In a more general sense, the market system of interaction operates only within a set of rules, a constitution, which itself must be explicitly political. But the classical economists, as well as modern social scientists and philosophers, failed to make the categorical distinction between political-collective action aimed at establishing and maintaining the rules, the constitution, within which the economic process takes place, and political-collective action that interferes with or attempts to replace the economic process itself.

It is, of course, necessary to acknowledge here that disagreement may arise, even among scientists, concerning the appropriate dividing line between elements of a constitutional framework and politicized intrusions in a post-constitutional setting. Two areas of disagreement have described economists' discussion in this respect. First, does an operative market economy require constitutional enforcement and protection of competition? Are anti-cartel and anti-trust laws a necessary part of the legal order for laissez faire?

Or do legal guarantees for freedom of entry and exit provide sufficient insurance against exploitation through collusion? Secondly, and perhaps more importantly, and especially in the context of Fukuyama's thesis, can a market economy function in the absence of explicit constitutional rules that guarantee predictability in the value of a monetary unit? Will the market, if left to its own devices, establish a monetary unit, and, if established, will such a unit possess predictability in terms of value through time? Or, is some monetary rule or set of rules a necessary complement to the efficient working of a market economy?

Note that these two hotly disputed areas have offered the sources of much of the criticism of the market economy, and especially that advanced by the socialist critics inspired by Marx. The alleged tendency of unconstrained market forces to stifle competition through collusive arrangements, along with the vulnerability of the whole economy to cyclical fluctuations created by monetary disturbances—these have been employed as effective arguments aimed at demonstrating the failure of the idea of market order generally. Again, adequate recognition of the distinction between constitutional and in-constitutional politics would have allowed defenders of the central idea to acknowledge possible benefits from pro-competition framework rules and from the establishment of an operative monetary constitution. "Laissez faire within constitutional limits" is, and should be, recognized to be quite different from "laissez faire without limits." But does the failure of the socialist ideal imply that the relevant distinction here will be now easier to make convincing than was the case a century past?

## IV. The Fatal Conceit of Socialism

F. A. Hayek entitled his last book *The Fatal Conceit,* referring explicitly to socialism as an organizing principle for an economy.[2] This characterization is one-half correct. The serious consideration of socialism as a general scheme for economic order emerged as an unexamined notion from the presumptive arrogance of intellectuals who claimed to know something about the economic process. Given an artificial "understanding" of how an economy, as

2. F. A. Hayek, *The Fatal Conceit: The Errors of Socialism* (Chicago: University of Chicago Press, 1989).

organized through markets, allocates resources and distributes products, and then observing alleged failures of markets to work in accordance with their idealizations, it seemed relatively easy for these intellectuals to imagine, to conceive, how an ideally operative collective process could correct for all the "market failures," while, at the same time, accomplishing the separation between consumption and production that had been the stuff of utopian dreams for centuries.

We now know, of course, that those intellectuals who advanced the idea of socialism neither understood how markets do work nor took the elementary step of comparing less-than-idealized markets with less-than-idealized collective arrangements. Markets produce economic value if value is defined as that which persons, as participants in the process, themselves desire. The value scale upon which differing goods and services may be evaluated, one against another, emerges in the production-exchange process. Such a scale does not, and cannot, exist independently, and it cannot, therefore, be available for bureaucrats who may be procedurally directed to meet standards without meaning. Even more importantly, economic value must be brought into being by production. Value does not exist to be allocated among end uses. Production requires outlay of effort, mainly labor, and persons will make such outlay voluntarily only if they expect to secure a return flow of product value, in such form as they define to be valuable. This most elementary of all economic exchange is denied validity in the principle of socialism, as such, where the idealized arrangement is consumption without production.[3]

Even if collectivization itself could work in accordance with some ideal model in which the bureaucrats themselves are totally benevolent, efforts at duplicating the operation of a market economy would surely fail for the basic reasons noted, as well as others that might be added. But it is perhaps easier to understand why economists blundered in their implicit analyses of markets than it is to understand why they, along with their intellectual fellows, adopted without question the presumption that collectivization in practice would correspond with the modelled ideal. Why were the bureaucrats who

---

3. See James M. Buchanan, "Consumption without Production: The Impossible Idyll of Socialism" (Center for Study of Public Choice, 1992, typescript).

were to manage the controlled economy presumed to be immune to ordinary incentives? Who should have been surprised when bureaucrats in socialist regimes were revealed to enjoy the perquisites of authority and to seek to increase this authority through time? Who should have been surprised by the developing distinction between the classes, between the managers and the managed, a distinction that puts to shame any alleged worker-capitalist conflict in market regimes?

If this were the end of it, I could end the paper at this point with the summary conclusion that Fukuyama is basically correct in his diagnosis. The fatal conceit that was socialism amounted to scientific-intellectual error that has now been put right. Markets are now much more fully understood. We know how markets create value through utilizing localized knowledge and how they channel incentives to insure that the value produced is the value demanded. We also know how schemes for collectivization-politicization founder on the shoals of incentive incompatibility.

## V. Every Man His Own Economist

Unfortunately, the fatal conceit of socialism is not the end of the argument. And recall that I stated that Hayek was only one-half correct in his assessment. The monumental scientific error that socialism embodied would never have attained its practical successes without the acquiescent support that was grounded in ascientific and unreasoned public attitude. Such an attitude stands as a barrier to any generalized acceptance of the supremacy of market organization in delivering economic value, and especially as this attitude seems relatively immune to either empirical or logical argument.

I referred earlier to persons' natural proclivity to think that an economy must be "managed." The basic idea of an emergent *order* arising from the separated but interdependent choices and actions of many participants seems counter-intuitive to the ordinary citizen who thinks at all about economic process. Without someone in charge, without a manager or at least a management team, the noneconomist predicts chaos. And, since at least some patterns of order may be observed, the noneconomist is likely to impute managing roles to an elite, an establishment, or a clique in the absence of explicit political authority. For those who model the working of the market economy as the secret machinations of the "gnomes of Zurich," "Wall Street bankers," "the Trilateral Commission," or some other equivalent, the explicit take-over of authority by politicization seems both a small and a "democratic" step.

This generalized public attitude that the economic process requires micromanagement which might as well be explicitly political is strongly supplemented by the related imputation of artifactuality to the operation of economic laws. Common reference is made to the immutability of the law of gravity in specific comparison to the law of supply and demand, with the latter being deemed subject to manipulation aimed to produce desired results. If a particular price that emerges from market forces is "too high" (or "too low"), public attitudes tend to support political-collective action that, quite simply, sets price at some preferred level, as if such action arbitrarily settles the matter. This attitude carries with it little or no recognition that if market prices are not allowed to do their job, alternative means both of rationing supplies and of calling forth production must be found. The necessary enhancement of the state's coercive authority tends to be left almost totally out of account. Even in those national economies that are not, and have never been, organized on socialist principles, there is no general public understanding of the "principles of economics." Such economies remain always vulnerable to politicization in the small, whether aimed at micro- or macromanagement.

The absence of understanding would not, in itself, lead to political intrusions that are so directionally biased were it not for the public presumption that, indeed, the operation of markets is within the working knowledge of everyone. "Every man his own economist," or "do it yourself economics," has been a characteristic feature of policy discourse since the professionalization of the science.[4] Nowhere is this presumption more detrimental to the implementation of scientific analysis than in application to trade across national political boundaries. Even in settings where the citizenry, perhaps begrudgingly, acknowledges the efficacy of markets internally, there is likely to be the public conviction that the opening of markets to "foreign competition" is harmful. And even if direct management of the domestic economy is not politically in play, arguments for managed trade and industrial policy find widespread public support.

4. David Henderson, *Innocence and Design* (Oxford: Blackwell, 1986).

## VI. The Distributional Politics of Unconstrained Democracy

Supporters of Fukuyama's thesis with reference to the relative superiority of market organization of economies might acknowledge difficulties in securing public understanding of the truths revealed in the socialist collapse. At the same time, these supporters may express a faith in the ultimate efficacy of empirical and logical argument, and especially in the absence of socialism's underlying ideological thrust. In this Section, I propose to raise what is perhaps a more damaging criticism of the Fukuyama hypothesis that does not depend on any public failure to recognize the findings of science. For purposes of the discussion here, we may assume that the principles of economics are fully understood, and that no one questions the relative superiority of a market economy to generate economic value in the aggregate. We may even go further and suggest that everyone may also recognize that any politicization of the market does enhance the coercive power of the state.

In such a setting, an organizational regime that includes a viable market economy is clearly in each person's constitutional or generalized interest. At the same time, however, each person's differential or factional interest diverges from the generalized standard. Although all persons prefer a market regime for others, each person also prefers that his or her own industry, defined by product and resource category, profession, occupation, location, or other identifying economic characteristic be treated as an exception and protected from market forces by the agencies of politics.

Despite the possible widespread understanding that a market economy does, indeed, generate a relatively larger value, in the aggregate, than any politicized alternative, persons behave rationally when they engage in the political game among factions. No person is likely to express primary concern about aggregate value when there exist apparent opportunities to secure differentially advantageous shares in somewhat less-than-maximal totals. Five per cent of a total of one hundred is larger than one per cent of a total of two hundred; the arithmetic is as simple as that.

The impossibility that all claimant groups can succeed in getting differential treatment may be recognized, along with the overall effects of the political game. At the same time, however, the expected value of success may be such as to keep all groups in the continuing game. To return to the simple arithmetical illustration: even a fifty per cent prospect of securing five per cent of the total of one hundred exceeds the certain prospect of a "fair" one per cent of two hundred. And these odds are biased even further when it is recognized that, by opting out of the game among groups, the prospect of getting an "even shake" or "fair share" may be dramatically reduced.

At this point, it should be clear that the two parts of Fukuyama's argument cannot be separated. The triumph of economic science will come to be practically realized only if the institutions of liberal democracy are those that reflect an understanding of the dilemma created by the disparity between factional or group interest and the general or constitutional interest. In this context, it seems singularly unfortunate that the collectivist urges that motivated the socialist piecemeal experiments in nonsocialist regimes, many of which were general in purpose and intent, provided a protective cover for the rapid growth of factional politics, best described as a distributive game among competing groups, each of which seeks a differentially advantageous share in economic value without regard to the general interest.

This explosion of distributive politics, euphemistically called "the welfare state," particularly in the twentieth century, was aided and abetted by intellectual-academic failure to develop a behavioral science of politics itself.[5] From its ancient Greek origins, the dominant political "theory" modelled politics as a continuing search for "the true and the beautiful" rather than as a set of institutions established to allow persons to act collectively in pursuit of their own interests, whatever these might be. In the conventional model, the emergence of "democracy" means only that all persons are allowed to enter into the discussion and to express views about what is "best" for the collective whole. And in this idealized conceptualization, the actual decision rule for terminating the discussion takes on relatively little significance. Majority voting rules in representative assemblies developed almost without any accompanying legitimizing analytical base. Given this history of ideas in political theory, it is not surprising that little or no attention was devoted to the desirability, or even the necessity, of placing limits on the range and scope for politicization through majoritarian democracy.

---

5. James M. Buchanan, "Politics without Romance: A Sketch of Positive Public Choice Theory and Its Normative Implications," *IHS-Journal, Zeitschrift des Instituts für Höhere Studien, Wien* 3 (1979): B1–B11.

Under the alternative (the "public choice" or "economic") model of democracy, in which persons seek to accomplish collectively those objectives that they consider less effectively achieved privately or individually, it is self-evident that public behavior through politics must be constrained similarly to private behavior. Just as it is illegal for one person to take another's private holdings, it must also be "illegal," in some constitutional sense, for one particular majority coalition to take the holdings of members of the opposing minority. A legal regime that protects a person's property from predation by other persons or privately organized groups but which allows such property to be taken by majoritarian political action does not describe a setting within which the market economy can function effectively. Persons will find it relatively more advantageous to seek rents or profits through politics than through production and exchange. Further, to the extent that politics, no matter how "democratic" the process might be, is distributionally driven, no economic value is created. And, indeed, economic value will be destroyed, or wasted, by the rent-seeking activities of those who participate in the inclusive distributional game.[6]

## VII. Constitutional Legitimacy, Generalization, and the Rule of Law

Is it possible that the dialectic between the market and its collectivist alternative has run its course and that in this sense at least we can signal the triumph of economic science? Or can we predict that failures of public understanding along with rational pursuits of differential distributional interests will only produce the nonideological "churning state"?[7] That which seems to be missing from Fukuyama's treatment is the recognition that "liberal democracy" carries at least two categorically different understandings of its meaning, and that any triumph of economic science may be realized only on the acceptance of one of these alternatives. To what extent do the revolutions of 1989–91 have implications for the ultimate acceptance of that understand-

6. Gordon Tullock, "The Welfare Costs of Tariffs, Monopolies, and Theft," *Western Economic Journal* 5 (June 1967): 224–32; James M. Buchanan, Robert D. Tollison, Gordon Tullock, eds., *Toward a Theory of the Rent-Seeking Society* (College Station: Texas A&M University Press, 1980).

7. Anthony de Jasay, *The State* (Oxford: Blackwell, 1985).

ing of "liberal democracy" that is necessary for the effective operation of a market economy?

An attempt to answer this question requires a separation between those societies where the revolutions occurred, where socialist regimes were displaced, and those societies which remain organized democratically but which are described as operating with more-or-less strongly politicized market economies. In the first group, there is strong public reaction against the observed history of bureaucratic excesses, and at least nominal support is given, provisionally, to privatization of holdings as a basis for the development of market economies. The institutions, whether those of democratic governance or a market economy, will not, of course, emerge in ready-made patterns comparable to those in Western regimes. But the countries of Central and Eastern Europe face the genuine opportunity to establish both liberal democracy and a market economy, based on the understanding that democracy must be reined in by constitutional limits.

The situation seems quite different in the Western welfare states that combine democratic electoral procedures with distributive politics. Simple observation indicates that the political dialogue in these countries has been scarcely affected at all by the revolutions that have occurred. "Politics as usual" describes the state of play, and even the general movement toward privatization of government enterprise that seemed popular in the 1980's seems to have lost momentum.

Such simple observation may, however, be deceptive. The anti-socialist revolutions may have provided the origins of the generalized public attitudes toward the excesses of distributive politics that we can begin to recognize. In the United States in particular, but also in Italy and elsewhere, there is strong public or citizenry opposition to politics and politicians, to the bureaucratic intrusions into the personal and economic affairs of citizens. In the waning years of the century there may well be opportunities to correct the understanding of liberal democracy and to put in place constitutional restrictions on the wastage of value generated by the distributional competition of factions.

If Fukuyama's two-part thesis is to be corroborated, the politics of democracy must be reconstructed so as to remove differential distributional gains from constitutional legitimacy. Separately identified economic groups or interests must be constitutionally prohibited from taking political action (through majority coalition formation) that will provide differential benefits that are not enjoyed by all members of the inclusive polity. Democratic politics must be *generalized* in its effects, much like the long-acknowledged generalization expressed as the objective for the legal order. Particular persons and groups cannot be singled out for differential treatment, either beneficial or harmful, if the rule of law prevails, and, indeed, it is the absence of such treatment that defines the rule of law itself. Democratic politics must be brought within a comparable generalization principle, as expressly embodied in and enforceable through constitutional precepts.

As generalized, democratic politics would allow persons to choose among alternatives in terms of their generalized interests rather than their differential factional interests. And, in the choice process, so constrained, we might predict that economies would be organized on market principles.

In some summary analysis, the triumph of the science of economics in providing the foundation for the organization of economies through markets must be accompanied by a near-revolution in the understanding of what liberal democracy means. Without the ideological crutch that socialism provided, such a near-revolution in political understanding may be easier to accomplish than it now appears. Can the pursuit of differential factional interests stand exposure to the light that can no longer be filtered through Marxist lenses of class conflict, bureaucratic benevolence, and the march of history? At the very least, those who reject Fukuyama's theses and who predict only the workings of the churning state will or should be stimulated to invest in efforts to persuade others that the "end of history" need not be so dismal after all.

# Public Choice after Socialism

## 1. Introduction

"Public Choice" was born during a period of time of intense ideological conflict and grew to maturity more or less in parallel with the decline of the Marxian-socialist-collectivist ideal for the organization of socio-political-economic interaction. Public choice, as a set of ideas about politics, was not a causal influence in the demise of Marxian socialism, which would have taken place even if there had been no such emergence of a subdiscipline. On the other hand, public choice has been influential through its ability to offer an understanding-explanation of the observed failures of political processes, whether these are socialist efforts to control whole societies by command or particularized efforts at sector-by-sector politicization. The consequences of public choice will presumably be reflected in the increased difficulty that collectivist-control advocates will face in restoring the *status quo ante* in non-Western regimes and in expanding the range of politicization in Western settings.

With relatively few exceptions (e.g., George Stigler), dealers in ideas, whether first- or second-hand, agree with the summary statement that "ideas have consequences." And most of us, even if we totally reject Marxian monocausality, also accept the obverse statement that "consequences generate ideas." Especially with reference to ideas relevant to socio-economic-political orders of human interaction, the events of history must surely be allowed to affect both the models that social scientists advance in explanation and the normative models that are suggested by reformers. History is the

From *Public Choice* 77, no. 1 (1993): 67–74. Reprinted by permission of the publisher, Kluwer Academic Publishers.

only laboratory available for social science, even if its limitations in such a role are fully recognized. Indeed, we may suggest that the lags and gaps in the feedback loops between consequences and ideas allow phenomena analogous to the speculative bubbles familiar to theorists of financial markets to occur regularly.

Both the lags and the gaps are important here. The lags refer, of course, to the temporal dimension; participants in social interaction may be slow to recognize the accumulating results of changes in institutional structures. "Failures" may not be sensed for years, decades or possibly even centuries, and especially in the absence of data from competing societies.

The gaps in the effective operation of the loops are perhaps even more significant than the lags. Because of the inability of the social scientist to conduct experiments in closed and controlled laboratories, there is little prospect of generating results that are convincing to skeptics, at least as compared with the enterprise of natural science. In social science, there is nothing akin to "failure to fall off the edge," such as might have once convinced the flat-earther. Any particular set of historical results, as observed, may be explained-interpreted by more than a single theoretical framework: falsification in Popper's sense may seldom be possible. Discrimination among alternative hypotheses may require prior agreement on the imagination of an experiment.

## 2. Expanding the Explanatory Domain

What, then, can we make of the current and prospective state of "Public Choice," as an inclusive research program, in the postrevolutionary, post-socialist moment?

We live now in a setting where genuine "public" choice, that is, the set of attitudes held by the citizenry about the behavioral motivation of political actors may have extended beyond any of the models that have been carefully introduced by the academic theorists. The venality that is widely imputed to politicians and bureaucrats is surely misplaced in many instances, and concentration on overt misbehavior distracts attention from the organizational structure that allows the observed results to emerge. There is, in this respect, an important educational role for public choice to play, in its constitutional economics variant, in shifting the focus of discussion and understanding to the institutional-constitutional structure within which politics takes place.

I have addressed the issues of constitutional emphasis elsewhere.[1] Beyond this constitutional emphasis, however, is it time that positive public choice theorists make efforts to expand their domain of inquiry by moving beyond the relatively narrow behavioral limits that seem to be imposed by the economic model for behavior? Should we begin to examine the effects of other motivational postulates on political outcomes?

Consider an example, one that comes naturally to any neoclassical economist. There is a meaningful economic content in the notion of overall economic efficiency, provided that care is taken to place all of the definitions inside the necessary qualifiers. And economists know that any restriction on freedom of persons to exchange, domestic or foreign, tends to reduce efficiency. A smaller-valued bundle of goods is made available to citizens in the economy than would be available in the absence of the restriction.

Let us now allow some members of the legislature to act as if overall efficiency in the national economy matters. These legislators vote against any and all restrictions on trade. But how many members so motivated would be required to insure political support for a general policy of free trade, as opposed to a regime of "black hole tariffs"?[2]

The results suggested by this particular example, and others that might be introduced, are not encouraging for those who want to challenge orthodox public choice models. The single legislator who voted for the "public interest" and, hence, against any and all proposals to restrict trade would find his own constituency interests forced to sell competitively while buying from monopolists.[3] The distributive game that modern democratic politics represents forces the individual legislator to act contrary to any meaningfully defined "public interest." If the legislator does not so act, he or she will not survive in the competitive electoral process.

Introduction of the example into the discussion of the question initially

1. J. M. Buchanan, "The Domain of Constitutional Political Economy," in *The Economics and the Ethics of Constitutional Order* (Ann Arbor: University of Michigan Press, 1991), 3–18.

2. S. P. Magee, W. A. Brock and L. Young, *Black Hole Tariffs and Endogenous Policy Theory* (Cambridge: Cambridge University Press, 1989); J. M. Buchanan and D. R. Lee, "Cartels, Coalitions and Constitutional Politics," *Constitutional Political Economy* 2, no. 2 (1991): 139–69.

3. Buchanan and Lee, "Cartels, Coalitions and Constitutional Politics."

posed as to the motivational postulates for political actors suggests that at least a part of the traditional public choice emphasis, as well as the criticism, has been wrongly placed. Political actors are not necessarily motivated to depart from public interest motivational postulates because they initially are propelled by other objectives. Instead, the structure of the politics in which they act requires them to act contrary to public interests if they are to survive at all. We do not necessarily get the results we see because politicians, like the rest of us, are sometimes motivated by self-interest. We get the results we see because the incentive structures of politics insure the survival of those politicians who do depart from public interest norms. Politicians are forced to seek private interest objectives for much the same reason that private sector entrepreneurs are forced to seek maximal profits. The seminal Alchian analysis of the market's analogue to evolutionary selection can be extended to politics in relatively straightforward fashion.[4] The difference between the two evolutionary models lies in the compatibility with overall efficiency. The profit seeking of the private entrepreneur produces results that tend, when extended over the whole market and particularly to its dynamic growth, to maximize total economic value in the economy. By contrast, the private interest seeking of the elected politician, that is equally necessary with entrepreneurial profit seeking for survival, when extended over the whole political process, tends to shift results away from rather than toward any meaningful conception of "public interest," whether this be economic value or any other generalized objective.

The comparison between the evolutionary forces in market processes and in political processes that is suggested here may be extended generally. Economists have discussed at some length the spontaneous coordination that takes place in an operative market economy, even if there remain aspects of the process that warrant further attention. Public choice analysts, or indeed other political science theorists, have not, to my knowledge, examined in detail the "spontaneous coordination or discoordination" properties of political interaction structures. In both market and political orders, the mathematics of game theory offers a useful beginning, but this mathematics has not been exploited fully in either case. Beyond game theory, however, the in-

---

4. A. Alchian, "Uncertainty, Evolution and Economic Theory," *Journal of Political Economy* 58, no. 3 (1950): 211–21.

sights offered by some of the analyses of spontaneous orders that occur outside of equilibrium settings may prove useful in application to politics as well as to economics.[5]

## 3. Veils That Allow the Crossing of Bridges

How can the bridge between individual pursuit of private or special group interest and promotion of the general interest be crossed? Starting from the orthodox economic model of behavior in which persons are modeled as rational utility maximizers, the only readily available response involves the argument for the design of a choice setting in which the possibly diverging interests coincide, that is, a setting in which pursuit of private or special interest also promotes the general interest. Within a well-structured legal order, the operative market economy accomplishes this feat, provided only that the general interest is defined to be overall economic efficiency. But what is the political analogue that might accomplish the same purpose? Clearly, such an analogue cannot exist so long as politics is conceived as a distributive game among persons and groups in a community.

The distributional elements in politics must be eliminated if private or special interests are to be brought into line with the general interest. And these elements disappear only if the individuals who choose are placed in settings where their own positions (or those of the groups that they represent) are not identified. Such a setting is present if the individual is placed behind a veil of ignorance and/or uncertainty.[6] The individual's own interest becomes equivalent to that of the inclusive group that claims him or her as a member. That which is in the interest of the group, generally, defines the interest of the individual.

The discussion in the preceding section suggests that a somewhat different interpretation and usage of the veil of ignorance and/or uncertainty is pos-

---

5. J. M. Buchanan and V. J. Vanberg, "The Market as a Creative Process," *Economics and Philosophy* 7, no. 2 (1991): 167–86.

6. See J. Harsanyi, "Cardinal Utility in Welfare Economics and in the Theory of Risk-Taking," *Journal of Political Economy* 61, no. 5 (1953): 434–35; J. M. Buchanan and G. Tullock, *The Calculus of Consent: Logical Foundations of Constitutional Democracy* (Ann Arbor: University of Michigan Press, 1962); J. Rawls, *A Theory of Justice* (Cambridge: Harvard University Press, 1971).

sible. In the standard interpretation-usage, as noted, the question is how to design choice settings so as to exploit individual self-interest motivation. The motivation is, in itself, postulated for the whole exercise. The alternative interpretation-usage drops such a postulate. The individual, whether he or she acts privately or as an agent for a special group, may not be "selfishly" motivated; he or she may seek to promote the general or public interest for the inclusive membership of the community. But if the structure that defines the conditions for choice contains distributional features, the person who tries to further the general interest does not survive. In this formulation of the problem, something like a veil of ignorance and/or uncertainty becomes a necessary characteristic of the choice setting if individual participants who may seek to promote the generalized interests are to remain as effective players in the political game.

In this alternative formulation, the veil of ignorance and/or uncertainty offers a bridge that allows for the political survival of those who try to act in furtherance of the general interest, which, only coincidentally, involves action that promotes their own interests or those of the special group represented. The evolutionary perspective surely tempers considerably the criticism of public choice that has been directed at the underlying economic model for individual behavior in politics.

## 4. Public Choice and a Rule of Law

The suggested evolutionary perspective also allows a relationship to be established between the veil of ignorance and/or uncertainty and the rule of law. Critics of the veil, as a practicable device in the design of constitutions as opposed to the derivation of normative principles, à la Rawls, have pointed to the difficulty if not the impossibility of reducing the identifiability of political actors to any extent dictated to be useful in the choice-making exercise. But, if participants, whether at the constitutional or ordinary politics level, cannot fail to identify their own, or their group's, interests, how can the choice setting be modified so as to approximate as closely as possible the conditions provided by the thick veil?

Generalization in the objects for political choice is immediately suggested. If "players" in the political game are required to choose only among options that, if agreed upon by the required coalition of players, must apply to *all* participants, a major source of distributional conflict is removed. (In a simple two-person game, the requirement here removes all off-diagonal cells from the set of possible solutions; choice is reduced to one from among positions along the diagonal itself.) In this construction, any player would continue to have an identifiable distributional interest in securing a solution that will insure differentially advantageous benefit. But a generalization rule would serve effectively to prevent the realization of any such solution, to the differential benefits of anyone or any group.

Return to the free trade example introduced earlier. In the distributive game in which representatives vie for politically enforceable differential restrictions (or differential subsidies) for their constituent industries (or regions, professions, ethnic groups, gender categories, age groups, etc.) any efforts toward promoting a general interest result must be predicted to founder. If, however, a generalized constitutional rule should be in effect that would legally guarantee *equal* treatment for all contending parties (industries, regions, groups, etc.), no such outcome need be observed. If a particular industry should succeed in getting, say, tariff or quota protection that shuts out, say, twenty percent of foreign supply, the general rule would indicate that all imports be cut in like amounts. In this setting, the political choice reduces to the selection of one from among the several *general* alternatives (one from the several cells along the diagonal). While distributional elements are not totally eliminated, the sources of distributional conflict are very substantially reduced, so much so that the elements that remain can be taken to reflect genuinely differing conceptions of what might be the genuine public interest. At the least, in such a choice setting, the political agent who seeks to further the general interest is not faced with a survival threat. In a very real sense, the arguments reduce to those involving alternative visions of what the public interest is.

Modern United States jurisprudence has extended an enforceable rule of law in application to many personal rights; differential or discriminatory treatment by any political authority is prohibited. By dramatic contrast, constitutional interpretation has allowed a progressive narrowing of the rule of law in application to the economic treatment of persons and groups. Political authority may discriminate in treatment with little or no appeal to the violation of generality, as principle. As a result, modern politics, as it is observed, has become increasingly a politics of redistribution. The results follow the patterns predicted by the public choice models. Politicians are required by the nature of the choice settings that they face to act strictly in their own or in their constituents' interests. The politician who tries to do otherwise, who tries to further the public interest, is, at first, ineffective in the game that is played, and, second, is soon eliminated from the ranks of the players. Modern politics selects for those traits that succeed in the distributive game.

## 5. Beyond Science

In this final section, I propose to relate the discussion of Sections 2, 3 and 4 to the intent of the paper, as indicated both in its title and in the Introduction. I suggested that the disfavor toward politics and politicians that describes public attitudes in the postrevolutionary, postsocialist moment may have been extended beyond the limits supportable from either analytical or empirical science. The economic models for the behavior of public choosers that have informed public choice do offer highly useful insights into the political reality that can be observed. And, in this sense, these models produce an explanation-understanding of political failure, generally, and of the grand socialist experiments in particular. But in the postrevolutionary moment more is needed than this science-based understanding of what has happened in history. Extended positive analysis can also prove helpful in suggesting feasible means of achieving reform or moving beyond science into "better" political order.

Public choice, as a predictive-descriptive social science, is vulnerable to the charge that the whole exercise is, at best, amoral, and, at worst, immoral.[7] There is no space for genuinely public-spirited behavior in public choice, as an all-inclusive explanatory model of politics.

I have, first of all, suggested that public choice scholars should be sensitive to such criticisms, and that efforts should be made to examine carefully how changes in the basic motivational postulates might affect results. As I initially opened up discussion in this respect, an evolutionary perspective seemed to

7. S. Kelman, " 'Public Choice' and Public Spirit," *Public Interest* 87, no. 80 (1987): 93–94; G. Brennan and J. M. Buchanan, "Is Public Choice Immoral? The Case for the 'Nobel' Lie," *Virginia Law Review* 74 (March 1988): 179–89.

offer promise. What happens when and if a political representative, or a group of representatives, tries to act in furtherance of the general interest? Within the incentive parameters that describe modern politics, the response seems clear; such a person or group does not survive, as the game is played.

Once this point is recognized, the focus shifts *from* the motivational postulate for the behavior of political actors *to* the characteristics of structure within which the choices are made. (And I acknowledge that orthodox public choice theorists have perhaps been overly defensive of the economic motivational bases for analysis.) The directional effect upon research effort seems clear enough. More attention should be placed on the incentive structure of the politics-as-observed, on the institutions as they are, as opposed to the stylized and sometimes empty models that are driven primarily by the motivational postulate.

Consider two familiar and traditional examples. First, an organized political community, with a long-established, predictable and stable tax-sharing system confronts a genuine public goods decision, say, how much mosquito abatement to finance. The publicness characteristic of the good insures that there will be relatively minor differences among the separate legislative constituencies in benefits received from the program. The orthodox public goods, public choice model is helpful here, but there is nothing in the structure, as such, that makes it either difficult or impossible for a legislator to act in terms of his or her own assessment of the whole community's interest.

Second, a politically organized community without a stable and predictable tax-sharing system faces a collective choice as to the location of one or more special-benefit projects, projects that yield rewards only to identified constituencies. The legislative representative for any constituency must, in such a choice setting, act as an agent for the constituency's members. There is incentive incompatibility with any promotion of the overall general interest, an incompatibility that is not present at all in the first example. In sum, the public-spirited politicians can thrive in the political regime that adheres to general standards of publicness. The private-spirited politicians necessarily emerge in the regime that departs from publicness or generality.

Question: Which example comes closest to the descriptive reality of politics in modern welfare states?

The evolutionary perspective is helpful to the extent that it allows concentration on the survival traits under alternative regimes. More generally, however, an evolutionary perspective must be used with caution lest it be extended too readily to the evolution of regimes, as such, and be taken to imply acquiescence before the forces of history. As the observed politics of Western welfare states demonstrate, there is no assurance that the regimes that evolve are such as to satisfy criteria that include compatibility with the survival of public-spirited political leaders. Both modern Western regimes and those in transition from socialist structures must be treated as institutional variables subject to reform and change through deliberatively motivated action.

My assignment, in accordance with the request of the editors, was to consider possible developments in "public choice" over the course of its second quarter-century. I have made no effort to be comprehensive, and I have not tried to advance either general or specific predictions. I have, instead, outlined the prospects for a research program that seems to offer considerable promise, a program that does parallel developments in applied economic theory, and that does have a potential contribution for those who are trying to design the institutions for those societies in postrevolutionary transition.

# PART FOUR

# Reform without Romance

# Adam Smith as Inspiration

## I. Introduction

Intellectual historians classify Adam Smith as a leading member of the Scottish Enlightenment, taking his place alongside Adam Ferguson, David Hume, Francis Hutcheson and Thomas Reid. In the terminology of the eighteenth century, these were all moral philosophers, but, among them, it is Adam Smith in *The Wealth of Nations* who offers the foundational understanding of the market economy as a necessary and integral component of a free society, or, to use Smith's own term, a "system of natural liberty."[1]

How well are Adam Smith's ideas understood today, more than two centuries after their presentation? As surprising and as frustrating as it may be to many of us, we find the selfsame mercantilist ideas that Smith attacked being propounded daily by our politicians and pundits. In this respect alone, economics is categorically different from its natural science counterparts. We do not learn the principles of political economy in the same way that we learn the principles of physics. Despite the empirical evidence that we can observe, we continue to think, and to behave, as if we can, through political action, subvert the elementary laws.

It is, first, necessary to emphasize that economics is, indeed, a science in that the application of its principles allows us to separate feasible and nonfeasible alternatives. We must accord Adam Smith full credit for elevating confused economic discourse to genuinely scientific understanding. The

From *The Academic World of James M. Buchanan,* ed. Byeong-Ho Gong (Seoul, Korea: Korea Economic Research Institute, 1996). Reprinted by permission of Liberty Fund, Inc.

I am indebted to my colleagues David Fand, David Levy, Yong J. Yoon and Robert Tollison for helpful comments.

1. Adam Smith, *The Wealth of Nations* (1776; New York: Random House, 1937).

principles of this science are both simple and subtle, and the underlying behavioral reality can easily be observed. But how do these principles fit into the larger scheme of things? Adam Smith demonstrated that the growth in the wealth of society may be increased, while, at the same time, persons may enjoy the blessings of natural liberty. Or, conversely, he showed that politicized interferences with natural liberty must, almost necessarily, reduce a society's well-being. He did not, however, naively expect societies to evolve naturally toward some idealized order. And he did not think that the exercise of natural liberty was, in itself, sufficient to guarantee growth in the well-being of citizens.

To Adam Smith, the "laws and institutions," the political-legal framework within which persons interact, one with another, are important and necessary elements in the inclusive "constitution" for the political economy. At the same time, Smith took it more or less for granted that opportunistic behavior would be held in check by norms of mutual respect and reciprocal regard, norms that define a complementary "moral constitution."

Even so qualified, however, Adam Smith was not a naive optimist who predicted that the interdependent choices made by persons in a production-exchange-consumption network would insure growth in living standards through time. The size of this network of market interdependence was a critically important institutional variable. In addition, in a highly controversial and still misunderstood argument, Smith emphasized the importance of the relationship between labor in productive and nonproductive uses.

After all is said, however, why is Adam Smith so different from others of his time, and earlier, others who may have had roughly the same ideas about prosperity, liberty, politics and morals? Smith is, I think, deserving of the fame accorded him, then and now, because he was able to put the separate arguments together in a coherent intellectual package that, taken in total, amounted to a shift of perspective. Adam Smith was able to create "economic science" because he assumed the stance of a detached observer rather than that of either an adviser to governments or an advocate for organized interests. The ultimate addressee of Smith's discussion is the representative citizen who might participate in a continuing constitutional convention from which there emerges the structural framework for social interaction—those "laws and institutions" that act to channel man's seeking betterment of his own position in ways that insure the promotion of the interests of his peers.

It is not surprising that the basic ideas in Adam Smith's *The Wealth of Nations,* published in 1776, the same year as Thomas Jefferson's *Declaration of Independence,* should have been highly congenial to the American Founders, who were, almost to a man, engaged in genuine "constitutional" thinking, and who held, as bedrock convictions, profound dedication to individual liberty along with profound distrust of political authority. This philosophical stance, or *Weltanschauung,* that characterized the great minds of the late eighteenth century, is difficult for many of our peers in the late twentieth century to understand and appreciate, as we stand here, having soaked up, sponge-like, the historical experience of the intervening socialist epoch, as this experience exerted its impact both through its ideas and through the observed political consequences of these ideas in practice.

In this lecture, I shall try to flesh out and to elaborate the several related points outlined in this summary introduction. As my remarks suggest, I am setting up, or reconstructing, Adam Smith, if you will, as inspiration (hence my title) for participation in the continuing constitutional dialogue that must engage us all, whether actively or passively, as we reevaluate the foundations of socio-political order early in the post-socialist era.

## II. Adam Smith and the Science of Political Economy

*The Wealth of Nations* is a massive book—wealthy in historical, institutional and descriptive detail. The sometimes disparate material is integrated by Smith's nondeviating focus on a central thesis: the politically orchestrated network of regulatory controls—the mercantilist system—operates so as to reduce the level of economic well-being of citizens, while, at the same time, such a system arbitrarily restricts personal liberties.

To support this argument, it was necessary for Adam Smith to show how an economy, if freed of the whole regulatory apparatus, would work. The analytical description of a market economy became a complementary component to any demonstration of mercantilist failure. In this sense, and on a first consideration, the Smithean exercise seems to be the precise opposite to that of the welfare economics of the mid–twentieth century. In the latter, demonstrations of market failure were held to offer *prima facie* support for politicized correction. To Smith, demonstrations of regulatory failure offer support for depoliticization. Such a comparison is, however, much too simplistic because it fails to isolate a fundamental distinction between the two exercises, as separated by almost two centuries. The classical (Smithean) argument for decontrol (or depoliticization) and the welfare economists' argument for control (for politicization) are on all fours only if we presume the existence of the same underlying evaluative standard in the two cases. To suggest, with the welfare economists, that market failure supports politicization, there must be not only departures from the necessary conditions for efficiency, but also some presumption that political action is informed by a knowledge of what the allocatively efficient solution is, quite apart from the operation of politics itself. By contrast, to suggest, with Adam Smith, that regulatory failure supports market liberalization does not require any presumptive knowledge about what particular outcome is likely to produce maximal value. There is a categorical epistemological difference between the two comparative exercises, a difference that many modern economists still do not understand.

How can a regime be evaluated until and unless a standard has been first established? How can it be suggested that a market regime (Smith's regime of natural liberty) generates "better" results than a regime of politicized control until and unless some criterion for "betterness" is pre-selected? Adam Smith's answer to this question comes close to being genuinely revolutionary. A strictly subjective response would suggest that a regime that allows people liberty to make their own choices, whatever these may be, works "better" because the proper criterion for "betterness" is nothing other than the satisfaction of the preferences that such private choices reflect. The wealth of a nation is measured by the well-being of its members, and especially of its lower classes, as defined through their own separated but interdependent freely exercised choices. As noted, Adam Smith was not quite willing to go all the way to such a radical subjectivist vision, as Section V below indicates. Within the limits imposed by his productive-unproductive labor distinction, however, he was quite willing to allow persons to be free to choose, and, indeed, he was steadfast in his criticism of mercantilist efforts to quantify and measure national well-being by accumulation of treasure.

As I noted earlier, Smith's insight and understanding of how market exchange coordinates separated individual actions was, at the same time, simple yet subtle. Any such understanding must counter the natural way of thinking which associates coordination with control. To make the whole argument convincing, Adam Smith found it necessary to analyze in some detail the conjectural operation of a whole economy in which the many participants choose and act independently, each within the choice settings separately confronted. The coordinating properties of the network of production, exchange and distribution became the explananda of the inclusive intellectual enterprise. Economic science, as such, was born, and the explanatory purpose came to overwhelm any putative political or ideological motivation. In sum, in order to attack the mercantilist fallacies effectively, Adam Smith needed to show that a free market worked "better." But before he could get to an evaluative comparison at all, he found it necessary to carry out an analytical exercise that was divorced from the underlying motivation.

In the confines of a single lecture, I cannot, of course, sketch out, even in summary outline, the analytical content of Smith's total effort. Nor do I advance any claim that Adam Smith's work is free of ambiguity, confusion and internal contradiction, or that the particular insights were necessarily original with Smith. I do suggest that, nonetheless, the essential elements of what developed as the science first called "political economy" and later simply "economics" are to be found first in *The Wealth of Nations*. And, although indeed there have been major scientific innovations over the two and one-quarter centuries since 1776, we have advanced relatively little in fundamental economic understanding.

Recognition and acknowledgment of this fact brings me back to the distinction between economics and the hard or natural sciences—a distinction alluded to in my introduction. It is unnecessary for the ordinary natural scientist to teach the basic principles of her discipline to a public audience repetitively over a continuing sequence of periods. The elementary laws of physics or chemistry are taught in college classrooms, and the citizen, whether in her private or public capacity, accepts the authority of the science as espoused by the professionally accredited scientist. The feasibility spaces defined by the natural laws are acknowledged to exist. We do not act, in our everyday lives, public or private, as if these laws do not hold. We react with derision to arguments put forth by those who claim to deny the existence of physical reality. We read, but we do not believe, science fiction.

With economics, things are quite different. Despite the efforts of scientists over the two centuries since Adam Smith, the citizenry—and especially in its capacity to act collectively through the agencies of politics—does not acknowledge the authority of economic science or of economists. The feasibility spaces that are laid out by the behavioral postulates that define human nature are not considered to be constraining. We believe and act, every day, on the romantic fiction of the schemer who would have us think that economic reality is what we choose to make it. The crudest of mercantilist fallacies against which Adam Smith directed his finest rhetoric remain alive and well as we end the twentieth century.

Examples abound. But let one recurrent proposal for politically imposed interference with market process suffice—namely, the proposal for the imposition of, or an increase in, a legally enforceable minimum wage. We need to adduce only the most elementary of scientific principles here to predict that any increase in the legal minimum wage, above the level that would be maintained in the absence of political action, must reduce employment. Economic science, as such, must, of course, remain silent on the question as to whether increased unemployment is or is not a praiseworthy objective for policy. But the prediction that the inverse relationship between wage rates and employment exists is as solidly scientific as the elementary laws of physics in their practical application, for example, that water runs downhill.

To deny or to reject the prediction that emerges from this relationship requires a rejection of the fundamental behavioral postulates upon which the whole science of economics is constructed. Persons may be acknowledged to differ, one from another, along many dimensions: in capacities, endowments, preferences, values. And these differences generate predicted differences in behavior. But behavior may be brought within the scope of scientific inquiry if uniformities can be isolated—uniformities that transcend the differences noted.

Adam Smith, and his eighteenth-century peers, experienced the thrill that comes only on discovery when they recognized that the simple proposition that persons try, generally, to improve their own well-being could be used as the behavioral lynchpin upon which an understanding of the whole interaction structure could be erected. And the mark of an economist informed by this understanding, then and now, becomes the ability to reject, as scientifically untenable, implied propositions that deny this central behavioral norm.

Return, then, to the minimum wage example. To reject the prediction that increases in the legally imposed wage cause a reduction in employment requires that those who make hiring decisions, presumably either employers or those who act as employing agents for firms, deliberately choose to reduce rather than to increase their economic positions, their own or those of their principals, either before or after the political action that imposes the wage change.[2] Generalization of this departure from the behavioral uniformity postulated to be the coordinating element which makes the whole structure of market interaction work would, indeed, imply that claims to a scientific status for economics are bogus, and that the market interactions that we observe function without any internally coherent logic of their own. If this were, indeed, the situation, all of us who classify ourselves as professionals had best turn in our badges and return to the intellectual world as it was before Adam Smith—a world in which economic interests, along with sophisticated arguments in support, are omnipresent, but in which economic analysis, as such, does not really exist.

Francis Fukuyama, in his provocative book *The End of History and the Last Man,* suggested that with the demise of socialism, societies everywhere would organize their economies on the basis of market principles, and he interpreted this step to represent the ultimate historical validation of the scientific truths of classical political economy, as first enunciated by Adam Smith.[3] We may wish that Fukuyama's prediction might be corroborated, but the continuing resurgence of mercantilist arguments suggests that economics must face a never-ending struggle to secure and to maintain its sci-

2. For economist nitpickers, perhaps it is necessary to append two separate qualifying statements. First, the standard prediction holds under *ceteris paribus* conditions. This requirement serves to make empirical testing of the hypothesis almost impossible, but it does not, in any way, affect the scientific standing.

Secondly, the textbook curiosum demonstrating that under conditions of monopsony an isolated firm may increase employment in reaction to an imposed increase in wages requires the assumption that entry of other profit-seeking firms is, somehow, prohibited. The "competitive monopsonist," which covers cost only because it purchases labor inputs monopsonistically, will, of course, go bankrupt under an imposed increase in wages.

3. Francis Fukuyama, *The End of History and the Last Man* (New York: Basic Books, 1992).

entific respectability. When we look at intellectual history from the perspective of the here and now, as we must, we stand in awe at Adam Smith's achievement. *The Wealth of Nations* stands as the single great book which, both symbolically and in actuality, allowed economists to stake meaningful claims to admission in the academy of science.

Why did Adam Smith succeed when modern economists seem to falter, even in the face of the overwhelming empirical evidence of socialist-mercantilist failure? He did so because his work was embedded in a comprehensive and coherent vision of social order, some version of which must necessarily find new life in modern constitutional dialogue if liberal society is to survive. I shall explore prospects for such renewal in concluding parts of this lecture.

## III. The Institutional Framework

In the preceding section, I have discussed Adam Smith's criticism of mercantilist ideas that had as a by-product the development of scientific economic analysis. In this section, I propose to shift the emphasis and to discuss aspects of Smith's work that are often neglected, and perhaps especially by those who are among his most ardent and vocal advocates.

Adam Smith gave us an understanding of the internal logic of a system of interlinked market exchanges in which persons, exercising their natural liberties, are able to increase the nation's wealth, defined in terms of the satisfaction of their own preferences. Smith was not, however, so naive as to assume that a regime of markets would emerge, full-blown as it were, from the unconstrained exercise of natural liberties. He did not, to my knowledge, explicitly consider what we may call the Hobbesian problem—that of explaining the emergence of social order from the disorder of natural anarchy.

*The Wealth of Nations* is wide-ranging, but its scope is, nonetheless, limited. Adam Smith was concerned with analyzing the operation of an economy that was depoliticized in the sense of hands-on controls over the processes of economic interaction, whether over potential entry or exit or over terms and conditions under which exchanges are consummated. Smith emphasized, however, that the market economy works only within a functioning set of "laws and institutions," which is, in another sense, necessarily political in the more inclusive constitutional interpretation.

Adam Smith cannot, therefore, be classified as an advocate of *laissez faire,* in the sometimes vulgar extension of this term. The metaphor of the invisible hand was insufficiently expansive to comprehend the emergence of the legal-institutional framework. The concern was with explaining how an economy works without politicized direction but within the legal-institutional parameters summarized in the established laws of property and contract. The "mine and thine" issues that were so central in importance to Thomas Hobbes were presumed to have been settled. The institutional order was established; people were secure in their property; voluntary contracts were enforced.

Within this institutional framework, the wealth of a nation (defined as the expressed well-being of its citizens) depends on the degree to which people are free to choose. In a narrow sense, this institutional structure is one that sometimes has been called the minimal, protective or night-watchman state. But here it is noteworthy that Adam Smith did not propose that political-governmental action be kept strictly within such limits. He was quite prepared to acknowledge that there may be a "public works" role for government—a role that we may summarize under the "productive state" rubric. Another way of interpreting Adam Smith's position here would be to suggest that he raised no objection to the governmental provision of genuinely collective goods and services, at least directly.

The categorical dividing line, for Adam Smith, was drawn where putative claims are made that political direction of the ordinary processes of market exchange can, in some fashion, "improve" on the emergent patterns of allocative-distributive outcomes. As applied to these ordinary channels through which individuals produce, purchase, sell and consume goods and services that they value privately, Adam Smith was, indeed, a proponent of *laissez faire.* For such interactions, politicization could only reduce the value potential that might be generated from any existing resource base as well as decrease the projected rate of aggregate growth.

Adam Smith, along with his peers in the development of classical political economy, was understandably excited by the discovery that there need be no conflict between productive efficiency of the economy and individual liberty. Perhaps the most widely cited passage in *The Wealth of Nations* is the statement that relates the availability of meat for supper to the butcher's self-interest. As elsewhere, however, care must be taken to understand Smith's meaning here. He did not suggest that the unconstrained pursuit of self-interest in all settings will generate desired results. He suggested, instead, that the pursuit of self-interest within the constraints imposed by the discipline of open markets in a regime of private property and contract would tend to promote the well-being of all participants. The occasional deviant butcher, who places his hand on the scales when weighing up the mutton chops, will not survive; he will lose both respect and custom, quite apart from possible legal sanction.

Market discipline, which comes to be developed in settings where entry and exit are open, where property rights are protected and contracts enforced, embodies ethical norms that themselves describe the behavioral parameters for an effective system of natural liberty. The butcher need not sense, on each and every confrontation with a customer, either a threat from potential competitors, a potential lawsuit for fraud or the potential wrath of God. He will, in an effective social order, have developed patterns of behavior that involve the pursuit of self-interest, constrained by the ethics of the marketplace—patterns that are categorically different from those described to be opportunistic.

Critics have suggested that Smith's normative inferences about the efficacious working of the economy are temporally and culturally dependent. The claim is that Adam Smith's model reflects unwarranted generalization of the behavior that he observed in eighteenth-century Scotland—a relatively stable society described by mutuality of respect between economic actors, that is, by ethically constrained pursuit of self-interest. Smith, himself, would have conceded the point here, as evidenced by his throw-away remarks about the opportunistic behavior of the rude Highlanders. The proper target for criticism here is not Adam Smith, but rather those followers who have unthinkingly generalized his argument to make it apply to nonspecified parametric settings. Smith would have endorsed the distinction between the necessary and sufficient conditions for the effective operation of the invisible hand.

## IV. The Extent of the Market

The elements of Smith's construction outlined to this point have received disproportionate attention as economic analysis has developed, at least by comparison with Smith's own relative weighting. Markets will, indeed, generate high levels of well-being for participants if they are left free of political interference within an appropriate set of institutions. The extent or size of the market network or nexus is also critically important, however, because only with market outreach can the specialization of labor be extended. And here we recall that Adam Smith placed division of labor, or specialization, in the forefront of his explanatory enterprise. An appreciation of the relationship between market size, specialization and economic well-being allows implications to be drawn for policy direction that are related to, but subtly different from, those that involve the removal of politicized controls over the internal or domestic economy.

For any economy, measured by its labor force, specialization will be observed regardless of the organization of activity. Different persons will be seen to be doing different things, no matter what the degree of politicization. "The extent of the market" is, in this sense, fixed by the size of the resource base, and Adam Smith's arguments apply exclusively to the manner of specialization, or, in more familiar terms, to the allocation of the available resources. The relaxation of controls will "extend the size of the market," measured by output, but such language would seem unfamiliar to most economists.

Why did Adam Smith place such weight on the extent of the market? He must have considered the size of the exchange nexus to be an institutional variable subject to change. But, if the resource base is fixed, how can the size of the resource base for the market be modified?[4] The answer to this query is obvious once we recognize that the comprehensive mercantilist system, against which Adam Smith's whole construction is directed, involved political control over both internal and external trade, and that the internal controls were, themselves, motivated by their alleged effects on the external economic balance. Closing off, or otherwise restricting, access to exchanges with persons or firms from other economies reduces the effective size of the market, properly measured, and hence limits the degree of specialization. In the Smithean perspective, there is no distinction between internal and external trade, a principle that yields the proposition that if the well-being of its

---

4. To the extent that people may choose varying amounts of leisure (nonwork), the extent of the market may be varied, even for given resources, as usually measured. See James M. Buchanan and Yong J. Yoon, eds., *The Return to Increasing Returns* (Ann Arbor: University of Michigan Press, 1994).

members is the policy objective, any organized polity should open its economy to all potential traders. (Britain's repeal of the restrictive Corn Laws more than a half-century after the publication of *The Wealth of Nations* is often cited as an example of the influence of the ideas of classical political economy.) To appreciate the continuing strength of the mercantilist fallacies, we need only read our newspapers in 1996 to observe that our politicians act as if they are more interested in the well-being of members of other nations than of our own. More concretely, trade policy seems driven by an almost exclusive concern with our specialized roles as employees-producers rather than our generalized role as consumers. Why else should we be so single-minded in demanding that Japan, in particular, open its markets?

## V. Prudence and Profligacy: Productive and Unproductive Labor

As I noted in the Introduction, Adam Smith was not a subjectivist, in any sense that is descriptive of the methodological stance of modern economists of an Austrian persuasion. He did endorse a regime that allows persons to exercise their natural liberties in allocative, exchange and consumption choices. In part, this stance was dictated by his profound mistrust of political agents. But Adam Smith was also willing to evaluate normatively differing patterns of private choices in an economic nexus and to suggest relationships between these patterns and rates of growth in economic well-being.

Smith considered the choices that participants make in their final end-uses of resources to be important in determining whether or not aggregate value produced in an economy grows over time or remains relatively stagnant. The critical variable is the ratio defining the allocation of labor between productive and nonproductive uses. Smith's introduction of this distinction, along with his emphasis on its importance, has been subjected to more criticism than any other element in his whole construction. Even the most sympathetic of modern readers is required to acknowledge that Smith's discussion is both confused and confusing.

The radical subjectivist has no difficulty in labeling Smith's argument as absurd. The regime in which persons are free to choose will operate so as to satisfy whatever preferences are revealed in choices made, whether these choices be for material goods or for services that are provided simultaneously with consumption, e.g., menial servants' actions. But are we not forced to acknowledge that a society in which persons use scarce resources in exchange for currently consumed services is likely to generate a lower rate of growth than a society that produces relatively more material goods, defined to be capable of yielding benefits to users beyond the immediate periods during which they are produced? Modern economists, even those who are radical subjectivists, will, of course, acknowledge that accumulation through the production of capital goods will increase potential income flows through time. But Adam Smith's argument seems to go beyond the conventional distinction between consumption and saving as end-uses of income received. His productive-unproductive classification seems to suggest that the type of consumption matters—that the market purchase of a material good, say, a book or a chair, is different in kind from the market purchase of menial services, a theatrical performance or a live musical concert.

This lecture is clearly not the place to attempt clarification of what Adam Smith might have really meant by the productive-unproductive labor categorization.[5] Let me say only that despite my sometime self-identification in the radical subjectivist camp. I have considerable sympathy with the Smithean evaluative stance implied by the productive-unproductive breakdown. I am unwilling to relegate Smith's thesis here to the analytical dustbin. I agree, basically, with George Stigler, who suggested that, when we examine Adam Smith's arguments, we should always commence with the presumption that he was onto something, no matter how confused these arguments might appear to us, and no matter how different this approach is from that taken toward the ideas of any other economist, old or new.[6]

Interpreted generously, Smith was saying only that a country in which persons use up a large share of current income as it is provided is unlikely to grow rapidly, even if persons are allowed to exercise fully their natural liberties free of direct political intervention. In his listing of unproductive activities, Smith included the services of government officials and bureau-

---

5. For a limited and preliminary attempt, see James M. Buchanan, *Ethics and Economic Progress* (Norman: University of Oklahoma Press, 1994).

6. George Stigler, "The Economist as Preacher," *The Tanner Lectures on Human Values*, vol. 2 (Salt Lake City: University of Utah Press, 1981).

crats, including military personnel. This classification was used, by Smith as well as by his followers, early and late, as a basis for restrictions on the relative size of the public or governmental sector of an economy, on some implicit presumption that individuals' choices, as exercised in market interactions, would exhibit less profligacy than the indirect choices made by political agents. The hypothesis that governments and politicians are likely to behave as if their time horizons are short relative to those exhibited by private-sector behavior seems to have been corroborated by the socialist and welfare state excesses of the twentieth century.

## VI. Adam Smith as Constitutional Economist

In 1996, it is difficult for us to reconstruct, even in imagination, the reaction of informed readers to the publication of *The Wealth of Nations* in 1776. As many critics have noted, the ideas in Smith's treatise, taken separately, can be found variously in other eighteenth-century writings—some of which antedate Smith's book—including the principle of the spontaneous coordination of economic activity through the interlinked structure of markets. Smith's own genius is reflected in the integration of the whole set of ideas into a comprehensive and wide-ranging discourse that seemed to transcend the apparent immediate purpose of undermining alleged bases for mercantilist policies. The effect was to create the impression that Adam Smith was, himself, disengaged from partisan and interest-driven rhetoric, an impression that was fostered by his established repute as a moral philosopher and, importantly, by the sheer breadth of knowledge conveyed in the treatise itself. We may say that Adam Smith created for himself the authority that we came to associate with the true scientist. Indeed, his influence carried over, and, for many decades, classical political economy was accorded a status akin to that which was later reserved only for the natural sciences.

In part, Adam Smith was fortunate in being able to exploit the intellectual excitement that was already present in the developing recognition that markets work, provided that the essential framework parameters are in place. The political function of the market economy in making detailed direction of resource use unnecessary—this is an immensely powerful idea whose time had come, and an idea that had, and still can have, profound implications. We can appreciate how and why this central idea might have stirred the excitement consequent on any discovery.

In a somewhat more inclusive philosophical context, Adam Smith introduced his ideas in a setting for discussion that was highly congenial to the consideration and evaluation of genuinely radical alternatives. The spirit of the Enlightenment was in the air. Thinkers in France, Germany, England, Scotland and America were convinced that rational thought could be applied to the structure of social institutions, and that reason could become the basis for reform. With Smith, however, along with others of his peers in Scotland, the constructivist urge was tempered by a recognition of the distinction between structural (constitutional) and hands-on adjustments.

I should acknowledge here that my own intellectual prejudices prompt me to look on Adam Smith as a constitutional political economist and to associate him with the American Founders in a precursory relationship to that branch of modern constitutional discourse with which I have been associated, and particularly as it relates the political-legal framework to the operation of a market economy. The observed historical collapse of the great twentieth-century efforts at political direction and control of large national economies has surely justified a reexamination of the scientific propositions upon which all such efforts were supposed to rest. If it is now acknowledged that national economies cannot, at the same time, be widely politicized and produce satisfactory levels of personal well-being (quite apart from the suppression of individual liberties), a reiteration of the lessons taught by Adam Smith, and his classical economist peers, is in order. And, whether or not his prediction proves to be correct, Fukuyama's claim that the failed socialist experiments do, indeed, validate the central scientific hypotheses of political economy can scarcely be challenged, analytically or empirically.

It is, then, appropriate that, in 1996, early in the post-socialist epoch, we should celebrate Adam Smith's achievement anew. I may end this lecture on a speculative note by asking: How differently would we have written those bicentennial celebratory essays in 1976 had we been able to predict the events of 1989–1991? I suggest that we failed, on that occasion as on others, to appreciate fully Adam Smith's message. Shall we continue to fail as we confront repackaged mercantilist fallacies? Or are there now positive signs that suggest that we, as citizens of a constitutional democracy, are, finally, coming to understand the economic limits of our politics?

# The Potential for
# Politics after Socialism

## I. Introduction

We are living in a new epoch, and it is vitally important that we recognize the changes that have occurred, both in the events of history and in the way we think about this history and about prospects from future developments.

The century-long romantic vision that embodied the potential achievements of state-ownership of production along with centrally planned and controlled economic activity no longer exists. Socialism, in this sense, is dead, and its failures are acknowledged by both political leaders and intellectuals throughout the world. There exists widespread and pervasive skepticism about the effectiveness of state or governmental direction of economic affairs.

It seems appropriate, therefore, to examine the potential for politics in this post-socialist setting. How much can we expect to accomplish through the auspices of the political workings of the modern nation-state?

In particular, how much can the specialists in political economy, my own scientific discipline, contribute to ongoing problems of reform, especially when it is recognized that these reforms must be politically implemented? A warning against expecting too much from applying a "scientific" approach is in order here. But there is a positive role for the social scientist and social philosopher, provided the limits to this role are well understood. Within these limits, I shall try to set out and suggest specific steps that may be taken

From *Geschichte und Gesetz, Europäisches Forum Alpbach 1989,* ed. Otto Molden (Vienna: Österreichisches College, 1990), 240–56. Reprinted by permission of the publisher.

to insure that we can, on all counts, enter the 21st century with hope, without which there can be no creativity. I shall then relate some of the discussion to some projections of alternative futures.

In the developed nations of the West (Western Europe, United States, Japan) we live with a modern achievement described by the simultaneous presence of widespread individual liberty, economic prosperity, and both domestic and international order. This modern achievement is, however, fragile in the extreme, and its fragility must be recognized. It is vulnerable to destruction and erosion, both from deliberately fostered attacks and from nonattended historical evolutionary drift. This vulnerability increases as the philosophical underpinnings of the achievement come to be increasingly forgotten, neglected, and misunderstood. This lecture is a plea for simultaneous recognition both of the potential for deliberately organized change in institutional order and of the limits that history, human nature, science, technology, and resource capacity impose on efforts to move toward the betterment of humankind.

## II. Science, Understanding, and Control

It is critically important that we emphasize both the potential benefits of scientific discovery and the potential damages that might be caused by misunderstanding and misapplication of that which might be alleged to be scientific findings. It is incumbent on me to issue a cautionary warning. Many modern scientists, secure in their own achievement of genuine discovery of new laws of the workings of the physical universe, and observing first hand the extension of humankind's mastery as these laws are applied, exhibit a natural proclivity to attribute what seem to be flaws in the structure of social interaction to "scientific" backwardness, and to expect improvements from inappropriate extensions of science's domain into the realm of social control.

Let me be precise. I do not suggest that there is no "science" of economics, or of human behavior more generally considered. We have, indeed, made major progress in the development and testing of falsifiable hypotheses concerning how persons behave under specified sets of constraints, and these hypotheses enable us to make predictions concerning the effects of changes in constraints on human behavior patterns. The activity of those who derive, test, and extend these hypotheses in the human sciences is not different in kind from the activity of their counterparts in the ordinary hard sciences. And, indeed, we now understand the failures of attempts at centralized economic planning because of the scientific developments in economics over the last half-century.

A categorical difference emerges, however, from what I call the *public artifactuality* of the constraints that we observe as the domain for inquiry in the human sciences. There is no *natural* order within which we, as human animals, must confine our activities, one with another. We remain, necessarily, in a set of artificially constructed, or historically evolved, "zoos." There exists no natural habitat, no "jungle" to which we can return specimens for scientifically antiseptic observation.

Just as there is no natural order that confines our social interaction, there is no ideal order that is revealed to us transcendentally, or revealed to us as if it embodies the truth of scientific discovery. The set of constraints that define the limits on human interaction in society must be chosen from among a sub-infinity of alternatives. And there is no external standard—either embodied in "nature" or transcendentally revealed—that would single out one alternative as "objectively" best. If the image of scientific discovery and technological application by *experts* can be assumed to be characteristic of the perceived role of modern science, the closest analogy in the socio-political arena is the totalitarian regime where an elite separates itself from the others in the society and applies its scientific findings to control and direct human behavior toward a furtherance of the elite's own self-selected purposes. As modern history and modern economics have surely told us emphatically, all such efforts aimed at scientific control of human beings tend to fail, even to accomplish that which the masters seek.

As soon as one steps outside the mindset of the totalitarian model of social engineering, one cannot avoid recognition that the problems of social organization in nontotalitarian regimes are vastly more complex, and that the scope for any direct applications of the findings of science in the standard sense remains limited. If there is no expert-elite that can legitimately claim to know what, in some objective sense, is the ideal social arrangement, and, further, if individuals who participate in social interaction are acknowledged to be the ultimate judges, then even with major advances in our understanding of human choice behavior, there remains the problem of securing *agreement* among those who participate in the complex network of human social interaction. There are important implications if the problem of social organization is analyzed as one of securing agreement on the self-imposed set of constraints within which we engage with one another, from war to trade to love. Agreement on the rules by which we shall live, one with another, domestically and internationally, is, of course, informed by scientific inquiry and understanding. But, at base, the problem is not one involving technological application of scientific discoveries, and it seems a mark of folly to treat it as such, that is, as an engineering problem.

## III. The Role of the Social Philosopher

I have suggested that scientific inquiry into human behavior, as such, is not different in kind from the activity that describes the working of ordinary scientists. Discoveries are made, and these add incrementally to a stock of knowledge that, presumably, will prove helpful in some ultimate improvement in the human condition. For the physical scientist, as such, the task is done when a discovery is made. The results of inquiry are published, and there is left to the engineer the assignment of translating these results into valued practical application.

Things seem quite different with the sciences of human behavior. In non-totalitarian societies, there is no proper role for the "social engineer," for the expert who takes the results of scientific inquiry and applies these results in the furtherance of the specific end objectives whether desired by the engineer himself or dictated to him by a master elite. Who, then, is to make use of the findings that emerge from the sciences of human behavior? Who can assume the task of "constitutional design," the task of setting up or of modifying institutional rules so as to "improve" predicted patterns of results?

There is a subtle but vitally important distinction between the social philosopher who may assume the role of leader in discussions of constitutional design and the social engineer. By inference from the very word "engineer," there is implied some more or less direct translation of scientific findings into end-objects. Such an inference becomes misleading as applied to the social philosopher, who may make himself fully aware of the scientific laws, but who then takes on the role of persuading others in the body politic to reach agreement on principles of design that will further *commonly shared* objectives.

In the necessary dialogue on constitutional design, involving the continuing evaluation of the workings of existing rules of social order along with an evaluation of the working properties of potential alternative rules, two distinct elements must be separated. Persons may differ both in their theories as to how institutions work and in their *interests*, against which the expected workings of institutions are measured.[1] The conceptual separation of these two potential sources of disagreement in matters of social organization is of basic importance, even if in reality, a clear distinction between the theory and interest components is rarely present. The principal task of the social philosopher who assumes any leadership role in the discussion is to facilitate the initial distinction between these two elements, and to bring the fruits of scientific inquiry to bear on securing a reconciliation of conflicting theories. Beyond this basically scientific task, the philosopher can also assist in facilitating agreement among participants by reducing or dispelling bases for conflicts among identifiable interests.

I do not want to suggest that agreement or consensus on the set of rules within which we interact to generate complex patterns of outcomes (allocations, distributions, scales of value, growth rates, etc.) will somehow emerge spontaneously as if by some invisible hand. The social philosopher must, indeed, engage actively in the whole dialogue, analysis, and discussion. And, to the extent that his scientific competence and integrity are acknowledged, others may defer to his authority in the array of the alternatives of structural change.[2] But the social philosopher cannot assume the arrogance of the social engineer, and, ultimately, those changes in the rules that he proposes must be presented as hypotheses, the test for which is the generation of agreement among those who are to act within the chosen structure.[3]

## IV. Liberty, Prosperity, Peace—and Justice

All of the discussion to this point is preliminary to any suggestion or proposal on my part as to specific steps that might be taken, by socially organized

1. Viktor Vanberg and James M. Buchanan, "Interests and Theories in Constitutional Choice," *Journal of Theoretical Politics* 1 (January 1989).

2. James M. Buchanan and Viktor Vanberg, "A Theory of Leadership and Deference in Constitutional Construction," *Public Choice* 61 (April 1989).

3. James M. Buchanan, "Positive Economics, Welfare Economics, and Political Economy," *Journal of Law and Economics* 2 (October 1959).

groups, from local communities to nation-states to international organiza-tions, with a purpose of insuring a "better" 21st century. The precautions were necessary. It would be arrogant folly to parade my own privately derived pref-erences for social change under some guise of scientific validity. At best, the suggestions that I advance must be treated as hypotheses about the working properties of certain rules as well as about what persons may consider prefer-able, hypotheses to be tested in the continuing dialogue in which all persons participate under self-imposed limits of reciprocity and mutuality of respect. The suggestions made below emerge out of my own generalized knowledge of the findings of the human sciences and out of my application of these findings in the context of comparative institutional analysis.

I suggest that there does exist general agreement on some of the ultimate objectives to be sought for in socially organized communities. As individuals, we place a value on liberty, on the freedom to make choices for ourselves over a broadly defined private space. As individuals, we also place a value on the attainability of a sufficiently high level of primary goods and services without undue hardship and suffering. And finally, as individuals, we place a value on the existence and maintenance of peace or order, both within local communities as among persons and groups, and between separately orga-nized communities, including nation-states. Individual liberty, prosperity, peace—these are universally acclaimed values. But can these values be se-cured in the complex interaction processes that describe modern socio-political arrangements?

The central problem is, of course, that liberty, prosperity, and peace are sensed as *individualized* values, independent of any generalization to a social context. As an individual, I value *my own* liberty, *my own* economic well-being, *my own* peace, and it is only when I am forced to acknowledge that these values cannot differentially be made available to me, individually, that I shift my attention to the generalization of these values to all persons in-volved with me in the institutions of social interaction.

How can social interaction be organized to allow all persons, simulta-neously, to enjoy the values of liberty, prosperity, and peace? What are the limits that political equality, economic reciprocity, and mutuality of respect impose on the attainment of any or all of these values?

Historical experience offers empirical evidence demonstrating the neces-sary complementarity between individual liberty and economic prosperity.

Experiments in which liberties have been suppressed under centralized political direction allegedly aimed at expanding economic product are now acknowledged to have failed, universally so. Institutional reform now taking place, on what is literally a worldwide scale, is based on the developing recognition of this complementarity between individual liberty and economic prosperity.

There is an analogous complementarity between peace on the one hand and both prosperity and liberty on the other. Resources are wasted in negative-sum conflicts among persons, groups, and nation-states, and individuals find themselves deprived of liberties when their energies are coercively mobilized in the furtherance of communitarian objectives in social conflicts.

The great scientific discovery of the 18th century, out of which political economy (economics) emerged as an independent academic discipline, embodies the recognition that the complementary values of liberty, prosperity, and peace can be attained. It is not surprising that my 18th- and early-19th-century counterparts were so enthusiastic in their advocacy of market organization. So long as the state provides and maintains the appropriate structural constraints (the "laws and institutions," the rules of the game), individuals, as economic actors, can be left alone to pursue their own privately determined purposes, and in so doing enjoy the values of liberty, prosperity, and peace in reciprocal and mutual respect, one for another. The role of the state is critically important in maintaining and enforcing the rules that define the limits of the economic game, but the role is also minimal in that there is no place for detailed politicized intervention with the liberties of persons and groups to enter into voluntary exchanges. Policy reforms are to be concentrated exclusively on the rules, the structural framework, the constitution broadly defined.

This ideal of the great classical economists was never fully realized. There was a failure to understand the separation between political attention to structure, attention that is both necessary and appropriate, and political intervention into the socio-economic game itself. As a result, states have rarely, if ever, offered a satisfactorily supportive structure for the economy, and most notably as regards the monetary unit. And, as we know all too well, states failed everywhere to limit political manipulation to structure alone.

Why did the vision of classical political economy fail to capture the imagination of more than a few generations of intellectual leaders? Why did social philosophers from the middle of the 19th century forward lose interest in the classical teachings? Why did the socialist century emerge, and with the active support of social philosophers?

These questions admit of relatively easy answers once we recognize that my earlier listing of the universally desired objectives or values of liberty, prosperity, and peace is not complete. The listing omits *justice,* which is also a value, in both Aristotelian senses, *commutative* justice, an attribute of a system of rules, and *distributive* justice, an attribute of patterns of distributive outcomes that are generated in an economy. The vision of classical political economists of a regime that meets the norm of equal liberty implies nothing directly about access to primary goods, which depends upon the distribution of endowments and talents among participants.

The distributional experiments of the socialist century remain in the late 1980s, long after the promises of socialism are acknowledged to be romantic dreams. These experiments were and are charged with elevated moral purpose, that of furthering distributional norms as measured by enhanced equality. But these experiments have been generally characterized by an apparent incongruity between declared purpose and observed results, an incongruity that can and must be subjected to the scrutiny of scientific analysis. The failures of the explicitly totalitarian experiments in achieving distributive justice are now widely acknowledged. What is not yet generally realized are the threats that are inherent in the ordinary mechanisms of majoritarian democratic politics. The traditional perception of democratic politics has been characterized by an implicit acceptance of the post-Hegelian romantic image or model of politics and the state, based on the surprisingly unchallenged presumption that persons who assume roles as political agents shed off all individualized interests and behave both benevolently and omnisciently in their assigned public duties.

The incongruity between the justice-driven moral purpose and the realities of interest-motivated constituents and agents has produced results that surely could have been predicted with more careful scientific scrutiny. When the political dynamics that describe modern democracy comes into force, it is not surprising that efforts to redress economic results toward enhanced distributional equality should have become the cover for interest-driven efforts to gain distributional advantage. Under the aegis of welfare-state redistributionism, the interest-driven politics of modern democracy has given us the "churning state,"[4] which does, indeed, involve redistribution, but which is, to a large extent, unrelated to "legitimate" welfare-state objectives, and which has more or less openly been transformed into a negative-sum game among competing interest groups. Whether or not the redistributive activity of the modern state, constrained only within majoritarian electoral limits, "improves" at all upon the nondisturbed patterns that might be generated by the market remains an open issue, and one that cries out for both analytical and empirical research.[5] We do know that the redistributional game that we observe in the churning state motivates a very substantial wastage of valued production due to the investment in rent-seeking by competing groups seeking to curry political favors. And this wastage appears to be growing exponentially as we enter the last decade of the 20th century, at least in my own country.

I do not suggest quiescence before the very real issues of distributive justice, and I surely do not claim ethical legitimacy for the distributional patterns that the historically evolved distribution of premarket endowments along with the workings of the market itself might generate. I should, nonetheless, argue that, pragmatically considered, these patterns may well be preferred, *on agreed-on criteria of equality,* to those that are being generated in the rent-seeking politics of the churning state, as observed. But such politics is not the only institutional route toward the attainment of distributional norms. Once again, it becomes necessary to hold fast to the distinction between potential reform in the structure of an economic order and activity that is allowed to take place within that structure. There are prospects for building redistributional elements into constitutional regimes, elements that can be effectively insulated from the machinations of interest-group politics.

The demands of justice require, first of all, constitutional articulation and implementation of the rule of law, which itself embodies the principle of equality before the law. This basic precept must be extended to insure that all "play by the same rules," that differentiation or discrimination in political

4. Anthony de Jasay, *The State* (Oxford: Blackwell, 1985).

5. Geoffrey Brennan and James M. Buchanan, *The Reason of Rules* (Cambridge: Cambridge University Press, 1985).

treatment is strictly out of bounds. Secondly, the demands of justice require that, upon entry into the "game" itself, players face opportunities that are equalized to the extent institutionally feasible. I have often suggested that this principle implies equal access to and state financing of education at all levels. Beyond these constitutionally implemented steps, some rectification in the intergenerational transmission of asset accumulation may be dictated, again to be secured only via constitutional procedures rather than through ordinary politics.

If we use the analytical and empirical results of the social sciences to evaluate the prospects of politics realistically rather than romantically, we have good reasons to think that, beyond these limits of constitutional justice, the siren songs of the churning state masquerading under welfare-state arguments should be resisted. Submission to the false prophets of welfare-state expansion promises only the further sacrifice of liberty, prosperity, and, possibly, domestic peace, and without substantial gains, if any at all, toward the agreed-on norms of justice.

In a single lecture, I cannot describe in detail the political economy that would be both institutionally feasible and normatively preferred by citizens at the turn of the century. I have suggested that, building on the insights of the great classical economists of the 18th century, as appropriately modernized for the technology, resources, human capacities, and scientific advances that describe the late 20th century, we can secure a socio-economic-political order that would allow individual liberty, economic prosperity, peace, and justice to be achieved. This order is possible only if political activity is largely confined to structural reform and if politicized intrusions into the privately chosen lives of persons are severely limited by effective constitutional prohibitions.

My suggestions apply directly to the internal structure of a national economy, but the same principles lend themselves to ready extension to the increasingly interdependent international community of states. Interest driven politicizations of voluntary exchanges between citizens and associations of separate states reduces the economic well being and the liberty of all members of the international nexus. And constitutional sanctions against politicized interferences should extend equally in application to both domestic and international markets.

## V. After Socialism—What?

I have referred earlier to the end of the socialist century, and to the death of the socialist god. These statements are based on my reading of the history of this century. The romantic faith in the state and in politics that emerged and blossomed in the late 19th century and the 20th century no longer exists, and, once lost, such faith does not seem likely to reappear. In the preceding section, I have tried to outline the features of the "good society" that could emerge in our post-Hegelian epoch. However, as I stated before, this normative structure is advanced only as a set of hypotheses, the test for which becomes generalized agreement on the changes that are therein implied.

There are two complementary elements in the argument, or two sides of the coin, both of which are necessary for consensus to emerge. There must first be some convergence of opinion on the relative inefficacy of politics (including the bureaucracy) as it is observed to work. The romantic blinders must come off; persons must learn to view ordinary politics as it is, not as it might be if all actors were saints. Public choice, the new subdiscipline with which I have been associated, has done much to dispel the romance here, although direct observation of program failures of the agencies of the over-reaching modern state has perhaps been of much greater significance than any scientific demonstration.

But the shedding off of the romantic image is not sufficient unto itself. It must be accompanied by an understanding and appreciation of what Adam Smith called the simple system of natural liberty, by a generalized willingness to leave things alone, to let the economy work in its own way, and outside politicized interference. I am by no means convinced that this second element for constructing the "good society" is present. We seem, instead, to be left with a generalized public skepticism about the efficacy of ordinary politics to accomplish much of anything, but, at the same time, we seem publicly unwilling to allow the forces of voluntary agreement and association to work themselves out. We have, indeed, lost faith in the socialist god; but we are a long way from regaining any faith in the "laissez-faire" principle of the classical economists.

The combination of attitudes on the part of the citizenry, at least in my own country, lends itself to exploitation by those interest groups that have their own ready-made agenda for state action designed to yield these groups differentially high rents or profits. Building on the public's unwillingness to act on principle in support of market solutions to apparent problems, whether real or imagined, these interest groups secure arbitrary restrictions on voluntary exchanges, and in the process secure rents for their members while reducing both the liberties and the economic well being of other members of the economic nexus, both domestically and internationally.

A protectionist-mercantilist regime described by particularized and quite arbitrary politicized interventions into the workings of markets, both domestic and international, seems to represent a much greater threat to the achievement of the social order outlined above than any regime embodying socialist-inspired direction, planning, and control. In two centuries, we have apparently come full circle. The selfsame institutional barriers that Adam Smith sought to demolish are everywhere resurging, as if from the depths of history. And the same arguments are heard in the land, both in support and in opposition. It must seem, therefore, to those of you outside economics that any scientific impact of the discipline matters little, if at all, on how we order our affairs, how we construct the rules within which we carry on our lives, one with another, in social interaction.

That this experience could repeat itself demonstrates the public artifactuality of the structure of social interaction, the feature that I noted to be that which distinguished the human and the nonhuman sciences. And, as this experience indicates, this feature has implications for the didactic role of the scientist. For the physicist, there is no requirement to repeat the arguments that long ago convinced his peers concerning the validity of a particular theorem. For the political economist, the arguments that Adam Smith once advanced were compelling, but we have allowed the artifactual structure to be shifted. Our task begins anew.

Adam Smith occupies the place that he does among our intellectual heroes because he was the first to demonstrate that politicized interferences with voluntary market exchanges reduce both economic well being and individual liberties. But Smith himself remained naive in that he felt that once the generalized harm of protectionist-mercantilist measures came to be understood, governments would act, as if on principle, to eliminate all such restrictions. We now know that governments, as they operate, will do no such thing. They will act only in response to constituency interests, a response that is, in itself, desirable. But in the dynamics induced by the particular constraints that exist, the interplay of interests insures that the patterns of protectionist restriction will emerge.

There will be no escape from the protectionist-mercantilist regime that now threatens to be characteristic of the century's turn so long as we allow the ordinary politics of majoritarian democracy to operate in the absence of adequate constitutional constraints. We have learned to understand interest-group politics. What is required is that we look to principles that can be incorporated in constitutional structure, principles that dictate the imposition of constraints that will prevent the intrusions of ordinary politics into market exchange. Acceptance of the arguments for, and active support for, the constitutional-structural reforms implementing these principles may, but need not, require some conversion to a new morality of public interest, as such. Individuals and representatives of specialized producer groups can be led to support generalized constitutional constraints "in their own interest." So long as a person, as a specialized producer, knows that a constitutional prohibition against protection for his own industry will also be extended to all industries, he will recognize that his own interests will be served, not harmed, by such constraints. The protectionist-mercantilist thrust is necessarily fueled by the expectations that some interest groups can secure discriminatory advantage at the expense of others. If this expectation is removed, the protectionist-mercantilist regime must collapse.

The 21st century need not be ushered in by a cacophony of voices shouting for agricultural subsidies, textile tariffs, voluntary agreement on automobile imports, taxicab licensing, rent control laws, minimum wage regulations, retaliatory anti-dumping measures, and the myriad of other all-too-familiar modern variants of the mercantilist economic order. Depoliticized economic order is within the realm of the politically-constitutionally possible, whether accomplished within one nation-state or within and among the whole community of nation-states.

## VI. The Potential and the Limits

In concluding this lecture, I return to my somewhat grandiose title, "The Potential for Politics after Socialism." And let us clear the intellectual air by an early acknowledgement that without the benefits of social-legal-political organization, very few of us could be here today. We could not exist; the physical world would support only a tiny fraction of its population if we were forced to live in the almost unimaginable state of Hobbesian anarchy, or even under the tribal organization that described most of human history. We live now by the graces of those persons and forces that designed, constructed, maintained, and secured the institutions of order within which we live, work, and play.

A threshold was crossed in the 18th century when we learned how the rule of law, stability of private property, and the withdrawal of political interference with private choices could unleash the entrepreneurial energies that are latent within each of us. The modern age was born. Humankind seemed near to the realization of its socially organized potentiality only to have this future threatened, and in part forestalled, by the emergence of the socialist vision, a vision that has now been shown to be grounded in romance rather than scientific understanding. The central flaw in the socialist vision is its failure to recognize the limits of socialized organization. There can be no escape from the feasibility space that is defined by natural and human constraints. And if these constraints are ignored in well-intentioned but misguided efforts to realize more than we can socially achieve, irrevocable harm may be imposed on all persons in the international social nexus.

Recognizing the limits in order to avoid such harm is as important as recognizing the potential that may be achieved within those limits. The organized policies of the nation-states, and the association of these states, one with another, must be kept within the boundaries of the potential and the possible. As we enter soon into the 21st century, the prevention of politicized overreaching is perhaps our most obvious priority. The state-as-Leviathan described much of this century; we shall destroy all of our dreams if this "monster's" growth is not limited and its productive potential marshalled to guarantee the framework of order within which individuals can, indeed, pursue that which their own potential makes them capable of realizing.

# Ideas, Institutions,
# and Political Economy
## A Plea for Disestablishment

---

## Introduction

In early 1985 President Reagan seriously considered abolishing the Council of Economic Advisers, either temporarily through failure to make appointments or permanently by seeking legislative approval for formal disestablishment. In any event, the Council was not abolished, and the inclination of an administration in this direction does not seem likely to recur. The Council of Economic Advisers survives, and as the institution ages, pressures for continuation strengthen, quite independent of purpose or function.

The Council of Economic Advisers should have been abolished. The Council is an institution that finds its origins in a set of political and economic ideas that are no longer accepted. In the context of its originally claimed purpose, the Council is irrelevant. Any productive output now generated is peripheral to the primary objective. The institutional heritage that defined this objective, however, carries sufficient weight to the uninformed, and notably to the media, to insure counterproductive influence on the economic policy of the nation.

In supporting these arguments, I shall *not* introduce directly any of the three familiar complaints about the operation of the Council. (1) I shall not dust off the hoary notion that given its political setting the Council of Eco-

From *Real Business Cycles, Real Exchange Rates and Actual Policies, Carnegie-Rochester Conference Series on Public Policy 25,* ed. Karl Brunner and Alan Meltzer (Amsterdam: North Holland, 1986), 245–58. Copyright 1986. Reprinted by permission from Elsevier Science.

nomic Advisers cannot refrain from advancing the partisan objectives of the administration that it serves. It cannot, so the complaint goes, present its recommendations-findings with sufficient "scientific objectivity." (2) I shall not, on the other hand, reject the general claim of "economic science" which the institutionalization of the Council seems to advance. There is a science of economics, but this science, properly defined, tends to be weakened rather than strengthened by the formalization of advice that the Council represents. (3) I shall not, finally, base my position on the more sophisticated modern notion that governmental economic policy is rendered ineffective by the predictive competence of rational citizens.

My recommendation that the Council be abolished, as an institution, is based on its political history and its relationship to the ideas that were important in shaping that history. The argument for disestablishment is not analogous to the argument for deregulation that has motivated efforts in transportation, communication, and finance. There has been no interest-group capture, nor does the argument emphasize inefficiencies of bureaucratic apparatus. The damage or harm wrought by the Council is indirect and arises from the Council's very existence, rather than from any efficacy or inefficacy in what it does. Its existence, as an institution, distracts the attention of political leaders and the public from structural features of the political economy and insures the politicization of economic policy, either in reality or in appearance. Implicitly, the existence of the Council postulates a role for government that involves active participation within the rules of the political-economic game as opposed to government's more appropriate role in modifying the rules themselves.

I have leveled strong charges at an institution that has a very modest budget and which seems to exercise relatively little influence on politics. Admittedly, I am using the institution of the Council as the focal point of a whole mind-set that should be disestablished. It is, of course, possible that major features of this mind-set would persevere even if the Council should be abolished. On the other hand, so long as the institution continues to exist, as such, the mind-set that it embodies cannot be fully dislodged.

There are two separate elements in my inclusive argument. One of these is within the corpus of economic analysis, and it will be broadly familiar to modern economists. The other is based on elementary application of public-choice theory to the institutions of democratic politics. The first element is more significant in assessing the role of the Council in the context of its own origins and history. The second element is more important when assessing the legitimacy of the Council of Economic Advisers as an institution designed to offer professional guidance to political decision-makers. These elements are discussed separately below. I shall then examine the broader issue of professional guidance in the conduct of economic policy, and I shall emphasize the categorical distinction between advice to political decision-makers who act within existing rules and advice to citizens who take part in a continuing dialogue-discussion of possible changes in the rules (constitutional reform).

## The Keynesian Theory of Policy

The Council of Economic Advisers, as an institution, was established in the Employment Act of 1946. There is no question that the Council, and the more inclusive legislation that set it up, was intellectually grounded in the Keynesian theory of economic policy that had literally conquered the academic-intellectual community of Washington during the early 1940s. We need only recall the several projections of massive postwar unemployment generated by the application of simple macroeconomic models that now seem so grossly naive. But events occur in their own historical settings, and the events of 1946 were produced out of the ideas that were current at the time.[1]

The United States had experienced the Great Depression, and it was widely held that only the armament boom of the 1940s had pulled the otherwise stagnating national economy into high-level employment. The "natural" state of the economy was widely thought to be characterized by excessive saving relative to investment opportunities with accompanying high unemployment and excess industrial capacity. There was general acceptance of the normative principle that positive action by the national government should be taken with the precise objective of achieving and maintaining desirable levels of income and employment. This normative principle was itself based on the theory of relationships among economic aggregates that we associate with the name "Keynesian." A genuine revolution in the thinking of economists had

---

1. See Herbert Stein, *The Fiscal Revolution in America* (Chicago: University of Chicago Press, 1969), for the definitive history here.

occurred. Keynes had provided a framework within which the whole economy, not just the actors within it, could be analyzed. Economists were duped into thinking that they could "understand" the operation of a complex economic interaction process by the use of hydraulic-like models that embodied the interdependencies among a relatively small number of macroeconomic variables, with macroeconomic equilibrium being defined independent of that which described incentive-compatible states in the behavior of participating actors.

The macroeconomy equilibrium need not, however, embody, as any necessary consequence, the full employment of resources. Hence, the theory seemed to explain that which had been observed in the 1930s without direct references to the neoclassical hypotheses concerning market clearances. Attention was diverted from the operation of markets, whether for resource inputs, final products, or financial instruments, and toward the operation of the macroaggregates, as a system, and also toward the prediction-measurement of the gap between observed output and that which might be potentially attained if the equilibrating variables should assume values different from those emerging.

The step from Keynesian theory, as macroeconomic analysis, to economic policy, as the normative application of the theory, was a natural one that could scarcely have been resisted by economists who accepted the former. To anyone whose thinking was indeed revolutionized by the Keynesian theory, there could have been no pulling up short before the policy applications. Who could forswear effort to attain the objectives of full employment and high income? The real opportunity costs of underutilized resources seemed nonexistent, and the use of the budget to fill in the gap between predicted and desired levels of aggregate demand seemed to follow as a matter of course. Lerner's regime of "functional finance" was self-evidently the policy ideal.

At this point, it is necessary to examine the Keynesian impact on the theory of economic policy in a more inclusive historical context. With the acceptance of the Keynesian analysis, the role and responsibility of the central government in maintaining target levels of employment and output were made explicit. And the assignment of a major share of this task to the instruments of fiscal or budgetary policy again seemed a natural extension. What is missing from the narrative to this point is any reference to the pre-

Keynesian or even to the Keynesian theory of monetary institutions or to the assigned task of government in maintaining stability in the value of the monetary unit. An active policy role had been assigned to government in these respects prior to the 1930s. Keynes had, himself, discussed this role in detail in his early writings. The theory of central banking, developed in the 1920s, embodied an idealized policy norm along with implicit instructions to the monetary decision-makers. In practice, this theory of policy failed in the Great Depression, for reasons to be discussed later. The impact of the Keynesian teachings of the 1930s was to divert attention almost totally away from the workings, and the failures, of basic monetary institutions, and to build a theory of macroeconomic policy as an appended superstructure to an existing central-bank foundation that had been flawed in its origins.

The stage was set, at the end of World War II, for the institutionalization of the Keynesian theory of economic policy. The macroeconomic models were in place; improvements had been made in the collection and processing of data necessary for prediction. The responsibility of government for maintaining high employment was widely accepted in the setting where the achievement of the more specific war objectives was observed as reality. Legislation was required only to make the objective explicit and to establish in the Executive branch an agency charged with the functions of assessing the data, making the predictions, and offering the advice of the political decision-makers.

We know, of course, that the Council of Economic Advisers was unable to meet its promise from the very outset of its existence. We know that the mid-1940s predictions of the Keynesian macromodels were almost uniformly in error, while the simpler classical predictions proved basically accurate. There was no shortage of investment opportunities in the postwar years; there was no excessive saving. Inflation rather than unemployment was the economic policy problem.

Both ideas and their institutionalized embodiments, however, once created, tend to assume quasi permanence, regardless of their empirical validity or demonstrated achievement. This characterization is especially descriptive when the ideas in question are comprehensive rather than piecemeal, when they reflect a whole mind-set rather than particularized hypotheses. It is not surprising, therefore, that the Keynesian theory of macroeconomics, along with the theory of policy, was not simply abandoned as a result of its early record of predictive failure. The late 1940s and 1950s were years in which this dominant mind-set was adjusted, modified, and extended, all with the aim of making the basic models offer more plausibly acceptable "explanations" of observed economic reality. Difficulties in prediction were acknowledged; lags between the implementation and the effects of policy action were recognized; differences in results of dissimilar policy instruments were analyzed; possible conflicts among desired objectives were emphasized. The early Keynesian neglect of money and financial instruments along with the necessary complementarity and substitutability between fiscal and monetary instruments became the subject matter for intensive research inquiry.

The Council of Economic Advisers shifted its role from that originally envisaged to one that was in keeping with the changing content of macroeconomic theory. Its reports collected and presented data on macroeconomic aggregates; they assessed the record of performance *ex post;* they made cautionary projections of future movements; they presented briefs for the policy stances of the administration in office. The difficulties of translating ideas directly into policy formulation were acknowledged both by academic economists and by members of successive Councils.

The national economy is a much more complex reality than that incorporated into the models of the early American Keynesians. The function and purpose of any agency assigned the task of proffering economic advice in the sense initially intended was lost almost from the start. By the end of the 1950s, almost all economists were "Keynesian" in the sense that macroeconomic tools were used to "explain" the aggregates. At the same time, almost no economists were "Keynesian" in the sense that they retained the faith in the efficacy of simplistic macromanagement that had been expressed a decade earlier.

In the late 1950s and 1960s, the Phillips trade-off dominated macroeconomic policy discussion, and argument centered on the relative weights to be placed on the employment and monetary objectives, along with some debate as to the relative efficacy of fiscal and monetary instruments. The apogee of economic advice, as such, was perhaps attained in the early 1960s, when the political decision-makers seemed to act as economists suggested. Taxes were deliberately reduced for macroeconomic policy rather than for budgetary policy purposes, and with surprising success.

By the middle and late 1960s, however, the Keynesian neglect of monetary elements forced itself into recognition as inflationary dangers appeared. Economists, meanwhile, had commenced looking for the microfoundations of macroeconomic action. The historical record of the 1930s was reassessed and the Keynesian low-employment trap was called into question. Milton Friedman and E. S. Phelps introduced the "natural rate" of unemployment as that rate which could, at best, be only temporarily shifted by fiscal and/or monetary manipulation. Martin Bailey questioned the efficacy of fiscal policy in its claimed ability to accomplish any macroeconomic objective.[2]

Historically, the national economy moved from the low-inflation, high-growth years of the early 1960s into the accelerating-inflation, low-growth years of the 1970s. "Stagflation" was upon us, and the Keynesians had neither a satisfactory explanation nor a plausible policy suggestion for escape.

The monetarists gained the high ground in some academic citadels. Their testing was to come later. But the monetarists, at least in their early years of return to respectability, were almost as simplistic as the early Keynesians. And, had their substitute models been proven fully descriptive, there might have emerged an argument for the institutionalization of monetarist advice. However, the early monetarists did not shift attitudes to an extent remotely comparable to the Keynesians of the 1940s. At best, monetarist influences indirectly entered into the Council's reports but almost always through the language and data of the Keynesian macromodels. The results could scarcely have been otherwise. The Council of Economic Advisers was a product of the Keynesian mind-set, and this mind-set must be embodied in the institution itself, independent of the particular economists who may be chosen to serve and also independent of the economic stance of the administration in office.

In the mid-1980s (when this is written), macroeconomic theory is in disarray. The aggregative relationships described in neither the most sophisticated Keynesian models nor in the most advanced monetarist hypotheses describe the experience of the early 1980s. On the other hand, the severe recession of 1982 essentially refuted the extensive claims made by the rational

2. M. Friedman, "The Role of Monetary Policy," *American Economic Review* 58 (1968): 1–17, and E. S. Phelps, "Phillips Curves Expectations of Inflation, and Optimal Unemployment Over Time," *Economica*, n.s. 34 (1967): 258–81; M. Bailey, *National Income and the Price Level: A Study in Macroeconomic Theory* (New York: McGraw-Hill, 1971).

expectations advocates. There is no macroeconomic theory, as such, upon which economic policy advice might be based. The Council of Economic Advisers is a redundant agency, a leftover from the Keynesian era, an agency that could, at its best, present the case for its own ineffectiveness.

## The Politics of Policy

A different, and perhaps even stronger, indictment can be developed, independent of the validity or invalidity of the whole macroeconomic "scientific" enterprise. Even if macroeconomic theory, whether in its pristine Keynesian simplicity or in its modern expectational feedback variants, should be acknowledged to be descriptively adequate, the bridge between analysis and policy would still have to be crossed. Efficacy in policy would require resort to instruments that embody incentives compatible with the roles assigned to decision-makers within the governmental structure. The whole Keynesian edifice was constructed on the preposterous supposition that economic advice is offered to a genuinely benevolent despot, an entity devoid of its own interests, and presumably willing and able to implement, without resistance, the advice offered to it. The early monetarist challenge was directed to the Keynesian analysis and, in itself, did not question the implicit political supposition.

Policy decisions emerge from a process in which persons participate in accordance with established rules governing their behavior and authority. In order to advance any normative theory of policy at all, it is necessary to model the decision process. As noted above, the implicit Keynesian supposition is starkly simple; there is no decision process. An argument for a policy change need not go through a model of decision, either in terms of potential incentive compatibility for the individual or in terms of the reconciliation of possibly divergent individual interests.

For purposes of initial discussion here, I shall assume that there does exist a theory of the macroeconomy that allows economists to offer agreed-on policy advice. Further, I shall assume that the economists, themselves, are not directly motivated by their own career objectives in the governmental structure. Under these assumptions, the advice offered will be invariant over differing political decision structures, and it will, presumably, reflect the whole community's long-term interests. The same "independent" advice will be forthcoming whether the political authority is or is not responsive to the preferences of an electorate.

These assumptions allow me to focus attention on the behavior of the political agent when economic advice is offered. Only if the interests of the agent are coincident with those of the community would we expect quasi-automatic acceptance of the advice. Effective authority lodged with an hereditary monarch might represent the closest historical parallel to the implicitly presumed Keynesian model of politics. In all assignments of authority that are impermanent and that are not convertible into private-wealth equivalents, there will arise a necessary conflict between the interests of the agent and those of the citizenry. The impermanence of tenure along with the non-marketability of the "policy regime as a capital asset" insures that the interests of any designated political agent will be myopic relative to those that would be appropriate for the community. The agent would, therefore, tend to reject the advice of the economists when it embodies considerations of long-term gains at the expense of short-term sacrifice.

Applied to the whole set of choices among instruments and targets for macroeconomic policy, the political agent's decisions will tend to be biased toward demand-side rather than supply-side adjustments. More specifically, the agent's decisions will reflect biases toward public-spending increases as against tax reductions, toward deficit as against surplus financing, and toward monetary expansion as against monetary contraction.

This myopia exhibited by political agents will be accentuated if they are required to compete with potential replacements through electoral processes.[3] An authority or agent who is genuinely independent from politics possesses more flexibility in choice, and this may be exercised by closer adherence to the economists' advice. The absence of electoral feedbacks must, however, also allow more latitude for deviant behavior on the part of the agent.

Any plausible descriptive model of the political-decision process must yield the prediction that policy advice of economists will get, at best, only a

---

3. For a discussion of the differing effects of alternative political structures, see my paper "Can Policy Activism Succeed? A Public Choice Perspective," presented at Conference, Federal Reserve Bank of St. Louis, October 1984, Center for Study of Public Choice, George Mason University, unpublished manuscript.

biased acceptance. If political agents are to be made to conform more closely to the genuine "public interest" (on the presumption that there is no difficulty in defining such interest), their range of discretionary authority must be reduced or their incentives must be modified to induce closer conformity. The second of these prospects is severely restricted in democratic structures; politicians cannot readily be provided with effective incentives that run contrary to their survival in elected office. Meaningful prospects for reform may be limited to reduction in the range for discretionary action, i.e., to some introduction of *rules* within which action must take place.

To the extent that such constraining rules take the form either of specifically defined targets or instruments of policy, there is little left for advisory economists to do. As an extreme case, what would be the role for a Council of Economic Advisers in a setting where there exists a constitutional amendment for budget balance along with a Friedman-like rule for monetary growth? We do not, of course, have any such rules in place as a part of our constitutional structure. If constitutional reform is impossible, and hence if arms and agencies of government are to continue to be empowered to take policy actions that will affect the economy, is there a residual role for an agency designed to offer expert advice? Could it be argued that such an agency might exert a force, even if a limited one, toward policy directed in the community's interests?

My judgment is that such a potentially constructive role is more than offset by the delusion of effective policy activism that the very existence of such an agency tends to foster. This judgment is strengthened when we drop the provisional assumption, advanced above, that an agreed-on macroeconomic theory exists. The existence of an agency of experts in the setting of 1985 creates the appearance that a basis for agreed-on policy action exists which politicians could, ideally, implement but for their own narrowly defined interests.

In this setting, individuals will attempt to base their own economizing decisions on expectations concerning how political agents will, in fact, behave, both as against the idealized policy set and in terms of their own interests. The political agents in office will encourage the delusion by claiming credit for economic improvements, and their opponents out of office will reinforce the argument by blaming incumbents for economic disappointments. The very appearance of macroeconomic policy effectiveness or ineffectiveness on the part of an activist government tends to shift political debate to artificial if not false grounds of argument. The primary task of the Council of Economic Advisers, that of presenting an annual economic report, implies the assignment of "grades" to the stewardship over the national economy. Could we expect a council of economists to use the report for truth-telling? Could we expect them to expose the reality behind the appearance?

## Economics: Positive and Normative

I have not based my argument for the disestablishment of the Council of Economic Advisers on any claim that economics lacks scientific standing in the proper meaning of the term. There is a science of economics that yields testable hypotheses and allows conditional predictions to be made. Economists can predict the effects of shifts in the constraints within which persons act. These predictions are possible because of uniformities in the nature of man, who remains both natural and artifactual. At this level of inquiry, the science of economics is no different from the science of chemistry or biology. And the professional standards of the discipline operate similarly. An economist who advances a claim that trade restrictions increase the value of national product loses his credibility as a scientist. But, as noted earlier, there exist no comparable agreed-on standards in macroeconomics.

The comparison with other sciences is suggestive, however, because we do not observe agencies of government carrying the labels Council of Chemical Advisers, Council of Biological Advisers, etc. It is more or less taken for granted that the predictive properties of these basic sciences are utilized as inputs in any discussion of governmental action. There is no call, however, for the elevation of the practitioners in these disciplines to positions of particularized political influence. The role of such institutions as the President's Science Advisory Council or the Office of Technology Assessment is much more limited than that occupied by the Council of Economic Advisers. In general, it is taken for granted that scientists will do their work in academic and research communities, and it is also presumed that such work is best performed in relative isolation from the political forum.

Economists, as positive scientists, can contribute much to our understanding of the interactions among us and of the institutions within which such interactions take place. But what of the role for the economist reformers, for those who seek to use the predictions emergent from positive economics to suggest what governments "should" do? Even if there is no agreed-on "science" of macroeconomics, the predictions of microeconomics offer a basis for normative advice to governments, or so it may seem. Consider the simple case of minimum-wage legislation. Economic science predicts that increases in the level of real minimum wages, legally enforced, will increase unemployment, and especially among low-skill workers. This prediction has been empirically corroborated. Does it not follow directly that the economist, armed with these findings of his science, can suggest to governmental decision-makers that such legislation be repealed? Can the economist not use the familiar efficiency criterion to advance this argument?

The economist who takes this position must, however, place himself in the arrogant role of assuming a private knowledge of the preferred "social" rankings of alternative policy steps. In this position, there is nothing whatsoever in the economist's "science" that allows his own value rankings to be superior to those of anyone else in the polity. Enhanced employment of the low-skill workers, increased value of real product in the economy, extended sphere for voluntary contractual exchanges—these may be valued results, but they may well be relegated to rankings below those of maintaining higher wages among the employed or maintaining the existing geographical dispersion of employment by members of certain groups. The economist who implies that his "science" enables him to call for the repeal of minimum-wage legislation is on all fours with the nuclear physicist who implies that his "science" enables him to call for nuclear disarmament. In both cases, the genuine authority of the positive science is seriously undermined by the advancement of such false claims.

My own efforts in what we now call "constitutional economics" has often been classified as "normative economics." Does this suggest that I have been guilty of my own admonitions here? Careful reading of my position would suggest otherwise. I have called on my fellow economists to devote more attention to the working properties of alternative sets of rules within which persons, and especially those charged with political responsibilities, act. My continuing frustration has been with the refusal of so many of my fellow economists to recognize that the behavior of persons in public-choice roles is also subject to the predictions of our science. With Wicksell, I have urged those who seek reforms in policy, not as economists but as socially responsible citizens, to look to changes in the constraints placed on those we charge with political authority as opposed to changes in their behavior within existing constraints.

In my sense, again with Wicksell, my central purpose has been that of ridding our discourse of the benevolent-despot image, in all its forms. The Keynesian half-century in which this image was politically institutionalized through the creation of the Council of Economic Advisers is behind us. It seems time that we eliminate this relic of a past that has failed on so many counts, and that we get on with our business of engaging in constructive dialogue on the potential for reform in the framework of rules within which we may, both privately and publicly, pursue our individually defined purposes.

# Can Policy Activism Succeed?
## A Public-Choice Perspective

## 1. Introduction

The question posed in the title assigned to me presupposes the existence of an ordering of options along some scale of presumably agreed-on preferredness or desirability. Only if this presupposition is made does it become appropriate to ask whether or not politics, as it operates, can be expected to select the most preferred option on the ordering, or, less ambitiously, to select, on average, options that would allow the pattern or sequence of "choices" to be adjudged "successful." The generalized public-choice answer to the question, given the required presupposition, is reasonably straightforward, and it is essentially that of classical political economy. Those who make political decisions can be expected to choose in accordance with agreed-on or "public interest" norms only if the institutional structure is such as to make these norms coincident with those of "private interest." The public chooser, whether voter, aspiring or elected politician, or bureaucrat, is no different in this role than in other roles, and if incentives are such that the coincidence of interest is absent, there will be no "successful" political ordering over the feasible options. I shall return to the possible coincidence of interest following section 2.

The more fundamental question to be asked, however, involves the appropriateness of the required presupposition—that concerning the possibility of

From *The Monetary versus Fiscal Policy Debate: Lessons from Two Decades,* ed. R. W. Hafer (Totowa, N.J.: Rowman and Allanheld, 1986), 139–50. Reprinted by permission of the publisher.

any meaningful ordering of policy options, quite independent of any problems of implementation. This question has been obscured rather than clarified by those economists who resort to "social welfare functions." These functions impose a totally artificial and meaningless ordering on "social states" without offering any assistance toward facilitating choice from among the set of options feasibly available to the public chooser. Section 2 examines this fundamental question in the context of the issues that prompted the assigned title.

## 2. Is It Possible to Define an Ordering of Policy Options Along an Agreed-On "Success" Scalar?

In this section I propose to ignore totally all problems of policy implementation—all public-choice problems, if you will. For simplicity, assume the existence of a genuinely benevolent despot, who sincerely seeks to do that which is "best" for all of those who are members of the political-economic-social community. How can we describe the utility function of this despot? It is easy, of course, to list several desired end-states. Full employment, stable and predictable value in the monetary unit, high and sustainable rates of economic growth, stable international order—these may be mutually agreed-on objectives for policy action. But there may be conflict among the separate objectives (to raise a topic of much debate-discussion of the 1950s that has been relatively neglected in the 1980s). How are we to model the trade-offs among the objectives within the utility function of the benevolent despot, if indeed such conflicts should arise?

I presume that the despot can act so as to influence macroeconomic variables in the economy; I leave possible rational expectations feedbacks to the other paper in this session. But how "should" the despot act, and, in this model, how "will" he act? There is no definitive answer to these questions until and unless the utility function is defined more fully.

There is, of course, an empty response to the question posed in the title to this section. Clearly, if the despot can, by our presumption, influence macroeconomic variables by policy action, then, by some criterion of his own, he can be "successful." But presumably we seek to employ a more objective criterion for success, one that can at least conceptually be observed by others than the despot himself.

For simplicity, let us assume that the despot is concerned only about domestic employment and monetary stability; we ignore all nondomestic considerations, and we put aside problems of growth. Further, let us restrict attention to standard macropolicy tools. The despot here is assumed to be unable, at least in the time frame of the policy under consideration, to modify the structural features of the economy. With these simplifications, we can go further and specify the objective function more precisely. Let us assume that the despot seeks to guarantee that level of employment that is consistent with stability in the value of the monetary unit, given the institutional structure of the economy. The objective reduces to a single price level target.

Even in this highly restricted setting, which is by no means that which might command consensus as a normative posture, the despot cannot simply "choose" the ultimate end objective from an available set of options. That is to say, "stability in the value of the monetary unit" cannot be selected as if from off a policy shelf. The despot is further restricted by the tools of policy available, which in this setting are those of the familiar fiscal (budgetary) and monetary instruments. Nominal demand can be increased, directly or indirectly, or reduced, directly or indirectly, by the use of fiscal-monetary tools, either separately or in some mix. Even if we ignore, as indicated, the expectational-induced feedbacks generated by resort to any instrument, there remains the task of predicting accurately the relationship between the instrument, economic structure, and ultimate objective. The structural features of the economy are not invariant over time, and a policy thrust that might be successful under one set of conditions, say in $t_0$, may fail, say, in $t_1$, because of structural shifts. At best, therefore, the truly benevolent despot can only be partially successful, even given the most clearly defined target for policy.

## 3. Monolithic and Nonbenevolent Despot

The presumption of benevolence on the part of political agents is not, of course, acceptable within a public-choice perspective. It is precisely this presumption that has been a central focus of the overall public-choice critique of the theory of economic policy. Political agents must be presumed to maximize personal utilities in a behavioral model that is invariant, as between public and private roles or capacities. The structure of decision making may, however, affect utility-maximizing behavior through shifts in the effective constraints on choice.

In this section, I shall discuss briefly the simplest possible decision structure, one in which political decisions are lodged within a single monolithic authority (in the limit in one person) which (who) is not directly accountable to or subject to constituency pressures, whether or not these be explicitly "democratic" (electoral) in nature. In this model, it is evident, quite apart from any historical record, that the despot will find it advantageous to resort to money creation over and beyond any amount that might characterize the "ideal" behavior of the benevolent counterpart considered above. This result emerges, quite simply, because incentive effects must be taken into account, and the despot, even if totally immune from constituency pressures, must reckon with individual adjustments to alternative revenue-generating instruments. Through a policy of revenue-maximizing inflation, defined in a dynamic sense, the despot can extract the full value of monetary structure (that is, the value differential between a monetary structure and a barter structure).[1]

The amount of revenue that may be potentially raised through money creation is, of course, finite. And the totally uncontrolled despot may seek to utilize the taxing and debt-issue power over and beyond the inflationary revenue limits. The precise features of the despot's policy mix will depend, in part, on his time horizon in relation to the behavioral reactions of the population. These features need not be examined in detail here. It is sufficient, for my purposes, to conclude that the monolithic despot will be successful only in terms of his own criteria, and that by any of the more familiar criteria for policy success, the failure would be manifest.

## 4. Monolithic and Nonbenevolent Agent Subject to Electoral Constraints

The analysis becomes more complex once we introduce electoral feedback constraints on the behavior of the monolithic political agent. Assume now

---

1. For further elaboration and analysis, see Geoffrey Brennan and James M. Buchanan, *The Power to Tax* (Cambridge: Cambridge University Press, 1980), chap. 6, and *Monopoly in Money and Inflation* (London: Institute of Economic Affairs, 1981).

that decision authority remains concentrated, but that the holder of this authority is subject to potential electoral replacement at designated periodic intervals. In this model the "governor" cannot expect to use his authority for personal enrichment for any extended period. Under some conditions, simple wealth-maximizing strategy might involve revenue-maximizing exploitation during the period of office, with no attention to possible reelection. In other conditions, the wealth-maximizing strategy might involve the effort to remain in office, in which case, short-run revenue maximization via inflation, debt creation, and taxation will be mitigated. If the agent is modeled as a simple revenue maximizer, it seems unlikely that his pattern of behavior would be adjudged "successful" by external criteria under either of these circumstances.

The more interesting model is one in which the agent is motivated by other considerations than wealth, the simplest model being that in which political position is itself the single maximand. The agent's behavior will, in this case, be constrained by expectations of electoral support. The question then becomes one of determining to what extent voters, generally, or in a required winning coalition, will support or oppose patterns of policy outcomes that might be deemed "successful" by external criteria. Given the postulated motivation here, the agent will base behavior strictly on constituency response.

Consider this question in the terms introduced earlier, that of a unique objective of monetary stability. Will a sufficiently large voting constituency support a regime that seeks only this policy objective? This question may be examined in the calculus of the individual voter or potential voter.

Two separate difficulties arise. The first involves the absence of individual voter responsibility for electoral outcomes in large-number constituencies. Even if the individual knows that the agent elected is fully responsive to the electoral process, because he knows that his own voting choice will rarely, if ever, be decisive, the individual may not vote. And if he does vote, he has little or no incentive to become informed about the alternatives. And if he votes, and even if he is reasonably well informed, there is little or no incentive for him to vote his "interests" rather than his "whims." Hence, there is only a remote linkage between what might be defined by the observing external "expert" as the "interest" of the voters and the support that is given to a prospective political agent who promises these externally defined "interests." This difficulty alone suggests that political agents cannot be "held responsible" by the electoral process nearly to the extent that is suggested by naive models of electoral feedback.

A second difficulty emerges even when the first is totally ignored. Even if all individuals are somehow motivated to vote and to do so in terms of their well-considered interests, these interests will not be identical for all voters. There are differentials among persons in the relative benefits and costs of any macropolicy action. Even the ideally responsive political agent will meet only the demands of the relevant coalition of voters, as determined by the precise voting rules.

Consider a single political agent who must satisfy a simple majority of constituency voters. If voters' interests in the employment-inflation trade-off can be presumed to be single peaked, the political agent's optimal strategy requires satisfying the median voter. It seems likely that this median voter will tend to be *myopic* in his behavior in the electoral process. He will place an unduly high value on the short-term benefits of enhancing employment relative to the long-term, and possibly permanent, costs of inflation. He will do so because, as a currently decisive voter, he can insure the capture of *some* benefits in the immediate future. By foregoing such short-term benefits in a "rational" consideration of the long-term costs, the currently decisive voter *cannot* guarantee against the incurrence of such long-term costs in future periods. This asymmetrical result follows from the potential shiftability of majority voting coalitions. A subsequent period may allow a different median voter or coalition of voters to emerge as dominant—a decisive voter or group that may choose to inflate from strictly short-term considerations. To the extent that this takes place, all of the initial benefits of policy prudence may be offset. In the recognition of this prospect, why should the decisive voter or coalition of voters in the initial period exhibit nonmyopic "rationality" in the sense indicated?[2]

The ultimate answer to the assigned question is clear in this highly sim-

---

2. For further elaboration of the analysis, see Geoffrey Brennan and James M. Buchanan, *The Reason of Rules* (Cambridge: Cambridge University Press, forthcoming), chaps. 5 and 6.

plified model for "democratic" politics. Policy activism cannot be successful if the criterion of success is long-term monetary stability, a criterion that seems most likely to emerge consensually in a constitutional process of deliberation.[3]

## 5. Nonmonolithic and Nonbenevolent Agents in a Political Structure Subject to Varying Electoral Constraints

The political models examined in sections 3 and 4 were oversimplified in the assumption that authority was placed in a single agent or agency. As we approach reality, it is necessary to recognize that policy-making authority is likely to be divided among several agents or agencies, who (which) may be subjected to quite different electoral controls or constraints and, hence, potentially affected by differing electoral pressures. For example, fiscal or budgetary policies may be made in a wholly different process, institutionally, from monetary policy, and, even within the institutional structure of budgetary policy, authority may be divided between executive and legislative branches of government, subjected to varying electoral constraints, as defined by such things as breadth of constituencies, length of terms of office, voting structure within agency (in legislatures and committees), legally defined responsibilities, and so on.

The direction of difference in effects between this more realistic political model and the monolithic model previously examined seems evident. To the extent that policy-making authority is divided, the proclivity toward response to short-term pressures is increased. Any array of results along the success criterion indicated would indicate that the divided-authority model ranks well below its monolithic counterpart.

3. I shall not develop the argument in support of the contractarian-constitutional criterion for measuring policy success or failure. Let me say only that such a criterion must be used unless we are willing to introduce external and nonindividualistic standards of evaluation.

A more controversial position is the one that suggests that the monetary stability criterion would, indeed, be the one that would emerge from the ideally constructed constitutional setting. I shall not develop the argument in support of this position, although I think it can be plausibly made.

## 6. Nonbenevolent but Monolithic Agent Divorced from Direct Electoral Constraints but Subject to Legal-Constitutional Rules Against Personal Enrichment

If there is little or no basis for expecting political agents to express benevolence in their policy behavior, and if, as suggested, the standard "democratic" controls will not themselves insure patterns of outcomes that meet reasonable criteria of success, alternative institutional structures must be analyzed. Consider, first, a model in which decision-making authority is lodged in a single agent or agency and one that is specifically divorced from the electoral process—an agent or agency that does not face continual electoral checks. To prevent that potential for excess under the model discussed in section 3, however, suppose that the agent or members of the agency are placed within enforceable legal-constitutional limits with reference to his or their personal or private enrichment, either directly or indirectly. That is to say, the agent or members of the agency cannot use the money-creation and/or taxing power to finance their own private consumption needs or accumulation (e.g., Swiss bank accounts) desires. Beyond this restriction, however, we shall assume that the agent or members of the agency is (are) not limited in behavior except in the overall and general mandate to carry out "good" macroeconomic policy.

This model can be recognized as one that is closely analogous to the monetary authority of the Federal Reserve Board in the United States. Some elements of the model discussed in section 3—that of the nonconstrained despot—describe the existing structure, and, more importantly, some political controls are exercised; but, for my purposes, the existing monetary authority fits the model reasonably well.

The problem becomes one of predicting the behavior of such an agent and of assessing this behavior in terms of the success criterion introduced. Neither economic nor public-choice analysis is capable of being of much assistance in this respect. To make a prediction, one must get inside the utility function of the agent (or of those who participate in agency decisions). In particular, it would be necessary to know something about the internal rate of time preference that will characterize behavior. If, as we have assumed, demand-enhancing action is known to generate short-term benefits at the expense of long-term costs, the behavior of the monopolistic and discretionary agent in making this trade-off will depend strictly on his own, private, rate of time preference, as expressed "for" the community. That is to say, under the conditions indicated, the agent will not, personally, secure the benefits or suffer the costs. By definition, the agent is not *responsible*, in the sense of a reward-penalty calculus.

This absence of responsibility itself suggests that the behavior of the discretionary agent is likely to be less carefully considered, to be based on less information, and hence to be more erratic than would be the case under some alternative reward-penalty structure. The model further suggests that the agent here is more likely to be responsive to the passing whims of intellectual-media "fashion" than might be the case in the presence of some residual claimancy status. To the extent that the agent is at all responsive to interest-group pressures, such response seems likely to be biased toward those groups seeking near-term benefits and biased against those groups that might be concerned about long-term costs, if for no other reason than the difference in temporal dimension itself. Organized pressures for the promotion of short-term benefits exist while there may be no offsetting organization of long-term interests. This bias might well be exaggerated if the agent or agency is assigned functions that cause the development of relationships with particular functional groups in the policy (e.g., banking and finance). In sum, although there is really no satisfactory predictive model for behavior of the genuinely discretionary agent or agency, there are plausibly acceptable reasons to suggest that policy failures will tend to take the directions indicated in the discussion here.

Viewed in this perspective, and in application to the Federal Reserve agency in the United States, and perhaps notably after the removal of international monetary constraints, there should have been no surprise that the behavior exhibited has been highly erratic. Any other pattern would indeed have required more explanation than that which has been observed. From both analysis and observation the ultimate answer to the question concerning "successful" policy activism in this model, as in the others examined, must be negative.

## 7. Nonbenevolent and Monolithic Agent Divorced from Electoral Constraints but Subject to Legal-Constitutional Rules Against Personal Enrichment but Also to Constitutional Rules That Direct Policy Action

The generally negative answer to the question posed in the title prompts examination of still other institutional structures that do not involve attempts at "policy activism," as such, but which, instead, embody sets of predictable and directed policy actions in accordance with constitutionally specified rules. In familiar terminology, if "policy activism," when applied in a setting of *discretionary authority*, must fail to meet the success criterion, can a setting of *rules* do better? It would be inappropriate to discuss at length the relative advantages of alternative regimes or sets of rules. But it is clear that almost any well-defined set of rules would eliminate most of the incentive and motivational sources for the failure of discretionary agency models as previously discussed.

In a very real sense there is no agency problem in an effectively operating rule-ordered regime. A fiscal-monetary authority, charged with the actual implementation of policy, but only in the carrying out of specified rules, defined either in terms of means or objectives, cannot itself be judged on other than purely administrative criteria of success or failure. More criteria must now be applied to the alternative sets of rules, with success or failure accordingly assigned. And working models of such alternative sets might be analyzed, just as the models of a discretionary agency have been analyzed here. But there seems to be a closer relationship between the rules that might be selected and the success criterion adopted than there is between the latter and the pronounced goals of a discretionary agency.

The potential for success of rule-guided macropolicy depends, in large part, on the *absence* of policy activism, not only for the removal of the potential for self-interested behavior on the part of discretionary agents, but also for the built-in predictability of such action that is inherent in the notion of rules, as such. The relative advantages of rule-guided policy over agency discretion could be treated at length, but this effort would carry me well beyond my assignment in this paper.

## 8. Fiscal Policy and Monetary Policy

There are two distinct policy instruments, or sets of instruments, both in the familiar textbook terminology and, indeed, in the overall subject of this conference: fiscal policy instruments and monetary policy instruments. To this point I have made no distinction between these two sets, and I have avoided altogether any discussion of relative efficacy as well as relative vulnerability to the sorts of influences on behavior that are emphasized in a public-choice approach. It is time to explore some of the differences that are directly relevant to the arguments that I have advanced.

Fiscal policy involves budgetary manipulation and, hence, a necessary linkage between any macropolicy objectives and the whole process of public-sector allocation. Given this necessary linkage, and given the institutional-political history, it seems totally unreal to suggest that any shift of authority over fiscal policy would be delegated either to discretionary or even to rule-bound authority. It seems highly unlikely that fiscal policy, in any sense, would be removed from the ordinary procedures of democratic decision making, with divided legislative and executive responsibilities and roles in its over-all formulation. It becomes unrealistic in the extreme to presume that we, in the United States, would transfer to an agency immune from electoral constraints any authority to manipulate either side of the budget in accordance with rules or intentions to improve macroeconomic performance. Decisions on tax rates, spending rates, and, in consequence, deficits and borrowing requirements are likely to remain within the responsibility of "democratic" determination, with the predicted result that any meaningful success criterion will fail to be satisfied. There will be a bias toward "easy budgets," with higher-than-desired deficits, to the extent that any considerations of macroeconomic policy enter the policy argument.[4]

Given this predicted bias, and quite apart from any consideration as to the independent efficacy of budgetary policy in effectuating desired results, any genuine hope for "success" in macroeconomic policy must involve a reduction or removal of budgetary manipulation from the potentially usable kit of tools.[5] If "fiscal policy" can be isolated so as to insure that its operation does not make the task of monetary management more difficult, a major step toward genuine reform will have been made. It is in this context that the ar-

---

4. For an early statement of this point, see James M. Buchanan, "Easy Budgets and Tight Money," *Lloyds Bank Review* 64 (1962): 17–30. For a more extended discussion, see James M. Buchanan and Richard E. Wagner, *Democracy in Deficit* (New York: Academic Press, 1977), and James M. Buchanan and Richard E. Wagner, eds., *Fiscal Responsibility in Constitutional Democracy* (Boston: Martinus Nijhoff, 1978).

5. Keynes and the Keynesians must bear a heavy responsibility for destroying the set of classical precepts for fiscal prudence that had operated to keep the natural proclivities of politicians in bounds. By offering what could be interpreted as plausible excuses for fiscal profligacy, modern politicians have, for several decades, been able to act out their natural urges, with the results that we now observe. For further discussion, see James M. Buchanan, "Victorian Budgetary Norms, Keynesian Advocacy and Modern Fiscal Politics," prepared for Nobel Symposium on Governmental Growth, Stockholm, Sweden, August 1984, working paper no. 4-02, Center for Study of Public Choice.

gument for a constitutional rule requiring budget balance becomes important in macroeconomic policy discussion.

If fiscal policy is so isolated, the task of policy action is left to the monetary agency or regime. A monetary agency can be made effective if the discretion of the agent is limited by the imposition of legally binding and enforceable rules for policy actions. These rules may take on any one of several forms, and it would be out of place to discuss these alternatives in detail here. The monetary agency can be directed to act on the defined monetary aggregates so as to insure prespecified quantity targets (as in some Friedman-like growth rule). Or the authority might be directed to act so as to achieve a specifically defined outcome target, such as the maintenance of stability in the value of the monetary unit. In either case the structure of the rules must be such as to invoke penalties for the failure of the authorities to act in accordance with the declared norms. Some allowance for within-threshold departures from targeted objectives would, of course, be necessary.

But only with some such feedback in place can the persons in positions of responsibility as monetary agents be expected to perform so as to further the success criterion that is implicit in the imposition of the rules. It seems at least conceptually possible to build in a workable reward-penalty structure for the compensation and employment of rule-bound monetary agents. And, in the limiting case, such a reward-penalty structure, appropriately related to the achievement of the desired policy target, may obviate the need for explicit definition of a rule for policy action. For example, if the compensations of all employees of the monetary authority should be indexed so as to insure personal penalty from any departures from monetary stability, perhaps nothing more need be required by way of rules. (Such a scheme might involve the maintenance of fixed nominal salary levels against inflation, and double indexing of salaries against deflation, or some more sophisticated formulae.)

If no incentive-motivational structure is deemed to be institutionally and politically feasible under the operation of any fiat money regime, the argument for more basic regime shift in the direction of an automatic or self-correcting system based on some commodity base is substantially strengthened. The relative advantage of all such systems lies in their incorporation of market-like incentives to generate behavior that will tend to generate at least long-term stability in the value of the monetary unit.

## 9. Conclusion

In this discussion, as elsewhere, the primary implication of public-choice theory is that institutional-constitutional change or reform is required to achieve ultimate success in macroeconomic policy. There is relatively little to be gained by advancing arguments for "better-informed" and "more-public-spirited" agents, to be instructed by increasingly sophisticated "economic consultants" who are abreast of the frontiers of the "new science." All such effort will do little more than provide employment for those who are involved. It is the *political economy of policy* that must be reformed. Until and unless this step is taken, observed patterns of policy outcomes will continue to reflect accurately the existing political economy within which these outcomes are produced. And we shall continue to have conferences and discussions about the failures of "policy activism."

# Society and Democracy

## I. Introduction

My thesis is simple. "Society" takes precedence over "Democracy." By this statement I mean that while democratic processes of governance, in which all persons have some participatory role, may well be necessary in any well-functioning civic order, the converse relationship does not hold. The presence of "democracy," as such, does not guarantee, or even promote, the construction and maintenance of those constitutional-institutional parameters which inclusively define the civic order (or "society"). In the absence of such parameters that define the very framework within which government as well as private agencies operate, no civic order, no "society," can exist that warrants positive evaluative designation.

I can summarize my argument by repeating here a statement made in an earlier paper. I stated that the political structure of any society that embodies respect for individual liberty must be one that is described by the term "constitutional democracy," but that of the two words in this couplet, "constitutional" is prior to "democracy."

I propose to develop this thesis with reference to the demonstrated proclivities of modern democratic politics to extend beyond meaningful constitutional, or within-parametric, limits, and to take on attributes of a negative-sum contest that becomes akin to a game without rules. In a very real sense, the distributional politics of what Anthony de Jasay has appropriately termed "the churning state," has become this age's version of the Hobbesian

From *The David Hume Institute—The First Decade*, ed. Nick Kuenssberg and Gillian Lomas (Edinburgh: David Hume Institute, 1996), 25–33. Reprinted by permission of the publisher.

war of each against all.[1] Particular interests seek to get, and succeed in getting, the assistance of the state at the expense of others, and all within the processes of democratic institutions. Until and unless we come to an understanding that the principle of generality must be operative in politics in some manner that is at least akin to that which is ideally present under the notion of equality before the law, the observed excesses of "democracy" will continue to undermine the public's confidence in our ability to govern ourselves.

## II. Politics without Romance

My inaugural lecture at the Institute for Higher Studies in Vienna, Austria, in 1979 was entitled "Politics without Romance."[2] I have since found this three-word title to be quite useful in summarizing the whole research program in public choice, that program within which my own work has been classified. This title is descriptively accurate because it contrasts the public choice conception or explanatory model of politics and political process with the traditional alternative one that could be described as "politics with romance." And, surprising as this may seem to Spanish realists, such a romantic model has been central in "political theory" since the ancient Greeks. In this traditional conception, the whole enterprise of politics is understood to be a continuing search for what is "good, true, and beautiful" for the polity. To the extent that individual participation is explicitly considered at all in this conception, the emphasis is on participation in the ongoing dialogue and discussion. The teleological nature of the whole enterprise suggests that the good and the true, once discovered, are to be universally accepted and acclaimed by all "right-thinking" and "morally responsible" citizens. In this romanticized conception of what politics is about, the specific features of a decision rule that may be used to close off discussion, temporarily or permanently, do not demand critical analytical attention. What matters is that the uniquely determinate results be attained and implemented, not that individual expressions of preference be embodied in such results. To the extent

1. Anthony de Jasay, *The State* (Oxford: Basil Blackwell, 1985).
2. James M. Buchanan, "Politics without Romance: A Sketch of Positive Public Choice Theory and Its Normative Implications," *IHS-Journal, Zeitschrift des Instituts für Höhere Studien, Wien* 3 (1979): B1–B11.

that separate individual preferences are counted or measured in some amalgamation process, such procedure qualifies only as one possible means of discovering that which exists. I have often referred to the multi-person jury as a means of determining guilt or innocence in criminal proceedings as an analogue to the place of democratic voting procedures under this conceptualization of politics. Individual preferences differ, one from another, here only because persons may be differently informed or may have differing theories as to how the good and the true may be generated. In this model, they do not differ because individuals have differing interests or purposes for the whole political enterprise.[3]

The realist or non-romantic conceptual model of politics is dramatically different from that just sketched out. First of all, there is no room for the notion that there exists some ultimate "truth" in the political enterprise, just waiting out there to be discovered, one way or the other. Secondly, the basic legitimization of politics, and of government as a coercive force, lies in the expressed consent of individuals, who judge that collective action is necessary for them, individually, to accomplish purposes that they cannot readily achieve through private action. And, in the organisation of collective action, that is, in the activity of politics, individuals express their own interests, which may differ, as well as their own theories. Politics is an enterprise in which persons and groups seek to further shared, but still private, purposes.

In this realist conception of politics, which informs the public choice research program, it is immediately evident that individual participation matters in quite a different way from its role in the romantic or idealist conception. Precisely because individuals do have separable interests, which may conflict, it becomes relevant and important that they be allowed access to the participatory enterprise. And not only potential access, but also the specific features of the decision rule become significant. A vote is more than a voice. Further, the domain of society over which politics is allowed to enter and to dominate emerges as a critical variable. In sum, politics as a "compromise of interests" is different in kind from politics as a "discovery of the good or the true."

---

3. For further discussion, see Viktor Vanberg and James M. Buchanan, "Interests and Theories in Constitutional Choice," *Journal of Theoretical Politics* 1 (January 1989): 49–62.

## III. The Electoral Fallacy

The intellectual leaders of the eighteenth-century Scots Enlightenment and the American Founders, in particular, were political realists; they were highly sceptical of politics, government, and politicians as promoters and guarantors of the public or general interest of the ordinary citizenry. They sought to constrain governmental intrusions into the lives of citizens, whether economic or personal. They interpreted constitutions to have such constraint as a primary purpose, and they did not distinguish between forms of government in terms of the applicability of constitutional limits. Whether or not governments qualified as democratic was not considered directly relevant to the need for constraint on the domain of society over which politics was allowed to operate.

Unfortunately, confusion emerged as previously despotic regimes came increasingly to be replaced by constitutionally guaranteed democratic electoral systems. What I have called "the electoral fallacy" emerged in the nineteenth century, reflected in the notion that so long as there existed constitutional protection that guaranteed universality in the franchise, open and periodic elections, freedom of entry into the formation of political parties, and the generality of enforcement of laws enacted through majoritarian processes, politics would be kept within bounds. Democracy was considered to be the guarantor of the discipline that it imposed upon itself. There was little or no understanding that electoral democracy, in particular, requires its own constitutional constraints. This absence of understanding was exacerbated by the resurgence of the romantic image of politics in early nineteenth-century political philosophy. The constitutional wisdom of the eighteenth century was lost, and democracy, treated as almost synonymous with majoritarianism, was allowed to move almost at will into areas of civic society that remained unprotected by constitutional barriers.

## IV. The Natural Limits of Majority Rule

In much modern discourse, democracy means majority rule. But this understanding is seldom followed up by its consequence. Majority rule means rule by the majority which, in its turn, means that those in the minority are ruled. They are coerced into an acceptance of political results that they do not prefer. This very elementary definitional starting point is too often overlooked because of an implicit assumption that the alternatives for collective or political selection are themselves exogenous to the process or rule through which selection is made. In such a case, while individuals in the minority may prefer some alternative other than the one imposed by the majority, there is no overt exploitation of the minority, as such. In this conceptual framework, the collective selection process contains elements of a coordination game within which members of both the dominant majority and the minority are predicted to benefit from the result, quite independent from status.

But where do the alternatives for political action come from? Are these alternatives "out there" as potentialities, waiting for some process, any process, to make a selection and put one of them into being? Or are the alternatives for political action themselves created endogenously by political entrepreneurs, who seek to further the interests of those persons and groups whom they represent? Do political entrepreneurs emerge to invent and discover alternatives for political action that are aimed primarily if not exclusively to promote the interests of those represented in the relevant coalition? In this perspective on democratic politics, the alternatives among which some selection is to be made do not exist independently at all. And in this perspective it is perhaps clear that, while alternatives may well be "public" along some relevant dimensions, the differential interest of members of the majority coalition is likely to be furthered by "private" elements.[4] It is equally clear that the set of political alternatives brought up for consideration will depend upon the decision rule in operation. A voting rule that requires only a simple majority of a legislative assembly will generate quite different options than would a voting rule that requires a five-sixths qualified majority.

Unless there exist explicit constitutional constraints on the type of alternatives to be considered, or, more generally, on the activities of society subject to politicization, the natural tendency of majoritarian decision processes is to move toward actions that benefit members of the majority at the expense of members of the minority. Aided and abetted by imaginative political entrepreneurs, majority coalitions will succeed in securing political ap-

---

4. Marilyn Flowers and Patricia Danzon, "Separation of the Redistributive and Allocative Functions of Government: A Public Choice Perspective," *Journal of Public Economics* 24 (August 1984): 373–80.

proval for programs that provide differential or special benefits to their own members, while imposing costs, either generally on all citizens, or differentially on members of the dominated minority. Or, conversely, majority coalitions will secure approval for programs offering general benefits to the whole citizenry while being primarily financed by taxes imposed differentially on members of the minority. Or, in further extension of this natural proclivity of political majoritarianism, programs that quite explicitly involve overt transfers from minority to majority members may become commonplace.

In any realist model or understanding of political process, majority rule becomes more than a means either of closing off discussion or of discovering truth. Majority rule becomes a means through which the interests of those who make up the successful coalition may be advanced, if necessary, at the expense of those who are outside this coalition. And when it is recognized that the makeup of majority coalitions shifts through time, we should scarcely be surprised at the growth of the politicized sector of society in the age of majoritarian democracy.

## V. Generality in Politics

What can be done to keep democracy within some appropriate limits? How can the natural extension of majority rule be held in check, while at the same time preserving those elements of political equality that are deemed necessary for the functioning of civic order? How can the game that is majoritarian politics be controlled to insure against minority exploitation? How can steps be taken to guarantee that this game be positive sum, that political action generate net benefits to all members of the inclusive polity?

These are, of course, questions that have been discussed through the ages. But they are, nonetheless, as relevant at the end of the twentieth century as they were in Athens in the centuries before Christ lived. The fears of democratic excesses expressed by the early Greeks also describe modern attitudes. The central problem of democracy has by no means been resolved.

James Madison, the most important of the American Founders, sought to forestall the emergence of coalitional or factional politics by incorporating several procedural checks and balances into the constitutional structure. Governmental authority was to be divided, deliberately, between executive, legislative, and judicial branches, each of which is responsive to a different constituency and with differing institutional traditions. The legislative branch itself was to be further limited by bicameralism, with separated, if overlapping, constituencies for the two bodies. Further, power was to be divided between the central and regional or provincial governments, with central domination restricted by the potential for secession. These several structural parameters for governance were to be implanted in an explicit constitution, which also stipulated the limits on the extension of political power, no matter how exercised.

We now know that the Madisonian enterprise failed. The great American Civil War in the 1860s removed forever the threat of secession by the states, and this basic constitutional change more or less insured that, eventually, the United States would be transformed into a centralized majoritarian democracy, with few, if any, checks on ultimate political authority. In this modern setting, democracy dominates society.

The parliamentary democracies of Western Europe were even less successful in holding back the forces for Leviathan. Confused by the electoral fallacy discussed above, these societies were allowed to drift into the politicized domination reflected in the modern social democracies of the expanded and intrusive welfare state, with little or no discussion of the appropriateness of limits to majoritarian control.

Observation suggests that democracy, in modern practice, is out of control. The great revolution of 1989–1991, which displaced centralized collectivism as a viable form of economic order, seems to have exerted little or no influence on the continued overreaching of majoritarian democracies, and on the ideas that sustain this movement. Is it possible even to imagine some means through which democracy can be limited, without, at the same time, replacing majority voting itself, which, unfortunately, has come to represent the meaning of democracy, at least in public attitudes? We do, indeed, find ourselves caught up in contradiction here. We want to define democracy as "majority rule," while, at the same time, we recognize that under any realistic modelling of politics majorities will act to exploit minorities.[5]

I suggest that the application and enforcement of the *principle of generality*

5. Norman Barry, in "F. A. Hayek's Theory of Spontaneous Order" (paper prepared for Liberty Fund conference, Chicago, November 1993), identifies a comparable contradiction in Hayek's position on parliamentary sovereignty.

can remove the contradiction here. We can reform our politics so as to reduce substantially if not totally eliminate majoritarian exploitation without
in any way removing majority voting from its central place as the basic decision rule, and, also, without placing specific areas of social activity beyond
the boundaries for politicization. The principle of generality is almost self-
explanatory. If political or collective action is to be taken at all, it must be
general in application over all persons and groups in the political community. Politics cannot be allowed to take differential or discriminatory action.
This principle would, indeed, close off many options for majoritarian choice.
But within the whole set of alternatives that satisfy the generality criterion,
majority voting may be allowed to make final determination.

The importance of the principle of generality was emphasized by Professor F. A. Hayek in his comprehensive treatise, *The Constitution of Liberty*, although he did not discuss its applicability in the context of majoritarian politics. Hayek recognized, however, the relevance of generality as traditionally
embodied in the rule of law, which he identified as a central norm in any
society that would lay claim to classification as a liberal order.[6] "Equality under the law" as a norm implies that specific exemption or special treatment
is out of bounds. In enforcing legal rules, the judiciary is simply not allowed
to differentiate among individuals and groups. Of course, this principle of
generality, even in law, has existed, and exists, only as a widely acknowledged
norm for judicial action rather than a strictly followed directive for behaviour. Violations have occurred, and do occur. Nonetheless, the rule of law
continues to retain its viability as an ongoing principle for legal order in all
Western societies.

Why have social scientists and social philosophers, other than Hayek, failed
to recognize that differential or discriminatory treatment in politics is, at base,
equivalent to differential or discriminatory treatment in law? Why can a legislative or parliamentary majority pick out particular constituency groups for
special treatment, either favourable or unfavourable, when a judge, in enforcing law, is prevented from comparable discrimination? The answer lies in the
combination of the idealist model of politics and the electoral fallacy, both of
which were discussed earlier in Sections II and III. Majority coalitions, both
because their authority is presumed subject to electoral feedback and because

6. F. A. Hayek, *The Constitution of Liberty* (Chicago: Henry Regnery Co., 1960).

they are presumed to be engaged in a search for truth rather than advantage, have been essentially immunised from critical behavioural scrutiny. And, indeed, the modern role for members of legislative assemblies has been transformed into one that involves the promotion of differential constituency interest as its defining characteristic.

Only if, as, and when effective constitutional constraints are imposed on the discriminatory actions of majority coalitions, can modern democratic politics be forced back into some appropriate relationship to the more inclusive society. It may be helpful at this stage to note several examples that would illustrate how a principle of generality would work if applied to politics.

Consider trade policy. The differential interest of each producer group (or industry) is to secure protection of its own market from potential competition by foreign suppliers. There are profits to be gained by investing in political activity that will impose such protection. And if a sufficiently influential coalition of producer groups can be organised, majoritarian politics will install the desired protectionist regime.[7] The groups that succeed in this effort will, however, increase profits only if the restrictive policy remains non-general. If a principle of generality is in place, protection for any industry or producer group would require that like protection be extended for all industries. But, in this case, the differential or particular interest of any single group in protection no longer exists. Given an effective generalization requirement, the interest of each group is in a non-restrictive regime of free trade. Support for protectionist majority coalitions would largely disappear.

As a second example, consider the familiar patterns of pork-barrel spending. A single legislator is deemed praiseworthy by constituents if a governmental project is located in his or her district, quite independent of the overall net benefits of the project. Under a principle of generality, the approval of any locationally specific project would require the comparable location of other projects in all districts, rather than only in those areas represented by the members of the majority coalition. In such a case, the interest of the electoral constituency shifts and support for cost ineffective projects disappears,

---

7. James M. Buchanan and Dwight Lee, "Cartels, Coalitions and Constitutional Politics," *Constitutional Political Economy* 2 (Spring/Summer 1991): 139–69.

but without in any way subverting the ultimate authority of a majority to take decisions for the whole electorate.

As a third, and final example, consider taxation. Somewhat interestingly, some elements of the generalization principle do describe tax structures in modern democratic regimes. Overtly discriminatory tax treatment of persons and groups as classified by political status would be deemed constitutionally out of bounds, and attempts to impose such treatment would be prevented by judicial mandates in most jurisdictions. But important features of constitutionally acceptable tax structures clearly violate any generality norm. Democratic majorities can impose discriminatory taxes on particular sources and uses of income, on particular professions, occupations, industries, or products and services, and, perhaps, most importantly, rates of tax can be different for persons in differing income categories. The progressive income tax clearly represents a departure from the generality principle, and only a uniform proportional or flat-rate tax, without exemption, deduction, or shelter would fully qualify.

## VI. Changing the Public Mind-set:
## From the Particular to the General

One way of interpreting the central argument advanced here is as a reconciliation between the teleological feature of the romantic notion of politics and the reality of interest-seeking political behaviour. Politics, as an activity, *should* be aimed at furtherance of "good" for society. But political activity as it is observed to take place in majoritarian democracy does not match this philosophically legitimating purpose. The infusion of the generality principle or norm, as a restriction on the domain of politics, as a limit on any ability of politics to further the defined interest of one group over another, would go far toward closing the gap between the ideal and the reality of democracy. Individuals will, of course, continue to seek to further their own interests, and these interests will differ among separately classified groups of persons. But potential disagreement over policy alternatives that are known to be generally applied are likely to be dramatically less intense than disagreement over non-generalizable polity options.

A shift in the public mind-set toward politics is required if the generality principle is to gain adherence as a prospective avenue for structural reform. The remaining residues of the romantic image of a disembodied political authority seeking the "good" and the "true" must be swept away. In such an image, the "good" might, of course, involve the furtherance of the particular. The genuinely benevolent government might discriminate among groups in terms of criteria for overall "goodness." But in the absence of any plausible presumption of benevolence, the "general welfare" cannot be promoted by other than *general* measures. Particular interests can be arrayed in support of generally applied alternatives only if and when the differentially superior profits from non-general alternatives are eliminated. A majority coalition will, of course, select a somewhat different mix of the feasible generalizable options than that mix preferred by members of the minority. But the difference would be reduced to a dimension along which all relevant alternatives tend to generate mutual advantage to all participants. The game of democracy would tend to be positive sum.

## VII. Society and Democracy

Only through the accomplishment of structural reform along the lines broadly suggested by the argument here can "society" and "democracy" be brought into the ultimately necessary symbiosis that is preferred by everyone. Democracy, as a basic organisational form, becomes the means through which persons in a civic order, a society, can secure the mutual benefits of peace and prosperity. Democracy cannot be allowed to trump society in the sense that the basic structure of civil order is determined by the relative success or failure of particular coalitions of persons and groups.

As such reform is implemented, politics, politicization, and the outreach of the state must recede from the extended current margins as elements in the inclusive civic order. Within its own limits, as defined by its constitutional structure and as guided by the generalization norm, the state can, and should, remain strong. A weak state insures only that factionalism, whether private or public, will emerge to subvert the genuinely productive collective action that a properly functioning constitutional democracy can facilitate.

Is it naive to hope that individuals can begin to think more seriously about the relationship between society and democracy so as to allow constitutional entrepreneurs to organise public support for specific reform?

Until and unless there comes to be a general public understanding of the philosophical grounding of democracy *in* society, rather than the other way around, the march of history offers little basis for optimism. Such an understanding, translated into practice through structural reform, can help to create a twenty-first century that is dramatically different from the twentieth, and better by all standards of comparison. Are living and future members of the post-socialist world up to the challenge?

# Reform without Romance
## First Principles in Political Economy [1]

At an Austrian meeting in August 1994, a distinguished philosopher surprised his audience by an emphatic insistence that he was no guru—that his role did not include the proffering of advice on this or that major issue of the day. I want to do the same thing. I want to preface any remarks by emphasizing that I am not sufficiently familiar with the historical, institutional or environmental particulars of any country to speak in a detailed way either on current economic policy or on ordinary politics. But I am a *political economist*—a scientist who does try to understand how political and economic structures actually work. And from this understanding certain first or basic principles emerge—principles that may be used to design reforms, provided that an agreed-upon set of objectives exists. But these principles are general, and they must in every case be applied in the knowledge of the particular time and place. My role is, therefore, to present and defend the general principles that can, indeed, tell us how economic prosperity, personal freedoms and domestic tranquillity can be achieved.

## Human Nature

Let me first explain my title "Reform without Romance." My primary emphasis is on "without romance." In many countries, decades (even centuries) have passed with far too much intellectual effort exerted in elaborating

From *Post-Socialist Political Economy: Selected Essays* (Cheltenham, U.K.: Edward Elgar, 1997), 233–39. Reprinted by permission of the publisher.

1. Material in this chapter was presented in a lecture in Romania in September 1994.

356

idealized or stylized constructions of how a political economy might work. Unfortunately, analysis and examination of how political and economic interaction takes place in nonromantic or realistic institutional settings, as populated by real persons, were largely ignored. The public choice research programme is basically aimed at correcting this error.

Once this basic shift in perspective is taken, we are well on the way towards understanding. Ordinary persons, no matter what roles they may occupy in political, administrative, bureaucratic or business structures, respond to private, personal incentives in roughly similar ways. That is to say, there are uniformities in behaviour patterns that can be used to help us in deriving some of the general or first principles about which I spoke. In this fundamental sense, persons do not behave differently over time and space. Persons in the nineteenth century responded to incentives in much the same way that persons respond in 1994. And persons in Romania respond similarly to persons in Austria, America or Africa. I am not denying the importance of culture here. I suggest only that the differences that we observe are to be attributed largely, even if not entirely, to the differences in the separate incentives structures, which range as widely among historical epochs as among polities.

## Classical Political Economy

The great eighteenth-century classical economists who called themselves moral philosophers, notably Adam Smith and David Hume, were successful in generating genuine and independent intellectual excitement with their discovery of how the basic uniformities in human behaviour, in human nature, could be institutionally channelled so as to serve the generally desired objectives of economic prosperity (as measured in terms of growth and stability) along with personal liberties and domestic tranquillity. Their discovery now seems simple enough, even if its implications are denied in practice in any and all political regimes in existence today, whether East or West. But a review might be useful.

Thomas Hobbes, who wrote a full century earlier than Smith and Hume and whose great book *Leviathan* was published in 1651, did, indeed, see through the romantic blinders when he looked at politics. Hobbes recognized that persons and groups have conflicting interests; that war, not peace, was the natural setting and that man's life would be nasty, brutish and short unless a political sovereign was established to maintain security and order. What he failed to recognize, however, was the prospect for controlling the interpersonal conflicts of interest by means that did not require the surrender of extensive personal liberties to the political sovereign. Hobbes failed to see that, provided only that the political authority establishes and maintains a regime that defines, protects and enforces a regime of private ownership of property (including property in person), the incentives for persons to promote their separate interests through voluntary exchange would result in benefits for all of a nation's citizens. And it is precisely this discovery that marks the contribution of the moral philosophers of the eighteenth century, as articulated best in Adam Smith's great book *The Wealth of Nations*, published in 1776.

Let me concentrate on the most familiar statement in *The Wealth of Nations*, the argument that the butcher offers meat for purchase not from some motivation of benevolence but, instead, out of regard to his own self-interest. The butcher has an incentive to sell us meat for supper because he secures money in exchange—money that he may then use in other exchanges to secure those goods which he most desires. That is to say, the whole interlinked chain or network of voluntary reciprocal exchanges allows all persons, as producers and consumers, to secure the bundle of goods they separately desire while, at the same time, retaining the liberties to do as each pleases, subject to no direct control by political authority.

## Natural Liberty

The simple system of natural liberty, to use Adam Smith's own designation, or as we would say, the market organization of economic activity, serves two functions simultaneously. Resources are directed by private owners into the most productive activities, as determined by the demands of final consumers, who get, in turn, the largest possible bundle of goods, again as measured by individuals' own evaluations. At the same time, however, over and beyond this economic or efficiency-enhancing function, the market reduces or eliminates the need for collective or political choices to be made concerning composition, organization, extent, and distribution of valued product. That is to say, the market serves a *political* as well as an *economic* function— one that may well be the more important of the two. Efficiency and economic liberty are two consequences of the same structural order of social interaction.

This summary sketch of the first principles of classical political economy is perhaps sufficient to suggest the excitement that was generated by the discovery of these principles in the eighteenth century. And a genuine understanding of these principles remains the basis for the arguments that place market organization at the centre of any institutional reform today, regardless of the current historical setting and independent of existing relationships.

## Laws and Institutions

These first principles do not, however, specify the nature of the political-legal-ethical framework within which individuals might be expected to carry on the many activities that make up an efficient and ongoing market economy. These first principles have been, and are, used by *laissez-faire* ideologues to suggest that free markets work well, anywhere and everywhere, and quite independent of the political-legal-ethical setting. Adam Smith did not make this mistake. He was careful to say that the market order, the system of natural liberty, works well only within the appropriate set of "laws and institutions." But Smith, perhaps, paid too little attention to precise definitions of these institutional requirements.

We, as political economists, have learned something in the two-and-one-quarter centuries since Adam Smith. We can now extend the first principles to include a specification of the political-legal-ethical framework that must be in existence for market order to work well—a framework that must be the central focus of any and all efforts at reform.

A preliminary principle emerges even prior to any such specification, however. A categorical distinction must be made between collective or political action directed at changes or reforms in the structural or constitutional framework for the market order and collective or political action directed at changes in resource usage within this order. An understanding of the first principles sketched out above should suggest that political reforms are or may be appropriate if aimed at the constitutional structure but are not often appropriate if aimed at modifying patterns of resource use within the operation of markets themselves.

But what are the political-legal-ethical parameters that must exist in order for a market economy to function effectively?

## Private Property

First of all, persons must be in possession of full ownership rights to the means of producing economic value, whether these means are in the form of human or nonhuman capacities. Only with private ownership can the appropriate incentives be exploited. The basic argument for private ownership has been known since Aristotle. Persons will care for, maintain and direct the use of productive resources properly only if there is a reciprocal relationship between effort expended and reward anticipated. A central Marxian socialist fallacy was the neglect of this ancient Aristotelian principle. How could persons be expected to produce economic value if the linkage between productive effort (work as well an entrepreneurship) and the distribution of rewards is severed. In a paper I wrote several years ago, I referred to the impossible socialist idyll of "consumption without production."[2]

Viewed from the Aristotelian perspective, any and all attempts to operate an economy on collective-command-central principles were foredoomed to failure. In modern terms, the structure of any such economy is incentive incompatible, quite apart from other central problems of management, such as the utilization and acquisition of knowledge concerning both consumer wants and producer capacities.

## Freedom of Entry

The assignment of private ownership rights is a first principle for viable economic order, and a basic political task is the enforcement of such rights. But privatization and enforcement are not, of themselves, sufficient to secure a well-functioning market economy. The ideologists of *laissez-faire* often neglect to note the limits that must be placed on the behaviour of those who participate in market dealings, even as fully protected owners of private property. Persons and groups must be prevented from erecting barriers to

---

2. See James M. Buchanan, *Consumption without Production: The Impossible Idyll of Socialism* (Freiburg, Germany: Haufe, 1993), 49–75.

entry into and exit from productive activity. Adam Smith's butcher offers meat for purchase out of his own self-interest, but this action is kept within nonexploitive limits only by the presumption that other prospective butchers, who may offer to sell at competitively determined prices, are present. The rights of private property cannot be extended to include rights to establish and enforce monopoly positions in markets.

The assignment and enforcement of rights to private ownership of property, along with the guarantee of rights to free entry into and exit from economic activity, are appropriate framework parameters, responsibility for which must be placed directly with the political-legal authorities. The market, standing alone and independent from political authority as defined by these basic functions, cannot be expected to accomplish the genuine miracle that remains possible if the parametric framework is in place.

## Monetary Stability

Beyond private ownership and free entry, what else is required that is appropriately guaranteed by legal-political authority? Recognition that viable activity—production, exchange and consumption—can take place only in a monetary economy draws direct attention to the function of money and to a possible political-legal role in establishing stability in monetary value. If exchanges are to be made in units of monetary value, if relative prices of goods and resource units are defined in nominal monetary terms, the vulnerability of the whole economy to unpredictable shifts and swings in the value of money becomes clear. Stability in monetary value becomes a much desired characteristic of the framework for market order.

There are certain advocates of markets who argue that *laissez-faire* will generate the emergence of a market-based monetary unit and that the forces of entry and exit will ensure adequate stability in its value, thereby leaving little or no monetary role for the political-legal authorities. I do not, personally, accept this argument, although I recognize its persuasive features. For my own view, I look upon monetary stability as a necessary element in the parameters of a viable market economy, and I think that such stability should be, and can be, guaranteed by political action. In saying this, I can be (and have been) accused of political naiveté, of myself maintaining a romantic vision of how politics actually works. Governments and politicians, anywhere and everywhere, have used their money-creating powers to extract value from citizens. Why, then, should I suggest that politics can, indeed, guarantee monetary stability?

Recall, however, that my self-assigned task in this chapter is to introduce some first principles for reform in the organization of a market economy. I am not, at this time, offering a realistic or hard-headed positive analysis of just how politics, or markets, work. The elementary fact is that throughout time governments may be observed to allow property rights to be confiscated or eroded to serve the interests of politicians; they may be observed to erect barriers to entry and exit in exchange, again to the interests of politicians, and they may be observed to use money-issue powers to extract value. This record does not, in any way, imply that such behaviour remains impervious to any institutional-organizational-constitutional reform. The whole normative purpose of the enterprise of "constitutional political economy" is to lay out first principles for institutional change that may constrain the natural proclivities of politicians to subvert the genuine interests to citizens as participants in the network of market exchange.

## Ethics

Private property, freedom of entry and exit, monetary stability—is the attainment of these objectives sufficient to allow the prediction that prosperity, peace and order will emerge? To this point I have said nothing specific about the place of ethical or moral norms in the workings of a market economy. The discussion has been grounded on the presumption that there exist behavioural uniformities in all cultures that allow the derivation of principles for institutional-organizational reforms independent of time and place. Nonetheless, the cultural norms of behaviour, which may differ substantially among nations and over time, can affect the efficacy of any efforts to apply the general principles for reform which have been outlined above. An economy in which participants behave, generally, in accordance with what we may call "the morality of the marketplace" will produce more economic value than an economy in which participants seek maximally to exploit each and every opportunity to realize personal gain, even at the direct expense of trading partners. There will exist productivity differences even if the formal institutional parameters are identical in the two settings. The ethical norm that dictates fairness in trading, rather than fraud, can be highly beneficial in generating mutually desirable results.

The importance of ethical standards in the successful workings of a market economy should, I think, be stressed in any discussion of first principles for reform in post-communist countries. A half-century's experience of life under command-control economic regimes has surely led to some erosion of the behavioural traits conducive to a regime of market exchange. The command-control economy, with its ubiquitous shortages, offered perverse incentives towards behaviour aimed opportunistically in order to secure differential advantage. Changes in behavioural attitudes should not be expected to occur suddenly, regardless of the institutional reforms that may be put in place.

I think that the years since 1989 have already done much to remove the early romantic dreams about the ability of the quick fix that seemed to be promised by dramatic reforms. But I fear that in some countries and among some observers the pendulum has already swung too far in the negative direction. There is no basis for any abandonment of the first principles of reform—principles that retain their validity and that continue to offer the best, and indeed the only, means through which citizens of a country can serve the joint blessings of liberty, prosperity and peace.

# Name Index

# Subject Index

agreement: in social interaction, 306–7; in taxing-spending choice (Wicksell), 142; in voluntary exchange, 141, 150–51; Wicksell's focus on, xvii. *See also* exchange, voluntary

allocationists: derivations for collectivity, xvii; diagnosis of market failure by, 137; differences from catallactic-coordination paradigm, 6–7; in modern normative economics, 147–48; of orthodox economics, 9

altruism: in welfare state (Tullock), 104–5

anarchy: conditions for, 198; constitutional, 177–79; Hobbesian, 317; order emerging from, 58, 174–75; potential in counterculture, 179; studies of, 58–59

Austrian economic theory: entrepreneurial choice (Kirzner), 156, 160; Knight's criticism of, 89

autobiography: conceptions of a person in, 66–70; as subjective record, 15; truth in, 64

biography, 66n. 2, 72–73

bureaucracy: of American government, 177–78, 183; economic incentives in, 235–36; economic theory of, 97–99; politics of, 97–99; response to restrictions of, 192–94; in socialist economy, 192–93, 237

capital theory: Austrian, 89; of Knight, 89–90

catallactic paradigm: difference from allocationist-maximization, 6–7; theory of exchange in, 7–9

catallactics: Buchanan's conversion to, 4, 24, 122

Center for Study of Public Choice, 44–45, 108–10

central banks: European Union nations, 207

choice: in allocation of labor (Smith), 300–302; as commitment, 159–60; consequences of, 159; among and within constraints, 245; creative and reactive, 154–56; informed by market order, 214; in market economy, 249; neoclassical definition of, 154–55; with scarcity, 223; Shackle's definition of, 153–61

choice, institutional: economic ignorance in, 219–20; understanding of, 212–15

Clinton Administration, 201

coalition, majority: constitutional constraints on, 351–52; disappearance of support for, 352; political approval, 348–49; selections under generality principle, 354

Coase theorem, 146

This book is set in Minion, a typeface designed by Robert Slimbach specifically for digital typesetting. Released by Adobe in 1989, it is a versatile neohumanist face that shows the influence of Slimbach's own calligraphy.

This book is printed on paper that is acid-free and meets the requirements of the American National Standard for Permanence of Paper for Printed Library Materials, z39.48-1992. ⊗

Book design by Louise OFarrell, Gainesville, Fla.
Typography by Impressions Book and Journal Services, Inc., Madison, Wisc.
Printed and bound by Worzalla Publishing Company, Stevens Point, Wisc.